Food Security, Nutrition and Sustainability

Edited by
Geoffrey Lawrence, Kristen Lyons and
Tabatha Wallington

publishing for a sustainable future
London • New York

First published 2010 by Earthscan   10 0681180 3

First published in paperback 2011 by Earthscan
2 Park Square, Milton Park, Abingdon, Oxon OX14 4RN

Simultaneously published in the USA and Canada by Earthscan
711 Third Avenue, New York, NY 10017

Earthscan is an imprint of the Taylor & Francis Group, an informa business

Earthscan publishes in association with the International Institute for Environment and Development

British Library Cataloguing in Publication Data
A catalogue record for this book is available from the British Library

Library of Congress Cataloging in Publication Data
Lawrence, Geoffrey.
Food security, nutrition and sustainability / Geoffrey Lawrence, Kristen Lyons and Tabatha Wallington.
p. cm.
Includes bibliographical references and index.
1. Food supply. 2. Food industry and trade. 3. Sustainable agriculture. 4. Diet–Research. 5. Nutrition–Research. 6. Agricultural innovations. I. Lyons, Kristen. II. Wallington, Tabatha. III. Title.
HD9000.5.L394 2009
338.1'9–dc22
2009026247

ISBN: 978-1-84407-775-5 (hbk)
ISBN: 978-1-84971-387-0 (pbk)

Typeset by JS Typesetting Ltd, Porthcawl, Mid Glamorgan
Cover design by Susanne Harris

At Earthscan we strive to minimize our environmental impacts and carbon footprint through reducing waste, recycling and offsetting our CO2 emissions, including those created through publication of this book. For more details of our environmental policy, see www.earthscan.co.uk.

This book was printed in the UK by MPG Books Ltd, an ISO 14001 accredited company. The paper used is FSC certified.

MIX
Paper from
responsible sources
FSC® C018575

Contents

List of Figures, Tables and Boxes

Figures

Tables

Boxes

List of Contributors

David Barling is Senior Lecturer at the Centre for Food Policy at City University, London. His research is focused on the government of the agri-food sector and of food supply, including its relation to sustainability and the politics of food standard-setting at UK, EU and global levels. He has written numerous journal articles and book chapters on food policy, and is co-editor of *Ethical Traceability and Communicating Food* (Springer, 2008) and co-author of *Food Policy: Integrating Health, the Environment and Society* (Oxford University Press, 2009). He was a member of the expert advisory panel for the UK Prime Minister's Strategy Unit project on Food Policy in 2007–2008.

Jayson Benge is the Field Research Manager for kiwi fruit in the Agriculture Research Group on Sustainability project – a six-year programme of research studying agricultural sustainability on New Zealand farms and orchards. This role primarily involves facilitating and undertaking research on participating orchards. He is a graduate of Massey University and gained a PhD from working on the nutritional aspects of kiwi fruit production. He is based in Tauranga, New Zealand.

Gianluca Brunori is Professor of Rural Development at the Faculty of Agriculture in Pisa, Italy. His research is focused on issues of rural governance, innovation processes in agriculture and in rural development, the survival strategies of small farms, and the link between food and rural development. He has published on a range of topics, including social representations and governance patterns in rural areas, local food and alternative food networks, and the relationships between multifunctionality, changing rural identities and institutional arrangements. Recent co-authored papers have appeared in the *Journal of Rural Studies*, *Anthropology of Food* and the *International Journal of Agricultural Resources, Governance and Ecology*.

David Burch is a Professor in the School of Biomolecular and Physical Sciences, Griffith University, Brisbane, Australia, teaching in the area of science and technology studies. He has published widely on agriculture and social change in Australia and Southeast Asia. His most recent works includes *Agri-food Globalization in Perspective: International Restructuring in the Processing Tomato Industry* (Ashgate, 2003), co-authored with Bill Pritchard, and

Supermarkets and Agri-food Supply Chains: Transformations in the Production and Consumption of Foods (Edward Elgar, 2007), co-edited with Geoffrey Lawrence.

Hugh Campbell is Associate Professor and Director of the Centre for the Study of Agriculture, Food and Environment (CSAFE) at the University of Otago, Dunedin, New Zealand. He is a member of the Project Executive which leads the Agriculture Research Group on Sustainability project – a six-year programme of research studying agricultural sustainability on New Zealand farms and orchards. His specialist research areas are rural sociology, sustainable agriculture, new forms of agri-food governance, and the emergence of food audits and quality assurance.

Peter Carey is a soil scientist with over 25 years' experience in analytical and applied research. He began his own company in 2004 (LRS – Land Research Services Ltd.) in Christchurch, New Zealand. He is currently leading the analysis of soils in the Agriculture Research Group on Sustainability project studying sustainability in New Zealand farming systems. Current research interests include sustainability of New Zealand farming systems, farm run-off and water quality, improving water quality of dairy effluent, nitrification inhibitor field trials and development of new soil test procedures.

Susan Cleary is a PhD candidate at the School of Land and Environment at the University of Melbourne, Australia. She studied gastronomy at the University of Adelaide. Her research is focused on understanding the relation between producing food and everyday practice and innovation. She also works on topics as broad as entrepreneurship and creativity, the ethics of agriculture and artisanal cheese-making. She has recently helped to develop and teach the graduate unit Transdisciplinary Thinking and Learning at the University of Melbourne.

Jane Dixon is a Fellow at the National Centre for Epidemiology and Population Health at the Australian National University, Australia. Her research interests focus on food sociology and the public health impacts of food system transformations, including the socio-cultural determinants of obesity, along with resilient food systems for population health in a changing climate. She has published in numerous international journals, including the *Journal of Sociology, British Food Journal* and *Critical Public Health*. Her most recent co-edited book is *The Seven Deadly Sins of Obesity: How the Modern World is Making Us Fat* (University of New South Wales Press, 2007).

Jago Dodson works as a senior research fellow in the Urban Research Program at Griffith University, Australia. He has published widely in the areas of urban planning, housing, transport and infrastructure. His recent research has focused on the problem of urban oil vulnerability and the distribution of adverse impacts of higher energy prices on urban households. He is also leading a major project funded by the Australian government which is examining Australian rural and regional oil vulnerability, and the implications for regional systems, including agriculture, of an energy-constrained future.

Kelly Donati is a PhD candidate at the University of Melbourne in the School of Land and Environment and a member of the teaching staff for the Gastronomy Program at the University of Adelaide, where she also completed her MA on the ethical, ecological and political dimensions of the Slow Food movement. Her research interests include gardening, cooking, and the politics and ethics of urban food practices. She is also the President of Slow Food Victoria.

Sharon Friel is a Fellow at the National Centre for Epidemiology and Population Health, the Australian National University, and Principal Research Fellow and Director of the Global Health Equity Group at the Department of Epidemiology and Public Health, University College London (UCL). She was Head of the Secretariat of the World Health Organization Commission on Social Determinants of Health (2005–2008), and a lead writer of its final report. She has been involved for many years in research and policy relating to global health – including social determinants of health inequities, food systems and food security, climate change, urbanization and health equity.

Angela Guarino is a sociologist with a research focus on rural development and food movements. She has a PhD in International Cooperation and Sustainable Development Policies from the University of Pisa in Italy. She is currently working at the Department of Agronomy and Agro-ecosystem Management at the University of Pisa. Angela is a member of the Laboratory of Rural Studies 'Sismondi'. She has previously been a visiting scholar with the School of City and Regional Planning at the University of Cardiff.

Libby Hattersley is a doctoral candidate at the National Centre for Epidemiology and Population Health at the Australian National University. She is researching the community health impacts arising from supermarket engagement in Australian food supply chains. She has previously worked with the New South Wales Centre for Overweight and Obesity. Recent co-authored papers have been published in *Public Health Nutrition, Australian and New Zealand Journal of Public Health* and *Health Promotion International.*

Megan Jennaway is a medical anthropologist specializing in women's health, climate change and social dislocation, in several Asian contexts, including Bali, Indonesia, East Timor, Vietnam and South Asia. She has been a lecturer in the School of Population Health, and in the Department of Asian Languages and Studies, at the University of Queensland. She is currently writing an ethnographic novel set in Afghanistan.

Helen Johnson holds degrees from Monash University and lectures in Anthropology in the School of Social Science at the University of Queensland,

Australia. She has received Visiting Fellowships at the French University of the Pacific in New Caledonia, the University of British Columbia and Dalhousie University in Canada, and the University of Hawai'i – Manoa, as well as the Five Colleges Centre for Women's Studies in the United States. Her articles and chapters have appeared in a range of international and national journals, and edited collections.

Tim Lang is Professor of Food Policy at City University's Centre for Food Policy in London. He was appointed Natural Resources and Land Use Commissioner on the UK Government's Sustainable Development Commission in 2006, and led the 'Green, Healthy and Fair' report on the government's relations with supermarkets in 2008. He has been a regular adviser to the World Health Organization at global and European levels, and a special adviser to four House of Commons Select Committee inquiries. He is co-author of 180 articles, reports, chapters and papers. His eight books include *Food Wars* (Earthscan, 2004) and *The Atlas of Food* (Earthscan, 2008).

Geoffrey Lawrence is Professor of Sociology and Head of the School of Social Science at the University of Queensland. His work spans the areas of agri-food restructuring, globalization and localization, rural and regional governance, and social aspects of natural resource management. In 2003, and again in 2009, he was appointed by the Federal Government to the Scientific Advisory Panel of the Lake Eyre Basin Ministerial Forum. During his career he has raised some AUS$10 million in research grants and has published 25 books. Recent co-authored and co-edited books include: *Supermarkets and Agri-food Supply Chains* (Edward Elgar, 2007), *Rural Governance* (Routledge, 2007), *Going Organic* (CAB International, 2006) and *Agricultural Governance* (Routledge, 2005). He is an elected Fellow of the Academy of Social Sciences in Australia.

Mark Lawrence is Associate Professor of Public Health Nutrition at Deakin University, Victoria, Australia. He has 25 years' experience working in food policy at local, state, national and international levels. He is currently a member of the Council of the World Public Health Nutrition Association and the National Health and Medical Research Council's Dietary Guidelines Working Committee. He is also a technical adviser to the World Health Organization. His research interests include the analysis of policies to protect and promote the nutritional health of populations from environmental, social, political, biological and economic perspectives. He has published extensively, including co-editing the reference book *Public Health Nutrition: From Principles to Practice* (Allen and Unwin, 2007).

Wieslaw Lichacz is an Accreditation Auditor with the United Nations Framework Convention on Climate Change Clean Development Mechanisms Accreditation Team, and Principal of WiseLaw Consulting and Trading. His interests include natural, indigenous and historic heritage, renewable energy strategies on a local and global scale, climate change impacts abatement, environmental impact assessment, and Clean Development Mechanisms under UN and Kyoto protocols. He has qualifications in applied environmental science, and constitutional and environmental law.

Stewart Lockie is Professor of Sociology in the Research School of Social Sciences at the Australian National University. His research addresses the governance and management of social and environmental impacts in agriculture and other resource-based industries. He is co-author of *Going Organic: Mobilizing Networks for Environmentally Responsible Food Production* (CABI, 2006) and co-editor of *Agriculture, Biodiversity and Markets: Livelihoods and Agroecology in Comparative Perspective* (Earthscan, 2009).

Kristen Lyons has been engaged in social research, advocacy and education on topics related to food, agriculture and the environment, as well as new technologies and social justice, for the last 15 years. She currently teaches food politics and science and technology studies in the School of Biomolecular and Physical Sciences at Griffith University, Australia. In her current research, Kristen is analysing the impacts of organic agriculture, along with the meaning of food sovereignty, in Africa. She is one of few social scientists examining the social and environmental implications of emerging agri-food nanotechnologies, including questions of governance, public participation and regulation.

Henrik Moller is Associate Professor and Co-Director of the University of Otago's Centre for Study of Agriculture, Food and Environment in Dunedin, New Zealand. Over the past 30 years he has applied population and community ecology principles to wildlife and conservation management in natural and production landscapes for sustainable agriculture and wild-food gathering. He currently leads the Environment objective of the Agriculture Research Group on Sustainability.

Sophia Murphy is a public policy analyst with degrees from Oxford University and the London School of Economics, UK. Her work is focused on agricultural trade rules, resilient agricultural practices and the right to food. She has published many reports and articles, including analysis of the effects of international trade rules on development and food security, the impact of corporate concentration in the global food system, and trade and poverty-related issues in the global biofuels sector. Sophia is a senior adviser on trade and global governance issues for the Institute for Agriculture and Trade Policy in Minneapolis, and has worked with the United Nations Non-Governmental Liaison Service in Geneva and the Canadian Council for International Co-operation in Ottawa.

Solis Norton has a background in agricultural science and veterinary epidemiology. He also has a growing interest and involvement in energy-related research, particularly with respect to Peak Oil. He is based at the Centre for the Study of Agriculture, Food and Environment at the University of Otago,

Dunedin, New Zealand. He is currently working as a Postdoctoral Fellow with the Agriculture Research Group on Sustainability project, comparing organic, integrated and conventional agricultural production systems.

Gerardo Otero is Professor of Sociology and Latin American Studies at Simon Fraser University in Vancouver, Canada, and Adjunct Professor in the Doctoral Program in Development Studies at Universidad Autónoma de Zacatecas in Mexico. He has written and edited four books, and over 60 scholarly articles and book chapters. His latest edited book is *Food for the Few: Neoliberal Globalism and Biotechnology in Latin America* (University of Texas Press, 2008). His current research is focused on the neoliberal food regime and its impacts on food vulnerability, the new division of labour and migration in North America.

Gabriela Pechlaner is a Social Sciences and Humanities Research Council Postdoctoral Fellow at the Centre for Economic and Social Aspects of Genomics (CESAGen) at Lancaster University. She works on the sociology of agriculture and food, with a particular emphasis on the legal and regulatory aspects of agricultural biotechnology. Her current research focuses on the effectiveness of legal mobilization as a strategy for social change in the technology's regulation in the US.

Lucinda Pike is a research assistant and a graduate student in Landscape Architecture at the Melbourne School of Design. Her research interests are based on the social dimensions of food production, and range from community gardens, contract farming and catchment management, to the relationship between governance structures and the realities of food production practices. She is particularly interested in the role of landscape design in creating sustainable and productive urban environments.

Roy E. Rickson is Emeritus Professor at the Griffith School of Environment, Australia. His primary research interests are in the changing structure of agricultural production, particularly the increasing importance of contract farming. The social assessment of development, and community democracy, are also research interests. Relations between globally organized corporate groups of companies and local rural communities are a consistent focus across these substantive areas. He has published widely on these topics in journals such as *Rural Sociology*, *Society and Natural Resources* and *Ecological Economics*.

Chris Rosin is a Research Fellow at the Centre for the Study of Food, Agriculture and Environment at the University of Otago, New Zealand, and a member of the social research team in the Agriculture Research Group on Sustainability project. His research interests include the justifications that are used to support particular sets of practices and courses of action in the production of food and fibre, including the commitment to organic principles. More recently he has begun to examine farmers' responses to the increased responsibility for environmental impacts associated with greenhouse gas emissions on farms.

Lisa Schubert is a lecturer and public health nutritionist at the School of Population Health at the University of Queensland, Australia. Her teaching and research interests lie at the intersection of the social and nutritional sciences. Her recently completed doctoral thesis – entitled *Diet and Domestic Life in 21st Century Australia: An Exploration of Time and Convenience in Family Food Provisioning* – used feminist ethnography and rationalization theory to explore dependency food work in households with working parents.

Gyorgy Scrinis is a research associate in the Globalism Research Centre at RMIT University in Melbourne, Australia. His research focuses on the ways that the technosciences shape structural, cultural and ecological relations, particularly across the food system. This includes the new biotechnologies and nanotechnologies of food production, and the way nutritional reductionism (or nutritionism) within the nutrition and food sciences frames the scientific and public understanding of food and the body, along with the production and marketing practices of food companies.

Rosalind Sharpe has an MA in English from Somerville College, Oxford, and an MA in Food Policy from Thames Valley University. After working for many years as a journalist, she now researches and writes on various aspects of food supply. Her contribution to this book is based on research into UK food security, self-sufficiency and sustainability conducted for the Centre for Food Policy at City University. She has also worked on food poverty for Sustain – the alliance for better food and farming – and on food and social justice for the new economics foundation (nef).

Neil Sipe is Associate Professor at the Griffith School of Environment, Australia. His research interests include energy security and patterns of oil vulnerability in urban areas, the influence of land use and urban form on travel behaviour, corner stores and neighbourhood sustainability, and the role of mediation in resolving environmental and public policy disputes. He has published on a range of these issues in journals such as *Ecological Economics, Australian Planner* and *Urban Policy and Research*. His recent co-authored book is *Shocking the Suburbs: Oil Vulnerability in the Australian City* (University of New South Wales Press, 2008).

Sean Sloan is a PhD candidate in the School of Resource Management and Geography at the University of Melbourne, where he is undertaking research investigating rainforest regeneration processes in Panama. Prior to commencing his PhD studies Sean worked as a Senior Research Assistant at Griffith University, where he contributed to a major project investigating rural and regional oil vulnerability.

Tabatha Wallington is a Research Scientist with CSIRO Sustainable Ecosystems, and an Honorary Research Consultant with the Institute for Social Science Research at the University of Queensland, Australia. Key research interests include the democratic governance of natural resource management, the role of lay and expert knowledge in environmental policy, and institutional designs for urban water management. Her work has been published in international journals such as the *Journal of Rural Studies*, the *Journal of Environmental Policy and Planning* and *BioScience*. She has previously lectured in environmental sociology in the School of Social Science at the University of Queensland.

Tony Weis is Assistant Professor of Geography at the University of Western Ontario, London, Canada. His research is principally concerned with the political economy of agriculture and the struggles of small farmers. He is the author of *The Global Food Economy: The Battle for the Future of Farming* (Zed Books, 2007), which examines the structural imbalances, social tensions and ecological instabilities in the global system of agricultural production and trade, and how these features have been institutionally entrenched.

Susan Williams is a Research Fellow in the Institute of Health and Social Science Research at Central Queensland University, Australia. Key research interests include bridging gaps between research, policy and practice through collaborative research with stakeholders, and understanding food consumption, food behaviours and health. Her research has focused on socio-ecological factors associated with adolescent obesity and associated behaviours. She has previously held academic teaching positions in the area of public health nutrition.

Acknowledgements

The idea for this book emerged from the 2007 annual meeting of the Australasian Agri-food Research Network. Formed in 1992, the Network is a loose affiliation of over 100 political scientists, sociologists, geographers, anthropologists, agricultural scientists, food policy experts, public servants and postgraduate students – all bound by a shared commitment to build theory, inform policy and shape practice in relation to agriculture and food futures. Through the presence of guest speakers, Network organizing committees have sought to provoke and enthuse conference participants and to bring new ideas to the Australasian agri-food table. Notable among past speakers have been Philip McMichael, Harriet Friedmann, Brian Wynne, Patricia Allen, Brian Ilbery, Reidar Almas, Katherine Gibson, Tim Lang and the late Fred Buttel. All have introduced fresh concepts, theories and debates to the group and most have penned chapters in the various collected volumes that have appeared, post-conference. Books that have emerged over the last two decades have included: *Globalization and Agri-food Restructuring* (Avebury, 1996), *Australasian Food and Farming in a Globalised Economy* (Monash University, 1998), *Restructuring Global and Regional Agricultures* (Ashgate, 1999) and *Consuming Foods, Sustaining Environments* (Australian Academic Press, 2001), along with a special Australasian edition of the influential US-based journal *Rural Sociology*.

On top of this, members of the Network – including David Burch, Hugh Campbell, Jane Dixon, Ian Gray, Richard Le Heron, Barbara Pini, Stewart Lockie, Bill Pritchard and Roy Rickson – have produced their own books dealing with topics as diverse as social dimensions of the 'triple bottom line'; cross-continental food chains; the cultural economy of the humble chicken; global restructuring in the processing tomato industry; masculinities and management in agricultural organizations; the social aspects of genetic engineering in agriculture; global governance of farming; organics and environmentally responsible production; the place of supermarkets in contemporary agri-food supply chains; and the future of rural communities in a globalizing world.

At the Agri-food XIV meeting held in Brisbane in 2007, the invited speaker was the internationally renowned scholar and food activist Professor Tim Lang from the Centre for Food Policy at City University, London. Not only were his talks at the conference inspirational, but he also made a concerted effort to speak with the many academics and postgraduate students in attendance, providing them with the most up-to-date ideas in the field of food and nutrition, and supporting their studies by helping them to make contact with leading scholars in their subfields of research. He encouraged the conference organizers to consider producing an edited book based on material presented at the conference – and then went one step further, talking to his friend and publisher, Tim Hardwick, the Commissioning Editor for Earthscan, based in London. We therefore acknowledge, and thank, Tim Lang for, ultimately, assisting us to publish what we hope will be a very important collection of papers on topics pertinent to the future of agri-food industries.

Tim Hardwick examined our initial proposal and provided some excellent feedback in relation to the focus of the book, the order of chapters, as well as some detectable weaknesses in our earlier draft outline. As a consequence – and along with Philip McMichael's assistance – we directly approached a number of new writers for various sections of the book. We trust that this collection will not only provide insights into the issues of food security, nutrition and sustainability, but will also discuss these issues on a global plane and thereby help to explain and unravel some of the 'big' issues of our time.

Given that the genesis of this book was the Agri-food meeting in Brisbane, we acknowledge the sponsors of that conference – the University of Queensland, Griffith University and Central Queensland University. We also thank the other members of our organizing committee – David Burch, Samantha Neal, Brendon Radford and Kiah Smith. Carol Richards provided some excellent comments on a number of original drafts of papers. Claire Lamont, Editorial Assistant at Earthscan, assisted us in the early preparation, and later production, of the book, while Sarah Thorowgood gave invaluable support during the editing phase. We would also like to acknowledge the support of Food First/Institute for Food and Development Policy for providing a supportive environment for Kristen Lyons during the compilation of this collection. Our partners and family members provided strong support and, from the beginning, backed our efforts in compiling this book – allowing us the 'space' to undertake the editing at nights and on weekends. In particular, Kristen's partner Sean assisted in the preparation of the index – at a time when both were supposed to be enjoying vacation fun along the sunny coast of California.

We also thank the many contributors to this volume. All delivered their manuscripts to us in a timely manner and in a form that allowed for ease of editing. They accepted our comments in a positive and collegial way – making the production of this volume a great pleasure. The book has a specific purpose: we trust that readers will, in assimilating the contents of this volume, recognize the many contradictory, harmful and destructive elements of current global agri-food production and seek – as we have, albeit in a limited way – to identify new alternatives to production regimes that undermine food security, polarize the world in terms of nutritional availability, pollute the environment and, ultimately, undermine attempts to move world agriculture onto a more sustainable footing.

We dedicate this book to Professor David Burch, the co-founder of the Australasian Agri-food Research Network, who will be retiring from Griffith

University at the end of 2009 after some 30 years of service. David not only helped to pioneer critical agri-food studies in Australia, but also introduced many of its important conceptual and theoretical underpinnings. He also inspired a generation of agri-food scholars to produce research which has become known internationally for its incisiveness and global relevance.

List of Acronyms and Abbreviations

ABS	Australian Bureau of Statistics
ACC	UN Administrative Committee on Coordination
ACF	Australian Conservation Foundation
ADM	Archer Daniel Midland
AGPS	Australian Government Publishing Service
AGRA	Alliance for the Green Revolution in Africa
AIHW	Australian Institute of Health and Welfare
AMAPs	Associations pour le maintien de l'agriculture paysanne
ANZFA	Australia New Zealand Food Authority
AoA	Agreement on Agriculture
ARGOS	Agriculture Research Group on Sustainability
BMI	body mass index
BSE	bovine spongiform encephalopathy
CAP	Common Agricultural Policy
CDCP	Center for Disease Control and Prevention
CLBA	Country Land and Business Association
COAG	Council of Australian Governments
DAA	Dietitians Association of Australia
Defra	Department for Environment, Food and Rural Affairs
DFID	Department for International Development
EC	European Commission
ECLAC	Economic Commission for Latin America and the Caribbean
ECOSOC	Economic and Social Council of the United Nations
EFFP	English Food and Farming Partnerships
EIA	Energy Information Administration
ER	energy ratio
EROEI	energy return on energy invested
ETC Group	Action Group on Erosion, Technology and Concentration
ETP	European Technology Platform
EU	European Union
EurepGAP	Euro Retailer Produce Working Group's Good Agricultural Practice – now GlobalGAP
FAO	Food and Agriculture Organization of the United Nations

FAOSTAT	Food and Agriculture Organization of the United Nations Statistics Division
FDA	Food and Drug Administration
FFA	Farmers for Action
FoE	Friends of the Earth
FRRC	Food Regulation Review Committee
FRSC	Food Regulation Standing Committee
FSANZ	Food Standards Australia New Zealand
G-20	Group of 20
G8	Group of Eight
GATT	General Agreement on Tariffs and Trade
GDP	gross domestic product
GlobalGAP	Global Good Agricultural Practice
GM	genetically modified
GMO	genetically modified organism
GoE	Garden of Eden
GRAS	generally recognized as safe
I$	International Dollars
IAASTD	International Assessment of Agricultural Knowledge, Science and Technology for Development
ICTSD	International Centre for Trade and Sustainable Development
IEA	International Energy Agency
IFPRI	International Food Policy Research Institute
IMF	International Monetary Fund
IPCC	Intergovernmental Panel on Climate Change
ISC	Implementation Sub-Committee
ITUC	International Trade Union Confederation
LEADER	Liaison Entre Actions de Développement de l'Economie Rurale
LOHAS	lifestyles of health and sustainability
MAFF	Ministry of Agriculture, Fisheries and Food
NAFTA	North American Free Trade Agreement
NCCR	Swiss National Centre of Competence in Research
NFA	National Food Authority
NFU	National Farmers Union
NGO	non-governmental organization
NHMRC	Australian National Health and Medical Research Council
NSW	New South Wales
OECD	Organisation for Economic Co-operation and Development
PCFF	Policy Commission on the Future of Farming and Food
PFFP	primary family food provisioner
PMA	The Prince Mahidol Award
PMSU	Prime Minister's Strategy Unit
R&D	research and development
RCEP	Royal Commission on Environmental Pollution
RCT	randomized controlled trial
RFid	radio frequency identification tags

RS and RAE	Royal Society and Royal Academy of Engineering
SCN	UN Sub-Committee on Nutrition
SFFS	Sustainable Farming and Food Strategy
SPG	Solidarity Purchasing Group
SPS	Single Payment Scheme
TNCs	Transnational Corporations
UK	United Kingdom
UNCTAD	United Nations Conference on Trade and Development
UNEP	United Nations Environment Programme
US EPA	US Environmental Protection Agency
US	United States
USDA ERS	US Development Association Economic Research Service
USDA NASS	US Department of Agriculture, National Agricultural Statistics Service
VAT	value-added tax
WFTD	Work for the Dole
WHO	World Health Organization
WRAP	Waste and Resources Action Programme
WTO	World Trade Organization

Foreword

Eric Holt-Giménez

A crisis is a terrible thing to waste.

Crises provide us with opportunities to change and improve the way we do things. They can also end up reinforcing the status quo that provoked them in the first place. Little wonder institutions leap to advance solutions even before the underlying causes of the problem have been determined. This is because crises are profoundly political events in which, in the words of Italian thinker Antonio Gramsci, 'the old is dying and the new cannot be born.'

The current global food crisis, decades in the making, is such a political event.

Everyone from the World Bank, the World Food Programme and the transnational agrochemical companies invite us to believe that the old formula of 'technology + food aid + global markets' will reverse the explosion of hunger, poor health and environmental disasters destroying the world's food systems. A review of the public-private partnership solutions coming from the latest global food summits indicates that the world's seed, grain and retail monopolies see the current food crisis as a perfect opportunity to further consolidate their hold over the world's food. This led the UN Special Rapporteur on the Right to Food, Olivier de Schutter, to warn the world's leaders that 'not all opportunities are solutions'.

An enquiry into the root causes of the food crisis and a review of the widespread grassroots responses to hunger, however, sheds light on an entirely different set of opportunities, and leads to quite different solutions to the problems of hunger, health and environment. Indeed, over the last 30 years, the chronic global food crisis has given rise to a virtual explosion of food and farming alternatives that have sprung up 'like weeds breaking through the asphalt' quite independently of each other, around the world. On the one hand, the growing number of farmers' markets, sustainable and agroecologically managed farms, community-supported agriculture, food policy councils and fair trade networks are working to forge equitable and sustainable food chains to replace the current, industrial forms of production and consumption. On the other hand, the political issues of entitlement and the human right to food are being actively addressed by food justice movements in the industrial North and growing agrarian movements for land reform, resource rights and food sovereignty in the global South. These developments reflect the spread of what is widely recognized as a global food movement. The increasing levels of integration and engagement among these movements signal the stirrings of a new food regime – one that is equitable, sustainable, that cools the planet, and provides healthy food and prosperous livelihoods.

The authors of the chapters in this book belong to the research wing of the global food movement. In the spirit of the path-breaking International Assessment on Agricultural Knowledge, Science and Technology for Development (IAASTD), their research delves deeply into the global paradox of 'the stuffed and the starved', analytically framing core issues and root causes before positing solutions. Their work not only engages the academic community and informs the general public, but also provides the 'advocates and practitioners' of the food movement with the information and analysis they need for informed engagement within the food system. Just as importantly, their writings amplify the voices of those working for change, particularly those for whom maintaining the corporate food regime is simply not an option.

Serious analysis into the political-economic nature of the current food regime, and an objective look at the growing social and environmental externalities, can be a brutally sobering exercise. For this reason, the focus on proximate over root causes and reformist, rather than transformational, solutions is the norm in the mass media and, unfortunately, in many global food policy circles. The possibility of a new, sustainable and equitable food regime, demands that food system researchers balance rigorous analysis with a vision of change, thus illuminating the path between the hydra-headed trap of facile solutions and the whirlpool of hopelessness. This road from old to new is made brighter with the contributions from *Food Security, Nutrition and Sustainability*. Readers are encouraged to walk it.

Eric Holt-Giménez, PhD
Executive Director
Food First/Institute for Food and Development Policy
Oakland, California, US

1
Introduction: Food Security, Nutrition and Sustainability in a Globalized World

Geoffrey Lawrence, Kristen Lyons and Tabatha Wallington

Introduction

Before the global financial crisis became acutely visible in late 2008, the crisis in food and agriculture had already taken hold. Accelerating food prices, combined with increasing numbers of low-income families dropping below the poverty line in the developing world, led to civil unrest on a large scale as people demanded access to affordable food – an idea long championed by many as a basic human right (Cresswell, 2009; Holt-Giménez et al, 2009). Between 2006 and 2008, global food prices had risen by 83 per cent and, even in the face of the price-deflating effects of the global recession, were predicted to remain high until at least 2012 (Loewenberg, 2008, p1209). In the lead up to 2009, close to 1 billion of the world's 6 billion people were chronically hungry, with this number expected to rise as prices for food staples continue to increase (Cresswell, 2009, p1). More than this, though – and notwithstanding the Food and Agriculture Organization's (FAO) calculation that there is currently enough food to feed the world's population (FAO, 2008) – it is anticipated that there will need to be an increase in food production of between 50 and 100 per cent over current levels if the world is to feed its people by the year 2030 (Cresswell, 2009, p2). Given the extent of the current food crisis, the arrival of peak oil and evidence confirming that climate change is 'real', it is no surprise that riots over food provision have become widespread (McMichael, forthcoming 2009).

Seeking to establish the reasons for the rise in food prices, economists and political leaders have explained the reduction in food availability as an outcome of a number of factors: declining growth in productivity due to drought, water scarcity and land degradation, along with the conversion of food staples into biofuels (or agrofuels, as they have also been termed)[1] – the latter as a response both to spiralling oil prices and to state-based incentives to reduce national dependency upon oil (Loewenberg, 2008; UNEP, 2009). Two additional reasons have also been given. First, with the growth of the middle classes in India and China, energy and food have been in high demand, reducing the availability of these resources to people without the necessary purchasing power. Second, there has been an increase in demand for artificial fertilizers and pesticides derived from petrochemical-based processes. Oil price hikes are therefore inflating the cost of agri-chemicals at the very time demand for them is increasing, exacerbating the cost-price squeeze in agriculture and ensuring that these farm-related costs are passed on to consumers as higher food prices (see, for example, Cresswell, 2009).

While such explanations are logically appealing, and while the factors listed above do, in combination, affect food availability, they nevertheless mask broader socio-economic settings, along with the actions of powerful corporations and global regulating bodies, which shape the ways foods are grown, distributed and ultimately end up – or for a growing number, don't end up – in the mouths of consumers. In his book *Food is Different*, Peter Rosset (2006, pxvi) argues that liberalized agricultural trade settings produce an 'inherent uncertainty' in commodity markets. Rosset reasons that food sovereignty – characterized by secure access to food across both local and national markets, and produced in ways that support socially and ecologically sustainable rural development (see for example Holt-Giménez et al, 2006) – will be compromised by the neoliberal-based insistence of the World Trade Organization (WTO) that the 'law' of comparative advantage should be the determining mechanism for where foods are produced and in which markets they are traded. For Rosset, liberalized trade in food reduces stocks of reserves (which provide a major contribution to food security) because of the imperative to sell into the global marketplace. Demonstrating this, by the end of 2008 world cereal stocks had dropped to 405 million tonnes, representing their lowest level since 1982, while US wheat stocks were at their lowest level in 60 years (FAO, 2008). Banks will not lend to farmers unless food is guaranteed to be sold (traded) for cash to repay loans. The trajectory is to sell agri-commodities at the highest price – which usually means ignoring local markets and local food needs. Rosset is reminding us that there are ingrained structural reasons that determine what foods will be produced, by whom and where, as well as to whom these foods are destined. Similarly, as Holt-Giménez et al (2006) have noted, agriculture should not be exclusively about trade. Rather, agriculture should support local economic development, address poverty and hunger, and support the sustainable management of natural resources.

Rosset (2006) was writing at a time when markets were being flooded by cheap agricultural goods. He rightly expressed indignation and dismay that the WTO-endorsed system of world agricultural trade was removing small-scale producers from the land in the developing world and re-orienting production in those countries to global rather than local markets. He also recognized and condemned policies that opened the door to the importation of cheap 'first world' foods that were not only subsidized by taxpayers, but were also produced in a manner that compromised ecologies in their country of production. What we know now is that if the developed world decides to convert its cropping system to make ethanol for cars – a scenario that government and industry appear increasingly committed to (see, for example, Jonasse, 2009) – those countries which are dependent upon the importation of food crops may find such crops are now beyond their reach. This scenario is set to play out at the same time as import-dependent countries continue to produce food – including crops for conversion to agrofuels – to supply the international market. The tragic irony in some parts of the global South is that people are starving while staring over fields of beans, plantations of coffee and tea, and stands of palms, all grown to meet the demands of already well-fed consumers in the North. For Raj Patel (2007), this is the polarized world of the 'starved' and the 'stuffed'[2] where the global agri-food system – from farm input manufacturers, to producers, packagers, suppliers and retailers – has been driven exclusively by profits rather than by any social or moral imperative to ensure that healthy, affordable foods produced in an ecologically sound manner are available to enrich and sustain the lives of peoples around the world. Today, we live in a world of hunger among plenty, at a time of a first-world obesity 'plague' alongside third-world starvation, and in circumstances where highly productive 'factory farms' sit within socially denuded, biologically fragile and heavily polluted agricultural landscapes.

How did this happen?

Why does the world continue to experience food insecurity? Why, given our ability to produce agricultural surpluses (albeit declining surpluses), do we not see all of the world's people reaping the benefits of adequate nutrition? And, why – given our considerable and sophisticated scientific knowledge of soil, water, bacteria, plants and animals, and the intricate biophysical connections between them – isn't the world producing foods in a more sustainable manner? We will address these questions briefly here, before outlining how each of the contributed chapters improves our understanding of food security, nutrition and sustainability.

Continuing world food insecurity

Droughts, floods, disease, plagues and other so-called 'natural disasters' have forever affected the amount of food available for human consumption. Such events will continue to impact upon agriculture, with affected regions almost inevitably experiencing food shortages. Since the 1960s, the applications of agricultural science have combined with improved global transport networks to increase food production and availability so that a drought in Ethiopia, or torrential rains in Bangladesh, will be met with humanitarian aid which – albeit sometimes constrained by national and international political agendas – aims to keep starving populations fed during times of adversity. And there is likely to be more adversity in a world experiencing increased climate change-related pressures (ITUC, 2009). Nevertheless, it is important to shift our sights beyond 'disasters' if we are to understand the structural conditions underpinning contemporary food insecurity.

Worldwide, agricultural development has been premised on de-peasantization in the global South and the continued corporatization of agriculture in both the global North and the global South – with the two outcomes underpinned by the dynamic of the concentration and centralization of capital (McMichael, 2006; Otero, 2008a). De-peasantization (or de-agrarianization – see Bryceson et al, 2000) occurs when small, previously self-sufficient, farmers who have been encouraged to go into debt to purchase the latest 'green revolution' technologies fail to achieve the necessary gains from the new agriculture and are displaced by a combination of crop failure and bank foreclosure (Weis, 2007). Many are literally forced from their farms as an inevitable consequence of having attempted to move to a more 'advanced' form of agriculture. The failures of this model of agricultural development are most powerfully manifested in the growing number of rural suicides, with an estimated 100,000 Indian farmers committing suicide between 1993 and 2003, and an average of 16,000 farmer suicides each year since this time, often via the ingestion of agricultural chemicals (Sharma, 2006). Despite such failures, the extension of 'green revolution' technologies is now under way through the Alliance for the Green Revolution in Africa (AGRA). AGRA puppets the policies being developed from the alliance forged between the Bill and Melinda Gates Foundation and the Rockefeller Foundation in the US. This alliance, by all accounts, is set to extend the inequities and injustices that characterized the 'green revolution' in the 1960s and beyond (Holt-Giménez et al, 2009).

Rural out-migration is encouraged by global bodies such as the World Bank, which consider that the removal of peasants will lead to an increase in food production (as larger, more labour-efficient farms prevail), while at the same time releasing peasant labour for the supposedly more 'worthy' task of employment in city-based manufacturing industries (McMichael, 2006, 2009c). The reality, though, is that the World Bank model of agricultural development has accelerated rural out-migration. It has, in fact, created a 'planet of slums' – those inhabited by many of the estimated 1 billion people who now live in urban hovels in the cities of the South (Davis, 2007). Meanwhile, other farmers are 'structurally adjusted' out of agriculture to enable the consolidation of larger units of production (Heynen et al, 2007). The consequence is that people who once had direct access to food are no longer connected to the land and the food that it produced, a situation that is destroying food sovereignty (or, according to Tim Lang, food democracy),[3] and overall food security (Otero, 2008a).[4]

Such dispossession does not happen in a regulatory or policy vacuum. According to Heynen et al (2007, p7), the World Bank and International Monetary Fund (IMF) both insist that the borrowing of funds for agricultural and other 'development' must be accompanied by neoliberal policies, which include trade liberalization, reduced regulatory impositions on private investors and structural adjustment policies. These policies combine to foster the growth of a dynamic, market-based economy in which small-scale (subsistence) farming is replaced by larger and more globally focused farms – an economy with a very different agenda from that of providing food security to local people (Patel, 2007; Weis, 2007; McMichael, 2008).

How might food provision under neoliberalism work? As Otero (2008b, pp137–138) has noted, prior to the signing of the North American Free Trade Agreement (NAFTA) in 1994, various Mexican governments had insisted that Mexico be self-sufficient in corn – albeit with some importation at times of unmet internal demand. With NAFTA's neoliberal reforms, a cheap-food-for-the-cities agenda replaced older policies which had subsidized peasant agriculture. Corn from the US flooded in, while the small-scale farming areas once responsible for domestic supply were labelled as zones of 'low productive potential' and became recipients of structural adjustment funding and welfare. Unfortunately, this neither led to lower prices of corn-based foods in the cities, nor to the creation of alternative work in the regions, with many displaced labourers having to migrate to large cities in the US and Mexico so as to earn wages to send back to relatives now impoverished in the once successful food-producing regions (Otero, 2008b, p139). With the demise of significant parts of local food production in Mexico, combined with increasing dependence upon US-subsidized corn,[5] it can be argued that food security, and certainly food sovereignty, has been considerably diminished in Mexico (Patel, 2007; Otero, 2008b) as a direct result of the application of neoliberal policies (Heynen et al, 2007).

There are other examples. The Philippines was once self-sufficient in rice but – with the removal of government incentives – is now a net importer. Cameroon was told by the IMF and the World Bank to cease supporting its rice farmers in 1994, and the country is now importing increasing volumes of rice. Haiti was largely self-sufficient in rice three decades ago, but was then persuaded to import cheap foods and to sell its forests to gain much needed foreign income (ITUC, 2009, pp20–29). The result has been the virtual collapse of domestic agriculture, the denudation of its forests, and the movement of rural workers into the slums of the capital, Port-au-Prince. Here, the people eat so-called 'mud cakes' – literally, patties made of clay and water – as a means of filling empty bellies (ITUC, 2009, p20). As De Neve et al (2008, p14) have argued, rather than delivering prosperity, global markets are – in concert with neoliberal policies of 'comparative advantage' – causing insecurity and 'immiseration'; they are destroying the livelihoods of many small producers, while delivering considerable economic benefits to large-scale corporate capital.

The price of agricultural commodities increased significantly during 2007 and 2008 as large cashed-up investors such as the hedge funds began speculating in foodstuffs as a basis for high-level gains (ITUC, 2009). According to ITUC (2009, p10):

> *investments in food commodities and futures have grown twenty-fold because deregulation has allowed non-commercial traders to seek profit gains in relatively small markets, causing sudden volatility and turmoil ... driving up the prices of basic food staples.*

It should be remembered that, for at least three-quarters of a century up until the 1990s, speculation in basic agricultural commodities such as wheat, corn and soybean was banned in the US. Then, deregulation of US and global agricultural markets followed in the wake of deregulation of financial markets. Between 2000 and 2007, world wheat prices increased by some 147 per cent, corn prices by 79 per cent and soybeans by 72 per cent (ITUC, 2009, p37). While the corporations made increasing profits, more people became hungry. Indeed, it has been concluded that every time global food prices increase by a percentage point, another 16 million people are condemned to hunger (ITUC, 2009, p37).[6] The financialization of agri-food industries (see Burch and Lawrence, forthcoming 2009) means that speculation is rife and food crops can be moved to more profitable areas (for example, to agrofuels), resulting in food price 'spikes' that affect the most vulnerable consumers (ITUC, 2009, p38). In other words, the expansion of financial derivatives ('shadow' financial instruments including forwards, futures, 'swaps' and other hedging options) in the agri-food industries have, by increasing the level of speculation, created inflationary pressures on food. As Pace et al (2008, p2) have written in *The Lancet*:

> *[I]t seems to us an infringement of human rights and an offence against humanity that large investors should speculate on food price rises knowing that families in the poorest countries will suffer hunger, malnutrition and death... The G8 should act quickly to regulate global trading in food commodities.*

Diversion of crops into agrofuels is about corporate profit-making. According to the ITUC, about 30 per cent of food price increases has been attributed to food crops being diverted into fuel production (see ITUC, 2009, p11) – a sure reminder that food crops are just another input into a global production cycle and go to the highest bidder, rather than being an intrinsic source of human sustenance. They have market (exchange) value, well ahead of any use value (McMichael, 2009a, p155). As McMichael (2009a, p155, p162) perceptively argues:

> *the agrofuels project represents the ultimate fetishisation of agriculture, converting a source of human life into an energy input at a time of rising prices ... the 'agrofuels rush' renders agriculture indistinguishable from energy production in a context where peak oil is making its presence felt in world prices.*

A second factor, here, is the declining purchasing power of those who are most vulnerable: a shortage of food, with resultant hunger, is a result of the incapacity of people on meager wages to pay for food. Agricultural produce might be available, but the ability to purchase diminishes as prices increase, leaving people bereft of the means to obtain enough food even for basic subsistence (ITUC, 2009, p18).

The issue of food security might seem less of a concern in the global North, given the large volumes of food produced and exported by nations like Canada, Australia, New Zealand and the US. But that is not the case, with 'security' taking on a very different meaning from that of food availability. It is one thing to produce large quantities of food, and yet another to do so in a manner that encourages agricultural diversity, nurtures regional prosperity, enhances environmental integrity, sustains biodiversity and rests upon a predictable and fair platform of production, sale and delivery. In these latter qualities, food security in the global North has been notably lacking. Instead, what has been witnessed in the last 30 or so years of capitalist farming and food distribution has been a significant increase in the amount of food available *at the same time* as the system for that delivery has been found to be environmentally damaging, and socially and economically polarizing. In short, food in the North is produced at significant environmental and social cost (Magdoff et al, 1998; Buckland, 2004; Mazoyer and Roudart, 2006).

Environmental costs associated with contemporary food systems include stream and river pollution caused by toxic agri-chemicals, the genetic pollution and biodiversity losses associated with the expansion of genetically modified (GM) crops, and the atmospheric impact of greenhouse gases (largely methane) produced by livestock. With the numbers of cattle predicted to rise along with the growing 'meatification' of global diets, there is concern that the adverse environmental consequences of farming will get worse rather than better (Weis, 2007).

Supermarkets, too, are implicated in increasing the level of pressure on the environment. It is the supermarkets that purchase foods from distant locations, thus adding to the 'foodmiles' associated with certain foodstuffs and depleting energy reserves in the process. And it is the supermarkets that are re-shaping the nature of the food system in a manner which, while purporting to provide environmental benefits, fosters wasteful practices and generates significant environmental impacts (see Burch and Lawrence, 2007; Lang and Barling, 2007).

Agricultural surpluses – but poor nutrition

The actual availability of food provides no guarantee of its nutritional quality. There is emerging evidence, for example, that as food prices have increased in the developed world, consumers have reacted by turning to cheaper foods with dubious health credentials (those which, in many cases, are sugar, fat and salt laden – see ITUC, 2009). At a time of global economic concerns, consumers have also begun to eschew potentially more nutritious organic foods – along with other ethically produced and health-enhancing foods – as a means of reducing their budget expenditures (Teather, 2008, p5).

As part of the so-called 'nutrition transition', consumers in the global North and South have been moving, seemingly inexorably, away from largely grain-based diets, towards predominantly meat-oil-fat-sugar-based diets (Dixon and Broom, 2007; Ambler-Edwards et al, 2009). This is the general trend. More specifically – and notwithstanding the pressures to reduce food budgets in a time of economic uncertainty – more affluent consumers have moved to healthier (green-leafy) diets, while the less affluent have embraced a supermarket-based convenience-food path – looking toward fast and prepared foods for energy intake. In the latter case, we have seen the emergence and impact of the so-called 'obesogenic diets' that are a feature of modern living in the North (Critser, 2003; Dixon and Broom, 2007).

The influence of the corporations should be highlighted here. The large corporations that currently dominate food provision – Heinz, Kellogg, Kraft, Nestlé, Cadbury and so forth – have been prominent players since the early 1900s, engaging in the production of convenience foods from at least the 1920s (Murton, 2000). The corporations became firmly entrenched after the Second World War when the automobile became increasingly affordable and people could drive to the supermarkets. From about the same time, the use of refrigerators in western households became widespread (Murton, 2000). With advanced food technologies allowing for the manipulation of foods to improve their look, taste, shelf-life and general appeal, along with the macro-changes in the ways people lived their lives (more urbanization, greater private travel, a growing interest in the purchase of convenience foods, and so on) the supermarkets and the fast-food firms were the ones most able to capitalize (Burch and Lawrence, 2007; Hendrickson et al, 2008).

The industrialization both of agriculture and of the processed foods sector also had important impacts, allowing the cost of foods – relative to other family purchases – to fall. This, in turn, fuelled the growth in demand for all varieties of novel foodstuffs. Packaging and advertising were geared to various new market segments, thereby better targeting and stimulating demand, and literally 'creating' markets for manufactured foods (Critser, 2003).

As Symons (2007), and later Dixon and Broom (2007), have argued, the supermarkets promote their 'labour saving' foods as those that are scientifically proven to be healthy and nutritious. They employ home economists, nutrition 'experts' and other scientists to endorse industrial products as wholesome and nourishing – as the very foods needed for the pursuit of a modern lifestyle (Symons, 2007). But processed foods are replete with the sugars, salts and fats that contribute to excessive weight gain and obesity (Dixon and Broom, 2007) and – along with a variety of food chemicals – combine to induce allergic reactions, poisonings and deaths (Nestle, 2003, 2006; Lawrence, 2004).

Science has been steadily applied to the areas of food preservation, packaging, storage and delivery. Chemical preservatives have allowed foods to last longer on the shelves of supermarkets and in family pantries. Demand for such foods has increased markedly in the decades since the Second World War as women – whose homemaking role had included food preparation – began to enter the workforce in ever larger numbers (see Dixon, 2002). Fast-food restaurants have taken advantage of increasingly more mobile populations in places like the US and their ready-to-eat takeaway products have been heavily advertised as a tasty, nutritious and relatively cheap means of feeding the family (see Critser, 2003). It was in this environment that the so-called 'junk food' revolution took hold (Dixon and Broom, 2007).

Nearly a decade ago, Lang and Rayner (2001) argued that public health should be central to the agricultural and food industries. They called for the emergence of an 'ecological public health' paradigm – one which ensured that the so-called 'three pillars' of nutrition, food safety and sustainable food production would be considered together in the evolution of public health policy. The aim was to 'deliver affordable, health-enhancing and accessible diets for all, not just those who can afford it' (Lang and Rayner, 2001, p4). Lang and Rayner's vision has, unfortunately, not been realized: the twin aim of providing a balanced diet to a growing population, and in a sustainable manner, has fallen well short of its target. Part of the reason lies in the failure to institute the conditions for such an ecological public health paradigm:

> *In order to advance both environmental and health goals there needs to be a switch from the production of animal-based foods to plant-based foods – particularly vegetables and fruit. There also needs to be an emphasis upon increasing bio-diversity in the agriculture system both to protect ecosystems and to ensure a varied diet* (Lang and Rayner, 2001, p10).

The achievement of these conditions remains the challenge to this day (see Lang, 2009a). Instead of people in the North having richer diets, there are now 'food deserts' in the middle of cities where local people have no access to fresh foods: where the small grocers have been forced out of business, and consumers must drive to distant hypermarkets to purchase their foods (see Lang and Rayner, 2001, p20). And, in the South, the nutrients which once provided local sustenance are destined for other lands. According to ITUC (2009, pp36–37):

> *The problem inherently wrong with the world food system is that local crops such as cassava and sorghum, for example, are not wanted by international agribusiness and therefore local farmers grow crops like coffee, cocoa, tea, cotton and flowers and afterwards use the export earnings to purchase food... [Farmers] are 'producing what they do not eat, and eating what they do not produce'. The fallacy of this policy is shown by the fact many developing countries are at this time paying high prices for imported food at the same time as the food multinationals [involved in both export and import] are reaping record profits.*

Knowledge of science – but little progress on sustainability

The highly productive seed/fertilizer/pesticide/farm equipment package provided to the poorer nations of the world by the 'green revolution' has been one based upon the petrochemical industry. The green revolution was initiated by the US government and its corporate allies as a means of achieving high-level production gains in countries facing both starvation and the threat of internal 'red' revolutions (Middendorf et al, 1998, p93). It led to gains in output – albeit dependent on the complete use of technological packages, including hybrid seeds and chemicals – some of which was destined for export; yet it also caused considerable ecosystem degradation (Middendorf et al, 1998, p94). When oil prices rose in the 1970s – and fertilizer costs increased as a consequence – many poor farmers with small holdings were driven from the land. In subsequent decades, many more have been forced to leave farming because of the rising costs associated with this so-called productivist model of agriculture, with the irony being that 'by the 1980s, every country revolutionized by the Green Revolution was once again an importer of those staple foods they had expected to produce in abundance' (Kiple and Ornelas, 2000, p15). As Magdoff et al (1998, p11) wrote over a decade ago:

> It is clear that the current food system in all its ramifications is not beneficial for the mass of farmers or the environment, nor does it ensure a plentiful supply of food for all people. However, it does meet the needs of a limited group of large farmers and, of course, the sellers of agricultural inputs as well as the processors, distributors, and sellers of food.

Along with many critical observers of the time, these authors questioned what might be done, and concluded that only 'substantial' changes to the system of food production and distribution would address the pressing issue of food security and sustainability. In short, if the commoditization of food and farming – whereby the generation of profit was the singular end of activity – was the cause of the problem, a more socially just and environmentally sound approach would need to come into being to replace it (Magdoff et al, 1998, p13; see also Allen, 2004; Lang, 2009a). The limits of profit-driven, market-based solutions are perhaps most clearly articulated in the activities of the global *La Via Campesina* movement – an international peasant movement that, in contrast to the export-led model of agricultural development, works to build local food sovereignty by feeding families and local communities via sustainable farming methods (Holt-Giménez et al, 2009). In addition to shifting the focus away from export-led crop production, one of the main elements of the food system targeted for replacement by this movement was so-called 'productivism' – an approach that placed human labour and crop/animal efficiency at the pinnacle of farming success (see Magdoff et al, 1998; Gray and Lawrence, 2001; Lang and Heasman, 2004).

Transnational farm supply firms have been particularly successful in encouraging farmers to use the latest technologies as a means of ensuring the continued application of such technologies in farming. The direct consequence of such strategies – at least in relation to agri-chemicals – has been an increasing dependence upon potent and toxic insecticides, weedicides, and fungicides in plant production, and upon various vaccines and hormones in animal farming, which have combined to foster the monocultural approaches that now dominate farming across the globe (Magdoff et al, 1998). The major technologies that have underpinned productivism are those associated with farm mechanization, genetic improvements in plants and animals, applications of agri-chemicals, as well as growth stimulants and antibiotics to assist animal growth and prevent disease (Altieri, 1998). The 'factory farms' that are dependent upon this potent mix cannot be considered sustainable production systems, however. They are structured in a manner that has both direct and indirect consequences for the social and ecological bases of sustainable farming:

- They generate wastes that are not re-used. This is particularly the case for intensive livestock production units where wastes are usually not recycled and are often discarded, causing environmental pollution. A topical example is the 2009 outbreak of Swine flu – renamed Influenza A (H1N1) – that has been linked to human exposure to pollution generated from pig-raising operations in Vera Cruz, Mexico (Patel, 2009).
- They reduce food crop diversification by relying on the planting of monocultures over large areas. These attract pests in large numbers and require toxic doses of poisons to keep the pests under control.
- They foster pest resistance, which means that ever-more powerful chemical concoctions need to be applied in future cycles.
- They reduce biodiversity and the functional redundancy associated with it. The aim is to plant crops and raise animals that have the highest energy conversion rates, thereby eschewing those species that have lower potential but which might, nevertheless, have other desirable characteristics (hardiness, for example).
- They lead to the adoption of propriety seed/pesticide 'packages' as a means of seeking continual productivity gains. This has the effect of making farmers – and therefore wider society – dependent on corporate agribusiness, while conferring increasing power on those companies to shape the future contours of (industrial) agriculture (see Altieri, 1998; Gray and Lawrence, 2001; Jansen and Vellema, 2004; Lang and Heasman, 2004; Patel, 2007).

There are voices, even in conservative global governance bodies, calling for things to change. As the director of the FAO's plant production and protection division, Shivaji Pandey, has stated current production systems will need to be altered for the world's agricultural ecosystem to be restored:

> In the name of intensification in many places around the world, farmers have over-ploughed, over-fertilized and over-irrigated, and over-applied pesticides. But in doing so we [have] also affected all aspects of the soil, water, land, biodiversity and the services provided by an intact ecosystem (quoted in Cresswell, 2009, p1).

Similarly, a report published by the International Assessment of Agricultural Knowledge, Science and Technology for Development (IAASTD) – an intergovernmental group of over 400 scientists and UN agencies – has linked high-tech and reductionist farming with environmental and natural resource degradation that includes deforestation, the introduction of invasive species, and increased pollution and greenhouse gas emissions. The report also associated capital-intensive and high-tech farming with rising food prices and increasing rates of poverty. The group concluded that the way the world grows its food would have to change radically if the poor and hungry are to be better served (IAASTD, 2008).

This would seem to be a damning condemnation of productivism. Nonetheless, the arguments for such a system continue to resound when the alternatives are as yet unproven. Productivism has been highly successful in producing ever-increasing volumes of food, with some arguing that any attempt to abandon this approach will increase global food insecurity and condemn millions of human beings to death from starvation (Avery, 1995). How will the world increase its food output by a minimum of 50 per cent over the next three decades to feed the expected population (see Cresswell, 2009)? Increased food provision will also have to take place in the face of climate change, fights over water for irrigation, competition for access to cultivable lands, and limited access to the nutrients and energy currently derived from fossil fuels. Not only this, but the increases in global agricultural production are arguably beginning to plateau (Cresswell, 2009). Although Lang and Heasman (2004) have reported strong challenges to productivism from both the life sciences industry[7] and from an ecologically integrated paradigm that includes organics, and while writers have identified the emergence of a 'post-productivist' countryside in the UK and Europe (Wilson, 2001), it remains true that agribusiness-based and petrochemical-dependent industrial agriculture is not only entrenched in food-exporting nations such as Canada, the US and Australia (see Gray and Lawrence, 2001), but is being delivered worldwide to nations like Thailand, the Philippines and China (Pritchard and Burch, 2003).

It has been proposed that one way forward will be to apply GM technology to boost productivity. Perhaps unsurprisingly, the World Bank has endorsed the biotech push, claiming that 'GM crops could offer a range of benefits over the longer term' (quoted in Cresswell, 2009, p2). Meanwhile, the AGRA is working to spread GM seeds across the African landscape, while simultaneously working to shape African policies and media opinion in favour of GM technologies (Holt-Giménez et al, 2009).

But GM appears little more than an add-on to productivism. While some fertilizers and pesticides might be abandoned in the GM 'revolution' (the irony of such a move being that the majority of GM crops currently being cultivated are modified to resist *increased* exposure to pesticides and herbicides), the system of intensive agriculture remains intact – with all its vulnerability to more devastating infestations of bugs able to kill, or to render sick, the industrially produced plants and animals that are feeding the developed world (see Hindmarsh and Lawrence, 2004). The supposed benefits of GM technologies are, nonetheless, based upon their purported environmental credentials. For example, McMichael (2009a, p252) has reported that large agro-biotechnology firms such as Monsanto, Bayer and Dupont are already filing patents on 'climate ready' genes, hoping that the global food crisis will induce farmers and governments to resort to genetically modified seeds as part of any 'adaptation' to drought, pest attacks and other manifestations of changing climatic conditions. Meanwhile, a number of universities and industries, both singly and in collaboration, are applying for patents on products and processes involving 'synthetic biology' – a result of the convergence of a number of technologies, including biotechnology, nanotechnology and information technology – many of which are being marketed as 'environmentally friendly'. Yet, their impacts are likely to introduce new environmental and social risks. As a case in point, synthetic biology is currently being applied to create new forms of agrofuels with increased efficiency both in terms of crop production and in terms of crop conversion into ethanol. Such developments are likely further to intensify the production of monoculture crops, as well as the transformation of increasing areas of agricultural land from food to fuel production and thus, notably, provide an opening for the energy sector to increasingly influence agricultural policies (ETC Group, 2007a).

High-tech and converging technologies such as GM, synthetic biology and nanotechnology are not the only future on offer, however. An alternative is so-called 'small-footprint' technology (Ambler-Edwards et al, 2009, p28). These new technologies aim to reduce the amount of material required for the manufacturing of products by using more energy-efficient technologies and by re-using waste through recycling. In agriculture, such technologies could include: methane 'digesters' that can generate energy; controlled fertilizer release that reduces run-off; use of on-farm waste as green fertilizer; and the application of drip irrigation (Ambler-Edwards et al, 2009, p28). This model of agri-food production holds the promise of providing viable livelihoods for people in a manner that ensures that nature is not compromised (Scherr and Sthapit, 2009, p33). In relation to the current challenges of climate change, this approach would include the absorption and storage of carbon in plants, the reduction of emissions from rice and livestock production systems, a major decrease in the burning of timber, and the cutting back of nitrous oxide emissions from inorganic fertilizers (Schahczenski and Hill, 2009).[8]

Systems capable of delivering enhanced sustainability would be those that can enrich soil carbon, employ high carbon-cropping approaches, reduce the impact of livestock-intensive production systems, conserve the current carbon that is stored in forests and grasslands, and encourage the planting of trees and other vegetation in areas of degradation (Scherr and Sthapit, 2009, p33). Organic production methods, conservation tillage and crop rotation, along with the grazing of livestock on grasslands and the replanting of once-cleared lands to forests, are five main ways of reducing the current impact of agri-food production systems on the environment (Lockie et al, 2006; Schahczenski and Hill, 2009; Scherr and Sthapit, 2009). Organic and agro-ecological methods are especially recommended as they have out-performed productivist approaches by providing environmental benefits such as soil water retention (and hence increased drought tolerance) and improvement in soil fertility (Altieri, 1998; Environmental News Service, 2009).

Moreover, according to Scherr and Sthapit (2009), the global consensus on the need to reduce the greenhouse gas 'footprint' implicates the entire agri-food system, in as much as up to one-third of greenhouse gas emissions (McMichael, 2009a, p139) must be reduced along all sections of the chain that deliver foods and fibres to consumers – production, transportation, refrigeration, packing, storing and point of sale. Waste, too, must also be addressed. Achim Steiner, the Under-Secretary-General of the United Nations Environment Programme (UNEP), has reported that over half the food produced in the world today is 'either lost, wasted or discarded as a result of inefficiencies in the human-managed food chain' (reported in Hill, 2009). Food loss in the US currently sits at around 50 per cent, with at least one-quarter of all fruits and vegetables being wasted between the farm gate and the fork (Environmental News Service, 2009). It has been suggested that recovering only 5 per cent of this wastage per day could feed 4 million people (Ambler-Edwards et al, 2009, p12). Altering the proportion of cereal crops dedicated to the production of animal feed would, finally, enhance the system capacity to feed the world's poorest people. UNEP (2009) has reported that up to 30 per cent of all cereals that are produced in the world are currently used for animal feeds, and that this is expected to rise to 50 per cent by 2050, limiting the ability of any expansion in crop production to directly feed the hungry through increased grain supply.

As Lang (2009a, p30) has cogently argued, food security 'can *only* mean sustainability'. Thus, food security will only be achieved when:

- the core goal is to feed everyone sustainably, equitably and healthily;
- culturally appropriate goals of suitability, availability and accessibility are pursued;
- the food system is ecologically sound and resilient in the face of environmental volatility;
- agriculture enhances the productive capacity of the land;
- the food system builds capacities and skills to ensure that future generations can continue to produce food in a sustainable manner (Lang, 2009a, p30).

In addition to this, Pinstrup-Andersen (2009) has suggested that it is not enough to focus on food security, or sustainability, if people continue to be exposed to poor sanitation and polluted water. Nutritional levels might be acceptable, but people will continue to suffer and die from exposure to water-borne diseases in rivers and streams polluted with sewage. The nutritional deficiencies of the world's poor and hungry should be viewed as just one element of a wider suite of needs that must be addressed *in toto* if progress is to be made in the creation of a world where healthy people live in healthy landscapes. In this regard, a 'health enhancing' food system will also need to be one that provides for carbon reduction while generalizing nutritional benefits across nations, and that ultimately seeks to abandon productivism (Lang, 2009b). Revisiting the economic thrust of the depression times characteristic of the Roosevelt years, this could be part of a so-called 'Green' New Deal in the current period of volatile global economic conditions (Lang, 2009b, p583).

The themes of the book

The book is divided into three parts: Part One 'Global Food Security'; Part Two 'Food Systems, Diet and Nutrition'; and Part Three 'Towards a Sustainable Agri-Food Future'. While each chapter takes one of these themes as its primary focus, we believe the content of each chapter will demonstrate that these themes are highly interrelated. Indeed, we hope this book will demonstrate the extent to which theoretical and practical approaches for addressing the global agri-food crisis will benefit from the consideration of issues as diverse as food security, nutrition and health, and social and environmental sustainability collectively, rather than as separate entities.

In Part One, the contributing authors deal with various aspects of global food security. In this first section of the book, authors explain some of the structural and regulatory circumstances that have shaped international agriculture and food trade, and then explore some of the implications of these circumstances for food security, food policy and fossil-fuel energy use. This section identifies some of the challenges for countries in both the North and South in achieving food security – including those challenges emerging in the broad context of climate change, peak oil and the 'meatification' of global diets.

In Chapter 2, Tony Weis explains the nature of the grain-livestock production complex in the US and Canada – which is at the heart of both contemporary energy-dense diets and global food trade for these nations. He examines the environmental, energy and other so-called 'quickening' contradictions that are emerging from this form of production. Weis considers that, despite the current dependence on this form of agriculture, there are clear signs that the US and Canada will need to move towards a 'post carbon' farming future. Opportunities will arise, he argues, for the rebuilding of localism in food economies, for the fostering of more effective forms of rural development, as well as for the creation of more sustainable and equitable farming alternatives. He argues that progressive forces in the US and Canada have the potential not only to transform farming in both nations, but also to assist in the re-localization of food provision in the South.

In Chapter 3, Gianluca Brunori and Angela Guarino examine how discourses about food and agriculture are changing in the EU in the context of the global food crisis. They compare the two prominent discourses in Europe – the discourses of 'mass agriculture' (industrial farming) and 'agriculture for rural development' (diversified, multifunctional farming systems) – and conclude that the various crises being experienced globally have begun to favour the second approach. There is now talk of the need for 'resilience' in farming communities, along with the application of local knowledge and the encouragement of more biodiverse, regional food systems. They call on those in the fields of education and communication to assist in changing the attitudes and behavior of consumers so that they may move away from the purchase of industrially produced foods and towards foods produced in a more sustainable manner.

Chapter 4 deals with the re-emergence, in the UK, of a national food security agenda. According to David Barling, Tim Lang and Rosalind Sharpe, the recent policy of UK governments has been to secure foods globally, under conditions of increasing trade liberalization, in the belief that imported foods help to reduce the risk of food shortages in the UK that might arise from domestic crop failures or from profound livestock disorders like 'mad cow' disease. Yet, questions are being raised about the resilience of global food supply and the extent to which international food sourcing is, in some way, connected to domestic attempts to move towards more sustainable systems of rural production. They argue that a mismatch is occurring. The government's commitment to a liberalized trade regime has driven farmers to adopt a more productivist-based efficiency regime while, at the same time, there is a distinctive push by both the UK public and by government to make agriculture more environmentally sustainable. There is no obvious resolution to this conundrum, at this time.

Gabriela Pechlaner and Gerardo Otero link growing food vulnerability to neoliberal economic policy. In Chapter 5, they highlight the hypocritical position of the North in advocating for free trade, while generously funding home-grown economic protectionism. To counter this, they consider that countries of the South should return to policies of self-sufficiency so that there is national control over food provision, as well as a fetter on corporate domination of the global food industry.

In the final chapter in this section, Jago Dodson, Neil Sipe, Roy Rickson and Sean Sloan focus upon global oil price vulnerability. They argue that, because the conventional agri-food industries are heavily dependent upon petroleum products for tractor fuel, chemical inputs and for the transport of products, fuel price hikes have a significant effect on the overall price of foods. Not only that, but any future oil shortages – requiring farm businesses to pay more for fuel and chemical inputs to farming – are likely to simultaneously intensify the concentration of land ownership and food processing. This, they argue, will result in the continued dominance of large-scale capital in farming and in the food industry.

Part Two of the book turns to an examination of food systems, diet and nutrition. Here, contributing authors explore the extent to which those structural aspects of global food systems – some of which are outlined in Part One – shape broader experiences of nutrition, diet and health. Authors explore various links between the structural inequities that characterize contemporary agri-food systems – including the increasing supermarket retailer concentration, the paradox of food regulations and the merger of the food and pharmaceutical industries – and the inequities in food access, as well as in the distribution of diet-related illness.

In Chapter 7, Sharon Friel and Wieslaw Lichacz link unhealthy diets to what they term 'unequal' food systems. These authors argue that the global system – in which major transnational firms determine the availability, quality and affordability of food – establish the conditions for the uneven distribution of food between, and within, nations. They comment upon the nutrition transition that occurred in India, indicating that globalization has altered middle-class diets so that they resemble those of the west – high in saturated fats and sugars. The reason for this is that the removal of domestic subsidies has undermined conventional food production, allowing cheaper western-style processed foods to become more readily available. As a result, there has been an increase in diet-related diseases, as well as the displacement of peasants from agriculture as the food giants and supermarkets increase their influence.

Convenience food consumption is the issue of concern for Lisa Schubert, Megan Jennaway and Helen Johnson. In Chapter 8, these authors present four 'frames' for understanding the consumption of convenience food. Each frame has a basic mantra ('there's not enough time in the day to cook', 'McDonald's made me fat', and so on), and each frame has particular weaknesses (in assuming, for example, that consumers are rational in their purchasing, or that consumers might be receptive to diet-related health messages). The authors critically assess approaches to the question of why consumers have embraced convenience foods and conclude that no single approach can provide an adequate explanation. They urge food researchers to be aware of both structure and agency in accounting for food demand, to improve the understanding of both consumption and production in household economies, and to provide historically rich descriptions of how fast foods and convenience foods have become so prominent in the marketplace.

In Chapter 9, Stewart Lockie and Susan Williams introduce various sociological perspectives to explain the emergence of the so-called 'obesity epidemic'. They argue that excessive weight and obesity became framed as an epidemic by the 1990s while, at the same time, equal numbers of media headlines also began to question the veracity of such claims. In this context, their chapter aims to establish the extent to which being overweight or being obese is really an issue. With an empirical focus on Australia, and with additional empirical and theoretical insights drawn from an international perspective, this chapter points to the need for new sociological approaches that will help us to better understand weight gain and obesity.

In Chapter 10, Mark Lawrence analyses the food and nutrition regulatory system in Australia and New Zealand. Through an examination of three aspects of food regulation, he demonstrates the tensions that persist in defining the boundaries of food regulation and food regulators. While, on the one hand, this chapter demonstrates the role of regulation in supporting the expansion of the food industries it argues, on the other hand, that regulators also have a mandate to ensure the protection of public health. As an outcome of this tension, Lawrence argues that modern food regulatory systems are limited in their capacity to protect public health, and remain largely disengaged from contemporary health, social and environmental considerations.

Shifting the focus of this part of the book from an analysis of food regulations to the activities of the food industries, David Burch and Geoffrey Lawrence trace the extent to which the agri-food industries are forming new alliances with the pharmaceutical industries. They explore, in Chapter 11, the way such industries are transforming their product ranges – including embracing so-called functional foods – as part of the 'wellness revolution'. This revolution is reflected in a growing consumer interest in, and demand for, healthy foods, as well as in the more general pursuit of healthy lifestyles. These authors trace the emerging alliances and strategic partnerships between the food and pharmaceutical industries, and evaluate some of the implications for agri-food companies and for the future of food and agriculture.

In the final chapter in this section, Libby Hattersley and Jane Dixon begin to explore a research agenda that would assist in understanding and analysing the impacts of supermarkets in the arena of public health. They begin by highlighting the concentration of retailer power across the agri-food system, describing supermarkets as the 'gatekeepers' in agri-food supply chains. Given the on-going support for self-regulation, supermarkets are effectively able to dictate what, where and how our food is produced. Nonetheless, there is currently a limited understanding of the impacts of the influence of supermarket corporate power on public health. The authors suggest a research agenda that might allow an interrogation of such public health impacts, and conclude the chapter by questioning where responsibility lies for public health.

Contributing authors to Part Three of the book map out some of the challenges and opportunities in moving towards a sustainable agri-food future. Chapters offer approaches for re-thinking the contributions of community gardens and urban agriculture in building sustainable cities, analyse the impacts of emerging agri-food industries – including agrofuels and nanotechnologies – and the extent to which they enable the further extension of industrial and unsustainable agri-food systems, and evaluate, in a critical fashion, the contributions organic agri-food systems might make to a sustainable future.

In Chapter 13, Kelly Donati, Susan Cleary and Lucy Pike focus upon the social, economic and ecological contributions of community gardens. While acknowledging the importance of previous analyses of community gardens, these authors draw on the concept of 'liveliness' to expand understandings and ways of thinking about community gardens and their impacts on urban life. In so doing, their research with participants at the 'Garden of Eden' demonstrates outcomes that far exceed policy objectives, including the opportunity to create new ethical and political associations between humanity and nature.

The recent rapid expansion in the global biofuels (agrofuels) industry reflects the coalescence of the food and energy crises. In Chapter 14, Sophia Murphy describes such expansion, which has been driven by both government and industry investment. Given the energy dependence of contemporary food systems – a theme explored in Part One of this book – biofuels have emerged as a potential energy solution. Despite the hopes of biofuels advocates, however, Murphy's critical evaluation demonstrates the entrenched nature of fossil-fuel based systems of agriculture, of food insecurity and of unsustainable farming methods.

In Chapter 15, a multidisciplinary team of researchers – Hugh Campbell, Chris Rosin, Solis Norton, Peter Carey, Jayson Benge and Henrik Moller – consider the contributions of organic farming towards achieving agricultural sustainability. They begin by outlining public debates and media representations associated with organics, including the range of mythologies frequently associated with organic food and farming. Such representations are often polarized, ignoring the nuances of scientific and other academic debates. This chapter builds upon those discourses that seek to move beyond these polarized debates. Drawing from a decade of research by the Agriculture Research Group on Sustainability (ARGOS) in New Zealand, the authors offer a preliminary assessment of the extent to which organic farming may be compatible with the broader goals of agricultural sustainability.

At the same time as the global organic agriculture sector continues to grow, so do a range of high-tech and capital-intensive agri-food options, many of which are also promoted on the basis of their capacity to contribute towards agricultural sustainability. The development and application of nanotechnologies across the agriculture and food sectors – from nano-seeds and nano-chemicals to nano-food packaging and nano-food itself – demonstrates the compatibility of yet another technological innovation with past 'technological treadmill' approaches to food production. In Chapter 16, Gyorgy Scrinis and Kristen Lyons discuss the ways in which agri-food nanotechnologies provide a techno-scientific platform to extend the industrial and corporate model of agriculture. They contend that agri-food nanotechnologies stand counter to moves towards agricultural sustainability and are set to introduce a new order of environmental, social and health risks. In light of these risks, the authors expect that resistance to nano-food and nano-farming will continue to grow, as communities seek alternative solutions to the challenges facing agriculture and food systems.

In the final chapter of this book, Tim Lang evaluates the prospects and challenges of weaving together agriculture and food policy in a way that addresses the many challenges relating to food security, nutrition and sustainability. He describes the looming environmental, health, social, cultural and economic problems that are faced by the world and talks of the need to 'recast' everyday food activities in a manner that provides sustenance while respecting nature. He outlines the policy settings that might assist in creating more environmentally sustainable food systems, and reflects upon the possibilities for banishing hunger. Lang is insistent that a new global agri-food trajectory needs to be one that utilizes the best of science, but does so in a manner that empowers people to identify healthy eating as a primary goal. It is a trajectory that will question the mass-marketing techniques of the fast-food industry, that will confront supermarket power and that will help to re-localize food provision. Are these changes possible? Lang argues that positive change will only occur when the state plays a more important role in ensuring that beneficial public health outcomes become better matched to sustainability goals in agri-food industries, worldwide.

Notes

1 'Agrofuels' is the term used by writers such as McMichael (2009a) to draw attention to the fact that the fuels are agriculturally based and hence have implications for the amount of food that is removed from markets due to their production. Biofuels and agrofuels are used interchangeably throughout the book.

2 Patel notes that it is not as simple as characterizing the 'starved' as all belonging to the South, pointing to entrenched food insecurity among the poor in the US (Patel, 2007, p3).

3 Tim Lang prefers the phrase 'food democracy' to sovereignty, pointing out that 'sovereign' refers to top-down approaches that can lead to the exclusion of grassroots democratic processes and accountability (see Lang, 2009a). McMichael (2009b) argues that the food sovereignty movement helps to politicize the commoditization of food and expose environmentally destructive practices in farming, helping to foster an 'ethic' that could result in the emergence, globally, of a more democratic food regime.

4 For a discussion of the various meanings and interpretations of the term 'food security' see Pinstrup-Andersen (2009).

5 Subsidies to US corn producers include those for farm machinery, fertilizers, transportation and credit (see Patel, 2007, p49).

6 In poor countries 60–80 per cent of income is spent on food, so any increase in food prices has a direct and often devastating effect upon purchasing power (Loewenberg, 2008, p1209).

7 It could also be argued that the 'life sciences' approach is nothing more than an extension of productivism.

8 Approaches to shift agriculture in ways that manage and/or reverse climate change stand in stark contrast to a range of radical techniques currently being experimented with to alter climatic systems and biological processes. Arguably one of the most radical among these new approaches includes geo-engineering, or the intentional manipulation of the earth's land, sea and atmosphere – using controversial techniques such as 'ocean fertilization' (dumping iron into the world's oceans) – in an attempt to combat climate change (ETC Group, 2007b).

References

Allen, P. (2004) *Together at the Table: Sustainability and Sustenance in the American Agrifood System*, Pennsylvania State University, Pennsylvania

Altieri, M. (1998) 'Ecological impacts of industrial agriculture and the possibilities for truly sustainable farming', in F. Magdoff, F. Buttel and J. Foster, *Hungry for Profit: Agriculture, Food and Ecology*, Monthly Review Press, New York

Ambler-Edwards, S., Bailey, K., Kiff, A., Lang, T., Lee, R., Marsden, T., Simons, D. and Tibbs, H. (2009) *Food Futures: Rethinking UK Strategy*, Chatham House, London

Avery, D. (1995) *Saving the Planet with Pesticides and Plastic: The Environmental Triumph of High-Yield Farming*, Hudson Institute, Indianapolis

Bryceson, D., Kay, C. and Mooij, J. (2000) *Disappearing Peasantries? Rural Labour in Africa, Asia and Latin America*, Intermediate Technology Publications, London

Buckland, J. (2004) *Ploughing up the Farm: Neoliberalism, Modern Technology and the State of the World's Farmers*, Fernwood Publishing, Nova Scotia

Burch, D. and Lawrence, G. (eds) (2007) *Supermarkets and Agri-food Supply Chains: Transformations in the Production and Consumption of Foods*, Edward Elgar, Cheltenham, UK

Burch, D. and Lawrence, G. (forthcoming 2009) 'Towards a third food regime: Behind the transformation', *Agriculture and Human Values*

Cresswell, A. (2009) 'Soaring food prices, global warming and natural disasters have experts worried that the world is facing a food crunch', *The Australian*, www.theaustralian.news.com.au/story/0,25197,25041144-28737,00.html, accessed 19 February 2009

Critser, G. (2003) *Fat Land: How Americans Became the Fattest People in the World*, Allen Lane, London

Davis, M. (2007) *Planet of Slums*, Verso, London

De Neve, G., Luetchford, P. and Pratt, J. (2008) 'Introduction: Revealing the hidden hands of global market exchange', *Research in Economic Anthropology*, vol 28, pp1–30

Dixon, J. (2002) *The Changing Chicken: Chooks, Cooks and Culinary Culture*, UNSW Press, Sydney

Dixon, J. and Broom, D. (2007) *The Seven Deadly Sins of Obesity: How the Modern World is Making us Fat*, UNSW Press, Sydney

Environmental News Service (2009) 'The environmental food crisis: A crisis of waste', Environmental News Service, www.ens-newswire.com/ens/feb2009/2009-02-17.01. asp, accessed 20 February 2009

ETC Group (2007a) *Extreme Genetic Engineering: An Introduction to Synthetic Biology,* Action Group on Erosion, Technology and Concentration, Canada

ETC Group (2007b) *Gambling with Gaia – Communique*, Action Group on Erosion, Technology and Concentration, Canada

FAO (2008) *Crop Prospects and Food Situation*, February, Food and Agriculture Organization, Rome

Gray, I. and Lawrence, G. (2001) *A Future for Regional Australia: Escaping Global Misfortune*, Cambridge University Press, Cambridge

Hendrickson, M., Wilkinson, J., Heffernan, W. and Gronski, R. (2008) *The Global Food System and Nodes of Power*, Oxfam, www.ssrn.com/abstract=1337273, accessed 2 March 2009

Heynen, N., McCarthy, J., Prudham, S. and Robbins, P. (2007) 'Introduction: False promises', in N. Heynen, J. McCarthy, S. Prudham and P. Robbins (eds) *Neoliberal Environments: False Promises and Unnatural Consequences*, Routledge, London

Hill, S. (2009) 'UN calls for green revolution to prevent food crisis', Foodnavigator. com, www.foodnavigator.com/content/view/print237025, accessed 20 February

Hindmarsh, R. and Lawrence, G. (eds) (2004) *Recoding Nature: Critical Perspectives on Genetic Engineering*, UNSW Press, Sydney

Holt-Giménez, E., Altieri, M. and Rosset, P. (2006) *Ten Reasons why the Rockefeller and the Bill and Melinda Gates Foundations' Alliance for Another Green Revolution Will Not Solve the Problems of Poverty and Hunger in Sub-Saharan Africa*, Food First Institute for Food and Development Policy, Oakland, CA

Holt-Giménez, E., Patel, R. and Shattuck, A. (2009) *Food Rebellions: Crisis and the Hunger for Justice*, Food First Books, Fahamu Books and Grassroots International, Oxford, UK and Oakland, CA

IAASTD (2008) *Summary for Decision Makers of the Global Report,* International Assessment of Agricultural Knowledge, Science and Technology for Development, US

ITUC (2009) *A Recipe for Hunger: How the World is Failing on Food*, International Trade Union Confederation, Brussels

Jansen, K. and Vellema, S. (2004) *Agribusiness and Society: Corporate Responses to Environmentalism, Market Opportunities and Public Regulation*, Zed Books, London

Jonasse, R. (2009) *Agrofuels in the Americas*, Food First Books, Oakland, CA

Kiple, K. and Ornelas, K. (2000) 'Introduction', in K. Kiple and K. Ornelas (eds) *The Cambridge World History of Food*, Cambridge University Press, Cambridge

Lang, T. (2009a) 'How new is the world food crisis? Thoughts on the long dynamic of food democracy, food control and food policy in the 21st century', paper presented to the Visible Warnings: The World Food Crisis in Perspective conference, April 3–4, Cornell University, Ithaca, NY

Lang, T. (2009b) 'Invited commentary: What President Obama can do in the world', *Public Health Nutrition*, vol 12, no 4, pp581–583

Lang, T. and Barling, D. (2007) 'The environmental impact of supermarkets: Mapping the terrain and the policy problems in the UK', in D. Burch and G. Lawrence (eds) *Supermarkets and Agri-food Supply Chains: Transformations in the Production and Consumption of Foods*, Edward Elgar, Cheltenham, UK

Lang, T. and Heasman, M. (2004) *Food Wars: The Global Battle for Mouths, Minds and Markets*, Earthscan, London

Lang, T. and Rayner, G. (2001) *Why Health is the Key to the Future of Food and Farming: A Report on the Future of Farming and Food*, Department of Health Management and Food Policy, City University, London

Lawrence, F. (2004) *Not on the Label: What Really Goes into the Food on Your Plate*, Penguin, Victoria, Australia

Lockie, S., Lyons, K., Lawrence, G. and Halpin, D. (2006) *Going Organic: Mobilizing Networks for Environmentally Responsible Food Production*, CAB International, Oxfordshire, UK

Loewenberg, S. (2008) 'Global food crisis looks set to continue', *The Lancet*, vol 327, no 9645, pp1209–1210

McMichael, P. (2006) 'Peasant prospects in the neoliberal age', *New Political Economy*, vol 11, no 3, pp407–418

McMichael, P. (2008) 'The peasant as "canary"? Not too early warnings of global catastrophe', *Development*, vol 51, no 4, pp504–511

McMichael, P. (2009a) 'Contemporary contradictions of the global development project: Geopolitics, global ecology and the "development climate"', *Third World Quarterly*, vol 30, no 1, pp247–262

McMichael, P. (2009b) 'A food regime genealogy', *Journal of Peasant Studies*, vol 36, no 1, pp139–169

McMichael, P. (2009c) 'Banking on agriculture: A review of the World Development Report 2008', *Journal of Agrarian Change*, vol 9, no 2, pp235–246

McMichael, P. (forthcoming 2009) 'A food regime analysis of neo-liberalism's food crisis', *Agriculture and Human Values*

Magdoff, F., Buttel, F. and Foster, J. (1998) *Hungry for Profit: Agriculture, Food and Ecology*, Monthly Review Press, New York

Mazoyer, M. and Roudart, L. (2006) *A History of World Agriculture: From the Neolithic Age to the Current Crisis*, Earthscan, London

Middendorf, G., Skladany, M., Ransom, E. and Busch, L. (1998) 'New agricultural biotechnologies: The struggle for democratic choice', in F. Magdoff, F. Buttel and J. Foster, *Hungry for Profit: Agriculture, Food and Ecology*, Monthly Review Press, New York

Murton, B. (2000) 'Australia and New Zealand', in K. Kiple and K. Ornelas (eds) *The Cambridge World History of Food,* Cambridge University Press, Cambridge

Nestle, M. (2003) *Safe Food: Bacteria, Biotechnology and Bioterrorism*, University of California Press, Berkeley

Nestle, M. (2006) *What to Eat,* North Point Press, New York

Otero, G. (ed) (2008a) *Food for the Few: Neoliberal Globalism and Biotechnology in Latin America*, University of Texas Press, Austin

Otero, G. (2008b) 'Neoliberal globalism and the biotechnology revolution: Economic and historical context', in G. Otero (ed), *Food for the Few: Neoliberal Globalism and Biotechnology in Latin America*, University of Texas Press, Austin

Pace, N., Seal, A. and Costello, A. (2008) 'Food commodity derivatives: A new cause of malnutrition?' *The Lancet*, vol 371, no 9625, pp1648–1650

Patel, R. (2007) *Stuffed and Starved: Markets, Power and the Hidden Battle for the World Food System*, Black Ink, Melbourne

Patel, R. (2009) 'Swine flu roundup', *Stuffed and Starved*, www.stuffedandstarved. org/drupal/node/481, accessed 7 May 2009

Pinstrup-Andersen, P. (2009) 'Food security: Definition and measurement', *Food Security*, no 1, pp5–7

Pritchard, B. and Burch, D. (2003) *Agri-food Globalization in Perspective: International Restructuring in the Processing Tomato Industry*, Ashgate, Aldershot, UK

Rosset, P. (2006) *Food is Different: Why We Must Get the WTO Out of Agriculture*, Fernwood Publishing, Nova Scotia

Schahczenski, J. and Hill, H. (2009) 'Agriculture, climate change and carbon sequestration', National Sustainable Agriculture Information Service, www.attra. ncat.org, accessed 24 February 2009

Scherr, S. and Sthapit, S. (2009) 'Farming and land use to cool the planet', in Worldwatch Institute, *2009 State of the World: Into a Warming World*, www.worldwatch.org/ stateoftheworld, accessed 24 February 2009

Sharma, D. (2006) 'Farmer suicides', *Third World Resurgence,* no 191

Symons, M. (2007, second edition) *One Continuous Picnic: A Gastronomic History of Australia*, Melbourne University Press, Melbourne

Teather, D. (2008) 'Austerity Britain: Crunch forces consumers to change habits', *Guardian*, 5 September

UNEP (2009) *The Environmental Food Crisis: The Environment's Role in Averting Future Food Crises*, United Nations Environment Programme, Geneva

Weis, T. (2007) *The Global Food Economy: The Battle for the Future of Farming*, Zed Books, London

Wilson, G. (2001) 'From productivism to post-productivism ... and back again? Exploring the (un)changed natural and mental landscapes of European agriculture', *Transactions of the Institute of British Geographers*, new series, vol 26, pp103–120

Part I
Global Food Security

2
Breadbasket Contradictions: The Unstable Bounty of Industrial Agriculture in the United States and Canada

Tony Weis

Introduction

Agricultural systems in the US and Canada are the most industrialized in the world. Defining characteristics of this system of industrial agriculture include massive machinery, heavy use of inputs, the predominance of monocultures, large populations of intensively reared livestock, exceptionally high levels of per farmer productivity, the disarticulation of agriculture from rural communities, the control of agricultural inputs and outputs by large transnational corporations (TNCs), and the illusion of diversity in supermarkets and other retail outlets. The productive bounty of industrial agriculture has led to an out-sized place in the global food economy. With some 5 per cent of the world's total population (1 in 20) and only 0.25 per cent of the world's agricultural population (just 1 in 400), the US and Canada produce 14 per cent of world agro-exports by value, account for 15 per cent of the world's agricultural GDP, and absorb roughly 12 per cent of all agro-imports (FAO, 2007a, Tables C.1, C.2).

Many of the technological innovations underpinning the industrialization of agriculture, from the John Deere steel plough in the 19th century to the rise of factory farming in the 20th century, were initiated in the US and were entwined with mounting corporate power over agriculture. As a result, the US is home to many of the world's largest TNCs in all aspects of these agricultural systems, from farm equipment (for example, Deere & Company, CNH Global and AGCO Corporation), to agro-inputs (Monsanto, Dow, DuPont-Pioneer and Cargill), food processing and distribution (ADM, Kraft, Bunge, PepsiCo,

Tyson, Cargill, Coca-Cola and Mars Inc.), fast food (McDonald's, Compass, Yum! Brands and Sodexo) and grocery retailing (Wal-Mart).

The productivity of industrial agriculture, combined with the extensive global reach of TNCs, has bound agricultural systems in the US and Canada into trading relationships that deeply affect the conditions of food security in many parts of the world, in two primary ways. First, the US and Canada are relatively low-cost 'breadbasket' exporters, producing food durables that not only have a powerful impact on world market prices, but also work to re-shape consumption patterns. Second, these countries are large-scale importers, assisted by the prominent influence of TNCs in connecting tropical and semi-tropical agricultural production (which typically constitute a large share of the export base of poor countries) to these sizable markets, while extracting value from commodity chains in the process (Robbins, 2003; Rosset, 2006; Weis, 2007). Consistently large surpluses, cheap food prices and effective corporate branding have long served to conceal (or even counteract) some of the contradictions associated with this inequitable, and ultimately unsustainable, trajectory. There are strong indications that the biophysical basis of this system is beginning to fracture and, as cheap food surpluses become more volatile in the short term and inevitably more costly in the longer term, such instability has implications for food security on a much broader scale – with rising food prices in 2006–2007 providing an indication of the uneven social fallout associated with this trend.

To assess this recent price volatility alongside the longer-term challenge of ensuring access to affordable food on a global scale, it is necessary to first examine the nature of the agricultural system in the US and Canada.

The industrial grain-oilseed-livestock complex

The booming productivity of mechanized, high-input, monocultures across much of the temperate world is closely coupled to the growing scale and intensity of farm animal rearing. Nowhere is this more true than in the US and Canada. Friedmann (1993) has described this system as the industrial grain-livestock complex, which should now be slightly nuanced as 'industrial grain-*oilseed*-livestock complex' to reflect the critical role of oilseeds in this system. In 2004, the US and Canada together produced 389 million tonnes of cereal grains, a 29 per cent increase from a quarter century earlier and nearly one-fifth of the world's total production (FAO, 2007a, Table B.1). Maize is by far the largest grain produced in the US by volume and land area, and the US produced more than two-fifths of the world's total in 2007, while wheat has long been Canada's most important grain (FAOSTAT, 2009). Soybeans are the primary oilseed in the US (as they are globally), and are connected to maize for both rotational and feed-mixing benefits. US soybean production has more than doubled by volume since the early 1970s, and accounted for roughly one-third of the world's total in 2007. Canola/rapeseed is the primary oilseed produced in Canada, accounting for nearly one-fifth of the world's total in 2007 (FAOSTAT, 2009).

The increasing cycling of concentrated feed through livestock in the US and Canada has allowed farm animal populations to far exceed rangeland stocking capacities, and has led to livestock productivity levels far above global averages. Together, the US and Canada produced 43.5 million tonnes of meat in 2004, representing a 62 per cent increase from the previous quarter century, which amounted to 17 per cent of the world's meat production by volume, including more than one-fifth of the world's poultry and beef by volume (it is notable, however, that despite this sizable increase their share in the world total actually fell slightly over this time as meat production grew even faster in some rapidly industrializing countries such as China). Livestock production in the US and Canada is centred upon three species – cattle, chicken and pigs – which account for virtually all animal flesh, as well as derivatives like eggs and dairy products (FAO, 2007a, Table B.2; FAOSTAT, 2009). Most of the livestock (including nearly all chicken and pigs) are raised in homogenized, warehouse conditions on a massive scale, arrangements that have been euphemistically termed 'concentrated animal feeding operations' but are more commonly known as factory farms.

To give a sense of the scale of these factory farm operations, in 2007, 99 per cent of 'broilers and other meat-type chickens' in the US were reared on farms that had annual sales in excess of 100,000 birds, two-thirds of which sold in excess of 500,000 birds; and 99 per cent of layer hens were reared on farms with an inventory of 10,000 birds or more, with 434 farms having more than 100,000 birds (USDA NASS, 2008, p24). The average pig farm in the US had an inventory of 900 pigs in 2007, compared with 130 three decades earlier, and over four-fifths of all hogs and pigs were reared on operations with more than 5000 animals. Meanwhile, the number of pig farmers fell sixfold from 1978 to 2007 (USDA NASS, 2008, p7, 23). The trajectory of rising scale and declining number of farms is the same in Canada. In 2006, the average poultry farm in Canada had 5518 hens and chickens, a more than sixfold increase from 1976, while the number of farmers raising chickens fell more than fourfold (StatsCan, 2007a, Table 2.16). The average Canadian pig farm had 1308 pigs in 2006, a fourteen-fold increase from 1976, as the total population of pigs in Canada roughly tripled over this period while the number of farms raising them fell more than five-fold (StatsCan, 2007a, Table 2.13).

Beef and dairy cattle are typically reared in considerably lower densities, though concentrated feedlots for beef cattle and factory conditions for dairy cattle are increasing, and the male offspring of dairy cattle have long been reared in tight confinement for veal production. In 2007, the average cattle farm in the US had an inventory of 100 cattle and calves, but 48 per cent of cattle farms had 500 or more (USDA NASS, 2008, p20). The average cattle farm in Canada had an inventory of 144 in 2006, a rough doubling in three decades, over which time the number of farms raising cattle had fallen by roughly half (StatsCan, 2007a, Table 2.12).

The increased cycling of grains and oilseeds through livestock, the intensification of rearing practices, alongside innovations in breeding and pharmacology, have all served to speed up the 'turnover time' of farm animals from birth to slaughter weight and in yielding dairy products and eggs. This acceleration of turnover time can be seen clearly in the annual total of pigs and chickens sold for slaughter, which has grown much faster than the total 'inventories' of these animals (i.e. the populations at a given date). This trend is most dramatic with regard to chicken production in the US. In 2007, more than 8.9 billion broilers and other meat-type chickens were sold, a threefold increase from three decades earlier (USDA NASS, 2008, p7).

Monoculture grains and oilseeds, and rising populations of intensively reared livestock are, in short, two sides of the same biologically simplified coin. The factory farms dotting the US and Canadian agricultural landscape are directly tied to a large share of both monoculture output and, by extension, to a large share of agricultural inputs and associated toxic waste. When aggregated, the grain-oilseed-livestock complex accounts for roughly 80 per cent of the total volume of agricultural production in the US and Canada (FAO, 2007b). Because of the inefficiencies of cycling grains and oilseeds through livestock to produce flesh and derivatives, the overall land and resources required for agriculture necessarily increase as livestock consumption increases – a relationship that might be conceptualized as the expanding 'ecological hoofprint' of agriculture (Weis, 2007).

The productivity of this system is reflected in comparatively low real consumer food prices, the low average share of income spent on food and high food consumption levels. Based on 2001–2003 data, Americans consumed 35 per cent more calories, 52 per cent more protein and 100 per cent more fat than the world average, while Canadians were also well above the world average for calorific intake (by 28 per cent), for protein intake (by 41 per cent) and for fat intake (by 88 per cent) (FAO, 2007b). A large part of this excessive consumption lies in the steady 'meatification' of diets, or the progressive shift of livestock products to the centre of societal food consumption patterns (Weis, 2007) – particularly poultry, beef, dairy and eggs. The average American consumes roughly 4 times more poultry, 3 times more beef and 6 times more cheese than world per capita levels, with the average Canadian not far behind in consuming 3 times more poultry, 2.5 times more beef and 5 times more cheese than the rest of humanity (FAO, 2007b).

Beyond US and Canadian shores, the global marketplace has also been impacted by the immense productivity of this industrial grain-oilseed-livestock complex, which is characterized by a strong export imperative and an influential position in world trade. In 2004, the US and Canada accounted for some 35 per cent of the world's cereal grain exports by value, including 53 per cent of all maize (primarily the US) and 41 per cent of all wheat (Canada's largest export). Together, these countries have secured an even larger share in the world's oilseeds, with the US being the world's largest exporter of soybeans, and Canada the dominant exporter of canola/rapeseed. For the period from 2001 to 2003, the US exported an average of 85 million tonnes of grain, over 2.5 times more than its total human domestic consumption (i.e. grain consumed as food rather than animal feed). This ratio was even higher in Canada, as average grain exports (18.5 million tonnes) were more than 5 times greater than domestic human consumption (FAO, 2007a, Tables C.16, C18, D.3). Industrial grains, oilseeds and livestock products are also central components in a huge range of globally traded processed goods.

The scale of these surpluses, coupled with long-term price declines, have masked the highly unstable biophysical foundation on which they depend – one that is linked to steady but differentiated processes of dislocation of farmers and consolidation of corporate power across the globe.

Instabilities, distortions and polarization

The nature of the industrial grain-oilseed-livestock complex, as just described, reflects one of the most basic tendencies of industrial capitalism: the progressive substitution of skillful human labour with capital and technology that is at the heart of economies of scale. Mechanization demands the standardization of the productive environment, which has driven the simplification of agro-ecosystems at progressively smaller as well as larger scales, from plant genetics to the celebrated 'amber waves of grain' in the US and Canadian Midwest. Though the scope of this transformation has been momentous, the process of standardizing and simplifying the biophysical foundations of agriculture has not come easy. Bare ground between planted rows, no rotation of crops or fallowing of the land, and the compaction of soil caused by heavy machinery and over-ploughing all pose problems for soil degradation, while the standardization of plant and animal life enhances vulnerability to the impact of weeds, insects, fungus and diseases.

An early and spectacular indication of the biophysical instability of industrializing agriculture occurred with the Dust Bowl of the 1930s in the Midwest, when layers of fertile soils that had accumulated over millennia were swept up and carried away, darkening skies and destroying many farm livelihoods. However, responses to the Dust Bowl did not question the nature of the problems. Instead, a 'technological fix' was sought to override them. For soils, by far the most crucial technological fix was the increasing application of synthetic fertilizer, manufactured using natural gas, with phosphorous and potassium substitutes also dependent upon a non-renewable resource base. In addition to its manufacture, the bulky nature of fertilizer means that its distribution and application also entails significant oil consumption. The post-war period also saw the development of an expanding array of agro-chemicals and animal pharmaceuticals, which were applied to contain the spread of weeds, insects, fungus and disease. While the state subsidized the rapid capitalization of agriculture, subsidies were concentrated amongst the largest producers, while doing little to support most farm households (see Weis, 2007, chapter 2).

Thus, although the Dust Bowl exemplified the instability of industrializing agriculture, subsequent responses accelerated its reliance on an array of external inputs. Increasing dependence upon input suppliers systematically undermined the importance of localized ecological knowledge in agriculture, an important aspect of the shift in control and income away from farmers. So while tractors, combine harvesters, balers and planter/seeders are the most obvious way that labour is substituted with technology, exceptionally high per-farmer levels of fertilizer and chemical consumption are no less central to understanding this trend. The US and Canada together account for roughly 20 per cent of the world's fertilizer production, consuming slightly less than this total (15 per cent), with Canada a major fertilizer exporter (FAO, 2007a, Tables A7, B4). In 2001, the US alone consumed over one-fifth of the world's pesticides, taken as the total of herbicides (which makes up the largest proportion), insecticides, fungicides and disinfectants (US EPA, 2001).

One of the clearest indications of the way that extensive corporate power has shaped the trajectory of agriculture in the US and Canada – as well as the close linkage between agro-input companies and relevant government ministries, regulatory authorities, and extension agencies – is that genetically modified organisms (GMOs) are diffused throughout the agricultural landscapes of the US and Canada more than anywhere else in the world. Conversely, low-input agriculture represents a mere blip on the landscape: certified organic production occurs on less than 1 per cent of all farms in the US (USDA NASS, 2008, p602), and only 1.5 per cent of all farms in Canada (StatsCan, 2007b, Table 1.16), though in both instances this is growing.

Along with rising input costs, control has also been systematically transferred away from farms on the output side of agriculture, and re-directed towards the corporate interests driving technological advances in processing, packaging, refrigeration, transportation and food safety (which have overridden the previous limits to centralization posed by perishability). US corporations were leaders in integrating these activities, as reflected in their prominent global role in processing, distribution and retail.[1]

On the consumption side, the disarticulation of agriculture from communities and the predominance of corporate intermediaries (as agents) and profit maximization (as motive force) are reflected in poles of over- and under-consumption. There are a host of epidemiological problems linked to the proliferation of unhealthy diets (such as the prevalence of excessive fat and cholesterol intake), with the US having the world's highest levels of obesity. Meanwhile, considerable food insecurity persists in spite of very high average consumption levels. In 2007, over 36 million Americans were found to have struggled with food insecurity during the year, including 12 million who went hungry at some point, with much higher percentages among minority populations (Nord et al, 2008). In Canada, some 2.3 million people were identified as being food insecure in 2004, with over 700,000 facing hunger – something particularly marked among the indigenous population (Agriculture and Agri-Food Canada, 2006).

For farmers, the net outcome of the escalating corporate control over agriculture is a rising cost-price squeeze. Farmers purchase machinery and inputs in retail markets while selling to a shrinking number of outlets, with prices further depressed by aggregate productivity gains. This combination of increasing costs, low prices and reduced margins has generated pressure to expand farm size in order to survive, which in turn produces heavy debt loads and bankruptcies – with bigger and more competitive farmers able to grow at the expense of smaller and less successful ones. The net result has been a profound polarization of landholding and productivity, and a steadily decreasing agricultural population. Only 2 per cent of economically active people in the US and Canada are now employed in agriculture (FAO, 2007a, Table A.3). While some see this as 'development' or 'modernization', it nevertheless depends upon fossil energy and derivatives to an extent that is rarely appreciated.

In the US, the largest 8 per cent of landholders (exceeding 1000 acres/ 405ha) possess 67 per cent of all farmland, and those with the largest 16 per cent (exceeding 500 acres/202ha) possess 83 per cent of all irrigated farmland. From 1974 to 2007, while the population of farmers declined slightly, the number of farms greater than 2000 acres (809ha) grew by 29 per cent to over 80,000 (USDA NASS, 2004, p6; USDA NASS, 2008, p7). Rather than helping to mitigate this tendency, US agro-subsidies are notorious for having exacerbated it, with a small percentage of the largest farms having long dominated subsidy receipts (see Environmental Working Group, 2009). Another important and oft-neglected aspect of the inequality of industrial agriculture is the exploitative working conditions faced by a poorly paid, insecure and mostly non-unionized labour force, with extremely violent conditions pervasive in slaughterhouses and factory farms (Majka and Majka, 2000; Human Rights Watch, 2005; Weis, 2007).

The same basic pattern of increasing scale and consolidation has occurred in Canada, except that agricultural subsidies are distributed more evenly in Canada and are therefore less implicated in the process of polarization. Between 1921 and 2006, the number of farms in Canada fell threefold (from 711,090 to 229,373) while total area of agricultural land increased by 20 per cent. This process is continuing apace: between 1986 and 2006, the number of Canadian farms fell by 22 per cent while the average farm size grew by 28 per cent. Furthermore, of those farmers remaining in agriculture, an increasing proportion need to seek off-farm employment to make ends meet. In 2006, 48 per cent of Canadian farmers reported engaging in paid off-farm work, a proportion that had risen from 37 per cent in 1991 (StatsCan, 2007a, Table 6.3).

Such dislocating pressures have also been projected outwards. As surpluses expanded in the post-war period, an intense export imperative arose and a range of state support mechanisms (e.g. food aid, export subsidies) were developed to foster external market growth. A range of motivations were at the root of this strategy, from helping maintain a measure of price stability in domestic markets to US geopolitics and support for allies in the Cold War. Over time, however, the primary beneficiaries of this state-supported export promotion came to be the fast-growing and increasingly globally oriented TNCs. Moreover, this export promotion cannot be disentangled from the range of domestic subsidies supporting the low cost production of vast surpluses. Nor do explicit subsidies, in themselves, represent the whole picture with regard to the distorted competitive advantage of the industrial grain-oilseed-livestock complex.

Compounding this explicit subsidization are the implicit subsidies contained in the non-valuation or under-valuation of a range of environmental impacts (for example, erosion, salinization, water pollution and consumption) and health burdens (persistent toxins, avian flu, listeriosis and 'mad cow disease'), as well as the ethical implications of factory farming and its ecological hoofprint. Environmental externalities extend far beyond their borders, as the industrial grain-oilseed-livestock complex is a significant part of a grossly outsized per capita greenhouse gas footprint (made even more reprehensible by the fact that the US and Canada have played prominent roles in impeding multilateral action on climate change). An incalculable 'geopolitical externality' also implicitly subsidizes industrial agriculture, given that the US consumes roughly a quarter of the world's oil, spends as much on its military as does the rest of the world, and has an entrenched and tension-filled military presence in the Middle East (Weis, 2007; Foster et al, 2008). Canada's growth into a major oil producer could reduce US dependence on the Middle East, but most of Canada's oil supply is in the difficult-to-extract Alberta Tar Sands, which a recent report describes as 'the most destructive project on earth' (Hatch and Price, 2008).

In sum, the competitive advantage of these large industrial surpluses ultimately rests upon an illusory accounting system, one that has bolstered powerful agro-food TNCs and profoundly influenced world markets and dietary change. Further accentuating this, the US was the most prominent actor in the design of the World Trade Organization's Agreement on Agriculture, which has institutionally locked in a measure of trade liberalization. For its part, Canada was an influential member of the pro-liberalization Cairns Group (Weis, 2007, chapter 4). The flipside of this aggressive stance on liberalization is the fact that many of the world's poorest countries, which have the largest agrarian populations, are net food importers and depend upon the cheap surpluses of a small number of temperate countries that includes the US and Canada. This dependence is expected to deepen in the coming years, especially in the arid and semi-arid regions of the global South where agricultural production is projected to be most severely impacted by climate change (IPCC, 2007), a situation made more precarious as the implicit subsidies to industrialized agriculture start to break down.

Quickening contradictions

The biophysical foundation of the industrial grain-oilseed-livestock complex is unstable on many levels, particularly as challenges associated with climate change, land degradation and water availability intensify and intersect. However, the most proximate reason that chronic instabilities are shifting into a state of increasing volatility and crisis – or what might be seen as the quickening of systemic contradictions – stems from the looming scarcity of fossil energy, especially oil.

The energy provided by fossil fuel is the veritable lifeblood of modern economies, accounting for 80 per cent of the world's total primary energy supply, of which oil makes up the largest proportion (34 per cent), followed by coal (25 per cent) and natural gas (21 per cent) (IEA, 2007). Indeed, the centrality of oil is much greater than even this figure indicates, as it provides virtually all of the liquid fuel used to power global transportation systems. It has, of course, long been known that fossil fuel derived energy is a limited resource, but the implications of this realization have been partially obscured by uncertainties about the precise extent of these limits and, hence, the pace at which they are being approached.

Although fossil fuels have continued to be marked by considerable price volatility in recent years, the limits to the world's fossil energy reserves are coming into clearer focus, with oil the most well-known and significant case. For roughly the past three decades there has been a protracted decline in new oil discoveries, despite the application of sophisticated geological assessment techniques. Leading industry estimates, including those given by BP Global and the *Oil and Gas Journal* (2006), place global oil reserves in the range of 1.2–1.3 trillion barrels, an amount equivalent to that consumed since the rise of the Industrial Revolution.

The term 'peak oil' is increasingly used to mark the fact that world oil production will soon peak and inevitably decline. Given that current consumption levels (84.6 million barrels per day in 2007) are much greater than in the past, and are projected to increase still further in the coming decades, the back half of the world's oil supply will be consumed in a much shorter space of time than was the first half. This is described, in bold terms, in a 2007 advertisement from one of the world's largest oil companies, Chevron: 'It took us 125 years to use the first trillion barrels of oil. We'll use the next trillion in 30'. Even an upper-end estimate of 2 trillion barrels of reserves, given by the US Geological Survey, would only delay the inevitable decline by a few decades at current consumption levels. Further, the fact that the remaining supply will be more difficult and more energy intensive to extract (Alberta's Tar Sands being the classic example) promises to compound price pressures associated with increasing scarcity. The decline of coal and natural gas reserves has drawn less attention and is slightly further away, although this trend would be accelerated if large-scale liquification of natural gas occurs.

As discussed, oil and natural gas have a pivotal role in substituting labour with technology, in overriding various biophysical constraints to large-scale monocultures, and in promoting the further centralized control of outputs. Thus, diminishing supplies and rising prices will inevitably filter into industrial agriculture in a range of ways, taking away a large source of implicit subsidization. While this impact is so diffuse that it is difficult to quantify, the dramatic increase in the volatility of food, oil and natural gas prices in recent years – and particularly their concurrently rising prices from 2006 to 2007 – is strongly suggestive of what peak oil will mean for industrial agriculture.

Yet, at the same time, industrial grains and oilseeds are being viewed as a partial 'technological fix' for the coming scarcity of liquid fuel, with the US leading the worldwide surge in biofuel production. The promise of biofuels is that the sun's energy can be captured in plant biomass and converted into liquid form on a renewable basis, with the added advantage that these fuels burn more cleanly. The primary biofuel is ethanol, produced from the fermentation of carbohydrate crops (predominantly maize in the temperate world and sugar in the tropics). Biodiesel production from soybeans is also growing quickly, albeit on a much smaller scale. Over the past decade, a steadily rising share of US grain production has been devoted to ethanol production, including more than one-fifth of the total maize harvest in 2007. More than 100 large-scale ethanol refineries came into production in the US in the past decade, and many more are under construction (WorldWatch and CAP, 2006). The Canadian government has also signalled its enthusiasm for expanding biofuels, though production and related government supports are much smaller than in the US in absolute and relative terms.

The biofuel boom is generating lucrative new opportunities for agro-processing TNCs like ADM, Bunge and Cargill, with the combination of surging demand and US government subsidies constituting a powerful dynamic that is, paradoxically, emboldening industrial agriculture even in the face of very dubious energy budgets. When the extensive fossil energy inputs that go into growing and converting most industrial crops into biofuels (farm machinery, fertilizer production and transport, agro-chemicals, irrigation systems, fermenting/distilling and so forth) are weighed against the liquid energy output, research is finding that it takes almost as much (rare best case) or more (typically) fossil energy to make biofuels than is contained in the fuel itself (Pimentel and Patzek, 2005; Patzek and Pimentel, 2006). 'Second generation' biofuels (including non-edible grasses, woody biomass, straw and waste by-products) hold the possibility of considerably better input-yield ratios – but which hinge on the development of enzymes capable of converting plant cellulose into liquid fuel – are not yet commercially viable, and would still require huge land areas to substitute even a modest fraction of current oil consumption.

Given the centrality of the US to global trade in maize and soybeans, combined with the dominant position and profit-seeking motivation of TNCs over this trade – and the fact that car-drivers possess vastly more consumer power than do the world's poor and hungry – it is not surprising that the biofuel boom poses serious threats to international food security. Escalating biofuel production has had a major role in the draw-down of the world's grain reserves, along with rising demand for livestock feed, and this was another important dimension of rising food prices in 2006–2007. The moral perversity of diverting increasing volumes of edible food into automobiles as hunger worsened was highlighted by Jean Ziegler, the UN Special Rapporteur on Human Rights, who described biofuel production as a 'crime against humanity'.

It seems clear that as the biophysical contradictions of industrial agriculture in the US and Canada intensify in the age of peak oil, without yet de-stabilizing the operative logic of the dominant actors, the implications for food security in the short-to-medium term are ominous and highly regressive.

Transformative possibilities

In the slightly longer term, the transition towards a post-fossil energy agricultural system in the US and Canada poses momentous challenges. But, as in any systemic crisis, there is the possibility for hopeful change – in particular, the possibility exists that as the substitution of labour with technology becomes more difficult and costly, powerful counter-pressures might mount. There will undoubtedly be a search for more technological fixes, but it is also possible that a new economic and ecological logic will compel more locally oriented and diversified knowledge- and labour-intensive agricultural systems to emerge. The need for more labour-intensive agricultural systems will not necessarily tend towards greater equity – with the increasing exploitation of labour being one possible outcome (and it is worth remembering that agro-labour in the US has been described as the 'super-exploited segment of the US working class' – see Majka and Majka, 2000). Nevertheless, it is also possible to envision new opportunities for shifting profits and control away from agro-inputs, trading, processing, distributing and retailing, and re-centring these on farmers and farming communities.

A range of new organizations, together with social activism and a changing ('greening') consciousness, are beginning to challenge the dominant agricultural system in the US and Canada. Some notable dimensions of this challenge include: increased support for progressive farmer organizations like the National Family Farmer Coalition and the National Farmers Union; efforts to organize farm workers and legalize 'illegal' workers (who constitute a sizable share of US farm labour); organic food movements (associations of ecological farmers and consumer co-operatives); the permaculture movement; community and guerrilla gardening; the resonance of the '100 mile diet'; the growth of community supported agriculture and local food boxes; the growth of fair trade networks; the widening base of the Slow Food movement; struggles for the introduction of GMO labelling laws; rural community resistance to factory farms; farm animal welfare movements; ethical vegetarianism; and growing public calls for action to reduce greenhouse gas emissions.

Critics could surely suggest that these influences are largely fragmented at present, and much stronger in some small pockets than they are across large areas of the agro-industrial heartlands. A case could also be made that some 'alternative food networks' hinge less on an anti-systemic understanding of industrial agriculture and more on a narrowly framed self-interest, as relatively wealthy consumers seek to escape chemical-laden, heavily refined food durables and begin to access more diverse, healthy, and organic food baskets.

This criticism points to an urgent challenge: if there are abundant but largely scattered seeds of alternatives, there is a need to find fertile common ground for their germination. At the core of this search for common ground is the task of finding practical answers to the big question of how agrarian livelihoods and landscapes can be re-made as agriculture de-industrializes, underpinned by the need for an array of supports needed in realms such as youth outreach; education and training programmes; agro-ecological research and extension; policies for land access and inheritance; marketing systems; and more equitable subsidy regimes. This will also involve the less tangible but no less central challenge of re-conceptualizing farming within modern societies as a vocation to which people will aspire – one that affords an invigorating, creative, skillful and stable living, and is accessible to non-farmers, particularly younger people.

Conclusion

Given the way that food import dependencies have been forged by cheap food surpluses, the quickening contradictions of industrial agriculture in the US and Canada pose a serious short-term threat to many of the world's poorest people. A longer-term transition towards less industrialized agricultural systems in the US and Canada, whatever shape this takes, is also bound to create difficult challenges for low income, net food importing countries. In the short term and transitional period, this presents rich countries like the US and Canada with a responsibility to significantly increase food aid – not in the form of food surpluses, but in the form of funding to nations in the South to purchase supplies as locally as possible. In the longer term, as the price-deflating pressures of distant industrial surpluses subside, the need to rebuild and re-localize food economies could also open spaces for shifting income – as well as for reforming large-scale holdings currently in low-value tropical commodities – towards small farmers. But any hopeful prospects for small farm livelihoods in the South ultimately also depend upon the urgent reduction of greenhouse gas emissions in order to mitigate the worst impacts of climate change (IPCC, 2007), another way that the world's poor are tied to the economic activity of affluent countries like the US and Canada.

Notes

1   The ETC Group's *Oligopoly, Inc.* (2006) reports are an excellent asset for tracking the concentration of corporate power in agriculture.

References

Agriculture and Agri-Food Canada (2006) 'Canada's Fourth Progress Report on Food Security', Agriculture and Agri-Food Canada, Ottawa, www.agr.gc.ca/misb/fsec-seca/pdf/report-rapport_4_e.pdf, accessed 2 January 2009

Environmental Working Group (2009) Farm Subsidy Database, www.farm.ewg.org/farm/, accessed 2 January 2009

ETC Group (2006) *Oligopoly, Inc.*, www.etcgroup.org/en/materials/publications.html?pub_id=44, accessed 31 December 2008

FAO (2007a) *FAO Statistical Yearbook 2005-6*, Issue 1 – Cross-section by Subject, Food and Agriculture Organization of the United Nations, Rome, www.fao.org/statistics/yearbook/vol_1_1/index.asp, accessed 2 January 2009

FAO (2007b) *FAO Statistical Yearbook 2005-6*, Issue 2 – Country Profiles, Food and Agriculture Organization of the United Nations, Rome, www.fao.org/statistics/yearbook/vol_1_2/site_en.asp?page=cp, accessed 2 January 2009

FAOSTAT (Food and Agriculture Organization of the United Nations Statistics Division) (2009) Production Statistics Calculator, www.faostat.fao.org/site/567/DesktopDefault.aspx?PageID=567, accessed 20 April 2009

Foster, J., Holleman, H. and McChesney, R. (2008) 'The US imperial triangle and military spending', *Monthly Review*, vol 60, no 5, pp1–19

Friedmann, H. (1993) 'The political economy of food: A global crisis', *New Left Review*, no 197, pp29–57

Hatch, C. and Price, M. (2008) *Canada's Toxic Tar Sands: The Most Destructive Project on Earth*, Environmental Defence Fund, Toronto, www.environmentaldefence.ca/reports/pdf/TarSands_TheReport.pdf, accessed 2 January 2009

Human Rights Watch (2005) *Blood, Sweat, and Fear: Workers Rights in US Meat and Poultry Plants*, Human Rights Watch, New York

IEA (2007) *Key World Energy Statistics*, International Energy Agency, Paris

IPCC (2007) *Climate Change 2007: The Physical Science Basis*, Intergovernmental Panel on Climate Change, Geneva

Majka, L., and Majka, T. (2000) 'Organizing US farm workers: A continuous struggle', in F. Magdoff, J. Foster and F. Buttel (eds) *Hungry for Profit: The Agribusiness Threat to Farmers, Food, and the Environment*, Monthly Review Press, New York

Nord, M., Andrews, M. and Carlson, S. (2008) 'Household food security in the United States', United States Department of Agriculture Economic Research Service, *Economic Research Report* no 66, November, www.ers.usda.gov/Publications/ERR66/ERR66.pdf, accessed 2 January 2009

Oil and Gas Journal (2006) 'Worldwide look at reserves and production', *Oil and Gas Journal*, vol 104, no 47, pp24–25

Patzek, T. and Pimentel, D. (2006) 'Thermodynamics of energy production from biomass', *Critical Reviews in Plant Sciences*, vol 24, nos 5–6, pp329–364

Pimentel, D. and Patzek, T. (2005) 'Ethanol production using corn, switchgrass, and wood; Biodiesel production using soybean and sunflower', *Natural Resources Research*, vol 14, no 1, pp65–76

Robbins, P. (2003) *Stolen Fruit: The Tropical Commodities Disaster*, Zed Books, London

Rosset, P. (2006) *Food is Different: Why We Must Get the WTO Out of Agriculture*, Zed Books, London

StatsCan (Statistics Canada) (2007a) 'Selected historical data from the Census of Agriculture: Data tables', *2006 Census of Agriculture*, Government of Canada, Ottawa, www.statcan.gc.ca/pub/95-632-x/2007000/4129762-eng.htm#i, accessed 20 April 2009

StatsCan (Statistics Canada) (2007b) 'Agriculture overview, Canada and the provinces', *2006 Census of Agriculture*, Government of Canada, Ottawa, www.statcan.gc.ca/pub/95-629-x/1/4182377-eng.htm#0, accessed 20 April 2009

US EPA (2001) '2000–2001 pesticide market estimates: Usage', US Environmental Protection Agency, Washington, www.epa.gov/oppbead1/pestsales/01pestsales/usage2001.htm, accessed 31 December 2008

USDA NASS (US Department of Agriculture National Agricultural Statistics Service) (2004) '2002 Census of Agriculture', www.agcensus.usda.gov/Publications/2002/USVolume104.pdf, accessed 8 August 2009

USDA NASS (US Department of Agriculture National Agricultural Statistics Service) (2008) 'The Census of Agriculture, National Agricultural Statistics Service', www.agcensus.usda.gov/Publications/2007/Full_Report/usv1.pdf, accessed 20 April 2009

Weis, T. (2007) *The Global Food Economy: The Battle for the Future of Farming*, Zed Books, LondonWorldWatch and the CAP (Center for American Progress) (2006) *American Energy: The Renewable Path to Energy Security*, WorldWatch and the Center for American Progress, Washington

3
Security for Whom? Changing Discourses on Food in Europe in Times of a Global Food Crisis

Gianluca Brunori and Angela Guarino

Introduction: Food security as a key issue in Europe

Over past months, food security has become a familiar phrase in the European mass media – something unprecedented in recent decades. The reason for this renewed interest in food security is related to a sequence of events that has deeply altered public discourse on food, agriculture and – in a more general way – on the role of the state. Four specific crises – occurring in quick succession and thereby suggesting to the general public that they are strongly linked – are at the root of this change: the environmental crisis, the oil crisis, the food crisis and, more recently, the financial crisis.

Climate change has unified the discourse over the environmental crisis. The impact on public opinion of three well-publicized communications – Al Gore's film *An Inconvenient Truth*; the United Nations Intergovernmental Panel on Climate Change (IPCC) report, which provided evidence of global warming and its potential impact on global security; and the *Stern Review Report on the Economics of Climate Change*, which highlighted the social and economic costs of inaction – has been profound. Further, the endorsement of environmental issues by moderate or conservative leaders, such as Merkel in Germany, Cameron in Britain and Sarkozy in France, appears to have convinced the European public that the environmental crisis is real and not simply a social construction of radical groups.

The oil crisis became evident in the steady rise of oil prices during 2008, which has only recently been mitigated by a slump in demand following the global financial crisis. Oil prices reached a peak of US$140 per barrel in 2008, when the average price in the preceding two years had been below US$70 per barrel. Consumers have responded by reducing their oil consumption, including the modification of lifestyles heavily dependent upon the car. The link between the oil crisis and environmental crisis has been made evident by the emphasis on biofuels, proposed as a green alternative to oil on the basis that they would respond both to a need to reduce dependence on oil as well as to reduce carbon emissions (OECD, 2008). The interplay between biofuel production, food prices and food security is still hotly debated.

The food crisis was also made apparent in 2008, when escalating prices reached a peak. An announcement from the UN World Food Programme warned of the possibility that rising food prices would not allow the organization to bear the costs of its programme. The media also reported a dramatic sequence of food riots in several countries. As *The Economist* reported, these were the first food riots for some 30 years.[1]

Many news providers (including the *Financial Times*, Reuters and the *Guardian*) have set up a special web section on the 'food crisis'. Josette Sheeran, executive director of the UN's World Food Programme, stated that the global economy had created 'a perfect storm for the world's hungry, caused by high oil and food prices and low food stocks' (Darren, 2008).

Before emerging in its global form, the food crisis in Europe was identified as an internal problem, one related to low incomes (and especially the deteriorating economic conditions of the middle class), to inefficiencies in the distribution system and to speculation by strong players in the food chain. In Italy, farmers' organizations had been denouncing the gap between retail prices and producers' prices, asking for controls and activating initiatives to shorten the chain. Rifondazione Comunista, a radical left party of Italy, organized a demonstrative sale of bread for €1/kg. As the prices of bread and pasta increased by, respectively, about 13 per cent and 30 per cent in one month, consumers' organizations mobilized public opinion and launched 'shopping strikes' (Reuters, 2008). In Spain, consumers' organizations have demanded increased state controls of prices (*El País*, 2007). In Finland, the government is planning to reduce VAT on food during 2009 (Willoughby, 2008).

The food crisis has accelerated the debates over food security and has facilitated links between policies that were once anchored to narrow sectoral concerns. It has brought into focus the view that food security is not only a matter of national welfare, but is also a matter of global security. Germany's Angela Merkel underlined the point in her letter to the Group of Eight (G8) leaders ahead of the summit in Japan, stating that the crisis could 'threaten democratization, destabilize countries and lead to international security problems' (see Spiegel, 2008). The G8 Leaders' Statement on Global Food Security, produced at the summit held in Hokkaido, Japan, reports that:

> [w]e are deeply concerned that the steep rise in global food prices coupled with availability problems in a number of developing countries is threatening global food security... We have taken additional steps to assist those suffering from food insecurity or hunger, and today renew our commitment to address this

multifaceted and structural crisis (G8 Leaders Statement on Global Food Security, 2008, p1).

The sudden awareness of 'the end of cheap food' (Hawkes et al, 2008) has penetrated people's cognitive radar screens, bringing into focus the link between food security in the North and in the South. The UK Department for Environment, Food and Rural Affairs (Defra, 2008) has, in this regard, laid down the conceptual basis for the incorporation of food security into the policy agenda.

The financial crisis and the consequent fear of global economic recession has also embodied the food crisis within a broader economic crisis, undermining families' confidence about their future and calling into question the possibility of consolidated approaches to the economy, to the role of the state and to regulation.

Background: The European model and its ambiguities

European consumers are among the most concerned in the world about food quality. As a recent document from the UK Cabinet Office states, consumers 'have become more sophisticated and diverse in their food interests, and more people are now prepared to pay a premium for better food' (Cabinet Office, 2008, p9). This statement can be generalized across Europe.

The European model of agriculture and food – one which incorporated value-added commodities and high quality markets – was developed at a time of low global food prices:

> ... *alongside commodity production, many of our producers will compete best in the high-added-value, high-quality markets... We can do this because we have a food tradition that is the envy of the world. In fact I should say 'food traditions'. For centuries, in the various landscapes and climates which make up the wonderful diversity of Europe, producers have been choosing ingredients, refining techniques, building reputations. People all over the world want what we produce, and will pay well for it* (Fischer Boel, 2007).

The European model is one with multifunctionality at its heart. Along with the production of food, fibre and energy, farming is expected to deliver other benefits for society such as biodiversity preservation, the viability of rural communities and infrastructures, environmental protection and high animal welfare standards, along with food safety. It is purported to be a win-win solution both for farmers and consumers. In the liberalized global economic market, price competition would be highly unfavourable for European farmers. For small farmers in particular, high value-added products are seen as a way of escaping competition with large-scale commodity producers from abroad. For consumers, the European model satisfies their demand for 'healthier and more flavoursome food of higher nutritional value, produced by more environmentally friendly methods'.[2]

The European model has included the application of higher food standards than are the norm in other countries. The European Union (EU) has regulated organic farming since 1991, has regulated specific quality labels (geographical indications, traditional specialities), and has provided support to quality certification schemes covering criteria that include environmental protection, animal welfare, organoleptic (sensory) qualities, worker welfare, fair trade, climate change concerns, ethical, religious and cultural considerations, farming methods and origin (European Commission, 2008a). The framework provided by the Protection of Geographical Indications and Designation of Origin regulation has opened new markets, giving local producers and local food alliances a competitive advantage over the big food companies whose strategies were based on the homogenization of markets and sourcing. With its mandatory labelling scheme for food containing genetically modified organisms (GMOs) above 1 per cent and a regulation ensuring coexistence between GMOs and GMO-free crops – one which, at least in principle, defends GMO-free producers – the EU has given legal protection to food producers willing to carry out food production according to alternative paradigms.

The space for alternatives to standardized food products has been created by niche initiatives that have progressively gained widespread public support. Public institutions have played a mediating role, creating spaces for new initiatives and supporting them with rules and resources. The Liaison Entre Actions de Développement de l'Economie Rurale (LEADER), a European Community programme aimed at creating bottom-up processes of rural development, has promoted hundreds of successful examples where food is linked to rural development strategies and, in most cases, to the involvement of local institutions and stakeholders.

This approach has also grown as a consequence of an array of recent food crises. There is strong evidence, for example, that the bovine spongiform encephalopathy (BSE) crisis of 1996 led to the growth in demand for organic beef and for other high quality food retailing (Brunori et al, 2008a). Some food chain actors (particularly retailers) consider that the European model provides an opportunity for business because it meets an increasing demand by consumers for better environmental management and higher food quality. Most European retailers have been quick to follow this trend. Websites of many firms announce their intention to provide clean and green foods. Migros, the largest chain in Switzerland, accounts for 50 per cent of organic sales in the country. Many other large retailers (Tesco, ASDA, Marks & Spencer, Carrefour, Aldi, Coopitalia and Esselunga, among others) are applying a GMO-free policy in accordance with consumer preference for more 'natural' products.

From 1997 to 2008, European retailers joined EurepGAP, a body that set voluntary standards for the certification of agricultural products. As its website stated, *the EurepGAP standard is primarily designed to maintain consumer confidence in food quality and food safety. Other important goals are to minimize detrimental environmental impacts of farming operations, optimize the use of inputs and to ensure a responsible approach to worker health and safety (EurepGAP, 2008).*

In recent times EurepGAP has changed into GlobalGAP, underlining the importance of standards being 'generalized' on a worldwide basis. GlobalGAP is a global strategy to extend higher food quality and safety standards throughout the world. On the public side, a recent modification of specific EU quality schemes (labelling to guarantee quality) has opened registration procedures to non-European products, giving them the opportunity to be recognized and protected by the European authorities and, at the same time, to extend the European sphere of influence (as well as the European model of multifunctionality, and the creation and distribution of high value-added products) to the food industry overseas.

The new challenge

Analyses of the causes of the food crisis have revealed a world of unexpected interdependencies (see FAO, 2008a, 2008b, 2008c, 2008d). Drivers such as climate change, peak oil, fuel/food competition, nutritional transition in the emerging countries and financial speculation on food commodities have made evident the need to consider food security as a global issue – one that affects both the North and the South. In a recent food strategy paper produced by the UK government (Cabinet Office, 2008), food security enters into the strategic objectives for national food policies. A recent Communication of the European Commission (European Commission, 2008b) links the problem of rising food prices with food security. At the same time, the Commission recognizes that Europe has a responsibility to address food security and its implications for internal agricultural policy in non-member countries. This new scenario poses a challenge to the European model, pushing it towards a solution of its main contradictions, such as its biofuel policy, which is based on environmental concerns but contributes at the same time to food insecurity, and its decoupled subsidy scheme, which is based on land ownership rather than the provision of public goods.

According to *The Economist* (2008a) '[a]griculture is now in limbo. The world of cheap food has gone'. Indeed, there is general agreement that future food prices will remain at a higher average level than the prices that prevailed in past decades (OECD and FAO, 2008). The sudden awareness of 'the end of cheap food' (*The Economist*, 2007) has penetrated people's consciousness and has activated changes in the ways they think about and purchase food. In an era of cheap food, premium price strategies have proved very successful by meeting the demands of a very large segment of consumers for food quality and diversity while simultaneously conferring financial advantage to the farmers involved. But in a scenario in which food prices and/or lower incomes strike the purchasing power of the middle class, those strategies are challenged. As the UK Cabinet Office (2008, p10) states, '[h]igher prices will inevitably make it more difficult for some families to buy the foods they aspire to'.

The recession that started in 2008 has made this situation more evident. In Italy, there are an increasing number of press articles showing formerly affluent middle-class citizens queuing at charities to obtain free food. In Britain, press articles highlight the trade-off between food and fuel among poor families (Kelland, 2008). In general, analyses of consumer trends show that consumers try to cope with the crisis by changing purchasing strategies, for example shifting from high quality to lower quality products, and modifying their diets in other ways. Italian consumers are responding to the soaring food prices by altering consumption patterns (Russo, 2008) – a change which has generally involved reducing their consumption of meat, while increasing their consumption of pasta (Parise, 2008). The middle classes are discovering a quirky charm in discount supermarkets they once thought below their dignity to visit (*The Telegraph*, 2008). Increasing numbers of British consumers are shopping online as a way to save some money – with online grocery shopping having overtaken internet sales of electronic items for the first time as consumers seek cheaper foods. Sales statistics suggest that customers are looking for bargains on essential items such as bread and milk, and are turning to online supermarket sites for exclusive offers and discounts on home delivery (*The Independent*, 2008).

In times of recession, there is growing consumer resistance to the purchase of high-priced foods, with retailers responding to the new conditions by adopting a 'war on prices' strategy (Finch, 2008). Farmers' organizations in Italy have pointed to the gap – sometimes quite large – between producers' prices and retail prices, blaming this on the inefficiencies of the distribution systems as well as the excessive power of retailers. Coldiretti, the most important Italian farmers' organization, has launched a campaign to demonstrate that farmers are not beneficiaries of agflation (food price increases), as there are huge margins between the price paid to farmers for their produce and the prices paid by consumers at the point of sale (Reschia, 2008).

Indeed, there is a problem in the structure of the food chain relating to the present mechanisms of price transmission. The French government is reportedly concerned that the rise in milk and wheat prices has been used as a pretext to increase the prices of other products (Halliday, 2008). In a similar vein, a recent communication of the European Commission (2008a) has identified uncompetitive practices relating to purchasing agreements and exclusive supply agreements, among other things, and has set a 'roadmap' to improve the food supply chain.

The European model under attack

The European model of food production and consumption has become a target for criticism. On one side, the current crisis strengthens the arguments of those proposing that high value globalized food should better link 'spaces of poverty' with 'spaces of luxury' (Van der Ploeg, forthcoming 2009b). Others argue against the support of alternative food networks at the 'high end' of the European model (see Sonnino and Marsden, 2006). The critique mainly targets 'rent seeking' strategies that arguably address elite segments of consumers, and convey ambiguous messages to consumers.

There is some truth in the notion that elitism is a characteristic of some segments of 'alternative' food networks. So-called LOHAS (Lifestyles of Health and Sustainability) consumers, for example, are a market segment whose members have a strong interest in health, fitness, personal development and social justice, and put a high value on sustainability and environmental protection. Products purchased include 'green' building supplies, socially responsible investments (green stocks), organic products, alternative healthcare, and lifestyle and fitness products (LOHAS, 2008). Retail brands targeting these segments of the market – such as Whole Foods Market in the US, Champion in France, EatItaly in Italy and Tegut in Germany – all achieved rapid growth based on a strategy of excellence and premium pricing compared to standard products.

Another favoured target of the critics has been the Slow Food movement. Slow Food has sought to enhance the legitimacy (and sales volume) of premium-priced regional, environmentally friendly, foods with high sensory appeal. Its Taste Fair *Salone del Gusto* attracts hundreds of thousands of citizens on a biennial basis, the aim being:

> *to acquaint consumer-visitors with the other face of the food planet and understand the characteristics and history of top quality but little known food products. To learn to recognize quality is the best way to learn to understand the food we eat every day* (Slow Food, 2008).

Critics nonetheless accuse alternative food networks of elitism, although for different reasons. A debate on the recent regulation for organic production – held between Emma Bonino, former European Commissioner and now representative of the Italian Radical Party, and Carlo Petrini, Founder and President of Slow Food International – illustrates this point. Espousing a view from the left of politics, Petrini claimed that it is not organic food that costs too much, but conventional food that costs too little. From the other side of politics, high food prices become a key argument in support of the right's neo-productivist cause. Thus, Emma Bonino's response was:

> *I think we should say: let's make a healthy product and guarantee its safety for the consumer regardless of … method of cultivation. Thinking to benefit only those 2 per cent of Italians who buy organic is elitist. And asking to raise prices of conventional foodstuffs by 2–4 per cent as proposed by Petrini is disrespectful of the people who already have difficulty in shopping and, most importantly, does not ensure greater food security* (Bonino, 2008).

Should public policies give priority to technologies, agricultural models and trade regulations that promise to raise productivity and to keep food prices low? This would appear to be the position of UK Prime Minister Gordon Brown, who has called for the EU to relax regulations governing the import of genetically modified feed, which currently require that all incoming shipments of feed are subjected to strict testing (Crowley, 2008).

In situations of crisis, a more implicit critique of elitism, oriented to high quality and high valued products, can be found in some transnational food corporations' policies on food security for the poor. Corporate bosses consider that the global food crisis has its root in the increasing demand for food, and that part of the solution can be represented by the diffusion and development of productivity-boosting farming technologies. During the public World Food Day event on 16 Octobe 2008, Professor Sir Colin Berry of London and Martin Taylor, Chairman of Syngenta, both emphasized the need for agribusinesses to take a proactive stance on the role of crop protection and high performance seeds in food security and sustainable agriculture. They also declared that, for the first time since the food crisis of the early 1970s, hunger has to be seen not only as a consequence of inadequate buying power, but also in terms of inadequate staple food availability – with both being considered against a background of escalating overall demand. Thus, according to Marco Ferroni, Executive Director of the Syngenta Foundation (Syngenta Foundation, 2008), '[r]arely has Food Day assumed greater meaning than at the present time, as rising food prices in the face of insufficient production growth cause large numbers of people to go hungry in poor countries.'

In the same vein, the Nestlé company stated in its *Creating Shared Value* report that:

> *in order to build a successful business, we are convinced you have to create value for society and, in the case of a food company, we have to deliver more nutritious products at a lower cost to all parts of the population [and] not only the rich ones of this world. Our long term business strategy is 'Nutrition, Health, and Wellness' – selling food of higher nutritional value to all segments of society* (Nestlé, 2008; see also Chapter 11 of this volume).

Due to the food crisis, the European Commission appears to be increasingly open in relation to the application of food biotechnologies. After decades of suspicion about GMOs, a recent communication claims that:

> *The use of GMO crops can increase productivity. This may be particularly important in regions of the world which suffer from difficult climatic conditions. GMOs can therefore play an important role in mitigating the effects of the food crisis* (European Commission, 2008c).

Food movements facing the food crisis

From the left, elitism is an accusation addressed to alternative food networks such as the organic and Slow Food movements. While premium price is recognized as a reward for the full costs incurred by farmers for growing products of excellence and for preserving the environment, it can also be said that such pricing tends to reproduce inequalities in access to food, and therefore creates a division among those who can afford to sustain alternative models of farming and those who cannot.

The Slow Food movement has responded to its critics by arguing that Slow Food products are not expensive, and that conventional agriculture neither appreciates nor pays for the real costs of food. Initially focused on the sensory excellence of foods, the Slow Food movement has more recently adopted a discourse of 'good, clean and fair' products (Petrini, 2005). This shift is helping to open up debates about food security, food sovereignty, agro-biodiversity and the role of community action.

Here is the conundrum: how is it possible to give a fair reward to producers whose production will inevitably be limited, while making quality food both affordable and available to all? Such a question implies a conceptual framework that goes beyond sectoral approaches to question modes of production, styles of consumption and mechanisms of regulation.

In times of low food prices, aware consumers are willing to pay a premium as a means of giving farmers fair compensation for their work. But, in the new context, even wealthy consumers are modifying their attitudes and behaviour. As Harvey (2009) reports, sales of organic produce are predicted to fall by 7.5 per cent in 2009.

The issue of 'fair price' is thus becoming central to alternative food networks. Indeed, while refusing a commercial approach to producer-consumer relationships (Kirwan, 2004), consumers involved in alternative food networks are increasingly willing to consider prices as a matter for discussion. A symptom of this new approach is the growth of Solidarity Purchasing Groups (SPGs) in Italy. Unlike other similar alternative food networks, such as the Associations pour le maintien de l'agriculture paysanne (AMAPs) in France, SPGSs are initiated by consumers who not only have concerns for social justice and the environment, but are also concerned with their (diminishing) purchasing power (Brunori et al, 2008b).

Instead of centring their strategy on consumers' willingness to pay for foods of excellence, these groups are repositioning their discourse on *daily food* (food availability) and on *the right to high quality food* for all. This means dealing with aspects such as the transparency of food pricing mechanisms, the distribution of power along the food chain, and the reduction of unnecessary goods and services that are constituted in the product. An obvious example, here, is the amount and type of packaging that is used. The aim is to avoid waste and to encourage more sustainable consumption patterns, as well as cheaper products.

A shift of focus from production to consumption fosters synergies among food movements. The synergy between box schemes and gastronomy can elaborate consumption patterns that encourage consumers to eat less expensive meat cuts. For example, the price of beef cooked as a whole piece of steak is usually much higher than meat purchased for use in a stew, while local vegetables are often cheaper than those transported from distant locations. Local food movements can therefore stress the connection between the ecological component of local food, as well as the affordability of sustainable consumption patterns more generally.

One outstanding example is the diffusion of unpasteurized milk dispensers in recent years, mainly in Switzerland, Austria and Italy. Instead of selling their milk to cooperatives or to the dairies, an increasing number of farmers have started to distribute their milk directly to consumers – either on-farm or at chosen distribution points. The necessary investment for farmers is about €5000, which allows farmers to sell the milk at a price that is 20 per cent lower than that charged by supermarkets, but at a much higher price than they would receive from selling it directly to processors. Within a few months, the number of dispensers in Italy has reached some 566 in over 60 provinces (Pinducciu, 2008). Consumers have reacted enthusiastically to this initiative, encouraged by lower prices, the perception that 'raw' milk is a better quality product, and the satisfaction that they are supporting a local product. Food safety issues relating to the growing distribution of unpasteurized milk will, of course, need to be considered by food authorities.

Does the current crisis have the potential to permanently alter consumption patterns?

There is increasing agreement among the public that global crises are unlikely to be solved if existing consumption patterns remain unaltered. This point was recently made by Lester Brown in response to the question 'how many people can the earth support?' 'The correct question is: at what level of food consumption?' (Brown, 2008, p182). For example, while annual consumption of grain as food and feed averages some 800kg per person in the US, Brown notes that:

> a modest reduction in the consumption of meat, milk and eggs could easily cut grain use per person by 100kg (per year). People living high on the food chain, such as Americans or Canadians, can improve their health by moving down the food chain (Brown, 2008, p182).

Responding to the food crisis may thus prove to have multiple benefits. The opportunity to reflect on consumption styles may not only raise awareness of the strategies people can take to assist in the transition to more sustainable consumption patterns, but may also improve their wellbeing. If they are adequately supported by appropriate consumption infrastructures, the sustainable consumption strategies advocated by food movements can also generate the real win-win solution of improving quality of life while reducing expenditure on food.

At a broader level, the crisis has accelerated a convergence between food movements, sustainable consumers' movements and political movements inspired by non-conventional schools of economic thought. For example, in his radical critique of economic theories of growth and their extension in the common discourse, Serge Latouche (see Latouche 2004a, 2004b) inspired the so-called Movement for Happy De-growth, which now has units throughout northern Italy. The concept of de-growth adopted by this movement emphasizes the need to de-couple consumption from happiness, in both theory and in practice. The premise is that personal happiness will not necessarily decline if people reduce their levels of consumption. The key is to create a different ranking of values between goods. Rather than a focus on economic goods, the focus should be on both relational and public goods. Relational goods are those providing direct utility, such as conviviality and friendship, as well as goods that can be used as economic tools, as in the case of sharing and non-monetary exchange. Public goods can be indirect, as with amenities provided by the countryside, and direct, as with the provision of public facilities. Both relational and public goods are seen as crucial to building the foundations of a less consumption-oriented society (see Mas, 2009).

Food is among the most important areas of intervention for the Movement for Happy De-growth, just as it has been for the Slow Food movement. The latter has sought, over many years, to link the food and ecology movements. According to Carlo Petrini, the founder of Slow Food; 'a gastronomist who is not a bit an ecologist is a silly man; an ecologist who is not a bit a gastronomist is a boring man' (Petrini, 2005). A number of writers have begun to consolidate these connections by exploring the potential for alternative food networks to build ecological citizenship (Seyfang, 2006; Lockie, 2008).

The food crisis also brings into focus the significance of waste in the agro-food system. According to recent evaluations, about 30 per cent of food purchased in the UK is wasted. In Italy, the level of household food waste has been calculated at some 15 per cent for bread and pasta, 18 per cent for meat, and 12 per cent for fruit and vegetables (*Il Corriere della Sera*, 2008). Organizations such as LastMinuteMarket[3] in Italy have gained notoriety by reporting the amount of food that has been discarded by supermarkets (although it is absolutely safe to eat). The organization also arranges for such food to be distributed via a partnership between retailers, local administrators and charities. While uncovering the immense waste generated by modern food systems, LastMinuteMarket thus offers a practical solution by turning waste into a valuable resource.

The food crisis and the policy arena

The food crisis has contributed to an intense debate about the future of European agricultural and food policy. One of the main foci is the connection between the role of trade, markets and governments. A leader in free-trade discourse, *The Economist* journal, has pointed its finger at the European Union's Common Agricultural Policy (CAP) and, in particular, its stress on the need for high food safety, animal welfare and labour standards:

> *Marie-Antoinette would have been proud of Europe's farm ministers this week, as they debated what to do about the high price of food. True, ministers did not quite sigh 'qu'ils mangent de la brioche' ['let them eat cake'] as they discussed the hungry (as tradition alleges the French queen did when told that the poor of Paris had no bread). But that, in essence, was the message from the French, Germans, Spanish and Austrians, as they leapt to defend the common agricultural policy (CAP), which helps Europe to produce some of the priciest food in the world* (The Economist, 2008a).

In a similar vein, an article published in the *Financial Times* during the peak of the price crisis accused the French Minister of Agriculture, Michel Barnier, of protectionism:

> *The global food crisis should actually be a good opportunity to reform agriculture by lifting farmers off subsidy and tariff protection and getting global markets to work better. But though some emergency policies are going in the right direction ... many of the longer-term policy responses being mooted would make things worse. Raising tariff walls yet higher is one such [response]. Trade barriers provide a disincentive to developing countries to invest in agricultural production and export capability by removing a potential customer.*
>
> *Access to international markets raises incomes, often by several hundred per cent, for poor farmers. Cutting off that source of income reveals the emptiness of France's conception of itself as a country that truly cares about the developing world. This is not just a bad idea. It is a potentially lethal one. It should be discarded* (Financial Times, 2008).

Such provocative language brought an immediate response from the French Minister, who sought to reconcile the traditional interventionist policy of France with a concern for a fairer system of global trade:

> *You say that I wish to deny developing countries access to world markets. What I say is that food security can be achieved neither by protectionism nor by trade alone. The answer to global shortages must lie in developing production capacity throughout the world, and not only where it is most profitable. In this context, the losers of the Doha round will inevitably be the world's hungry and poor* (Barnier, 2008).

In taking this position, Barnier echoes some of the recommendations present in the 'Ecofair trade dialogue' promoted by Wolfgang Sachs under the Heinrich Böll foundation (Sachs and Santarius, 2007). The French government has shown itself to be very active in this field, organizing the timely conference 'Ou va a nourrir le monde?' ('Who will feed the world?') in 2008. In his address to the conference, Barnier stated that:

> *the adoption of agricultural policies aimed at local production adapted to suit each country must return to the top of our priorities. Without them, no state, and certainly not the poorest, can guarantee its population the elementary means of survival. Without them, the very conditions necessary for economic development will be undermined* (see Barnier and Kouchner, 2008).

This position is not confined to mainland Europe. According to the President of the Irish Farmers' Association, 'food security in Europe is even more important than energy security' (National Forum on Europe, 2009). Within Europe, a speech by Commissioner Marianne Fisher Boel synthesizes the EU position:

> *the future of our agri-food sector lies in playing an active role in a global trading system. This does not mean a system without any kind of limitation. We need a reasonable level of border protection, and that remains our position in Geneva. But a 'reasonable' level is a level that will allow some imports... So overall, the European Union has sensible policies in place with regard to domestic food production. There's space for market forces to work; but those market forces work within a strong policy framework* (Fisher Boel, 2008, p4).

In recent times, the EU has produced important documents aimed at adjusting policies in the fields of food and climate change, food security, biofuels, agricultural prices, food distribution for the most deprived citizens and the distribution of fruit in schools (European Commission, 2008a, 2008b, 2008c). In these documents as well as in the Commissioner's speeches, the emphasis on competitiveness and liberalization of markets has consistently softened compared to preceding years, while the emphasis on sustainability and equity has become stronger.

A comparative reading of these documents shows that their objectives are much more far-sighted than the measures taken, however. Although there is a clear effort to revise the language and to introduce new issues, sectoral policies constrain the ability to implement more sustainable practices. For example, in the case of biofuels, the existing policy approach (specifying a minimum biofuel proportion of the total fuel consumed) has been adjusted with the introduction of a sustainability certification scheme that would prevent biofuels being sourced from areas that have been deforested for the purpose of producing these fuels. Rather than modifying a questionable policy objective, a compromise has been chosen which does not take into account the considerable evidence that large-scale development of biofuels is detrimental to food security (see McMichael, 2007). While the need for coherence among policies is explicitly recognized by the European Commission (2007), it is clear that a transition to any new regime will require a more comprehensive effort to alter the current trajectory.

Some novel approaches to the issue of food security have emerged from national and regional governments. Morgan and Sonnino (2008) give the example of school food provisions in Europe and beyond:

> At first sight, the idea of serving fresh, locally produced food in schools looks very simple. But nothing could be further from the truth... Part of the explanation, we believe, has to do with the fact that in many countries, particularly the UK and the US, the idea runs against the grain of some very powerful cultural conventions – like the notion that there is nothing special with food, that food is just one industry among others.

The growth in the number of projects related to school food provisioning points to a new area of government intervention, linking public procurement with sustainability and food security.

Conclusion, and principles for a research agenda

In this chapter we have argued that the food crisis has combined with the contemporary environmental, oil and financial crises in a manner that is altering discourses about food. These global crises have shaken the most consolidated policy paradigms, providing the impulse for better connections among food and ecology movements which have, typically, existed independently of one another. In particular, the European policy discourse has brought together very different actors and strategies (Erjavec and Erjavec, 2008).

Whether these different actors have the necessary bonds to formulate new policy paradigms and turn them into a reframing of daily production and consumption routines is yet to be determined – but there are hints that this might be possible. What is clear at this time is that no one group, or government, has a ready solution to the food crisis. As we have sought to demonstrate in this chapter, there are many inherent contradictions in any of the strategies chosen, and a transition to a fairer equilibrium needs considerable thought, along with practical and focused adjustment processes. In this regard, social research has much to offer.

As food security becomes increasingly central, vulnerability/resilience will be among the principles that will drive the reformulation of social research, as well as social intervention policies. Consideration of the best means to improve food security will expand the possibilities for alternative paradigms to emerge and challenge conventional thinking about food provision.

In the field of trade, a multilateral approach will be essential given that the bilateral agreements which have featured throughout the last decade appear to disadvantage developing countries. Specifically, mechanisms to increase the openness of markets will need to be considered in the context of principles of food sovereignty and food security.

In the field of production, as the ideals and settings of the green revolution are called into question, there is the need to build a new paradigm. Here, resilience, biodiversity, multifunctionality, local knowledge, family farming, local food systems and fair trade are among the keywords of an emerging paradigm (see IAASTD, 2008), with the pledge for coherence in both policy measures and research strategies opening the way for the formulation of non-contradictory strategies.

Another of the central points of the research agenda should be consumption and the role of consumers. European food policies emphasize a consumer-centred approach. But what does it mean now? Should policy follow the expectations and concerns of consumers, revealed as market demand? Should the private sector be encouraged to measure success in terms of its capacity to satisfy consumers' needs, whatever those needs might be? Or might it be possible to ensure that the 'nutrition transition' in developing economies does not reproduce the levels of obesity prevalent in developed nations?

The food industry's focus is upon consumers and their need for 'affordable food of high quality and diversity' (ETP, 2008). However, consumers' attitudes and behaviour evolve in response to various influences, including education, communication, information and other social, economic and material drivers. Will it be possible to involve the food sector in a process that may lead to changes in dietary patterns, food lifestyles, food purchasing patterns and even, perhaps, a reduction in the level of food consumption? What instruments might be employed to ensure that consumers' needs, concerns and behaviour fit within emerging requirements for sustainable production and consumption?

Based on the principle that values, education and information are at the basis of consumption patterns, there is scope to create more discerning and knowledgeable consumer-citizens through the targeted provision of information about the sustainability of farming systems and food distribution networks. There are a growing number of consumers willing to purchase sustainably produced items – even though some might not have an in-depth understanding of the connections emphasized here between food and environmental, energy and global finance issues. Information and education become crucial tools in allowing people to make such connections, and to understand the links between issues such as water use, carbon and energy footprints, 'food miles', the importance of seasonality in food production and so forth. Communication tools can assist consumers to orient their choice and to activate learning processes.

Above all, the transition toward a sustainable, secure and equitable food regime will require a capacity to link the micro to the macro – to link daily routines to macro trends, and grassroots initiatives to global policies.

Notes

1   'Over the past dozen years, world farm output has barely kept pace with increased demand. In the past three years, output actually fell short: the world was eating more food than it grew. In 2009, output will increase again, relieving some of the pressure on developing countries that, in 2008, caused the first global outbreak of food riots for more than 30 years, Parker, 2008).

2   According to the European Commission on Agriculture and Food (2008) '[f]or some years now, European consumers' choices have tended to favour healthier and more flavoursome food of higher nutritional value, produced by more environmentally friendly methods. In other words, the guiding principle behind this development is quality'. See the web page of the European Commission on Agriculture and Food, www.ec.europa.eu/agriculture/food/index_en.htm, accessed 21 November 2008.

3   *LastMinuteMarket* is an initiative born of the University of Bologna in 1998, when a group of young researchers – coordinated by Professor Andrea Segrè – started to study the life cycle of food. They focused their research on the last link in the chain, the large retailers. The group has since evolved into a university spin-off enterprise that offers a service which assists private companies and public administrations to link the surpluses generated to charities that provide food for poor people. 'This system was tested in a concrete initiative that allowed the transfer of perfectly eatable unsold food products (otherwise transported and destroyed elsewhere) from a food shop to a number of charity associations assisting marginal people. The trial was performed in large retail shop in the metropolitan Bologna area. In 2003, some 140 tons of high quality foods were recovered each day providing meals for 250 persons and 500 animals' (see www.lastminutemarket.it; Segrè, 2004, 2008).

References

Barnier, M. (2008) 'CAP could be model for food security in Africa', *Financial Times*, 2 May, www.ft.com/cms/s/0/24be2eea-17e5-11dd-b98a-0000779fd2ac.html, accessed 8 August 2009

Barnier, M. and Kouchner, M. (2008) 'Who Will Feed the World? Towards diverse, sustainable forms of agriculture as drivers of development', 3rd July, European Parliament, Brussels, *www.parlonsagriculture.com/file/get?path=/var/docs/DossierENG.pdf*

Bonino, E. (2008) 'Ogm, Perché la norma ue garantisce i consumatori', *La Repubblica*, 25 November, p26

Brown, L. (2008) *Plan B 3.0: Mobilizing to Save Civilization*, Earth Policy Institute, New York

Brunori, G., Cerruti, R., Medeot S., Rossi A. (2008a) 'Looking for alternatives: the construction of the organic beef chain in Mugello, Tuscany', *International Journal of Agricultural Resources, Governance and Ecology*, vol 7, no 1–2, pp126–143

Brunori, G., Rossi, A., Guidi, F. (2008b) 'On the new social relations around and beyond food. Analysing consumers' role and action in Solidarity Purchasing Groups', Paper presented at the conference Sustainable Consumption and Alternative Agri-Food Systems, May, Arlon

Cabinet Office (2008) *Food Matters: Towards a Strategy for the 21st Century*, July, www.cabinetoffice.gov.uk/media/cabinetoffice/strategy/assets/food/food_matters1. pdf, accessed December 2008

Crowley, L. (2008) 'Debate ignites over GM's role in aiding food crisis', *The Foodnavigator*, 20 June, www.foodnavigator.com/Financial-Industry/Debate-ignites-over-GM-s-role-in-aiding-food-crisis, accessed 8 January 2008

Darren, E. (2008) 'World Food Program warning on soaring food prices', *The International Herald Tribune*, 6 March, www.iht.com/articles/2008/03/06/business/FOOD.php, accessed December 2008

Defra (2008) 'Ensuring the UK's food security in a changing world', Department for Environment, Food and Rural Affairs discussion paper, July, London, www.defra.gov.uk/foodrin/policy/pdf/Ensuring-UK-Food-Security-in-a-changing-world-170708.pdf, accessed December 2008

El País (2007) 'Investigación sobre la subida del pan y de la leche', *El País*, Madrid, 23 October, www.elpais.com/articulo/economia/Investigacion/subida/pan/leche/elpepueco/20071023elpepieco_4/Tes, accessed December 2008

Erjavec, K. and Erjavec, E. (2008) 'Changing EU agricultural policy discourses? The discourse analysis of Commissioner's speeches 2000–2007', *Food Policy*, vol 34, no 2, pp218–226

ETP (European Technology Platform) (2008) 'European Technology Platform on food for life: Implementation action plan', May, http://etp.ciaa.be/documents/Broch%20ETP_IAPlan_1.pdf, accessed 8 January 2009

EurepGAP (2008) EurepGAP (GlobalGAP) homepage at www.eurepgap.org/Languages/English/about.html, accessed 8 January 2009

European Commission (2007) *Report on Policy Coherence for Development*, COM(2007) 545 final

European Commission (2008a) *Green Paper on Agricultural Product Quality: Product Standards, Farming Requirements and Quality Schemes*, COM (2008) 641 final, 15 October, Brussels, ec.europa.eu/agriculture/quality/policy/consultation/greenpaper_en.pdf, accessed December 2008

European Commission (2008b) *Tackling the Challenge of Rising Food Prices: Directions for EU Action*, COM(2008) 321 final, 20 May, Brussels, ec.europa.eu/commission_barroso/president/pdf/20080521_document_en.pdf, accessed December 2008

European Commission (2008c) *Commission's / EU's response to the High Oil and Food Prices*, MEMO/08/421, 19 June, Brussels, europa.eu/rapid/pressReleasesAction.do?reference=MEMO/08/421, accessed December 2008

Fischer Boel, M. (2008) 'Global food demand: Role of the EU', speech by Mariann Fischer Boel, Member of the European Commission responsible for Agriculture and Rural Development, General Assembly of the CGB (Confédération Générale des Planteurs de Betteraves), Speech/08/694, Paris, 9 December 2008, http://europa.eu/rapid/pressReleasesAction.do?reference=SPEECH/08/694&format=HTML&aged=0&language=EN&guiLanguage=en, accessed 8 August 2009

FAO (Food and Agriculture Organization of the United Nations) (2008a) 'Bioenergy policy, markets and trade and food security', HLC/08/BAK7, Technical background document from the expert consultation 18–20 February, presented at the Conference on Climate Change, Energy and Food, 3–5 June Rome

FAO (2008b) 'Climate change adaptation and mitigation in the food and agriculture sector', HLC/08/BAK1, Technical background document from the expert consultation 5–7 March 2008, presented at the Conference on Climate Change, Energy and Food, 3–5 June, Rome

FAO (2008c) 'Declaration of the high-level conference on world food security: The challenges of climate change and bioenergy', 5 June, Rome, www.fao.org, accessed December 2008

FAO (2008d) 'High-level conference on world food security: The challenges of climate change and bioenergy', Report of the Conference, HLC/08/REP, 3–5 June, Rome, www.fao.org, accessed December 2008

Financial Times (2008) 'Barnier's barriers', the *Financial Times*, Editorial, 27 April, www.ft.com/cms/s/0/92b90e20-1483-11dd-a741-0000779fd2ac.html, accessed 8 January 2009

Finch, J. (2008) 'Supermarkets: Tesco and Asda slash food prices to stem flow of defectors to discounters', *Guardian*, 17 September, www.guardian.co.uk/business/2008/sep/17/tesco.asda, accessed December 2008

Fischer Boel, M. (2007) 'Quality is the (present and) future for European agriculture', SPEECH/07/64, Conference on Food Quality Certification – Adding Value to Farm Produce, 5 February, Brussels, www.europa.eu/rapid/pressReleases Action.do?reference=SPEECH/07/64&format=PDF&aged=1&language=EN&gui Language=en, accessed December 2008

G8 Leaders Statement on Global Food Security (2008) Hokkaido Toyako Summit: Special Address by H.E. Mr. Yasuo Fukuda, Prime Minister of Japan, www.mofa. go.jp/POLICY/economy/summit/2008/doc/doc080709_04_en.html, accessed 8 August 2009

Halliday, J. (2008) 'France suspects industry of fiddling food prices', *The Foodnavigator*, 26 February, www.foodnavigator.com/Financial-Industry/France-suspects-industry-of-fiddling-food-prices, accessed 8 January 2009

Harvey, F. (2009) 'Tough year ahead for organic farmers', www.ft.com/cms, accessed January 2009

Hawkes, S., Hurst, G. and Elliott, V. (2008) 'Era of cheap food ends as prices surge', *The Times Online*, 23 April, www.business.timesonline.co.uk/tol/business/industry_sectors/ consumer_goods/article3799327.ece, accessed December 2008

IAASTD (International Assessment of Agricultural Knowledge, Science and Technology for Development) (2008) *Executive Summary of Synthesis Report*, February

Il Corriere della Sera (2008) 'Cibo, il grande spreco: buttate 4 mila tonnellate al giorno, nella pattumiera 584 euro a testa', *Il Corriere della Sera,* 17 February, pp10-11

Kelland, K. (2008) 'To heat or to eat? Britain in court on fuel poverty', Reuters, 7 October, accessed 21 October 2008

Kirwan, J. (2004) 'Alternative strategies in the UK agro-food system', *Sociologia Ruralis*, vol 44, no 4, pp395–415

Latouche, S. (2004a) *Survivre au développement. De la décolonisation de l'imaginaire économique à la construction d'une société alternative*, Ed. Mille et une nuits, Paris

Latouche, S. (2004b) *De-growth Economics*, Le Monde Diplomatique, Paris

Lockie, S. (2008) 'Responsibility and agency within alternative food networks: assembling the "citizen consumer"', *Agriculture and Human Values*, vol 25, no 4, www.springerlink.com.ezproxy.library.uq.edu.au/content/lp36786370043645/fulltext.pdf, accessed 21 October 2008

LOHAS (2008) www.lohas.com/, accessed January 2009

McMichael, P. (2007) 'Sustainability and the agrarian question of food', paper presented at the European Congress of Rural Sociology, August, Wageningen University

Mas, M. (2009) 'Dieci Consigli solidali per sopravvivere in tempo di crisi', www. decrescitafelice.it/?p=405, accessed 8 January 2009

Morgan, K. and Sonnino, R. (2008) *The School Food Revolution: Public Food and the Challenge of Sustainable Development*, Earthscan, London

National Forum on Europe (2009) 'Food security more important than energy security – IFA leader tells Forum', www.forumoneurope.ie/index.asp?locID=366&docID=1 212, accessed 9 January 2009

Nestlé (2008) 'Creating shared value: The Nestlé report', March, Vevey, Switzerland, www.nestle.com/NR/exeres/1C69EF88-F4CB-4D52-96AB-8CB0B8724DAF.htm, accessed 8 January 2009

OECD (Organisation for Economic Co-operation and Development) (2008) *Draft Report on the Economic Assessment of Biofuels Support Policies*, TAD- CA (2008) 6-ENG, 13–15 May, Paris

OECD and FAO (2008) *Agricultural Outlook 2008–2017*, OECD Publications, Paris

Parise, L. (2008) 'Un mese di stipendio in più grazie al boom della pasta', *La Repubblica*, 24 December, http://bari.repubblica.it/dettaglio/Boom-della-Divella-la-crisi-impenna-le-vendite/1566568?ref=rephp, accessed 24 December 2008

Parker, J. (2008) 'Old Macdonald gets some cash. After the year of food crisis, the year of the farmer', www.economist.com/theworldin/displayStory.cfm?story_id=12494668&d=2009, accessed 8 January 2009

Petrini, C. (2005) *Buono, Pulito e Giusto: Principi di Nuova Gastronomia*, Einaudi, Turin

Pinducciu, D. (2008) 'Esperienze di filiera corta: la vendita diretta del latte crudo attraverso distributori automatici', *Working Paper no 4*, Laboratorio di Studi Rurali Sismondi

Reschia, C. (2008) 'Coldiretti: grano come petrolio. Cala il prezzo ma non per il consumatore', *La Stampa*, 3 September, www.lastampa.it/redazione/cmsSezioni/economia/200809articoli/36176girata.asp, accessed 8 August 2009

Reuters (2008) 'Italy consumers call for "loaf strike" over prices', 25 August, www.reuters.com/article/GCA-Agflation/idUSLP73225220080825, accessed December 2008

Russo, A. (2008) 'Rapporto COOP 2008 Consumi e distribuzione, Assetti Dinamiche e Previsioni', A cura di ANCC-COOP, Casalecchio di Reno [BO], www.e-coop.it/portalWeb/resources/jsp/popupDocumento.jsp?cm_path=/CoopRepository/COOP/CoopItalia/documento/doc00000058245, accessed 28 October 2008

Sachs, W. and Santarius, T. (2007) *Slow Trade – Sound Farming: A Multilateral Framework for Sustainable Markets in Agriculture*, Heinrich Böll Foundation and Misereor, Berlin

Segrè, A. (2004) *Lo spreco utile. Il libro del cibo solidale. Trasformare lo spreco in risorsa con i Last Minute Market: Food & Book*, Pendragon editore, Bologna

Segrè, A. (2008) *Elogio dello – SPR+ECO. Formule per una società sufficiente*, EMI, Bologna

Seyfang, G. (2006) 'Ecological citizenship and sustainable consumption: Examining local organic food networks', *Journal of Rural Studies*, vol 22, no 4, pp 383–395

Slow Food (2008) 'Slow Food Press Kit' http://content.slowfood.it/upload/3E6E345B0f10c2A053sNk3DA437D/files/PressKit2.pdf, accessed 20 December 2008

Sonnino, R. and Marsden, T. (2006) 'Beyond the divide: rethinking relationships between alternative and conventional food networks in Europe', *Journal of Economic Geography*, vol 6, no 2, pp181–199

Spiegel (2008) 'Merkel Warns Food Crisis Could Destabilize Nations', *Spiegel Online International*, 7 May, www.spiegel.de/international/world/0,1518,564063,00.html, accessed December 2008

Syngenta Foundation (2008) 'World Food Day lecture 2008: Agribusinesses need to become better at communicating the merits of scientific commercial agriculture', Sygenta Foundation, www.syngentafoundation.org/world_food_day_2008.htm, accessed 8 January 2009

The Economist (2007) 'Food prices: Cheap no more', 6 December, www.economist.com/displaystory.cfm?story_id=10250420, accessed 11 October 2008

The Economist (2008a) 'Let them eat cake', 22 May, *The Economist* print edition, www.economist.com/world/europe/displaystory.cfm?story_id=11413126, accessed December 2008

The Independent (2008) 'Online grocery shopping overtakes sales of electronic goods', *The Independent*, 28 October, www.independent.co.uk/life-style/gadgets-and-tech/news/online-grocery-shopping-overtakes-sales-of-electronic-goods-975831.html, accessed 28 October 2008

The Telegraph (2008) 'With soaring food costs, every Lidl helps', Telegraph.co.uk, 27 April, www.telegraph.co.uk/news/1904269/With-soaring-food-costs-every-Lidl-helps.html, accessed 10 October 2008

Van der Ploeg, J. (forthcoming 2009) 'The third agrarian crisis and the re-emergence of processes of repeasantization', *Rivista di economia agraria*, no 3

Willoughby, K. (2008) 'Finland to lower VAT on food, France on oil', in *Food International*, Elsevier, 28 May, www.foodinternational.net/articles/news/1293/finland-to-lower-vat-on-food-france-on-oil.html, accessed December 2008

4

The Re-emergence of National Food Security on the United Kingdom's Strategic Policy Agenda: Sustainability Challenges and the Politics of Food Supply[1]

David Barling, Tim Lang and Rosalind Sharpe

Introduction

The rises in commodity and food prices through the period 2006–2008 stimulated a renewed political concern and debate around the security of world food supply. The price peak also served to amplify an emerging domestic political debate in the UK questioning the government's assessment of the resilience of the food supply at the national level. The UK government's policy approach to the security of the national food supply is framed by its belief in the effective workings of an increasingly liberalized global trading environment. The increased sourcing of food from overseas is seen to allow for greater flexibility of supply for different products (including agricultural inputs), evidenced by the efficiency of modern integrated commercial food supply chains, and a reduced exposure to the risk of disruptions in domestic food production from situations such as harvest failure and livestock disease.

Debates about the security of the UK's food supply have illuminated the uneasy coexistence at the level of strategic policy formulation of two parallel policy approaches to the role of UK farming and food. The predominant and well-entrenched strategic policy approach is shaped by a continuing belief in the ability of a liberalizing global food economy to deliver sufficient food for the UK. The other identifiable strategic policy dimension is around sustainability for farming, food production and the food supply chain, primarily encapsulated in the Sustainable Farming and Food Strategy (Defra, 2002). These policy strategies informed a strategic review of national UK food policy conducted by the Prime Minister's Strategy Unit (PMSU), which was charged with addressing environmental and public health challenges, but not the issue of agricultural policy reform. The subsequent Cabinet Office report (PMSU, 2008) covered the security of the UK's food supply, reaffirming the government's belief in the resilience of the prevailing international food supply approach.[2] In contrast, the UK government's earlier policy review of its farming and food policy conducted in 2000 had identified the policy priorities as: first, enhancing the efficiency and competitiveness of British farming in both its domestic and international markets; and second, improving the environmental impact and sustainability of domestic farming and food production (PCFF, 2002). However, these policy priorities coexist in an uneasy manner (Barling and Lang, 2003). In particular, there is an increasingly evident disjuncture in strategic policy thinking between current food supply practice and its environmental and social sustainability.

The synergies between economic and environmental policies are highlighted and promoted in the concept of ecological modernization. Ecological modernization stresses the need to integrate environmental policy priorities not only in the implementation, but also in the formulation, of other public policy areas (such as industry, agriculture, energy and transport). However, such integration has proved difficult to achieve in practice. As one study of ecological modernization observed, synergies need to take place at both the micro-economic scale (e.g. adoption of environmental technologies at the firm level) and at the macro-economic level in terms of the strategic long-term integration of environmental considerations into policy (Gouldson and Murphy, 1997). In terms of strategic policy integration, the UK situation was depicted in 1997 as one of 'institutional inertia' (Jacobs, 1997). A decade later, the UK's approach to the security and sustainability of its food supply is characterized by two separate established policies, which remain in need of closer integration despite their location within the same policy sector and under the responsibility of the same government department – namely, the Department for Environment, Food and Rural Affairs (Defra). The conflicts between these two strategic policies and the limited and hesitant degree of integration between them are examined and illustrated in this chapter.

Food security and national food security

Food security as a term is deployed in a number of ways. A prominent use is to describe the challenges of feeding people adequately in developing countries both at the household and at the national or regional levels – notably in times of external stress such as poor harvests, which impact upon food supply in such regions and are transmitted down to vulnerable populations. Given that approximately 923 million people in the world are currently classified as living in hunger (FAO, 2008), this is a paramount concern. At the household level, the term food security is also used in both developing and developed countries in relation to food affordability and access issues for low income consumers.

The conventional definition of food security is that given by the Food and Agriculture Organization of the United Nations (FAO): '[F]ood security exists when all people, at all times, have access to sufficient, safe and nutritious food to meet their dietary needs and food preferences for an active and healthy life' (FAO, 1996).

The notion of food security has been used, also, in the context of national 'self-sufficiency' to describe whether a country, such as the UK, can meet its own food needs. The Organisation for Economic Co-operation and Development (OECD) describes this approach to food self-sufficiency as a '[c]oncept which discourages opening the domestic market to foreign agricultural products on the principle that a country must be as self-sufficient as possible for its basic dietary needs' (OECD, 2008). Within the OECD's description there are negative policy connotations of greater national protectionism and of moves to national autarky.

The UK government, through its Department for Environment, Food and Rural Affairs (Defra), states that: 'A national food security policy must ... address availability, access and affordability' (Defra, 2008a, p2). It defines these three aspects as follows:

- Availability is about how much food there is and how reliable is the supply.
- Access covers the transportation and food distribution system that gets food to where it is needed.
- Affordability is about food being available at prices that people can afford to pay, and in particular, whether low-income consumers can afford to buy enough nutritious food to meet basic health needs.

In contrast, for Defra, the issue at the global level is 'whether enough food is being produced to meet demand, and whether there are efficient and effective trading and distribution systems to get food to where it is needed' (Defra, 2008a, p2). Thus, the affordability criterion is absent in Defra's formulation of food security at the global level.

Beyond the UK, recent food price increases have resulted in social and political unrest in a wide range of countries, from Mexico to Italy, from Indonesia to Egypt, and from Haiti to Argentina. Social protests have provided clear reminders to governments that an adequate food supply is of fundamental importance for political stability. National governments have responded, in turn, with a range of measures that have included reductions in import tariffs, caps on domestic prices, and the application of export tariffs among producing countries to reduce prices – a move that has caused further protest from some producers (HM Treasury, 2008).

UK policy debate on national food security has raised questions about the future resilience of its food supply. In a general sense, resilience is understood in terms of 'keeping the show on the road' in terms of the UK's food supply. The resilience of the UK food supply system has been taken up by the responsible government departments such as Defra, HM Treasury and the Department for

International Development (DFID), by other interested groups in the agri-food sector, and by political parties. As part of this debate, questions are frequently asked regarding the extent to which the UK should be producing food for its own use, compared to the production of food for export to world markets as a contribution to the world's food basket. These concerns and others have garnered a great deal of public debate and policy-makers' attention due to the rise in food prices that occurred globally between 2006 and 2008, with the rate of price rises for UK consumers peaking around August 2008 (Office for National Statistics, 2008). Despite this price peak, it was nonetheless expected that prices would remain 'higher as a proportion of household income than they have been in the past' (Davies, 2008).

UK policy and the security of national food supply

The UK government's approach to national food security was set out by the Defra Minister, Margaret Beckett, in a speech made in March 2006:

> *Another key concern in the changing policy environment is the question of food security – something which lay at the heart of the Common Agricultural Policy's (CAP's) ambitions when it was first developed. We do not take the view that food security is synonymous with self-sufficiency... It is freer trade in agriculture which is key to ensuring security of supply in an integrating world. It allows producers to respond to global supply and demand signals, and enables countries to source food from the global market in the event of climatic disaster or animal disease in a particular part of the world ... it is trade liberalization which will bring the prosperity and economic interdependency that underpins genuine long term global security* (Beckett, 2006, paragraphs 48–51).

Beckett's approach reflected the thinking that informed the earlier HM Treasury and Defra joint paper *A Vision for the Common Agricultural Policy*, released in December 2005, which reinforced the belief that an active role in international markets was a key to ensuring efficient food production and an internationally competitive farming industry in the UK (HM Treasury and Defra, 2005). This paper was one in a line of government position papers on national food security, which are listed in Table 4.1 along with earlier national policy commitments.

The UK government's policy position towards national food security was detailed further in Defra's (2006a) *Food Security and the UK: An Evidence and Analysis Paper*. For Defra, national food security was not an issue of primary concern for the UK:

> *Poverty and subsistence agriculture are root causes of national food insecurity. National food security is hugely more relevant for*

Table 4.1 *Major statements on UK food security*

Date	Policy / document	Comment
1947	Agriculture Act	Drive to increase agricultural production with state support
1972	Treaty of Rome and other EU treaties signed by the UK	Signalled intention to shift to CAP
1975	Food From Our Own Resources	White Paper (MAFF, 1975)
2005	A Vision for the CAP	HM Treasury and Defra (2005)
2006	Food Security and the UK: An Evidence and Analysis Paper	Defra (2006a)
2008	Global Commodities: A Long-Term Vision for Stable, Secure and Sustainable Markets	HM Treasury (2008)
2008	Ensuring the UK's Food Security in a Changing World	Defra discussion paper (Defra, 2008a)
2008	Food Matters: Towards a Strategy for the 21st Century	Cabinet Office food policy strategy document, which includes food security (PMSU, 2008)

Source: the authors

developing countries than the rich countries of Western Europe (Defra, 2006a, p23).

Furthermore, a high level of national food self-sufficiency was not seen as a precondition of national food security. Rather, the analysis argued that national food security and the security of the UK's food supply were strengthened by the UK's role in international trade, as evidenced by its long history as a trading nation. The integration of the international supply of food commodities into UK food chains was seen as offering flexibility, for example as a means of compensating for unexpected harvest loss. The resilience of the UK food supply was also depicted as being enhanced by the flexibilities and expertise of supermarket food supply chains, which dominate the delivery of food to the point of sale to the public.

From the point of view of world food stocks and the adequacy of global food supply, climate change was also identified by UK government analysts as having greater impacts upon less developed countries than developed economies. The diversion of cereal and oil seed crop plantings towards biofuels was also seen as manageable in a global context (Defra, 2006a). For UK food supply chains, a number of past shocks (such as the fuel protests in 2000, and the foot-and-mouth disease outbreak of 2001) were assessed alongside future potential supply chain shocks (such as a flu pandemic or a shortage of non-renewable energy, or reduced availability of certain food commodity crops). The key risk identified in this assessment was disruption to energy supply, upon which food supply chains are dependent (Defra, 2006a). Overall, the view was expressed that such risks are potentially manageable with appropriate contingency planning and flexibility of supply – as found in both current international trade arrangements and contemporary commercial supply chains. The analysis did warn, however, that the challenge of shocks to the supply systems depended upon their 'scale, pervasiveness and duration' (Defra, 2006a, p63).

In contrast, the UK government put a quite different policy position forward 30 years earlier. In the mid-1970s, the UK government felt that a changing set of circumstances warranted a new assessment of the UK's ability to feed itself. There were concerns about the rising cost of imports and energy when considered alongside the expanding population and low global levels of cereal stocks, and the recognition that 'the influence of the UK as a buyer in world markets is changing' (MAFF, 1975, p3). The government produced a White Paper entitled *Food From Our Own Resources*, which took the view that 'a continuing expansion of food production in Britain will be in the national interest' (MAFF, 1975, p1), both to reduce the national bill for imported food, and to reduce 'the risk to the economy ... involved in a relatively high level of dependence on imports' (MAFF, 1975, p7). The paper acknowledged that the policy implications of increased food production were long term: involving the protection of agricultural land against development, the provision of a skilled young workforce, and effective research and development. The report went on to state that the government would 'frame their agricultural policies in the light of these conclusions', and ended by optimistically envisaging a partnership approach in which the government would 'look to the agricultural and food industries, with their fine record of past achievement, to work with them in bringing about an expansion of economic agricultural production in the interests of the nation' (MAFF, 1975, p17).

Over the past 30 years or so, the strength of this position has dissipated as the pace of trade liberalization has increased, underpinned as it is by World Trade Organization (WTO) agreements governing agricultural supports and food standards. As Defra (2006b) has pointed out, the UK has not been self-sufficient in terms of food production since before the Industrial Revolution. Table 4.2 provides a guide to the fluctuating levels of UK food self-sufficiency. Within these overall figures for food production, Table 4.3 indicates that there has been a further decline over the past two decades not just in the overall

Table 4.2 *Indicative UK self-sufficiency rates for food production at different periods*

Pre-1750	Around 100% of temperate produce
1750–1830s	90–100% except for poor harvests
1870s	Around 60%
1914	Around 40%
1930s	30–40%
1950s	40–50%
1980s	60–70%
2000s	60%

Source: Defra (2006b)

Table 4.3 *Decline in UK self-sufficiency rates for food production,*
1988–2007

	1988	1998	2007	Percentage change 1988–2007
All foods	71.1	67.5	60.5	−14.9
Indigenous-type foods	82.6	81.9	73.9	−10.5

Source: Defra (2007)

self-sufficiency ratio, but also in the ratio for 'indigenous type' foods, meaning those that could be grown in the UK.

The more recent declines in self-sufficiency ratios have raised the alarm bells of interests around food and agriculture policy, as is explained further below. First, however, there are qualifications that need to be made when interpreting these data. To begin, self-sufficiency figures are calculated by value, not by volume or calorific content.[3] Secondly, imports and exports of processed foods are re-valued so that they represent their constituent ingredients. This is done by multiplying the imports and exports by a 'revaluation factor', determined by the degree, or average value-added, of processing (Defra, 2006a). Whether a food is highly or lightly processed depends on the increase in value, not on the complexity of the nature of processing. Thirdly, the self-sufficiency statistics mask the extent to which goods ostensibly produced in the UK depend on imported inputs, notably oil and gas, fertilizer, feed and machinery. The government has estimated that 69 per cent of pesticides and 63 per cent of primary energy used in the UK for agriculture were imported (HM Treasury and Defra, 2005, pp47–48), while the import figure for fertilizer was put at 37 per cent, up from around 10 per cent in the 1970s (Defra, 2006a, p46).

Of the UK's food imports, 68 per cent come from European Union (EU) member states (PMSU, 2008, p32). Notwithstanding the unreliability of self-sufficiency data, a different picture emerges when looking at self-sufficiency ratios within the EU market. Table 4.4 illustrates higher levels of self-sufficiency in the production of a range of key commodities – the industrial and feed ingredients derived from soybeans are the main notable exception in these selected commodities. The EU dimension to the security of UK food supply is considered more fully in the sections below.

UK food and sustainability policy: CAP reform and food regulation

The UK's approach to food and sustainability is nested within its broader sustainability policy goals. The principles, priorities and indicators by which the UK government wanted to see the nation assist in the delivery of sustainable development were presented in *Securing Our Future* (HM Government, 2005). This strategy gave a more explicit focus to environmental limits, citing four agreed priorities – sustainable consumption and production, climate change,

Table 4.4 *EU-25 / EU-27 self-sufficiency, selected products, 2005–2006 (per cent)*

Durum wheat	88
Common wheat	103.5
Sugar	104.8
Olive oil	113.6
Sunflower oil	52
Rape seed oil	92
Soya oil	5
Soya cake and equivalent	2
Pig meat	108.2
Beef/veal	96.4
Poultry meat	102.7
Sheep and goat meat	78.2
Eggs	102.5
Honey	56

Source: European Commission (2007)

Table 4.5 *Major UK government policy statements on food and sustainability*

Date	Policy / document	Comment
2002	Farming and Food: A Sustainable Future	The Policy Commission on the Future of Farming and Food suggested bringing farming more into line with markets while delivering environmental goods (PCFF, 2002)
2002	Strategy for Sustainable Farming and Food (SFFS): Facing the Future	The Defra response to the Policy Commission report above (Defra, 2002)
2005	Securing our Future	Cross-government position and commitments to sustainable development, championing five principles (HM Government, 2005)
2006 (July)	Sustainable Farming and Food Strategy: Forward Look	Government priorities for delivery of the SFFS strategy (Defra, 2006b)
2006	Food Industry Sustainability Strategy	Industry-led sustainability strategy in line with the government's overall Securing Our Future and the SFFS Forward Look (*Food Industry Sustainability Strategy*, 2006)
2008	*Food Matters*	Prime Minister's Strategy Unit review of UK food policy with a focus on health and environmental dimensions (PMSU, 2008)

Source: the authors

natural resource protection and sustainable communities. Within its broader sustainability policy, the UK government has developed core strands of work around UK food and farming provision (see Table 4.5 for an overview of key documents).

The *Sustainable Farming and Food Strategy* (SFFS) laid out the priorities for the UK government's policy direction for agriculture and food production and its sustainability (Defra, 2002). The longer-term goals are to engage British farmers with their partners in the food supply chain, including consumers, and to ensure that farmers are efficient enough to compete in the international market place, ultimately without any further state supports. The SFFS policy priority areas were reaffirmed in 2006 (Defra, 2006b). One such priority focused on key structural challenges facing the sustainability of UK food production, such as the protection of the environment and natural resources (e.g. water, soil, air and biodiversity). Another priority area was the need to reduce the contribution of agriculture to climate change and to enhance its potential for mitigating such change. A third sustainability priority was to maintain high levels of animal health and welfare. Finally, the strategy reaffirmed initiatives to link sustainable consumption with production (Defra, 2006b). To supplement the consumption and production links, the food industry – notably manufacturing and retailing – were engaged in a range of voluntary initiatives under the *Food Industry Sustainability Strategy* (2006) to reduce the environmental impacts of the food supply chain, including water use, packaging and product waste, and greenhouse gas emissions. The initiatives were conducted with the aim of producing a lighter regulatory touch for industry from the state (*Food Industry Sustainability Strategy*, 2006).

The SFFS and its goals were framed by the trajectories of Common Agricultural Policy (CAP) reform which, in turn, were considered to fit the state supports for agriculture permitted within the green box categories, a type of subsidy category defined as the minimal or non-trade distorting category under the rules of the WTO. The 2003 CAP reforms accelerated the process of de-coupling permissible state and EU supports away from production to the provision of public goods through a single payment scheme (SPS) for farmers. The public goods principle was realized through 'cross compliance' with a set of sustainability related regulations and directives. Under the SPS, payment recipients are obliged to keep land in 'good environmental and agricultural conditions' which were targeted towards: combating erosion, avoiding the loss of soil organic matter, preserving soil structure and ensuring a minimum level of maintenance, including maintenance of historical levels of permanent pasture. In addition, the direct payments to farmers were dependent upon their compliance with 19 statutory EU directives and regulations covering environment, food safety, plant and animal health, and animal welfare standards.[4] Hence, sustainability criteria are built in as conditions for the payments to farmers.

The European dimension is not properly addressed in current UK government thinking on security of food supply. Not only are agricultural supports decided at EU level and currently linked to regulatory cross compliance, but the UK's food standards are largely regulated at the EU level as part of the single European market. These quality standards – particularly the sanitary and phytosanitary measures – provide a barrier to any food and feed imports that cannot match the required specifications. In particular, these standards have an impact on the international trade of GM food and GM feedstuffs, as well as international trade in meat produced in regions infected by certain diseases, such as foot-and-mouth disease. The Europeanization of food standards and of agricultural supports compromises the notion of a UK food supply that is free to source imports from any place where comparative economic advantage exists, for such advantage may be at the expense of standards necessary to enter the European market. Similarly, the UK Treasury's advocacy of an end to the CAP and its supports when the current budgetary agreements end after 2012 is not shared among some other member states. For example, the French Agriculture Minister, Michel Barnier, opposed the UK's ambitions to seek future reductions of CAP supports against the background of rising commodity and food prices, and argued for increased food safety and quality standards within the European market – seeking 'protection, not protectionism' for EU consumers and producers (Hall and Thornhill, 2007).

Emerging political discourse around the UK's food security

Economic and political groups in the UK have taken differing positions on the issue of UK national food security. Within the farming sector the Commercial Farmers Group – a small collection of medium-sized commodity farmers – has advocated greater national food self-sufficiency since 2004 (Commercial Farmers Group, 2004). Linked to this is a broader concern about support for the rural fabric, to which the farming industries are key contributors. One study estimated that by 2006, the farm share of the food basket had dropped by 23 per cent from the farm share in 1988 (Hampson, 2006). To this end, Baroness Byford – in her role as the Conservative spokesperson on Food and Rural Affairs in the House of Lords – raised questions about national food security from the floor of the chamber from 2005 to 2007. It was the view of this Conservative spokesperson that it was largely impossible to separate food production from the broader social and other rurally related concerns of the countryside (Byford, 2002). Groups such as the Countryside Alliance also advanced the interlinking of economic and social elements of rural pursuits, and associated the growing economic crisis in UK farming in the late 1990s with opposition to the proposed ban on fox hunting made by the incumbent Labour government at the time.

For the National Farmers Union (NFU) of owner-producers, mounting concerns associated with rising food commodity prices from late 2006 offered a policy opportunity to press the case for governmental supports for UK farming, such as increased investment in research and development, in the wake of the shift from production subsidies to support for public goods under the CAP. The NFU President Peter Kendall became more vocal about UK national food security from 2007 onwards, focusing on the need for the government to support British agriculture's contribution to both national and global food production (NFU, 2008). At the more activist end of the farming community were Farmers for Action (FFA), who had coordinated the fuel depot blockades in 2000 that caused such a significant degree of dislocation to food distribution. In the election campaign for the NFU presidency (won by Kendall), David Handley of FFA had been the only candidate to promote food security as the key election theme (*Farmers Weekly*, 2006). The Country Land and Business Association (CLBA), representing large landowners in the UK, linked the need to ensure adequate food production with the CAP reform context of environmental stewardship and in relation to future environmental change. The CLBA have called for food production levels to be considered within the wider complex of debates around land use, environmental change and resource depletion (Aubrey-Fletcher, 2008).

The Conservative Party produced a position paper titled *Blueprint for a Green Economy* that identified food security as a key vulnerability issue for the UK (Quality of Life Policy Group, 2007). In its report, the Group challenged the conclusions of the Defra (2006b) analysis paper by arguing that food security was something currently ignored by government. It contended that the:

> UK therefore needs a food and farming policy which fully acknowledges the importance and value of domestic production; otherwise, climate change, international insecurity, a growing world population with rising standards of living will make us increasingly vulnerable (Quality of Life Policy Group, 2007, p160).

In an effort to distance this position from the advocacy of farming commodity growers, the paper nonetheless concluded that: 'This is not a policy driven by the need to safeguard our ability to provide the commodities that our people need' (Quality of Life Policy Group, 2007, p160). Subsequently, the Shadow Agriculture spokesperson Jim Paice stressed that 'food security was at the core' of the Conservative Party's 'Quality of Life' agenda, emphasizing a clear policy difference from the Labour government (Gleeson, 2007).

The challenges of environmental change and resource shortage, particularly the prospect of the end of peak oil upon which the global food supply is highly dependent, have been a central platform of the Green Party's stance, as articulated by the party leader Caroline Lucas MEP, particularly with the publication of *Fuelling the Food Crisis* (Lucas et al, 2006). The policy path advocated in that paper is for a retreat from trade liberalization and for recourse to a more local and regionally based economic exchange and food supply system. Growing awareness of the environmental limits – including limits to fossil fuel reserves, to fresh water and to land availability – has been reflected, to varying degrees, in the Conservative Party's stance and in a study by Chatham House, an international affairs think tank on food supply resilience (Chatham House, 2007).

A discourse around food security already existed among development policy-makers and analysts focused on developing and least developed countries vulnerable to external shocks to their agriculture sectors, particularly those counties with large sections of their populations existing on subsistence farming. One area of expansion for developing country farmers has been the export of food, notably fruit and counter-seasonal vegetables, to European consumers – not least the UK. Development policy in the UK has supported these developments as a market-led instrument for poverty reduction among African farmers trading on their comparative advantage. In addition, UK development policy has advocated the further de-coupling of supports for producers to allow this comparative advantage to flourish. However, this policy direction was challenged by the concept of 'food miles', raising questions about the cost of environmental externalities caused by a reliance on air freight over long distances to ensure freshness at the final retail location. The issue of reducing food miles – like that of national food security – was enthusiastically taken up by British farmers and their trade press, as well as by UK retailers (Gairdner, 2006). For the development lobby, UK national food security was also a potential basis on which to justify a retreat to state or CAP supports for UK domestic production, which would potentially disadvantage the perceived comparative advantage of African producers. The sensitivities of the development lobby were most graphically illustrated when the Soil Association, an organic trade association steeped in environmental activism, canvassed its members for their views regarding a standard on imported organic food (Soil Association, 2008). The outcome was an acceptance of air freighted organic food imports that have a clear economic gain to poorer producers, such as those underpinned by fair trade designations. This led Gareth Thomas, a UK Minister of State for International Development, to berate the Soil Association for its actions – despite organic food contributing a little over 3 per cent of the UK food market (Thomas, 2007).

Questioning the resilience of contemporary UK food supply

The policy stances that have emerged in the UK range from the protection of existing policy positions, to the promotion of new or additional policy support by existing protagonists within food policy. In this, Defra's faith in the resilience of the current UK food supply strategy is increasingly questioned. Further criticism of the government position has come from Chatham House (an international affairs think tank) and other groups, which have argued that the sustainability challenges facing contemporary and future food supply are of a much more systemic nature than identified by the government (Chatham House, 2007). These systemic challenges include the UK's own sustainable farming and food criteria of adequate water, soil and air quality, biodiversity and the impacts of climate change. The systemic challenges also include the problems of energy supply and the oil-based dependency of farm inputs (fertilizers, pesticides and machinery) and food distribution systems, as well as the resultant greenhouse gas emissions. In addition, there are the increasing international demands upon food supply from growing urbanization and affluence in industrializing nations, and the impacts of the nutrition transition on the public health of these countries (Barling et al, 2008). In sum, these systemic challenges question the actual resilience of both current food supply and the underlying strategic approach. Clearly, there are disagreements with

Defra over the 'scale, pervasiveness and duration' of the external shocks to UK food supply (Defra, 2006a, p63).

There are also concerns along contemporary food supply chains about the resilience of current supply strategies. Interviews with stakeholders in UK food supply chains undertaken between late 2007 and early 2008 also revealed concerns when they were asked for their views on the sustainability of their current food supply strategies. Three examples of such concerns are cited below:

> *A sense across the global supply chain that whereas in the past, as a retailer, we have been able to shift very rapidly between countries if there was a problem – so if country X has a problem, we can go to country Y, that may be a problem for the country itself, but it's not a problem for me – there is now a recognition that the ability to hop between countries is being constrained, as climate change and other issues, such as the price of oil, kick in ... [There is] a growing awareness in the food industry that things aren't going to be the same in the future* (national food retailer).

> *We are on the cusp of quite a shift in food and what we have seen in the past year in terms of increased prices is just the most tangible change. We are shifting to where we have to be more focused on sustainable supply in the most broad definition of sustainable, and it might be that we can't eat as much, say beef, as we used to, because it takes too much grain to feed beef animals* (national food service brand representative).

> *If I'm absolutely honest, I have to say I don't know how fragile the whole system really is, and I suspect no one does* (global food manufacturer).

UK food security policy refined

The rise in commodity prices, global shortages in food commodity reserves and widespread rising food prices have together triggered public protests across the globe and international protests and policy responses, as outlined in the previous section. Against this backdrop, the issue of food security has risen up the agenda in British policy debates. Reflecting this, Gordon Brown, who was installed as Prime Minister in June 2007, authorized his strategy unit to provide an investigation into food and food policy in the UK. The issue of food security was also included in the final analysis, which echoed Defra's position that food security was different from self-sufficiency, and was integrated within international trade. This integration of UK food production within the international economy was illustrated by key inputs that are internationally traded and produced, such as oil, fertilizers, pesticides and feed, as well as a healthy export trade from British producers (PMSU, 2008).

The Prime Minister's Strategy Unit prescriptions were followed by a further Defra discussion paper *Ensuring the UK's Food Security in a Changing World* (Defra, 2008a), which raised the question of how to monitor the resilience of the UK's internationally traded food supply. Defra's updated current working model of the influences upon food supply incorporated some of the external factors influencing contemporary food supply changes. To this end, Defra (2008a) put forward a set of indicators for food security. The striking feature of the indicators is that many of the systemic challenges gathering around contemporary food supply, notably concerning environmental change and sustainability, are relatively marginalized. The proposed indicators reflect an analysis that, while rooted in past experience where retrievable data exist, remained insufficiently forward looking. The themes and related key indicators for monitoring national food security are presented in Table 4.6.

The proposed indicators highlighted the global food production capacity to meet consumption needs at the macro level, as well as social dimensions of the food vulnerabilities of low-income households at the micro level. Two key resilience features are identified: namely, energy supply, and the concentration versus the diversity of food supply. The latter feature centres on growing capacity

Table 4.6 *Defra's proposed headline and supporting food security indicators (July 2008)*

Theme	Proposed headline indicators	Potential supporting indicators
Global availability	Trends in global output per capita	Real commodity prices Stock to consumption ratios International trade as a percentage of global production Agricultural research spending Sustainability related indicator
UK trade and diversity	Concentration/diversity of supply	Share of UK imports from EU EU-wide productive capacity UK potential in extremis
Food chain resilience	Energy dependence of the supply chain	Energy reliability Diversity of oil and gas imports IGD (Institute of Grocery Distribution) retailer stock levels Cereal stock ratios Retailer concentration ratios Business continuity planning Port capacity
Affordability	Share of spending on food by low income households	Food inflation for low income groups Fruit and vegetable purchases by low income households Fruit and vegetable inflation
Safety and confidence	Public confidence in food safety measures	Trends in cases of pathogens Food covered by assurance schemes Consumer confidence in food availability

Source: Defra (2008a, p29)

across the EU, as well as on UK food growing capacity in extremis; that is, on measures of self-sufficiency at both levels (Defra, 2008a). However, neither the affordability indicators, nor the food safety and consumer confidence indicators, include the health impacts of diet and their true costs. Furthermore, there is a compelling case for a complete set of environmental sustainability indicators to be added. On the one hand, indicators need to be based upon measurable data but, on the other hand, environmental indicators are being developed under the SFFS and other sustainability and environmental policy initiatives. The need to monitor and measure new and appropriate data is part of the challenge of sustainable development policy. A revised draft of the indicators, in early 2009, added a separate category on global resource sustainability, covering fertilizer intensity, water withdrawal and global fish stocks. The concerns over the sustainability of natural resources and ecosystems for UK farming remained sidelined with the continuing emphasis upon the flexibility offered by the geographical diversity of imported food supply. However, Defra had introduced a new departmental strategic objective, following a reorganization in late 2008, to 'ensure a sustainable, secure and healthy food supply' (Defra, 2008b). There is little evidence of a proper integration of these two strands of policy work to consider food security indicators alongside food sustainability indicators; yet, clearly, the new departmental strategic objective will need the integration of these strategic policy strands if it is to be realized.

Conclusions

The renewed political interest and debate around the security of the UK's food supply has underlined a number of residual tensions within the government's farming and food strategies. The government's approach to UK food production has been framed by an overarching commitment to the liberalization of international trade. This has entailed efforts to direct the farming industry towards greater efficiency, and better marketing and supply chain relationships to improve its international competitiveness, in both domestic and international markets (Barling and Lang, 2003). Juxtaposed with this is the policy priority of improving the public goods derived from agriculture, notably: lessening farming's environmental impacts and contributing to improved use of natural resources and their sustainability, and to improved environmental quality, including the mitigation of greenhouse gas emissions and climate change impacts. From an ecological modernization perspective, these dual policy aspirations would seem to provide a good example of matching up sector economic growth with environmental gain. Closer examination, however, reveals limited and hesitant policy integration at the strategic level. This is illustrated through an examination of the UK government's food security policy.

A set of interrelated tensions can be identified from this examination of contemporary policy initiatives, and from the subsequent policy debates. Criticisms have emerged over just how resilient the internationally based supply of food and feed, and of key inputs into farming and food production, actually are. Furthermore, an important criticism relates to the sustainability of the current environmental trajectories of food production and supply. Stakeholders in food supply chains are beginning to address these environmental constraints (Lang and Barling, 2007; Barling et al, 2008). However, these environmental constraints are only partially embraced in the UK government's food supply and security policy statements. Conversely, the environmental constraints upon UK farming practice are high on the policy agenda and are being addressed, for example, under the Sustainable Farming and Food Strategy. Indeed, the CAP supports for farming are based upon compliance with a variety of regulations that are designed to improve the sustainability of agriculture and food production. At the same time, the UK government is committed to a reduction in the costs of the CAP as part of its desire to reform the EU budget and the UK's contributions. Another call in domestic policy debates is the need to rebuild and support UK food producers by such means as exerting a lighter regulatory touch, and providing more research and development support. These challenges, in turn, are part of an ongoing discourse around how much food Britain should produce. The environmental sustainability policy dimension raises complementary questions around how such food should be produced. It is clear that these policy tensions are far from being resolved, and that they are likely to be exacerbated as the consequences of global environmental change and uncertainty increasingly come to the fore.

Notes

1 We would like to acknowledge the support of the Esmée Fairburn Foundation and the Soil Association who funded research projects upon which this chapter is partly based. The views expressed here are entirely the authors' own.
2 In addition, there have been other strategic policy formulations and directions taking place around other dimensions of food policy such as food and health, and a national obesity strategy. However, neither of these initiatives has addressed the relationship between domestic farming and agricultural production and food supply in any substantive fashion. In addition, a voluntary government and industry initiative has sought to address environmental sustainability along the food supply chain with the *Food Industry Sustainability Strategy* (2006).
3 According to Defra, self-sufficiency is the value of production of raw food, divided by the value of raw food that is used for human consumption.
4 See Council Regulation (EC) No 1782/2003 establishing common rules for direct support schemes; Council Regulation (EC) No 1234/2007 establishing a common organization of agricultural markets.

References

Aubrey-Fletcher, H. (2008) Letter to *The Times*, March 8, www.timesonline.co.uk/tol/comment/letters/article3507292.ece, accessed 10 October 2008

Barling, D. and Lang, T. (2003) 'A reluctant food policy? The first five years of food policy under Labour', The Political Quarterly, vol 74, no 1, pp8–18

Barling, D., Sharpe, R. and Lang, T. (2008) 'Towards a National Sustainable Food Security Policy: A Project to Map the Policy Interface Between Food Security and Sustainable Food Supply', Centre for Food Policy, City University, London

Beckett, M. (2006) 'Action in Response to Opportunity and Challenge', Speech by Rt. Hon Margaret Beckett, Secretary of State for the Environment, Food and Rural Affairs at the Agra-Europe Outlook Conference, 23 March, London, www.defra. gov.uk/corporate/ministers/speeches/mb060323.htm, accessed 10 October 2006

Byford, Baroness (2002) Speech to LEAF Conference on World Rural Woman's Day, 14 November, www.assuredcrops.co.uk/_code/common/item.asp?id=4029605, accessed 10 October 2008

Chatham House (2007) *UK Food Supply in the 21st Century: The New Dynamic*, Chatham House, London

Commercial Farmers Group (2004) 'Food Security: The Pressure on Global Food Supply', Commercial Farmers Group, Barton-on-Humber, www.commercialfarmers. com/CFGDoc2004.pdf, accessed 12 October 2008

Davies, J. (2008) 'Has food price inflation peaked?' *Farmers Guardian*, 31 October, p12

Defra (2002) *The Strategy for Sustainable Farming and Food: Facing the Future*, Department for the Environment, Food and Rural Affairs, London

Defra (2006a) 'Food Security and the UK: An Evidence and Analysis Paper', December, Food Chain Analysis Group, Department for Environment, Food and Rural Affairs, London, www.statistics.defra.gov.uk/esg/reports/foodsecurity/foodsecurity.pdf

Defra (2006b) *Sustainable Farming and Food Strategy: Forward Look*, Department for Environment, Food and Rural Affairs, London

Defra (2007) 'Agriculture in the UK Tables and Charts, Chart 7.4', at https://statistics. defra.gov.uk/esg/publications/auk/2007/excel.asp, accessed 8 October 2008

Defra (2008a) *Ensuring the UK's Food Security in a Changing World*, Department for Environment, Food and Rural Affairs, London

Defra (2008b) 'Defra Departmental Strategic Objectives', www.defra.gov.uk/corporate/ busplan/spending-review/psa2007.htm, accessed 3 June 2009

European Commission (2007) 'Agriculture in the European Union: Statistical and Economic Information 2007', www.ec.europa.eu/agriculture/agrista/2007, accessed 10 October 2008

FAO (1996) *Rome Declaration on World Food Security*, Food and Agriculture Organization of the United Nations, Rome

FAO (2008) *The State of Food Insecurity in the World 2008*, Food and Agriculture Organization of the United Nations, Rome

Farmers Weekly (2006) 'Candidates vie for the presidential top spot', 27 February, www.fwi.co.uk/Articles/2006/02/27/92944/nfu-candidates-vye-for-the-presidential-top-spot.html, accessed 11 October 2008

Food Industry Sustainability Strategy (2006) *Food Industry Sustainability Strategy*, Department for Environment, Food and Rural Affairs, London

Gairdner, J. (2006) *Local Food is Miles Better: The Farmers Weekly Food Campaign*, Reed Business Information, Crawley

Gleeson, C. (2007) 'Food security at the heart of policy', *Farmers Guardian*, 5 October, p6

Gouldson, A. and Murphy, J. (1997) 'Ecological modernisation: Restructuring industrial economies', in M. Jacobs (ed) *Greening the Millennium? The New Politics of the Environment*, Blackwell, Oxford

Hall, B. and Thornhill, J. (2007) 'Paris for "protection, not protectionism"', *Financial Times*, 25 October, p6

Hampson, S. (2006) *Differentiation: A Sustainable Future for UK Agriculture*, John Lewis Partnership, London, p4

HM Government (2005) *Securing Our Future: The UK Government Sustainable Development Strategy*, HMSO, London

HM Treasury (2008) *Global Commodities: A Long Term Vision for Stable, Secure and Sustainable Global Markets*, June, HM Treasury, London

HM Treasury and Defra (2005) *A Vision for the Common Agricultural Policy*, HM Treasury and Department for Environment, Food and Rural Affairs, London

Jacobs, M. (1997) 'Introduction: The new politics of the environment' in M. Jacobs (ed) *Greening the Millennium? The New Politics of the Environment*, Blackwell, Oxford, p10

Lang, T and Barling, D. (2007) 'The environmental impact of supermarkets: Mapping the terrain and the policy positions in the UK', in D. Burch and G. Lawrence (eds) *Supermarkets and Agri-Food Supply Chains: Transformations in the Production and Consumption of Foods*, Edward Elgar, Cheltenham, UK, pp192–215

Lucas, C., Jones, A. and Hines, C. (2006) *The Fuelling of the Food Crisis*, The Greens/ European Free Alliance, Brussels, www.carolinelucasmep.org.uk/2006/12/08/ fuelling-a-food-crisis/, accessed 11 October 2008

MAFF (Ministry of Agriculture, Fisheries and Food) (1975) *White Paper on Food From Our Own Resources*, HMSO, London, National Archives catalogue ref: cab/129/182/24

NFU (National Farmers Union) (2008) 'Action on Food Security Should Start at Home', 18 July, Press Release, www.nfuonline.com/x29277.xml?action=preview, accessed 11 October 2008

OECD (2008) *OECD Glossary of Statistical Terms: Food Security*, Organisation for Economic Co-operation and Development, Paris, http://stats.oecd.org/glossary/ detail.asp?ID=5006, accessed 19 June 2008

Office for National Statistics (2008) 'Consumer Price Indices July 2008', Office for National Statistics, London, www.statistics.gov.uk/pdfdir/cpi0808.pdf, accessed 16 August 2008

PCFF (2002) *Farming and Food: A Sustainable Future*, January, Policy Commission on the Future of Farming and Food, London

PMSU (Prime Minister's Strategy Unit) (2008) *Food Matters: Towards a Strategy for the 21st Century*, Cabinet Office, London

Quality of Life Policy Group (2007) *Blueprint for a Green Economy: Submission to the Shadow Cabinet*, Quality of Life Policy Group, p160, www.qualityoflifechallenge. com, accessed 9 October 2008

Soil Association (2008) *Air Freight Consultation – Recommendations for Standards*, March, Soil Association, Bristol

Thomas, G. (2007) 'New organic labelling rules threaten poor farmers', *Guardian*, 2 November, www.guardian.co.uk/commentisfree/2007/nov/02/comment. lifeandhealth, accessed 11 October 2008

5

Neoliberalism and Food Vulnerability: The Stakes for the South

Gabriela Pechlaner and Gerardo Otero

Introduction

Agriculture has historically represented the greatest stumbling block for promoters of neoliberal ideology and trade liberalization across the global marketplace. Having been set apart in the post-Second World War trade regime, neoliberal globalizers have consistently sought to bring agriculture into the free-trade fold since the Uruguay Round of the General Agreement on Tariffs and Trade (GATT) (1987–2003), and later through the Doha 'Development' Round. With agriculture's products having the distinction of being the means to sustaining life, it is hard simply to designate them as commodities to be exchanged according to the dictates of national comparative advantage. Furthermore, advanced capitalist countries have been glaringly inconsistent in preaching free trade while practising protectionism in agriculture. In a market context, with such inconsistent liberalization the revenues generated from agriculture for export are far from predictable, stable and equitable. Similarly, the cost of purchasing food internationally is equally subject to the vagaries of the market. Consequently, food security based on market access is less risky for high-income nations, and national food sovereignty is of far greater concern to lower-income nations. Nonetheless, developing countries of the global South – many of which produce a surplus of food – have signed on to free-trade deals with hopes of ensuring market access to the developed countries of the North.

Given the power inequalities at play in the jockeying over trade liberalization in agriculture, trade negotiations shaping the international division of labour in agriculture and food have become regionally polarized. These slow and unwieldy policy negotiations have been jolted more recently, however, by the shocks in world food prices experienced in 2007–2008. Consequently, even prior to any resolution of the issue of agriculture at the World Trade Organization (WTO), theoretical arguments about trade liberalization have been dislodged by the wealth of empirical evidence demonstrating the disproportionately negative impact of food dependency on lower-income countries. While the food crisis affecting developing countries has resulted from a mix of natural and policy factors, subscription to trade liberalization is increasing both their dependence and their peripheral status with respect to countries of the North. There is strong evidence that the resulting food vulnerability in developing countries is not only increasing national inequalities, but is also exacerbating the dependence of lower-income countries on their Northern neighbours. While more equitable arrangements are clearly required, we do not believe that an isolationist strategy is the only solution. Instead, we propose an internationalist form of food nationalism, one that privileges food sovereignty without cutting off opportunities for international trade or resorting to protectionism.

In the first section of this chapter, we discuss the main legal tenets of neoliberal globalism at the supra-state level, which we refer to as 'neoregulation'. Specifically, we outline those international trade-liberalization efforts in agriculture related to the Agreement on Agriculture (AoA) made under the auspices of the WTO. In the second section, arguments around trade liberalization are cast in the context of the ongoing food crisis. Given the likely exacerbation of this crisis by the severe economic problems triggered by the US financial 'meltdown', we focus on painting a broad picture of the impacts of the food crisis on the ability of developing countries to address issues of food vulnerability. The third section examines such food crisis impacts for one country, namely Mexico, which was chosen based on its status as a developing country that has a trade agreement with two developed neighbours to its north. In the final, concluding, section we argue that promoting food sovereignty and retaining national control over agriculture is the safest bet for developing nations of the South. Specifically, we call for an 'internationalist nationalism' in regard to food and agriculture, which has the potential to achieve these gains without resorting to isolation or protectionism.

Neoregulation in agriculture

As we have argued elsewhere (Pechlaner and Otero, n.d.), regulation for trade liberalization is an ideological project, conducted under what we call 'neoliberal globalism'. Rather than the power of the state 'withering away' under globalization, as the situation is sometimes characterized, we see strong evidence that states are active participants in regulatory restructuring that aims to support the market as a self-regulating mechanism. Consequently, we prefer the term '*neo*regulation', rather than the more popular '*de*regulation', to better characterize state participation in restructuring. Vast economic and power differentials between states, however, mean that some states are more able to drive the creation of global regulatory regimes, while others must concentrate on strategies aimed at adapting to the resulting conditions – conditions frequently not in their favour (see Ó Riain, 2000; McMichael, 2004). In this context it becomes easier to understand why current efforts to incorporate agriculture into international trade agreements are rife with contention, despite the strong role of agriculture in global trade throughout history.

Trade liberalization in agriculture is an important component of the full implementation of neoliberal ideology in international regulations. In many ways, the argument for free trade echoes historical discussions regarding comparative advantage. It is argued that trade works best when each country specializes in what it can produce best, or most efficiently, and then trades with other countries that have done the same, but have specialized in other products. With respect to agriculture, it has been argued that it would be inefficient for each country to seek to produce all its own food. As Pascal Lam, Director General of the WTO, has argued 'if Egypt had to be self-sufficient in food, there would be no water left in the Nile' (cited in Bradsher and Martin, 2008). In short, it is assumed that global food production would decrease if each country – no matter how ill-suited – attempted to produce all of its own food. Further, while agricultural products have been traded internationally for centuries, agriculture has also been strongly protected at the national level, with the most protectionist (or farmer-subsidizing) countries being advanced capitalist societies, namely the US, member countries of the European Union (EU) and Japan. Given that developing countries do not have the resources to compete with the subsidies provided to the sector in these regions, signing on to trade liberalization would theoretically provide access to otherwise highly protected markets.

The locus for negotiations over trade liberalization in agriculture is the WTO. While some dictates for trade in agriculture existed in the WTO's predecessor, GATT, it was only during the Uruguay Round of negotiations – resulting in the transformation of GATT into the WTO in 1994 – that an agreement dedicated to agriculture was initiated. The resulting Agreement on Agriculture (AoA) was a preliminary step towards reducing trade distortions in agriculture. At its core are three 'pillars' for reforming trade – market access, export competition and domestic support – with different phase-in periods being specified as appropriate for developing and developed countries.

The market access pillar requires the conversion of all non-tariff barriers (such as quotas and voluntary export restraints) into tariffs, through a process called 'tariffication'. Once each country's barriers had all been converted into tariffs, the tariff amount was set and could not be increased. The tariffication process aims to create a more predictable system, and to facilitate the numerical reduction of tariffs over time according to set targets. The second pillar, export competition, relates to export subsidies. Export subsidies are by their very nature trade distorting because they encourage the export of goods through various government measures (such as tax relief), thus increasing sales on the international rather than the domestic market. It is easy to see how these two pillars distort trade, either by increasing the costs for those trying to import goods into the country (thus keeping local prices artificially high), or by helping local producers export their goods outside the country (thus driving market prices artificially low). In either case, producers outside the country who are not similarly protected face a trade disadvantage as a result of these measures. The last pillar is the domestic support pillar. Domestic supports are problematic in a free trade regime because they encourage overproduction, which affects the potential for imports and can lead to 'dumping' on world markets (WTO, 2007).

Importantly, the AoA categorizes domestic support measures in terms of 'boxes', which are somewhat analogous to traffic lights. Green box measures include subsidy programmes around environmental protection, regional development and direct income supports to farmers that do not affect production levels (WTO, 2007). While green box subsidies are permitted, these subsidies must not deliberately distort trade, although some minimal trade distortion effects may be acceptable. In contrast, amber box forms of domestic support are known to distort trade by supporting price or production levels, although only a minimal amount of such distortion is permitted. Finally, while not named as an actual 'box' in the AoA, any domestic support measure that exceeds the permitted amount of amber box subsidies could be considered 'red'. Beyond the traffic light metaphor are blue boxes, which are essentially amber boxes with restrictions, and which have no subsidy limit (WTO, 2002). Thus, an amber box policy that has a condition requiring farmers to limit production is placed in a blue box.

The AoA has numerical targets for the reduction of tariffs and subsidies, with a six-year phase-in period for developed countries starting in 1995; a 10-year phase-in period for developing countries; and no reductions required for least-developed countries. The average cut in tariffs for all agricultural products and export subsidies was to be 36 per cent for developed countries and 24 per cent for developing countries. Cuts to domestic supports were to be 20 per cent for developed countries and 13 per cent for developing countries (WTO, 2007). Implementation of these targets has had some very unequal effects. Essentially, there is a significant difference between implementation according to the spirit of the agreement, and implementation that – while still technically in compliance – nonetheless manages to maintain agricultural protection. Trade liberalization is not as transparent as touted. Consequently, while these trade liberalization strategies appear to make provisions for the relatively weaker status of developing and least-developed countries, there are indications that the changes are nonetheless significantly disadvantaging these countries. According to a WTO 'backgrounder' published near the end of the phase-in period for developed countries:

> *Many developing countries complain that their exports still face high tariffs and other barriers in developed countries' markets and that their attempts to develop processing industries are hampered by tariff escalation (higher import duties on processed products compared to raw materials) (WTO, 2004).*

Another frequently-made critique of the trade-liberalization programme is that the 'box' process of subsidies has been manipulated to the advantage of developed countries, thereby circumventing the opening of their markets while developing countries have followed through with agreed trade liberalization measures. For example, the organization ActionAid claims that since the AoA has been in place, developed countries have been shifting their subsidies between boxes in order to avoid their reduction commitments, and as a consequence have actually managed to increase their agricultural subsidies by some 9 per cent between 1986–1988 and 1999–2001 (ActionAid.org, n.d.). Through such box manipulation, developed countries are able to maintain their subsidies, and to continue the practice of 'dumping' agricultural products on the world market at prices below the cost of production – a practice that damages the domestic agriculture sectors of developing countries unable to match such subsidized production. In the decade prior to 2003, for example, ActionAid estimates that the US has sold various agricultural products at prices significantly below the cost of production: for example, maize has been sold at 5–35 per cent below cost, with figures cited as 20–55 per cent for cotton, 20–35 per cent for wheat, 15–20 per cent for rice, and 8–30 per cent for soybeans (ActionAid.org, n.d., p8).

Subsequent negotiations towards agricultural liberalization were to be pursued during the 9th Round of WTO negotiations in Doha in 2001. Despite its billing as the 'development round', supposedly prioritizing the issues of developing countries, these countries found their concerns over the non-trade values of agriculture and food – such as food security, poverty alleviation, rural development and rural migration – insufficiently represented in negotiations. In 2006, a number of developing-country groups issued a joint statement emphasizing that for negotiations to work, the protectionist tendencies of developed countries had to be addressed:

> *The most substantial results must be achieved in the areas where the greatest distortions lie, in particular on trade-distorting subsidies in agriculture that displace developing country products and threaten the livelihoods of hundreds of millions of poor farmers* (G-20, 2006).

Consequently it is not agricultural trade as such that is the concern for developing countries – to be sure, such trade might be to their advantage. The issue, rather, is trade between countries with vast power differentials, and with no provisions for the special status of food and agriculture in disadvantaged countries. The discord over agriculture ultimately caused negotiations to completely collapse in July 2006, and again in November 2008.

The food crisis

While numerous developing countries have fought against the unqualified liberalization of agriculture, recent shocks to world food prices have moved these debates out of the sidelines and on to the world stage. The Food Price Index of the Food and Agriculture Organization of the United Nations (FAO) recorded a steady increase in international food and feed prices from early 2006, a situation that reached crisis proportions by 2008. Demonstrations and food riots have flared up in developing countries such as Guinea, Mauritania, Mexico, Morocco, Senegal, Uzbekistan and Yemen (Bradsher, 2008). People have died in violent protests in places such as Haiti (Associated Press, 2008) and Africa, where government stores were burned and looted in the rampages (Walt, 2008). While prices began to drop by October 2008, they still were 28 per cent above October 2006 levels (FAO, 2008a). Food prices are responsive to many factors, and shifts can be expected, but a majority of the factors precipitating the crisis are likely to continue their upward pressure on prices.

The causes of the current food crisis are manifold. As noted by the Economic and Social Council of the United Nations (ECOSOC), while there is wide agreement on the factors that caused the crisis, there is 'less agreement on their relative importance,' no doubt in part due to the political significance of this weighting (ECOSOC, 2008). The concerns noted by ECOSOC and many others include rising food demand, declining productivity growth, weather events such as the multi-year drought in Australia, rising energy prices, and competition from 'biofuels' – referred to more accurately by McMichael (2009) as 'agrofuels'.

While food demand is in part a factor of population growth, it is also a factor of increased income in developing countries, where between 1970 and 2005 the per capita income has almost tripled (Rosen and Shapouri, 2008, p12). This has increased food demand and, more specifically, the demand for higher-value foods such as protein (including meat), which require more resources to produce than grain. Despite the predictability of many of these factors, years of agricultural surplus in the US and the EU have seemingly biased perceptions about the need for agricultural research and development, with a consequent reduction in investment. As a result, yield growth decreased from 3 per cent in the period from 1961 to 1984 to its current level of 1 per cent – close to the world population growth rate (Reguly, 2008).

A related issue is that of high energy prices, which have pushed up the cost of food production through the increasing cost of fuel, fertilizer and pesticides. These same energy concerns have driven the demand for agrofuels, which compete for crops and cropland (McMichael, 2009). We attribute greater significance to the contribution of agrofuels to increasing food prices, than to politically neutral explanations of the food crisis triggers, for two reasons. First, the push to develop agrofuels has become an accelerating policy train. The leading agrofuel producers are the US and Brazil (together accounting for almost 90 per cent of ethanol production), and the EU (accounting for approximately 60 per cent of biodiesel production), with a growing number of other countries – including China, Canada and India – joining the policy train (FAO, 2008b, p15). A wide range of government support programmes at various stages of production and consumption have accelerated agrofuel production since 2003. A report by the Global Subsidies Initiative estimated that by 2007, support for the industry in Organisation for Economic Co-operation and Development (OECD) countries was approximately US$13–15 billion per year (Steenblik, 2007, p4). While disputed, there is ample evidence of the significant contribution of agrofuel development to the increase in food prices. For example, despite US assertions that agrofuels contributed just 2–3 per cent to global food price increases (Borger, 2008), the International Food Policy Research Institute estimates that the US contribution to global commodity price increases is between 25 and 33 per cent (Martin, 2008). Moreover, the OECD has estimated that agrofuels accounted for nearly 60 per cent of the increased demand for cereal and oils between 2005 and 2007 (Borger, 2008).

The second point regarding the relationship between agrofuels and food price increases is that, while many of the factors that affect food prices are difficult if not impossible to control – factors such as drought, rising incomes and population growth – the decision to prioritize fuel over food as the purpose of agricultural production is a policy decision. Moreover, it is a decision that is currently being implemented by the very countries that are simultaneously advocating trade liberalization in agriculture. Brazil, the one developing country which stands to profit from significant agrofuel production – and, importantly, whose production of sugar ethanol does not compete with food crops – is subject to high import tariffs in the EU (Cronin, 2008). Future subsidy and policy commitments to agrofuel development in OECD countries (such as the EU commitment to 10 per cent mandated agrofuel content by 2020) suggest that the pressure on food prices will be maintained, if not increased. Despite the predictability of many of the food crisis triggers, their confluence was allowed to unfold into a 'perfect storm' that acted on the price of food staples such as rice, wheat and corn. Rice prices differ by type, but in 2006 most types hovered around US$300/tonne and peaked in May 2008 at almost triple that price. Thailand, for example, has been the top rice exporter since 1980 (FAO, 2004) and the price of Thai white rice increased by 310 per cent, from US$311/tonne in 2006 to US$963/tonne in 2008 (FAO, 2008c). Similarly, the price of US No 2 Hard Red wheat increased by some 227 per cent, from US$212/tonne in 2006 to peak at US$481/tonne in March 2008, while US No 2 yellow maize increased 201 per cent from US$145/tonne in 2006 to peak at US$292/tonne in July 2008 (FAO, 2008d). While such price increases may cut into the discretionary spending of the middle-income earner in a developed country, its impact is far greater on those in developing countries – most notably on the low-income, food importing countries in Africa and Asia.

The leaders of developing countries consequently have good reason to doubt the rosy 'everybody wins' hypothesis articulated around trade governed by the neoliberal paradigm. A document from the EU issued prior to the collapse of the Doha Round stated that Doha would help reduce food prices on the basis that reducing subsidies and barriers would encourage the agriculture sector to respond to market signals and to increase production in developing countries (Europa, 2008). In the immediate term, however, the food crisis has sent governments and international agencies scurrying for solutions and either backtracking on, or defending, policies with regard to any factor that could be said to influence food prices. A key topic of the FAO's High-Level Conference on World Food Security held in June 2008 was the question of agrofuels and the extent to which they were a contributing factor to the world food crisis. The resulting declaration called for an international dialogue on agrofuels in the context of food security and sustainable development goals. More pointedly, the same OECD countries that are behind the push for agrofuels are facing increasing pressure to tone down their agenda in the face of the food crisis. Specifically, the EU faces pressure to suspend its mandated 2020 agrofuels target (Martin, 2008). It seems doubtful that – even in the context of an agricultural production system more closely responsive to the wider market – future production could be sufficiently raised to mitigate all demand pressures from a greatly expanded international agrofuels industry.

Speculation aside, the crisis has provoked real-time policy responses. National governments in countries hardest hit by the food crisis have reacted with a wide range of policy responses: reducing the tax on imported foodstuffs (such as in Congo, Azerbaijan and Brazil); eliminating or reducing import duties and tariffs (such as in Ghana, Kenya, Nigeria, Mauritania, China, Pakistan, Brazil, Mexico and Nicaragua); banning exports of selected foodstuffs (Liberia, Egypt, Bangladesh, India, China and Argentina) or otherwise imposing export controls, duties or taxes (Kyrgyzstan, Belarus and Argentina); subsidizing distribution (Honduras, Panama, Ethiopia and Rwanda); placing a freeze on food-item prices (Mexico); and using ration card systems (Egypt). Some governments have also tried to stimulate production by such means as providing subsidies or increasing the prices paid to farmers (Zambia, Azerbaijan, China, India and Malaysia), distributing seed (Guyana), or attempting to ameliorate the impact of high energy prices on farmers through fuel and fertilizer allocations and subsidies (China and Indonesia). These are just some examples of the wide range of responses (FAO, 2008e). Of course, the availability of responses depends both on international trade rules and on the financial abilities of the countries involved.

The differing abilities of countries to respond to crises make it impossible to consider neoregulation in agriculture and food without considering the issue of power in food dependence. A historical example of the consequences of such food dependence is the role of Japan in the 1973 US embargo on soybean exports, in response to a surge in demand and the price increases that followed as a consequence. Given the importance of soybeans to the Japanese diet, the 'embargo-induced shortage created panic' and induced 'the worst food crisis in Japan since the war' (Katsuro, 1984). In fact, given Japan's inability to produce food to meet its own needs, the 1973 events are often cited as the reason for Japanese investment in, and the subsequent growth of, the Brazilian soybean industry (Ray, 2004a). The 1980s US grain embargo on Russia as a foreign policy response to Russia's invasion of Afghanistan is another case in point. While the embargo did not have its intended impact (Ray, 2004b) as Russia sourced its needs elsewhere, it remains an important example of the risks of food dependence. Nonetheless, as current world events indicate, food shortages can evolve in the absence of such foreign policy interventions.

The tone of national self-preservation is already clear in the post-2006 food crisis. By June 2008, 29 countries had limited or banned food exports in such commodities as rice, wheat, corn and even sunflower seeds in order to ensure sufficient and affordable food for their own populations (Bradsher and Martin, 2008). As an outcome of such actions, which have reduced the available market stocks and thus further increased the cost of remaining supplies for import-dependent countries, international relief groups such as the World Food Programme in Rome are also having trouble purchasing stocks for emergency operations and food aid programmes (Bradsher and Martin, 2008). Despite the drive to liberalize trade in agriculture and the risks that are inherent in food-import dependence, such food-export restrictions did not garner significant attention in agricultural trade liberalization negotiations until the current crisis. Japan and Switzerland (both food import-dependent) have responded to the crisis by calling for a considerable strengthening of the rules on export restrictions in the current draft of the WTO. Notably, they have called for new rules to constrain export restrictions to the 'extent strictly necessary', for export restrictions to be subject to extensive pre-authorization and consultation requirements, and for disputes over export restriction proposals to be subjected to binding arbitration (ICTSD, 2008). A discussion paper by the Swiss National Centre of Competence in Research (NCCR), to cite another example of such rule-strengthening, emphatically asserts that '*A failure to discipline export restrictions would be particularly damaging when trade liberalisation increases competition on domestic markets*' (NCCR, 2008, p6, emphasis in original).

While many of the national governmental policy responses are efforts with predominantly local-level impacts, the impacts of those who resorted to so-called 'starve-thy-neighbour' export bans and related policies are devastating for those low-income countries dependent on the global market for their food. Significantly, but not surprisingly, these policies are not always evenly applied, as trade is never far from the reach of foreign policy. Politics are evident, for example, in the exceptions to export bans such as those associated with China's exports to the Democratic People's Republic of Korea, Argentina's exports to Brazil, and Ecuador's exports to Venezuela (FAO, 2008e). Such exchange agreements can be based on historical precedent or in-the-moment strategizing; for example, Malaysia's announcement that it will exchange palm oil for rice (FAO, 2008e). When the conditions for mutually beneficial trade break down, as they inevitably will, countries with little economic, military or other forms of global power will be without recourse.

A view from the ground: The food crisis in Mexico

Let us further interrogate the case of Mexico. When considering aggregate data, Mexico is not self-sufficient in agriculture, although these aggregate data narrow the definition of agri-food (which we prefer to define broadly) and exclude more broadly defined agri-food exports, such as beer and distilled alcoholic beverages. With this wider definition, the country is self-sufficient. In either case, if Mexico is not yet self-sufficient in agriculture, it is nonetheless very close to being so. Consequently, given its high level of agricultural production and its involvement in agricultural trade liberalization through the North American Free Trade Agreement (NAFTA) since 1994, Mexico is a good case from which to consider the impact of trade liberalization in the context of high food prices. We do this using per capita food consumption data, which we compare with that of its two NAFTA partners, the US and Canada.

Unfortunately, per capita food consumption data are not available up to and including the current food crisis, but we can nonetheless extrapolate from data up to 2003, the latest year for which they are available from FAOSTAT (see Figures 5.1–5.4 below). Comparing data for the three countries of the NAFTA region for per capita food consumption, we note several trends and shifts. First, while consumption in the US is clearly above that of both Canada and Mexico, it may be surprising to some that Mexico had a slightly higher per capita food consumption prior to 1994, the starting year of NAFTA. Starting exactly in that same year, however, Canada's per capita food consumption exceeded that of Mexico, and approached that of the US by 2003. Finally, there is an upward trend in per capita food consumption throughout the period, but this is considerably more pronounced for the US and Canada than it is for Mexico, where the increase is barely perceptible. Going on this aspect alone, Mexico was left behind in per capita food consumption by its northern partners, even prior to the sharp food price increases that occurred in 2006.

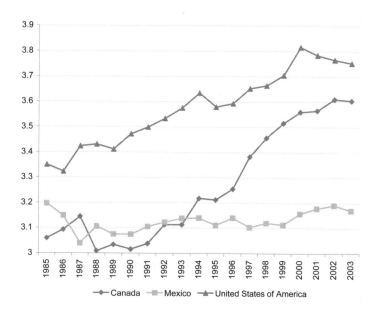

Source: FAO (2006)

Figure 5.1 *NAFTA region food consumption*

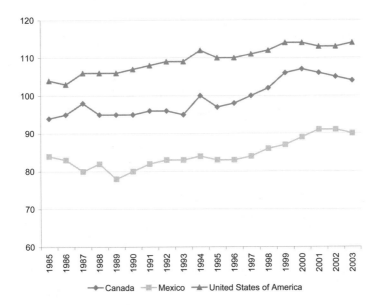

Source: FAO (2006)

Figure 5.2 *NAFTA region protein consumption*

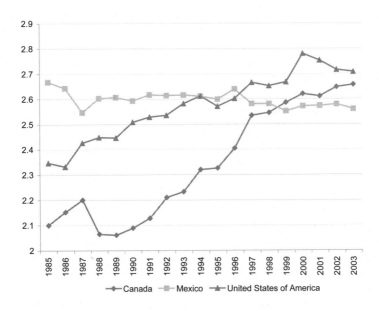

Source: FAO (2006)

Figure 5.3 *NAFTA region vegetable consumption*

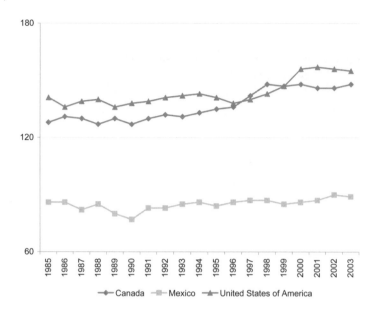

Source: FAO (2006)

Figure 5.4 *NAFTA region fat consumption*

If we break down the analysis by components of food: protein, vegetables and fats, we can ascertain some additional interesting contrasts. Once again, each of the three countries experienced slight increases in per capita protein consumption, but consumption in Mexico is 15 to 25 grams per day below that in Canada and the US, respectively, at any given time between 1985 and 2003 (see Figure 5.2). It should be acknowledged that the most likely catalyst for Mexico's increased per capita protein intake was the importation of cheaper meat from the US after 1994. Nonetheless, per capita protein intake in Mexico still falls far below that of the other two countries. The contrasts change when we move on to vegetable consumption per capita; while the US still has the highest consumption level, and has increased its per capita vegetable intake over time, Canada's consumption jumped from below that of Mexico to a level considerably higher. Indeed, Mexico's vegetable intake, which started out higher than Canada's, experienced a slight decline. This is quite ironic, as during the same period Mexico increased its vegetable exports to Canada and the US (Pechlaner and Otero, n.d.). Evidently this means that, while capitalized farmers were able to take advantage of liberalized trade through NAFTA, average Mexican consumers experienced declining purchasing power, affecting their ability to buy vegetables (see Figure 5.3). Lastly, per capita fat consumption in Mexico has always been something over half that of Canada and the US. While fat consumption in Mexico has remained fairly stable since 1984, with a slight decline at the start of the neoliberal turn in 1987–1990, the trend for its northern neighbours has been to increase fat intake since that time (see Figure 5.4).

Academic economists in Mexico corroborate these trends, clearly indicating an unfavourable evolution of food consumption for Mexico relative to Canada and the US. To start with, 2 million jobs were lost in the Mexican countryside, with many of these people migrating to cities or to North America, in most cases without immigration documents. According to José Luis Calva of the National Autonomous University of Mexico, the country's economy grew by a yearly average of 6.1 per cent from the 1940s to 1982. In the 14 years of NAFTA to 2007, however, Mexico's economy grew by a mere 1.7 per cent annually. While there was growth in Mexico's agriculture sector from 1.7 to 2.0 tonnes per hectare, such growth was much lower than that in the US, which increased from 7.0 to 8.9 tonnes per hectare.

Further, a United Nations Economic Commission for Latin America and the Caribbean (ECLAC) report estimates that the 2006–2007 consumer price indexes in Latin America and the Caribbean have risen at rates between 6 per cent and 20 per cent annually, with the average being around 15 per cent. The report goes on to state that 'a 15 per cent rise in food prices will increase indigence [the state of extreme poverty] by almost three points from 12.7 per cent to 15.9 per cent. This means that elevating food prices will lead another 15.7 million Latin Americans to destitution' (CEPAL News, 2008, p1). Even adjusting for income increases, ECLAC estimates that the figure will be 10 million.

For Mexicans, corn is a significant foodstuff both nutritionally and culturally. At the same time, market competition has meant that corn is not just directly consumed, but is also a very versatile ingredient found in processed foods such as corn oil, corn flour, high fructose corn syrup (used as a sweetener in many products), as well as in livestock feed. Most recently, it has also become a highly controversial input to agrofuel production, thus further increasing demand for the crop. This versatility goes some way to explain the role of corn in the global food-price crisis, with significant negative impacts for Mexican consumers. Oxfam estimates that between January 2007 and April 2008, tortilla prices in the country have increased 66 per cent (Shikoh and Shuriah, 2008). Indeed, the Bank of Mexico has revealed that of the 24 products with the highest price increases during 2008, 15 were food products, with some price increases being enormous. The price of green tomatoes, for instance, was 110 per cent higher – an increase 18 times greater than that of general inflation. As for developing countries generally, food-price inflation in Mexico disproportionately affects lower-income households.

From the above data we can see that the recent food price increases are more likely to have a significant impact on food import-dependent countries like Mexico. From a situation in which per capita food consumption hardly increased since 1985, we are already seeing declining consumption alongside these price increases. When prices increased by 15 per cent during the month of December 2008, consumption dipped by 30 per cent (Notimex, 2009). This trend has occurred for at least two primary reasons: first, the proportion of family budgets spent on food is about four times as large as in developed nations; and, second, overall income levels are substantially lower in developing countries. In Mexico, this means that for people making three times the minimum wage inflation in 2008 was 8.02 per cent, but for those making six or more times the minimum wage inflation was 5.98 per cent (Martínez, 2009).

In short, what we can observe is that any negative impacts of trade liberalization have been far greater for Mexico than for Canada and the US, even prior to the post-2006 food-price crisis (for more on this topic, see Otero and Pechlaner, 2008). Once the crisis ensued, these disproportionately negative impacts have only deepened. We argue that these results can be largely generalized to other low-income developing countries. For low-income countries, the impact has a real and negative effect on people's well-being. Even those developing countries that are surplus agricultural producers suffer from these negative impacts, as we can project from the price increases.

Conclusion

In this chapter we have discussed the uneven impacts of the post-2006 food-price crisis for Southern developing countries. The severity of the food crisis has provided a unique opportunity to reflect on the impact of neoregulation in agriculture, on the promotion of a new international division of labour in agriculture and food, and on the particular consequences of agrofuel production. As we have seen, even developed countries such as Japan and Switzerland are subject to the risks of food-import dependency. As exemplified by Japan's influence on soy production in Brazil, however, these countries have considerable recourse to other forms of power on the global stage. The developing countries of the South have fewer endowments to deploy in order to safeguard their national food self-sufficiency in such cases. In short, food-import dependence has risks, but these risks are substantially greater for developing nations.

While some countries have no choice but to be food-import dependent, other countries that are self-sufficient in agriculture (or close to it) are confronted with a choice between producing luxury products for export under a liberalized trade regime, or prioritizing a nationalized agricultural sector that promotes the production of staples for domestic consumption. The implications of our analysis here lead us to favour the latter approach. Although there is little doubt that future international trade agreement negotiations will dedicate far more attention to such issues as export bans, they are unlikely to be able to cover all the eventualities. In the context of production for export – with likely restrictions on many of the policy measures taken by developing country governments in response to the current crisis – many of these governments would find themselves even more deeply dependent on the benevolence of other nations. In the context of insufficient purchasing power, the freedom to purchase on the open market is a rather weak freedom. Finally, it goes without saying that even perfectly equitable trade agreements that are attentive to national inequalities are still subject to political influence in their ongoing execution. In short, agreements can be broken.

The food crisis has provided some insight into the drawbacks of neoregulation for agricultural trade liberalization in an international context rife with power differentials. In this context, wholesale subscription to the ideology of neoliberal globalism can carry a very high price for the people in developing countries. Cuts to farm assistance programmes, such as have occurred in Mexico as part of a neoregulatory effort to eliminate masses of 'inefficient' farmers, have had the desired effect of reducing the farm sector. But the costs have been far reaching: the creation of masses of ex-peasants which the domestic economy has been unable to absorb; and increased local food vulnerability.

We argue that such consequences, and others detailed in this chapter, point away from neoregulation and toward the reinstatement of policies that support local agriculture and, with it, an increase in local food production, and that reduce reliance on imports. Supporting small-scale peasant producers has at least two long-term advantages. Firstly, they have demonstrated that even if they are not nearly as efficient as the more capitalized farmers of the North, they have been able to produce subsistence for millions of peasant families. Keeping farmers on the land, as opposed to economically expelling them from the country in the form of increased out-migration, also preserves rural communities as more vibrant entities. Studies have found that out-migration from rural communities sharply increases work for women in communities populated primarily by the elderly, women and children (Preibisch, 1996; Hanson, 2007). Secondly, small-scale peasant production has also been found to be important for preserving plant biological diversity (Bartra, 2004; Fitting, 2008). Such diversity is a fundamental insurance policy to buffer against future food vulnerability across the globe.

In short, peasant production fulfils both social and environmental 'services' that are rarely recognized when made to compete with the capitalized and subsidized farmers of the North (Bartra, 2004). Rather than taking an anti-trade stance (we must recognize that agricultural trade can, in fact, be an important economic generator for developing countries), we argue that maintaining local food self-sufficiency is an important national policy objective, wherever this is agronomically feasible. Trade agreements must either be supportive of this 'special' status of food and agriculture in developing countries, or developing countries should continue to resist further subscription to the neoregulatory regime crafted by countries of the North. This is what we mean by the need for an 'internationalist nationalism' in regard to food and agriculture, which involves promoting a hegemony of a new form of nationalism focused on democratic and environmental sustainability concerns.

References

ActionAid.org (n.d.) 'The WTO Agreement on Agriculture', www.actionaid.org.uk/_content/documents/agreement_3132004.pdf, accessed 25 June 2007

Associated Press (2008) 'Haiti: Thousands protest food prices', *New York Times*, 8 April, www.nytimes.com/2008/04/08/world/americas/08briefs-THOUSANDSPRO_BRF.html?fta=y, accessed 21 November 2008

Bartra, A. (2004) 'Rebellious cornfields: Toward food and labour self-sufficiency', in G. Otero (ed.) *Mexico in Transition: Neoliberal Globalism, the State and Civil Society*, Zed Books, London

Borger, J. (2008) 'US biofuel subsidies under attack at food summit', www.guardian. co.uk/environment/2008/jun/03/biofuels.energy?gusrc=rss&feed=networkfront, accessed 21 December 2008

Bradsher, K. (2008) 'High rice cost creating fears of Asia unrest', *New York Times*, 29 March, www.nytimes.com/2008/03/29/business/worldbusiness/29rice.html?ex=13 64443200&en=01bc00d1ab0307ee&ei=5088&partner=rssnyt&emc=rss, accessed 21 November 2008

Bradsher, K. and Martin, A. (2008) 'Hoarding nations drive food costs ever higher', *New York Times*, 30 June, www.nytimes.com/2008/06/30/business/worldbusiness/ 30trade.html, accessed 20 November 2008

CEPAL News (2008) 'Food price hikes may increase poverty and indigence by over ten million people in Latin America and the Caribbean', *CEPAL News*, vol 28, no 4, United Nations Economic Commission for Latin America and the Caribbean (ECLAC)

Cronin, D. (2008) 'Energy: Report challenges EU subsidies for biofuels,' Inter Press Service, 4 October, www.ipsnews.net/news.asp?idnews=39515, accessed 19 December 2008

ECOSOC (Economic and Social Council of the United Nations) (2008) 'Issues note for special meeting of the economic and social council on global food crisis', 20 May, www.un.org/ecosoc/docs/pdfs/Food_crisis_Issues_note_may_2008.pdf, accessed 21 November 2008

Europa (2008) 'Doha and the bigger picture,' www.trade.ec.europa.eu/doclib/docs/2008/ july/tradoc_139795.pdf, accessed 20 November 2008

Fitting, E. (2008) 'Importing corn, exporting labor: The neoliberal corn regime, GMOs, and the erosion of Mexican biodiversity', in G. Otero (ed.) *Food for the Few: Neoliberal Globalism and Biotechnology in Latin America*, University of Texas Press, Austin

FAO (Food and Agriculture Organization of the United Nations) (2004) 'International trade in rice, recent developments and prospects,' Report from the World Rice Research Conference, Tsukuba, Japan, 5–7 November, www.fao.org/es/esc/ en/15/70/81/highlight_79_p.html, accessed 21 November 2008

FAO (2006) FAOSTAT, www.faostat.fao.org/site/609/DesktopDefault. aspx?PageID=609#ancor, accessed 6 January 2009

FAO (2008a) 'World food situation: Food price indices, November 2008', www.fao. org/worldfoodsituation/FoodPricesIndex/en/, accessed 21 November 2008

FAO (2008b) 'The state of food and agriculture. Biofuels: prospects, risks and opportunities', ftp://ftp.fao.org/docrep/fao/011/i0100e/i0100e.pdf, accessed 21 December 2008

FAO (2008c) 'The FAO rice price update – November 2008', www.fao.org/es/ESC/ en/15/70/highlight_533_p.html, accessed 21 November 2008

FAO (2008d) 'Statistical appendix,' *Crop Prospects and Food Situation*, no 3, July, www.fao.org/docrep/010/ai470e/ai470e09.htm, accessed 21 November 2008

FAO (2008e) 'Policy measures taken by governments to reduce soaring prices,' *Crop Prospects and Food Situation*, no 3, July, www.fao.org/docrep/010/ai470e/ai470e05. htm, accessed 24 November 2008

G-20 (2006) 'Joint Statement. G-20, the G-33, the ACP, the LDCs, the African Group, the SVEs, NAMA-11, Cotton-4 and CARICON', 1 July, www.g-20.mre.gov.br/ conteudo/statement_01072006.htm, accessed 3 March 2008

Hanson, C. (2007) 'The both of us have battled: The practices and politics of female partners in the Canadian Season Agricultural Workers Program', *Masters Thesis in Latin American Studies*, Simon Fraser University, Canada

ICTSD (International Centre for Trade and Sustainable Development) (2008) 'Japan, Switzerland propose stronger WTO curbs on use of food export restrictions', *Bridges Weekly Trade News Digest*, vol 12, no 15, 30 April, www.ictsd.net/i/news/bridgesweekly/11075/, accessed 20 November 2008

Katsuro, S. (1984) 'Food exports and the U.S.-Japan trade deficit', *Asian Studies Backgrounder*, no 15, www.heritage.org/research/asiaandthepacific/asb15.cfm, accessed 20 November 2008

McMichael, P. (2004) 'Biotechnology and food security: Profiting on insecurity,' in L. Benería and S. Bisnaith (eds) *Global Tensions: Challenges and Opportunities in the World Economy*, Routledge, New York

McMichael, P. (2009) 'Contemporary contradictions of the global development project: Geopolitics, global ecology and the "development climate"', *Third World Quarterly*, vol 30, no 1, pp247–262

Martin, A. (2008) 'Fuel choices, food crisis and finger pointing,' *New York Times*, 15 April, www.nytimes.com/2008/04/15/business/worldbusiness/15food.html?pagewanted=print, accessed 19 December 2008

Martínez, J. (2009) 'Los productos que más subieron en 2008', CNNEXPANSIÓN.com: www.cnnexpansion.com/economia/2009/01/08/los-precios-que-mas-subieron-en-2008, accessed 8 January 2009

NCCR (Swiss National Centre of Competence in Research) (2008) 'World food crisis: Are trade rules a problem or a way forward?', Discussion paper for the WTO Public Forum 'Trading into the Future', 25 September 2008, Switzerland, www.wto.org/english/forums_e/public_forum08_e/session16_paper_wti_e.pdf, accessed 8 August 2009

Notimex (2009) 'Subieron 15 per cent los alimentos básicos y cayó 30 per cent el consumo', *La Jornada*, 7 January, www.jornada.unam.mx/2009/01/07/index.php?section=economia&article=022n2eco, accessed 7 January 2009

Ó Riain, S. (2000) 'States and markets in an era of globalization', *Annual Review of Sociology*, vol 26, pp187–213

Pechlaner, G. and Otero, G. (2008) 'Latin American agriculture, food, and biotechnology: Temperate dietary pattern adoption and unsustainability,' in G. Otero (ed.) *Food for the Few: Neoliberal Globalism and Biotechnology in Latin America*, University of Texas Press, Austin

Pechlaner, G. and Otero, G. (n.d.) 'The neoliberal food regime: Neoregulation and the new division of labor in North America,' unpublished paper

Preibisch, K. (1996) 'Rural women, Mexico's "comparative advantage"? Lived experiences of economic restructuring in two puebla ejidos,' Masters Thesis in Latin American Studies, Simon Fraser University, Canada

Ray, D. (2004a) 'Japan's 21-year aid program helped put Brazil on the soybean map', Agricultural Policy Analysis Centre, article no 216, originally published in *Mid America Farmer Grower*, vol 21, no 39, 23 September, www.agpolicy.org/weekpdf/216.pdf, accessed 20 November 2008

Ray, D. (2004b) 'Nothing intensifies food security concerns like food unavailability', Agricultural Policy Analysis Centre, article no 217, originally published in *Mid America Farmer Grower*, vol 21, no 40, 1 October, www.agpolicy.org/weekpdf/217.pdf, accessed 20 November 2008

Reguly, E. (2008) 'All about the yield,' *The Globe and Mail,* www.theglobeandmail.com/servlet/story/LAC.20080628.RCOVER28/TPStory/TPBusiness/?query, accessed 20 November 2008

Rosen, S. and Shapouri, S. (2008) 'Obesity in the midst of unyielding food insecurity in developing countries,' *Amber Waves,* vol 6, no 4, www.ers.usda.gov/AmberWaves/September08/PDF/ObesityCountries.pdf, accessed 21 November 2008

Shikoh, R. and Shuriah, N. (2008) 'Global food crisis: A bowl of opportunities for Muslim world,' *Dinar Standard,* www.dinarstandard.com/current/GlobalFoodChallenges100108.htm, accessed 27 November 2008

Steenblik, R. (2007) 'Biofuels – at what cost? Government support for ethanol and biodiesel in selected OECD countries,' Global Subsidies Initiative, www.globalsubsidies.org/files/assets/oecdbiofuels.pdf, accessed 20 December 2008

Walt, V. (2008) 'The world's growing food-price crisis,' www.time.com/time/world/article/0,8599,1717572,00.html, accessed 21 November 2008

WTO (World Trade Organization) (2007) 'Agriculture: Fairer markets for farmers', www.wto.org/english/thewto_e/whatis_e/tif_e/agrm3_e.htm, accessed 30 June 2007

WTO (2002) 'Agriculture negotiations: Background fact sheet. Domestic support in agriculture', www.wto.org/english/tratop_e/agric_e/agboxes_e.htm, accessed 2 July 2007

WTO (2004) 'Agriculture negotiations: Backgrounder: Developing countries', www.wto.org/english/tratop_e/agric_e/negs_bkgrnd14_devopcount_e.htm, accessed 2 July 2007

6
Energy Security, Agriculture and Food

Jago Dodson, Neil Sipe, Roy Rickson and Sean Sloan

Introduction

This chapter explores the effects of the changes in global energy security for agriculture and food production systems. The discussion centres on a set of emerging problems in the global petroleum environment and the potential consequences of these shifts for the future of agriculture and food production, including agricultural production and transport systems. Given the urgency of these problems, the chapter concludes by advocating much greater research and policy attention to energy issues within agriculture and food production.

Since 2004, the world has witnessed dramatic changes in the global petroleum security environment. This changing energy security environment has enormous implications for agricultural systems and food production, given the acute dependency of agricultural and food systems upon petroleum. The economic, social and environmental impacts associated with changes in energy security are both insufficiently recognized and poorly understood, particularly in terms of the direct consequences of these changing conditions for food and agriculture. While global oil shocks have occurred before, most prominently during the 1970s, the recent volatility in global oil prices and supplies has taken place in a far more internationally integrated – and arguably more petroleum dependent – world than that which existed three decades ago. International trade, including trade in agricultural commodities and food, occurs in much greater volumes than was the case just a decade ago, linking a wider web of international producers and consumers. As a major petroleum-consuming economic sector, global agriculture faces an inevitable adjustment to a more volatile petroleum era.

Conventional agriculture is heavily reliant on petroleum for production processes and for the transportation of produce to distant markets. Since at least the 1960s, energy consumption has increased alongside the growing volume of agricultural production (Miranowski, 2005). Similarly, the capacity for agricultural producers to deliver their outputs to distant markets relies increasingly on transport fuels in the form of petrol, diesel and aviation gasoline. The globalization of agriculture and the new logistics systems associated with it are therefore heavily dependent on petroleum. In this context, a pronounced deterioration in the global petroleum supply would inevitably increase the costs of petroleum fuels raising, in turn, the market cost of agricultural production. This is likely to produce systemic effects – effects with the potential to reduce the viability of some markets and the competitive advantage of distant producers.

Energy supply shocks are likely to exert effects beyond the production and transport of agricultural products. Changes in energy supplies would inevitably intersect with other forces that are currently transforming agricultural production, including globalization and the organizational reconfigurations of agriculture (Busch and Juska, 1997). In recent decades, agriculture has undergone increasing corporatization and capital intensification, along with the consolidation of holdings within larger organizational forms. This chapter examines the links between these broader structural transformations and the shifts in energy supply associated with an increasingly volatile petroleum era.

Global energy security

The period from 2004 to 2008 witnessed a remarkable transformation in global petroleum supply. Oil prices had been relatively low and stable during much of the preceding decade but accelerated sharply and became highly volatile after 2004. Demonstrating this, global oil prices increased from around US$25 per barrel in early 2004, to over US$140 per barrel by mid-2008. The real price of oil in 2008 far exceeded levels seen during the oil shocks of the 1970s. Explanations for the high oil prices highlighted a number of problems in the global petroleum supply system, especially the trajectory of growth in demand for oil. Global petroleum consumption has grown sharply over the past decade from 69.5 million barrels per day in 1995 to 82.5 million barrels per day in 2004, reaching 86 million barrels per day by 2007 (IEA, 2008). The International Energy Agency (IEA) predicts that by 2030, global oil demand will grow to 116 million barrels per day, a 37 per cent increase on 2006 levels (IEA, 2008). This sudden acceleration in the demand for oil can be explained by high levels of economic growth in western nations, accompanied by rapid growth in developing economies such as China and India. China's economy, for example, grew by at least 9 per cent between 2002 and 2007 (IMF, 2007). The IEA (2007) has projected that demand for oil in both China and India will double by 2030, adding an additional 13.8 million barrels per day to current levels of global oil consumption.

Other factors driving volatility in global oil markets include growing geopolitical instability, most obviously in regions such as the Middle East, central Asia and the Niger River Delta, as well as frictions between the US and oil-producing nations such as Venezuela and Iran. Some observers have suggested that a new 'great game' is now being played between wealthy and powerful nations and those holding large petroleum reserves (Kleveman, 2003; Klare, 2005). Threats of terrorism against oil facilities and shipping lanes have also raised anxieties in a high growth environment (EIA, 2005). Concerns about the capacity of oil production facilities to cope with growing demand have also contributed to rising oil prices, both in terms of ageing infrastructure and of the availability of investment in new oil production facilities – with the latter concern amplified by the current financial crisis (Simmons, 2005). In 2006, the IEA estimated that US$4.3 trillion worth of oil wells, pipelines and refinery investment would be needed by 2030 to satisfy projected global oil demand (IEA, 2006). A 2008 estimate suggests that at least US$50 trillion would be required (see Izundu, 2008).

The declining energy security environment since 2004 has also drawn attention to the longer-term sustainability of global petroleum production, with the problem of declining petroleum reserves being highlighted by a growing chorus of commentators. A considerable body of analysis now lends support to the view that continued exploitation of petroleum reserves in a world of finite resources means that production will eventually hit a maximum 'peak' level, followed by declining output (Campbell, 2003; Roberts, 2004; Leggett, 2005; Simmons, 2005; Strahan, 2007). The 'peak oil' scenario is expected to play out as the increasing effort to extract oil from more and more remote and complex oil reserves fails to maintain prevailing production levels. The problem of peak oil has generated considerable controversy in the petroleum sector. Early proponents of the notion were initially drawn from independent or dissident members of the petroleum industry (Campbell, 2003; Leggett, 2005; Simmons, 2005). The uncertainty around peak oil has generated an extensive independent literature, particularly on the internet where numerous websites are now dedicated to various dimensions of oil depletion. Recent years have seen increasing, if reluctant, acceptance of the likelihood of a future decline in oil supplies by major oil companies and governments. An Australian Senate (2007) inquiry, for example, found that peak oil could be expected by 2030, while the head of economic forecasting at the IEA has suggested that a peak in oil production by 2020 is probable (Birol, quoted in Monbiot, 2008). Meanwhile, the Chevron Oil Company (2005) has warned that 'the age of easy oil is over' and the head of Shell Oil has warned of a dangerous geopolitical 'scramble' for remaining oil reserves (van der Veer, 2008).

A decline in global petroleum security, whether due to the depletion of oil reserves or to some other factor such as geopolitical tensions, implies a destabilization of the relationship between growing energy demand and global production capacity. There are presently few substitutes for liquid petroleum fuels, especially in transport where the portability of such fuels is a key factor in their useability. Declining petroleum supply thus implies much higher prices for oil, potentially escalating far beyond the high levels experienced in 2008. While the effects of higher fuel prices on logistics and freight systems are reasonably well understood, little research has been undertaken into the recent effects of higher oil prices on agricultural systems, or on the longer-term energy trajectory of agricultural systems. While some research was undertaken on this issue in the 1970s and early 1980s in response to the oil shocks of 1973 and 1979, this work has now considerably dated. In the intervening decades, agricultural production patterns and the global integration of markets for agricultural products have undergone extensive changes. These circumstances underpin the contemporary imperative for research that evaluates the effects of higher oil prices on agricultural systems, and undertakes a wider rethinking of the relationship between food, agricultural production and energy. Improving knowledge in this area also requires understanding the links between agricultural systems and other influences, including broader economic and institutional patterns and their interdependencies at various scales of comprehension.

The remainder of this chapter explores the challenges and consequences of higher oil prices for agricultural systems and for our understanding of food and energy. The following sections present a review of the relationship between energy consumption and agricultural production, and an assessment of the ways in which energy and transport systems interact with agricultural production, before considering the structural vulnerabilities of agricultural systems and their capacity to respond to constrained petroleum supplies.

Agriculture and energy

Agricultural production has long been linked to the availability of energy sources. Early sources of energy used in agriculture were primarily derived from the kinetic forces of wind and water power. With the advent, and subsequent proliferation, of mechanized farm implements in the 19th century, agricultural production has grown increasingly dependent on fossil fuels. Modern cultivation and harvesting methods almost inevitably involve petroleum-fuelled machines such as tractors, cultivators and harvesters. Many agri-chemicals such as fertilizers and herbicides are also derived from petroleum sources. In some agricultural regions, the supply of water to crops also requires energy-intensive irrigation systems. Given the long-run uncertainty associated with global petroleum supplies, there is a pressing need to better comprehend the role of fossil fuel energy in maintaining the viability of agricultural systems.

Scientific attention to the role of fossil energy sources, including petroleum, in agriculture has varied over the past four decades. The oil price shocks of the 1970s spurred a flurry of research into the role of energy in agriculture, but this concern abated in the late 1980s as the price of oil moderated considerably. Much of this earlier literature attempted to quantify the direct and indirect energy requirements of agricultural systems at diverging levels of analysis, including the nation (Gifford, 1976), the wider food system (Brown and Batty, 1976), and the individual farm unit (Handreck and Martin, 1976; Pimentel, 1980). Some studies also assessed the degree of technological advancement between different crop and production system types in order to compare energy consumption levels, and to identify potential avenues for improved efficiency (see Pimentel and Pimentel, 1979). Pimentel's (1980) *Handbook of Energy Utilization in Agriculture,* for example, provides a comprehensive and highly detailed catalogue of agricultural energy inputs and outputs by crop type and the various forms of energy that are factors in on-farm consumption.

The scholarship of the 1970s and 1980s revealed the extensive dependence of agricultural systems on energy inputs. Estimates for the US indicated that the food system consumed 17 per cent of the nation's fossil energy, a figure comparable to the 25 per cent consumed by automobiles. Roughly one third of national agricultural energy consumption (5.6 per cent of total energy consumption) occurred in the cultivation stage of production, with the remainder in processing and preparation (Brown and Batty, 1976; Pimentel, 1980).

Around this period, researchers also began to use new measures to assess energy use in agriculture. The notion of the 'energy ratio' (ER) – developed as an expression of the efficiency of agricultural production and calculated in terms of energy inputs relative to food energy outputs – was among these new approaches. For example, Gifford (1976) suggested that Australian agriculture, with an ER of 2.8, was better situated than US agriculture (ER=0.7) or UK agriculture (ER=0.5) to adapt to changing energy costs and related constraints. Progress was also made at this time in comprehending the complexity of energy use across agricultural production types, especially in relation to other input factors such as labour and capital.

Interest in the role of petroleum in agriculture waned from the mid-1980s, as the drop in oil prices served to weaken the imperative to understand this area of activity. Since that time, new imperatives linked to energy use in agriculture have gained the attention of agricultural scientists. Organic production, in particular, has achieved prominence for its claimed environmental benefits – including lower use of petroleum-based inputs such as fertilizers and pesticides. Pimentel et al (1999), for example, report large energy savings for organic maize cropping systems compared to conventional production. Similarly, Dalgaard et al (2002) have calculated that converting the Danish national cropping and livestock sectors to organic production would reduce their direct and indirect energy consumption by 52 per cent and 28 per cent, respectively – although this would also cause their respective outputs to decline by 40 per cent and 30 per cent. In contrast, Wood et al (2006) found that an Australian sample of organic farms exhibited greater *direct* energy use, energy-related emissions and greenhouse gas emissions than a sample of comparable conventional farms, but that the conventional farms had much higher *indirect* energy use and emissions via energy embodied in other farm inputs. These various results help to highlight the vulnerability of food systems based on conventional agriculture to constrained fossil energy supplies.

The role of agricultural production in generating greenhouse gas emissions has been of particular interest since the mid-1990s. Part of this interest has focused on the biophysical generation of greenhouse gas emissions in agricultural production, such as via soil microbiota or livestock digestive processes (FAO, 2006). Weber and Matthews (2008) have also shown that sourcing food locally could reduce energy consumption by 5 per cent at most, because the vast majority of energy consumption related to food occurs in the production phase. The same level of greenhouse gas reduction could be achieved, they argue, via consumers halting meat and dairy consumption on one day per week, given the high energy intensity of meat and dairy production.

With the higher global petroleum prices seen since 2004, there has been a more general resurgence of interest in the relationship between energy and agriculture. The outstanding example of this work is the third edition of Pimentel and Pimentel's *Food, Energy and Society* (2007), which includes updated energy input tables, including energy ratios, for a range of crop types. For example, spinach has an ER of just 0.23, compared to potatoes with an ER of 1.33, and sugar beets with an ER of 3.22 (Pimentel and Pimentel, 2007). There have been few studies with this comprehensive level of descriptive detail across such a wide range of crop types.

Food, energy and transport

Energy ratios have returned to the fore in recent debates as high oil prices and concerns about renewable or greenhouse-neutral fuels have spurred interest in alternatives to petroleum. In turn, the high energy content of some agricultural products has seen such products emerge as potential *energy sources* in the form of biofuels. The emergence of a biofuel sector has focused considerable attention on the notion of the 'energy return on energy invested' (EROEI) with regard to alternative fuel types. Conventional gasoline has an EROEI of approximately 15:1 – meaning that every unit of energy expended in production generates 15 units of energy output (Cleveland, 2005). By contrast, ethanol biofuel has an EROEI as low as between 1.2:1 and 1.6:1 (Cleveland, 2005). Despite this recent work, the relationship between energy, agriculture and biofuel output remains highly contentious within the scientific community, as the vigorous flurry of letters on the topic in a 2006 issue of *Science* attests.

Debates related to the emerging biofuel industries can also be discerned beyond issues of on-farm production and agricultural logistics systems. One of the most dramatic effects of the changing global energy supply context over the past five years has been a sudden increase in the price of grain resulting from the increasing use and government subsidization of biofuels as a petroleum substitute. For example, US legislation passed in 2004 provided a domestic subsidy of US$1 per gallon for biofuel production, stimulating a more than tenfold growth in US biofuel output between 2005 and 2007 (Mitchell, 2008 and see Chapter 14, this volume). The effect of this biofuel surge has been twofold: first, existing grain supplies, especially corn and wheat, have been redirected to biofuels, which has had the effect of raising grain prices across the board through substitution effects; and second, the increase in grain prices has encouraged the conversion of non-grain land to grain production, which has reduced the supply of other food crops, causing sudden price hikes globally for food. This wider biofuel effect has been driven both by higher fuel prices, and by environmental concerns over fossil-fuel emissions in conjunction with new government subsidies for biofuel production (FAO, 2008). Given that most of this new biofuel production will be consumed in the US, there is considerable anxiety that subsidization of biofuels has the effect of taking food from the world's poor to support the mobility of the wealthy. The European Union became so concerned about the global effect of biofuel development that it reviewed its mandate on biofuel use in 2008, while the Food and Agriculture Organization of the United Nations convened a series of conferences in the same year on the effects of biofuel production on food prices and supply.

Clearly, the emerging links between energy, agriculture and the wider economy – especially transport – exhibit many contradictions that are yet to be resolved. The energy involved for transportation in agricultural production is estimated to be between 11 and 14 per cent of total farm energy use (Brown, 2008; Roberts, 2008). While energy use for transport is a relatively minor part of the agricultural energy picture, transportation's profile has been considerably raised with the popularization of the 'food miles' concept. Food miles are considered to be the distance that food travels as it moves from the farm to the consumer, and are used as a simple way to gauge the impact of food on climate change (Engelhaupt, 2008, and see also Paxton, 1994). Calculations of food miles are also increasingly used to depict the contribution, or otherwise, of particular food items to sustainability. An example is provided by the Australian Conservation Foundation (ACF, 2009):

> *A recent German study found that a 240ml cup of yoghurt in a supermarket shelf in Berlin entails over 9,000km of transportation. In the United States, the food for a typical meal has travelled nearly 2,100km, but if that meal contains off-season fruits or vegetables the total distance is many times higher.*

While the food miles concept has directed public and policy attention to the links between agriculture, food and energy, fundamental problems with the idea and its use as a sustainability measure nonetheless remain. Roberts (2008) has argued that food miles is a simplistic measure of a complex set of practices. The flows of transport energy in agriculture are more widely distributed than simply from farm gate to consumer. When the complexities of these energy flows are considered, as represented in Figure 6.1, at least four difficulties with the food miles concept can be identified. The first of these is scale. The size of the truck or ship used to freight the food is important because, on a unit basis, the more the transport mode can carry, the larger the volume able to be carried, and the lower the per-unit energy costs. The second problem is transport mode. The concept of food miles does not relate to a specific transport mode – only to the distance travelled. The energy costs of shipping navel oranges from California to Australia, for example, will be different if they arrive by plane than by ship. Similarly, the energy cost of road freight is typically much higher than rail, such that local produce carried by truck may consume more transport energy than distant food conveyed mostly by rail. The third problem involves fuel type, which will vary even if the same mode of transport is used. A truck using diesel will have a different energy and greenhouse gas emissions profile than one running on petrol. Finally, as noted at the beginning of this

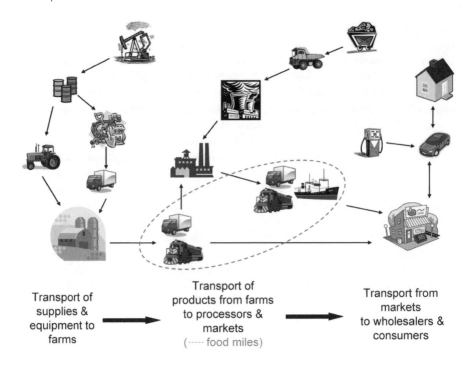

Transport of supplies & equipment to farms ➡ Transport of products from farms to processors & markets (----- food miles) ➡ Transport from markets to wholesalers & consumers

Source: the authors

Figure 6.1 *Transport energy flows in agricultural production and consumption*

section, transport energy is only 11–14 per cent of the total energy picture, a picture that typically excludes the significant energy use involved in getting the products from the market to the consumer.

Two examples assist to illustrate these conceptual problems with food miles. Saunders et al (2006) have shown that the energy-related impacts associated with New Zealand lamb and dairy products consumed in the UK were less than those for locally produced lamb and dairy consumed in the UK – with energy use being 75 per cent less, and climate impacts being 50 per cent less. Hence, even after accounting for transporting the products half-way across the globe, New Zealand lamb and dairy products are less energy intensive because they deploy grazing and husbandry methods that depend less on fertilizers and processed feed than do comparable methods for lamb production in the UK.

A second example derives from a recent Defra (2005) case study, which found that tomatoes grown in Spain and transported to the UK had a lower carbon footprint than tomatoes grown in heated greenhouses the UK. Coley et al (2008) argue that the concept of food miles is of little value as typically used, and that it is the *carbon emission per unit of produce over the transport chain* that really matters in terms of accounting for the energy dependence and greenhouse impact of agricultural transportation. This argument is supported by others (see, for example, Brown, 2008; Roberts, 2008), who also suggest that the ecological footprint concept might be a better way to assess the energy-related impacts of agricultural production.

Problems with the calculation of food miles notwithstanding, there are some valid insights that flow from the concept. First, if production energy were equal between two producers, then long-distance shipping of food would make no sense from an energy or environmental perspective. Cheap oil has made the global movement of food possible. This global movement has also resulted in changes to systems of agricultural production. Although the global movement of food is not new – wheat, for example, has been shipped around the world for decades – the global movement of perishable fruits and vegetables is a relatively recent practice. This means that farmers now breed fruits and vegetables for long journeys to the exclusion of other product qualities. Second, cheap and rapid transport has meant that global producers can often get products on to the market as quickly as local producers can. Third, food miles take on a different complexion when viewed from a petroleum security perspective, rather than from a greenhouse emissions perspective. Food miles primarily reflect, however accurately, the transport energy associated with agricultural products rather than the total energy those products embody. For this reason, food miles may provide an indicator of the risk or vulnerability of food products – or of the community consuming them – to petroleum shocks that raise transport prices, but offer a poor representation of overall energy consumption. Such observations further demonstrate the complexity of accounting for energy consumption in agricultural production.

Wider structural change and vulnerability in agriculture

Starting in the late 1970s and extending to the current period, the way we think about agriculture has undergone fundamental change – from how we produce food and fibre, to the natural resources used in that production, to the structure of agricultural systems more broadly. It is clear that structural, demographic and spatial factors interact to affect not only the production of food and fibre, but also the social and market relations across regional and rural areas. These, in turn, affect how we use, conserve and exploit natural resources. Emerging and relatively recent 'environmental shocks' are changing the way we see and use natural resources, as well as challenging deep-seated cultural understandings about farming – particularly about so-called family farms, as well as the question of who and what organizations will influence farm production in the future. Thus, agriculture is more than a defined set of economic activities, however important such activities are. Ultimately, agriculture is a *social system of production* (Hollingsworth and Boyer, 1997, p2).

Production systems are more than technology, economy and – for the purposes of this chapter – energy systems. Production systems rely upon and include concepts of equity, fairness and justice, ethnic identity and citizenship, relations of trust and cooperation, power and autonomy, knowledge and experience, technical skills, concerns about food, income and environmental security, including access to water, land, and largely petroleum-based technologies such as agri-chemicals and machine technologies. Farmer credit and market access, the cost of buying and using technologies, and access to professional advice, are also part of this process. Networks of relationships between farmers, non-government organizations (farmers' federations), agencies of the state, and private and public professionals representing private organizations (companies, usually members of international groups of organizations), are equally critical because they not only control or influence farmer access to credit, markets, knowledge, land and water resources – these networks also exert a substantial influence over how farmers use their land to grow food and fibre (Burch and Lawrence, 2007). Many of these relationships, especially those at the local or regional scale, are underpinned by transport systems that depend on petroleum fuels.

Productionist – or industrial – agriculture is primarily based upon chemical and biological inputs and its principal drivers are large-scale, centralized, corporate ownership that usually rests with international groups of companies. The primary goals of such corporations are economic efficiency, commercial competitiveness, strategies of vertical integration through the incorporation of local dealers and farms through production contracts, and horizontal integration through the purchase of seed and machinery by agri-chemical companies, for example – not to mention the goal of sustaining growth and shareholder value through market share. Because of their dominance in all phases of conventional food production and distribution, corporate economic activity and power are central driving forces, decisively shaping the future of agriculture and thus the ways that natural resources (including petroleum and other energy sources) will be consumed and conserved (Lawrence, 1999; Gray and Lawrence, 2001). Any question of a vulnerability to petroleum shortages, for example, necessarily implies a potential challenge to the relationships that farmers have with companies promoting oil-based technologies such as agri-chemicals and machinery, as these are critical inputs to contemporary food and fibre production. The central role of agribusiness in networks of agricultural production means that farmer autonomy in relation to crop, land and animal management, and to energy choices and alternatives, is narrowing. As a result, farms are becoming more specialized and more fully integrated, as well as becoming more dependent upon the organizational networks that provide the flow of external inputs – inputs such as fertilizers, seeds, pesticides and herbicides – and the machinery and information required to efficiently use these technologies.

Norgaard's (1994) concept of co-evolution helps to explain how changes in one part of a production system engender change in another, related, part. As companies consolidate for the sake of economic efficiencies, competitiveness and market control, they are less willing to spread and promote their commercial services among large numbers of small- and medium-sized properties, preferring instead to concentrate their services and sales among relatively few farmers with large holdings who can guarantee a substantial annual output to food processors and retailers. As a consequence, selling, buying and advisory strategies are directed to those farmers operating in a manner that is most compatible with the strategies and structures of large-scale corporate or organizational agriculture (Rickson and Burch, 1996), disadvantaging others and promoting the concentration of productive rural land ownership.

According to Wolf and Nowak (1999, p294), these agribusiness strategies create a mismatch between capacity and need; that is, a mismatch between farm inputs (fertilizer, pesticides and water) and the needs of crops and soils, and between such inputs and the needs of farmers for ongoing expert advice on how best to use them on their land. Private sector, corporate, resources focus mostly on intensive cultivation – leading to environmental vulnerability. However, areas of higher environmental vulnerability are characterized by weak private sector markets and a lack of information provision. These issues point to an institutional failure to provide good outcomes for the environment, which stems from the basis of private and public sector policies in models that assume a homogeneity (rather than a heterogeneity) of farm service needs.

This insight, in turn, has relevance for understanding the energy dimension of agricultural production. Not all agricultural organizations will have the same exposure to energy risks, just as not all agricultural regions experience the same relative exposure to the impacts of a changing energy security environment, because their access to alternative forms of energy will differ. The degree to which various structural formations in agriculture are arranged in terms of their reliance on energy types is potentially a key issue for the sector. Accordingly, any assumptions about farm sector homogeneity and capacity to absorb institutional changes driven by a transformed energy environment must be sensitized to local institutional and geographic conditions.

Corporate economic goals are most compatible with large-scale monocultures that, together with the direct reduction of biodiversity, have a range of often indirect social and economic consequences. As such, corporatization has led to the direct and indirect support of land and farm consolidation, leading to larger farms and fewer farmers. Although the agricultural production network is collectively vulnerable to resource scarcity in the form of oil shortages, for example, the vulnerability experienced by particular actors varies considerably depending on the institutional position of the actor within a supply or production chain. Farmers, for example, are 'price takers' rather than 'price makers', which conveys a distinct advantage to those companies most capable of passing on any increased costs, such as transport fuel expenses, to primary producers and consumers. Rather than being directed by an anonymous mass of consumer preference and choice, the 'market' for farm products is actually influenced more by what organized agribusiness is willing to pay. This situation also implies considerable restrictions on the capacity of individual farmers to pass on any additional production costs from higher energy prices to consumers, except within the bounds set by their corporate 'partners'.

Corporate mobility, or locational flexibility, means that companies are relatively free from supply dependence on any given group of farmers in any particular place. Indeed, national and international company groups are able to move their economic operations across regional, national and ecosystem boundaries, playing off, on an international scale, one group of farmers against another to reduce the price they pay for farm products. This allows them to increase their cost efficiencies and often ensures access to cheap local labour for use in their food processing companies. This flexibility, however, is highly dependent on the transport networks that link a disparate array of producers, processors or intermediaries, and consumers. The modelling of modern, conventional agriculture in this way thus reveals a dense and complex network of farmers, corporate sellers of information and technology, farm produce buyers, processors and retailers. Similarly, as corporate economic activities have become increasingly concentrated, companies that had previously sold agri-chemicals, farm machinery and information independently to farmers, while also buying farmers' products, are now rapidly consolidating so that fewer and more expansive companies control access to farm inputs and markets. As noted in a recent publication from Canada, government deregulation, coupled with corporate consolidation, has transformed farmers' competitive landscape from one defined by a single-desk seller to one defined by a single-desk buyer (National Farmers Union, 2003, p17). In this complex network of producers, processors and retailers, land ownership is increasingly severed from the power to make strategic decisions about how land will be used and what agri-chemicals and technologies will be employed to grow crops and animals (Rickson and Burch, 1996).

In other fields of enquiry, authors such as Tainter (1990) and Homer-Dixon (2006) have identified increasing complexity as a key risk factor associated with societal and institutional breakdown. Modern agricultural systems, with their institutional forms and their intricate and extensive web of relations suffused by uneven relations of power and control, could prove highly fragile in an environment where the security of the petroleum that sustains the system is threatened by an external shock. Recognition of the fragile complexity of global agricultural systems has been amplified by both oil price inflation in 2004–2008 and the 2005–2008 food price hikes, as exemplified by such titles as Robert's (2008) *The End of Food* and Pfeiffer's (2006) *Eating Fossil Fuels*.

Conclusions: The future of energy and food production

This chapter has addressed the rapidly emerging problem of recognizing, accounting for, and comprehending the role of energy in sustaining agricultural production. We have argued that there are now considerable uncertainties in the sustainability of global petroleum supplies, whether due to resource exhaustion or to increasing competition for a finite resource. This uncertainty was made dramatically apparent in the period 2004–2008, which saw a steady increase culminating in a sharp spike in global oil prices. Governments, scholars and private firms are all recognizing the increasing significance of the energy constraints facing global economies and societies. We have argued that the task of addressing this problem is yet to gain substantive momentum.

Agriculture is a key sector in which energy resources, especially petroleum, are consumed. Many of the key inputs into contemporary agriculture derive from petroleum sources, while the extended reach at which mechanized implements are deployed in agriculture further increases agricultural petroleum dependence. Transport systems often compound this reliance on petroleum energy. Although petroleum costs do not comprise a major proportion of energy use in agricultural production, the absolute reliance on petroleum and its critical transportation role in sustaining global production and consumption networks means that the question of energy security will remain a critical issue for agriculture.

While investigation into the role of energy in agriculture is undergoing a contemporary revival, many gaps in our understanding remain. Scientific understanding of petroleum energy consumption, and of the flows of petroleum products and associated emissions through agricultural systems, is reasonably good. There is much less robust understanding, however, about the wider significance of petroleum energy in sustaining organizational forms, social relations and institutional structures within regional, national and global agricultural systems. Although scientists must continue to respond to the imperative to better chart the flows of energy through agricultural production systems, much greater levels of research effort must also be dedicated to comprehending the extent to which petroleum energy also supports the wider social relations of production within agriculture.

References

ACF (Australian Conservation Foundation) (2009) 'Food mile facts', www.acfonline. org.au/articles/news.asp?news_id=491, accessed 20 March 2009

Australian Senate (2007) *Inquiry into Australia's Future Oil Supply and Alternative Transport Fuels: Final Report*, Australian Senate, Canberra

Brown, L. (2008) *Plan B 3.0: Mobilizing to Save Civilization*, Norton and Company, New York

Brown, S. and Batty, J. (1976) 'Energy allocation in the food system: A microscale view', *Transactions of the American Society of Agricultural Engineers,* vol 19, no 4, pp758–761

Burch, D. and Lawrence, G. (2007) *Supermarkets and Agri-Food Supply Chains: Transformations in the Production and Consumption of Foods*, Edward Elgar, Cheltenham, UK

Busch, L. and Juska, A. (1997) 'Beyond political economy: Actor networks and the globalization of agriculture', *Review of International Political Economy*, vol 4, no 4, pp688–708

Campbell, C. (2003) 'The peak of oil: A geological and political turning point for the world', in N. Low and B. Gleeson (eds) *Making Urban Transport Sustainable*, Palgrave Macmillan, Basingstoke

Chevron Oil Company (2005) Advertisement in *The Economist,* 16 July, pp6–7

Cleveland, C. (2005) 'Net energy from the extraction of oil and gas in the United States', *Energy*, vol 30, pp769–782

Coley, D., Howard, M. and Winter, M. (2009) 'Local food, food miles and carbon emissions: A comparison of farm shop and mass distribution approaches', *Food Policy*, vol 34, no 2, pp150–155

Dalgaard, T., Halberg, N. and Fenger, J. (2002) 'Can organic farming help to reduce national energy consumption and emissions of greenhouse gases in Denmark?' in E. van Ierland, A. Lansink and O. Dordrecht (eds) *Economics of Sustainable Energy in Agriculture*, Springer and Kluwer Academic Publisher, The Netherlands

Defra (Department for Environment, Food and Rural Affairs) (2005) *The Validity of Food Miles as an Indicator of Sustainable Development*, UK government, London

EIA (Energy Information Administration) (2005) *World Oil Transit Chokepoints*, Department of Energy, Washington, DC

Engelhaupt, E. (2008) 'Do food miles matter?' *Environmental Science and Technology*, 42, p3482

FAO (2006) *Livestock's Long Shadow: Environmental Implications and Options*, Food and Agriculture Organization of the United Nations, Rome

FAO (2008) *Soaring Food Prices: Facts, Perspectives, Impacts and Actions Required*, Food and Agriculture Organization of the United Nations, Rome

Gifford, R. (1976) 'An overview of fuel used for crops and national agricultural systems', *Search* vol 7, no 10, pp412–417

Gray, I. and Lawrence, G. (2001) *A Future for Regional Australia: Escaping Global Misfortune*, Cambridge University Press, Cambridge, UK

Handreck, K. and Martin, A. (1976) 'Energetics of the wheat/sheep farming system in two areas of South Australia', *Search*, vol 7, no 10, pp436–443

Hollingsworth, J. and Boyer, R. (1997) *Contemporary Capitalism*, Cambridge University Press, Cambridge, UK

Homer-Dixon, T. (2006) *The Upside of Down: Catastrophe, Creativity and the Renewal of Civilisation*, Text Publishing, Melbourne

IEA (2006) *World Energy Outlook 2006*, International Energy Agency and Organisation for Economic Co-operation and Development, Paris

IEA (2007) *World Energy Outlook 2007: Focus on China and India*, International Energy Agency and Organisation for Economic Co-operation and Development, Paris

IEA (2008) *World Energy Outlook 2008*, International Energy Agency and Organisation for Economic Co-operation and Development, Paris

IMF (International Monetary Fund) (2007) 'World economic outlook database', April, www.imf.org/external/pubs/ft/weo/2007/01/data/download.aspx, accessed 10 April 2009

Izundu, U. (2008) '$100 trillion needed to rebuild energy infrastructure', Oil and Gas Journal, 106 (18), 12 May

Klare, M. (2005) *Blood and Oil: The Dangers and Consequences of America's Growing Petroleum Dependency*, Penguin Books Ltd, London and New York

Kleveman, L. (2003) *The New Great Game: Blood and Oil in Central Asia*, Atlantic Monthly Press, New York

Lawrence, G. (1999) 'Agri-food restructuring: A synthesis of recent Australian research', *Rural Sociology*, vol 64, no 2, pp186–202

Leggett, J. (2005) *Half Gone: Oil, Gas, Hot Air and the Global Energy Crisis*, Portobello Books, London

Miranowski, J. (2005) 'Energy demand and capacity to adjust in U.S. agricultural production', *Proceedings of Agricultural Outlook Forum 2005*, US Department of Agriculture

Mitchell, D. (2008) *A Note on Rising Food Prices*, World Bank, Washington

Monbiot, G. (2008) 'When will the oil run out?' the *Guardian*, 15 December

National Farmers Union (2003) *The Farm Crisis, Bigger Farms, and the Myths of 'Competition' and 'Efficiency'*, National Farmers Union (Canada), Saskatoon

Norgaard, R. (1994) 'The co-evolution of environmental and economic systems and the emergence of unsustainability', in R. England (ed.) *Evolutionary Concepts in Contemporary Economics*, University of Michigan Press, Ann Arbor, MI

Paxton, A. (1994) *The Food Miles Report: the Dangers of Long Distance Food Transport*, Safe Alliance, London

Pfeiffer, D. (2006) *Eating Fossil Fuels: Oil, Food and the Coming Crisis in Agriculture*, New Society Publications, US

Pimentel, D. (ed.) (1980) *Handbook of Energy Utilization in Agriculture*, CRC Press, Boca Raton, US

Pimentel, D. and Pimentel, M. (1979) *Food, Energy and Society*, Edward Arnold (Publishers) Ltd., London

Pimentel, D. and Pimentel, M. (2007) *Food, Energy and Society*, CRC Press, Boca Raton, US

Pimentel, D., Pimentel, M. and Karpenstein-Machan, M. (1999) 'Energy use in agriculture: An overview, *Agricultural Engineering International, CIGR eJournal*, Congrès International du Génie Rural, France

Rickson, R. and Burch, D. (1996) 'Contract farming in organizational agriculture: The effects upon farmers and the environment', in D. Burch, R. Rickson and G. Lawrence (eds) *Globalization and Agri-Food Restructuring: Perspectives from the Australasia Region*, Avebury, Aldershot, UK

Roberts, P. (2004) *The End of Oil: The Decline of the Petroleum Economy and the Rise of a New Energy Order*, Bloomsbury, London

Roberts, P. (2008) *The End of Food*, Houghton Mifflin Company, Boston

Saunders, C., Barber, A. and Taylor, G. (2006) *Food Miles – Comparative Energy/ Emissions Performance of New Zealand's Agricultural Industry*, Report no 285, Agribusiness and Economics Research Unit, Lincoln University, New Zealand

Science (2006) 12 June, vol 312

Simmons, M. (2005) *Twilight in the Desert: The Coming Saudi Oil Shock and the World Economy*, John Wiley and Sons, New Jersey

Strahan, D. (2007) *The Last Oil Shock*, John Murray, London

Tainter, J. (1990) *The Collapse of Complex Societies*, Cambridge University Press, Cambridge, UK

van der Veer, J. (2008) 'Two energy futures', 18 March, www.shell.com/home/content/ aboutshell-en/our_strategy/shell_global_scenarios/two_energy_futures/two_energy_ futures_25012008.html, accessed 10 April 2009

Weber, C. and Matthews, H. (2008) 'Food-miles and the relative climate impacts of food choices in the United States', *Environmental Science and Technology*, vol 42, no 10, pp3508–3513

Wolf, S. and Nowak, P. (1999) 'Institutional failure in agro-environmental management', *Research in Social Problems and Public Policy*, vol 7, pp 293–310

Wood, R., Lenzen, M., Dey, C. and Lundie, S. (2006) 'A comparative study of some environmental impacts of conventional and organic farming in Australia', *Agricultural Systems*, vol 89, pp324–348

Part II
Food Systems, Diet and Nutrition

7

Unequal Food Systems, Unhealthy Diets

Sharon Friel and Wieslaw Lichacz

Introduction

Unequal food systems and unhealthy diets prevail in a world with increasing nutritional inequities across a distinct social gradient. Although stocks of food have fallen recently, global food production per capita has risen steadily since the 1960s, and yet over 900 million people are undernourished and living in hunger (FAO, 2008). At the same time, the world has become fatter. Ultimately, individuals become obese if they consume more energy than they expend. Genes, while playing an important role in individual susceptibility (Khamsi, 2007), cannot explain the shifting societal-level patterns over the acute time period in which the global 'obesity epidemic' has occurred. A nutrition transition towards diets of highly refined foods, and of meat and dairy products containing high levels of saturated fats, occurred in the developed world around the mid-20th century and is increasingly evident in developing countries. For example, in countries such as South Africa, Egypt and Mexico, numbers of overweight and obese people have reached around 60 per cent in urban adult populations (Mendez et al, 2005). The global nutrition transition, together with marked reductions in energy expenditure through physical inactivity, is believed to have contributed to the rise in levels of obesity (Friel et al, 2007).

This chapter explores the reasons for 'overnutrition', focusing upon the nutrition transition towards obesity, particularly in low- and middle-income countries. It will examine how the policies and processes of globalization encourage consumption of excess calories in a world still plagued by undernutrition (United Nations Standing Committee on Nutrition, 2000; Garrett and Ruel, 2005). The chapter also investigates how the global food system affects nutritional quality and the availability, accessibility, affordability and acceptability of food. It does so by examining food trade and the unbalanced deregulation of the market, and the subsequent expansion of transnational food corporations via foreign direct investment. It also comments upon the role of global food advertising and promotion. Changes in global social systems also appear to be playing a significant role in altering diets through the inter-related issues concerning household livelihood and income, shifting global demographics and increasing levels of urbanization (Mendez and Popkin, 2004; Monteiro et al, 2004; Hawkes et al, 2009). Using the example of India, the chapter will illustrate how underlying inequities in the global food system, combined with the social determinants of health, affect dietary habits and bodyweight.

The unequal transition towards weight gain and obesity

The world now faces a double burden of malnutrition: insufficient calorie or protein intake and undernutrition in relation to micronutrients on the one hand, and overnutrition as a result of excess calorie intake (and the associated increased risk of many non-communicable diseases, including obesity, diabetes and some cancers) on the other. Inequities occur in the prevalence of malnutrition between countries, within countries, within communities and sometimes even within households (Drewnowski and Popkin, 1997; Doak et al, 2000; Friel et al, 2007). As a country's gross domestic product (GDP) increases, so too does the prevalence of obesity, while undernutrition tends to decrease. It is evident from World Health Organization (WHO, 2006) data that at low levels of GDP per capita (below about I$4000) (I$ = International Dollars)[1] relatively high levels of child growth stunting (20–40 per cent) occur, while at higher levels of GDP (above about I$4000), higher levels (20–35 per cent) of adult obesity occur (see also Garrett and Ruel, 2005). The prevalence data for underweight and overweight people in urban and rural areas of selected developing countries show levels of weight and obesity exceeding 20 per cent in urban areas in most countries, and peaking at above 60 per cent in Mexico, Egypt and South Africa in both rural and urban areas (Mendez et al, 2005). Urban areas in India had roughly similar proportions of underweight and overweight individuals, registering 23 per cent and 25 per cent respectively (see Mendez et al, 2005).

Within countries, undernutrition is disproportionately higher among groups of lower socio-economic status, and the same trend is emerging for the overweight and obese (Griffiths and Bentley, 2001; Gupte and Ramachandran, 2001; Chhabra and Chhabra, 2007; Hong et al, 2007; Apfelbacher et al, 2008).

Understanding the nutrition transition: Energy balance

In industrialized countries, the transition to diets higher in fats, sweeteners and highly processed foods has been gathering momentum over time (Grigg, 1995). In England, one of the first countries in the world to become industrialized, it is estimated that the consumption of fat and refined carbohydrates per person has increased five to tenfold over the past two centuries, whereas the consumption of fibre-rich grains has decreased substantially (Uusitalo et al, 2002). More recent trends show that this nutrition transition is now taking place at a much faster rate in middle- and low-income countries (Popkin, 2002). Data from a number of countries between 1980 and 2000 show a dramatic increase in dietary energy availability in some instances (FAO, 2004). In South Africa, the daily energy availability per capita was 2800Kcals in 1980, increasing by a further 200Kcals by 2000. Over the same time period, the figures for Nigeria show an increase of 700Kcals from 2100Kcals to 2800Kcals, while in India levels increased by roughly 500Kcals from 2250Kcals to about 2700 Kcals (FAO, 2004).

On the basis of such global data, which show that more calories are now available for consumption, it is important to ask: where do those calories come from? One explanation might be the greater availability of processed foods. Looking at food balance sheet data from the 1960s through to the late 1990s, the increasing availability of dietary energy in the high-income countries of Asia, for example, corresponds with an increase in overall energy – particularly from added vegetable oils and added sugars, ingredients usually found in highly processed foodstuffs (FAO, 2004). Therefore, one hypothesis gaining strength is that such foodstuffs become more readily available with increasing national wealth (Popkin and Gordon-Larsen, 2004).

Increases in calorific intake are also associated with shifts in eating habits. The increases in per capita calorific intake in the US over the past decade match longer-term shifts in eating patterns, which are increasingly showing a greater intake of sugar and other calorific sweeteners, greater consumption of foods away from the home and greater consumption of fast foods. The nutritional quality of meals or snacks prepared at home can be quite different to that of meals sourced at away-from-home locations such as vending machines, restaurants and fast food outlets (Nielsen and Popkin, 2004). Generally, out-of-home food consumption reduces a person's control over both the total calories consumed and the nutritional quality of foods consumed, particularly in relation to the types of fats and sugars compared with foods prepared and consumed at home. Analysis of household expenditure data from a high-income country such as the Republic of Ireland identified an explosion of foods consumed out of home. Between 1951 and 2000, household expenditure on meals prepared away from home increased by more than 15 per cent across all social classes. Among higher social classes, expenditure on away-from-home meals was significantly higher, coming close to 30 per cent of total food expenditure (Kuchler et al, 2005; Friel et al, 2006). These Irish data probably reflect household food expenditure transitions experienced in other middle- and high-income countries also undergoing times of major economic and social change (Friel et al, 2006).

As suggested earlier, in terms of energy balance, it is not just what goes into the body that matters – the amount of energy expended also matters. Significant changes have taken place globally in terms of the amount of energy expended and the way in which this energy expenditure takes place.

Swinburn and colleagues (1999) characterized 'obesogenic' environments as contemporary environments that proffer not only an abundance of high-energy foods, but also an abundance of jobs, leisure and transport options that are predominantly sedentary and require little energy expenditure.

Working patterns in particular have changed dramatically, especially in urban areas where they are dominated by the service sector – a work environment that is not physically demanding, hence contributing little in the way of energy expenditure. These work-related energy shifts are certainly apparent in high-income countries, but now appear increasingly in low- to middle-income countries (Hawkes et al, 2007). With respect to transport, the escalation of private car use is evident globally, resulting in increasingly fewer people expending energy through active modes of travel such as walking, cycling and the use of public transport (Friel and Broom, 2007; Hinde, 2007). The amount of, and opportunity for, incidental energy expenditure has also reduced. Many domestic innovations and labour-saving devices have reduced the incidental energy expenditure that once took place in households around the world. Although addressing these changes does not mean going back to scrubbing the floor and beating the carpets to get rid of the dust, it is clear that modern day living for more and more people around the world nonetheless provides fewer opportunities to address obesity (Friel and Broom, 2007).

Drivers of the nutrition transition

With dietary energy availability increasing, and with greater calorific intake per person per day in all but the poorest countries around the world, body weights have increased dramatically in the latter part of the 20th century and early 21st century. The questions thus arise as to what is causing these profound individual-level dietary and physical activity changes on a mass scale, and why they are unequally distributed across social groups?

One possibility is the corresponding changes that have taken place in the socio-economic, socio-environmental and socio-cultural circumstances in which people function. Changes in global and national socio-political and macro-economic contexts – particularly since the current processes of globalization took off in the mid-1980s – have not only influenced global food systems, but have also re-shaped the make-up of societies and changed the nature of people's living and working conditions, physical and social environments, and local commodity markets (including food). All of these changing circumstances convey benefits and harms for human health (OECD, 2005; Burns et al, 2007).

Re-balancing the increasing prevalence of energy-rich, nutrient-poor diets across the world requires action on both global and national socio-political fronts. It also requires an examination of the macro-economic and micro-social arrangements that influence food systems, and have contributed to making less healthy food more easily available, more affordable and more acceptable to all. These issues will be examined in more detail in the following sections.

Increasing availability of less healthy food: 'more of it to more people'

Greater liberalization of the global food system – coupled with food subsidies and more direct foreign investment, and the changing nature of food distribution systems – have each played an important role in shaping the global nutrition transition. These three contributors to increasing food availability will be discussed in turn.

International food trade   Changes in international trade and food policy have led to profound changes in the composition and availability of food supplies. Recent analysis by Blouin and colleagues (2009) concludes that trade liberalization has enabled greater availability of highly processed, calorie-rich and nutrient-poor food in developing countries.

Structural adjustment in low- and middle-income countries, coupled with increasing trade liberalization (IMF, 2001) – particularly the agriculture trade agreement in the 1994 Uruguay Round of the General Agreement on Tariffs and Trade (GATT) – opened up these countries to the international market. Regional trade agreements multiplied, increasing at a rate of 15 per year in the 1990s. Subsequently, in the 1994 Uruguay Round of the GATT, the ability to protect national markets was revoked with the Agreement on Agriculture, which pledged countries to reduce tariffs, export subsidies and domestic agricultural support. While trade liberalization has helped to move food around the world – making more food available and increasing dietary diversity, at least for some – the conditions of trade have arguably distorted the food supply and corresponding prices in favour of less healthy foodstuffs, including an overproduction of foods that are high in saturated fats (Elinder, 2005). Many developing countries experienced more than a doubling of food import bills as a share of GDP between 1974 and 2004, while the amount of trade in processed agricultural products increased at a much faster rate than trade in primary agricultural products (FAO, 2004; Hawkes, 2006; Rosen and Shapouri, 2008).

When India became part of the GATT international trade treaty in 1994 (ICIS, 1994), a distinct shift occurred in the number and type of foodstuffs imported into India. At the same time, rapidly increasing economic growth – combined with other societal changes – helped to accelerate the convergence of middle class Indian dietary habits with those of the western world. This diet was high in saturated fat and refined sugar, a likely cause of the increasing rates of diet-related non-communicable diseases. Some detail of how changes in food system trade – along with wider societal change – has helped contribute to the nutrition transition in India is provided in Box 1.

Foreign direct investment   Via the removal of trade barriers, trade liberalization can affect availability of certain foods. Increasing levels of foreign direct investment by multinational food companies in developing countries have stimulated both the production of processed foods and the importation of such

BOX 1 IMPLICATIONS FOR DIET: CHANGES IN THE INDIAN FOOD AND SOCIAL SYSTEM

India, a nation of over a billion people, is in the process of rapid demographic, economic, nutritional and epidemiological transition. India's emergence as one of today's most rapidly growing economic forces arises partly because of a shift in the late 1980s away from the historical commitment to non-alignment and self-reliance, greater international trade liberalization, liberalization of direct foreign investment, liberalization of the financial sector and fewer restrictions on large enterprises. Since 1997, the Indian economy has grown on average by 5.4 per cent each year, resulting in a burgeoning urban middle class that is roughly the same size as the whole population of the US. Juxtaposed with national wealth are the persistently high rates of poverty that, while declining, remain a very serious problem in rural and urban slum areas. Both the economic growth and workforce changes were enjoyed most acutely by the urban middle-class professionals and skilled workers, and helped to fuel increases in market demand for high-value foods such as meat, fruit, vegetables and edible oils – a highly import-intensive process that has created a boom in certain consumer goods (Ghosh, 2002). Through globalization of the economy, middle-class Indian dietary habits have converged with those of the Western world – they are now high in saturated fats and refined sugars. During this period of globalization, work in the Indian agriculture sector stagnated (Papola, 2005). The reduction in state subsidies supporting domestic produce and the depression of domestic prices due to cheaper imports, in addition to technological and infrastructural factors, have impacted on food availability and access both through the nature of the national food supply, and through the employment and working conditions of those in the agricultural sector.

Source: Friel et al (in preparation)

foods, with the effect that more national marketplaces are now crammed with energy-dense food products (Hawkes et al, 2004; Friel, 2007). US investment in foreign food-processing companies grew from US$9000 million in 1980 to US$36,000 million in 2000, with sales increasing from US$39,200 million in 1982 to US$150,000 million in 2000. Processed food sales rose by 29 per cent annually in developing countries, compared to the 7 per cent growth in nations with high incomes (Blouin et al, 2009).

Thailand, for example, experienced a flood of highly processed, high-fat, high-sugar foods on to its domestic market from 1999 through to 2004. As shown in Figure 7.1, the actual volume of snack foods, potato chips and other extruded foods[2] increased by more than 20,000 tonnes over that period, from 35,000 to 55,000 tonnes. The bulk of this food came from foreign direct investment from US-based transnational food corporations, one of which was the food distributor Frito-Lay, which is a division of PepsiCo.

Food distribution systems Transnational food companies now increasingly organize food production, distribution and marketing on a global scale

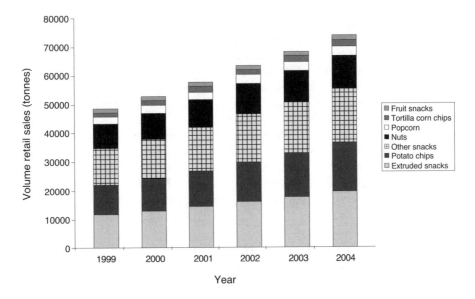

Source: Hawkes (2006)

Figure 7.1 *Retail sales of sweet and savoury snacks in Thailand*

(Hawkes et al, 2007). In middle- and high-income societies, the type and quantity of food that makes its way to consumers is very much determined by supermarkets and the food services sector (Reardon et al, 2003; Dixon et al, 2007, and see Chapter 11 this volume). The nature of the national and local food distribution systems plays an important role in determining the range and quality of foodstuffs available for purchase, and the prices paid.

The modern marketplace is increasingly one dominated by the retail, supermarket and food service chains (Martinez and Kaufman, 2008). Historically, and certainly in low- to middle-income countries, the traditional marketplace has tended to have attributes that are more beneficial to a healthy diet. However, the extent to which a shift in the type of distribution systems affects body weight seems to vary from country to country (see Chapter 9 this volume). For example, a study by Morland and colleagues (2006) in the US found that, while the availability of supermarkets is associated with a decreased prevalence of obese and overweight people, the availability of grocery stores and convenience stores is associated with an increased prevalence of weight gain and obesity among residents.

This finding notwithstanding, the influence of the shift in national food distribution systems towards supermarkets and food service chains does increase the availability of energy-dense foods, with increases in fat intake being seen progressively more in the transitioning countries (Dixon and Broom, 2007; Fisher et al, 2007). An illustration of this phenomenon is evident in data from Gambia, where gradations in energy density and the fat content of food are clearly observed across different food outlet types, accompanied by increasing levels of obesity (Prentice, 2006). With increased household wealth, mainly through remittance money, Gambians are demanding greater diversity in local shops, resulting in increased availability of foodstuffs that are high in fat and energy dense. Similarly, fast foods are becoming more readily available in urban areas. As may be expected, these foods are also very energy dense and have a high fat content (Prentice and Jebb, 2003; Prentice, 2006).

India, too, is starting to experience a shift in its food distribution system (Rabobank, 2007), although the market share of organized food material outlets like supermarkets remains a relatively small proportion of the total food retail market in India, where family-owned shops still dominate the food retail sector. However, the market share claimed by supermarkets is projected to rise.

Making less-healthy food more affordable

Trade and agricultural policy affect food prices. The drop in average global food prices prior to the price hikes of 2007 and 2008 was driven by subsidies supporting very cheap calories from oils, sugars and starches (Ray et al, 2003; USDA ERS et al, 2004; Elinder, 2005). In the US, agricultural policy decisions between 1995 and 2000 resulted in price increases for fruit, vegetables and cereals. Meanwhile, foods that were high in saturated fats and high in sugars decreased in price. Although the data do not allow for cause and effect to be established, there was, at the same time, an increase in average consumption of foods high in sugar and oils (Kantor, 1998; USDA ERS, 2003).

But changes are afoot in the nature of global agricultural trade and production – the production of food for fuel is displacing the production of food for human consumption, exacerbating already falling food stocks (FAO, 2008, and see Chapter 14 this volume) and contributing to food price hikes (OECD and FAO, 2007). More generally, the uneven distribution of existing food stocks resulting from protectionist import and export tariffs and subsidies, alongside population growth and the accelerating demand for certain food commodities such as meat and dairy – particularly among the urban middle classes – is impacting upon international and domestic food stocks and pushing up food prices (OECD and FAO, 2007). Speculative investment in food commodity futures and derivatives – a fairly recent development – is also contributing to inflationary pressures that affect food prices (Pace et al, 2008).

Data sourced mainly from rich countries demonstrates that the foods recommended in healthy eating guidelines are often more expensive than the less healthy options. The cost of the food relative to the amount of money that people have to spend is illustrated in Figure 7.2 for the Republic of Ireland, where the costs of a healthy basket of foods are compared to weekly welfare entitlements. Such disparities are significant in relation to food access. For example, in order to comply with the national dietary guidelines, a lone parent with one child would have to spend 80 per cent of the weekly household income on food. Dobson and colleagues (1994) have shown that financially

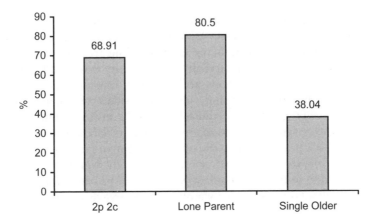

Source: Friel et al (2006)

Figure 7.2 *Healthy food basket cost as a proportion of weekly welfare entitlements, Republic of Ireland, June 2003*

constrained households consider food as a flexible item within the controllable household budget, and when other necessary household expenditure is taken into consideration, the food budget is reduced. There is little chance, therefore, that a low-income household would be able to spend 80 per cent of its weekly income on food (Fleming, 2008). In this context, complying with national dietary guidelines is not only a health policy matter, but also clearly requires coherent social policy.

As the cost of a basket of household goods increases rapidly relative to income, all but the very rich will feel the effects. Some will be able to purchase a healthy diet, some will only be able to purchase the cheapest sources of calories – energy-dense, highly processed products that increase the risk of obesity and diabetes – and many millions will be unable to afford even that (Friel et al, 2008).

Shaping food acceptability: 'Making more people want to eat unhealthy food'

Food companies engage in considerable market forecasting, including measures to assess the public acceptability of food. Food marketing divisions in large companies are very cognizant of the relative food demand within different countries, and aim to influence this through targeted advertising. Countries and sub-populations are at various stages of evolving food demand. For example, Australia is considered to be in the high-technology band – focusing on functional foods, organic foods and diet-related products. In comparison, China's consumer demands are evolving around snacks and prepared meals. And, if China continues along the regular demand curve, the next category of food will be convenience foods, followed by functional and diet foods. The evolving food demand curve helps shape the sorts of foods that citizens in different marketplaces consider acceptable and desirable (Rabobank, 2007).

Large food corporations carefully consider the evolving food demand curves in various countries, along with shifting demographics, in order to determine their market orientation and advertising strategies. Global food companies actively aim to contribute to the shift in food demand through advertising, and particularly through the medium of television. In an analysis of television advertising in the UK, and more generally across high-income countries, the 'big five' foods that are high in fat and high in sugar – sugared breakfast cereals, soft drinks, confectionery, savoury snacks and fast foods – are the foods that are most frequently and aggressively advertised (see Hawkes et al, 2009).

Similarly, global food advertising expenditure is increasing steadily in developing countries, particularly in relation to processed, energy-dense foods (Hawkes et al, 2009). In China, television ownership has tripled in the space of a decade. By 2004, about 10 per cent of the Chinese population had television. That viewing audience has now increased to about 50 per cent in 2009. With the purchase of Western satellite channels and programmes on the rise, the Chinese public is being increasingly exposed through advertising to foods that are high in fat, sugar and salt (Du and Zhao, 2007; Parvanta et al, 2008). Expenditure on advertising within the US by Coca-Cola and McDonald's, compared with expenditure in low- to middle-income countries outside of the US, is quite different for each company. Coca-Cola appears to have already captured its US market, as a large portion of its advertising spending now goes overseas in an attempt to capture foreign markets. In contrast, McDonald's has mainly concentrated its relatively large spending capacity within the US, although it is expanding its market elsewhere (AdAge Global, cited in Hawkes, 2002).

Conclusion

Food availability, affordability and acceptability are not evenly distributed between and within countries. This has enormous implications for inequities in the distribution of obesity. Reshaping the nutrition transition and the transition towards obesity requires closer scrutiny of the policies and practices of global and national food and social systems.

A systemic approach to healthy body weight is needed – one that considers the social determinants of diet, physical activity and body weight. Governance arrangements for trade, direct investment and subsidies need to be viewed through a health lens. Assurance of an adequate and nutritious food supply is essential. There are also issues in relation to material security. The data from Ireland concerning the cost of a healthy diet raise social policy issues and demonstrate the urgency of ensuring that healthy food is priced to make it more competitive than high-fat and energy-dense foods. A built habitat that influences energy expenditure and ensures the easy uptake of healthier food options needs to be part of a health-oriented food system. Finally, in a much broader sense than has been fully covered here, it is necessary to consider the home, educational and working environments and how these can help reinforce healthy behaviour, including the empowerment of people so that they can be confident in making healthy food choices.

Many consider that the processes of globalization are directly contributing to the nutrition transition, and thereby resulting in poorer quality, energy-dense diets and the rise of chronic disease. There is sufficient evidence to begin to redress the socio-environmental and socio-political drivers of weight gain and obesity. But more research is needed.

Notes

1   This is a hypothetical unit of currency that has the same purchasing power that the US dollar had in the US at a given point in time.
2   Extruded foods are highly processed foods. Grains and food additives are processed for a short time at high temperature and then 'extruded' through tubes, allowing later formation of human-made products such as muesli bars, breakfast cereals and snack foods.

References

Apfelbacher, C., Loerbroks, A., Cairns, J., Behrendt, H., Ring, J. and Krämer, U. (2008) 'Predictors of overweight and obesity in five to seven-year-old children in Germany: Results from cross-sectional studies', *BMC Public Health*, www.biomedcentral. com/1471-2458/8/171, accessed 10 February 2009

Blouin, C., Chopra, M. and van der Hoeven, R. (2009) 'Trade and social determinants of health', *The Lancet*, vol 373, pp502–507

Burns, C., Friel, S. and Cummins, S. (2007) 'Economically, geographically and socially disadvantaged communities', in M. Lawrence and T. Worsley (eds) *Public Health Nutrition – From Principles to Practice*, Allen and Unwin, Sydney

Chhabra, P. and Chhabra S. (2007) 'Distribution and determinants of body mass index of non-smoking adults in Delhi, India', *Journal of Health, Population and Nutrition*, vol 25, no 3, September, pp294–301

Dixon, J. and Broom, D. (2007) 'Introduction: Seven modern environmental sins of obesity', in J. Dixon and D. Broom (eds) *The Seven Deadly Sins of Obesity: How the Modern World is Making us Fat*, UNSW Press, Sydney

Dixon, J., Omwega, A., Friel, S., Burns, C., Donati, K. and Carlisle, R. (2007) 'The health equity dimensions of urban food systems', *Journal of Urban Health*, vol 84, supplement 1, pp118–129

Doak, C., Adair, L., Monteiro, C. and Popkin, B. (2000) 'Overweight and underweight coexist within households in Brazil, China and Russia', *Journal of Nutrition*, vol 130, no 12, pp2965–2971

Dobson, B., Beardsworth, A. and Keil, T. (1994) 'Diet, choice and poverty: Social, cultural and nutritional aspects of food consumption among low-income families', Family Policy Studies Centre, London

Drewnowski, A. and Popkin, B. (1997) 'The nutrition transition: New trends in the global diet', *Nutrition Reviews*, vol 55, no 2, pp31–43

Du, Y. and Zhao, X. (2007) 'The role of media in childhood obesity: What we learned from the case of Chinese children', Paper presented at the annual meeting of the International Communication Association, 23 May, San Francisco, www.allacademic.com/meta/p169740_index.html, accessed 18 December 2008

Elinder, L. (2005) 'Obesity, hunger, and agriculture: The damaging role of subsidies', *British Medical Journal*, vol 331, no 7528, pp1333–1336

FAO (2004) *The State of Agricultural Commodity Markets 2004*, Food and Agriculture Organization of the United Nations, Rome

FAO (2008) *The State of Food Insecurity in the World 2008*, Food and Agriculture Organization of the United Nations, Rome

Fisher, J., Liu, Y., Birch, L. and Rolls, B. (2007) 'Effects of portion size and energy density on young children's intake at a meal', *American Journal of Clinical Nutrition*, 86, pp174–179

Fleming, S. (2008) 'US consumers cut down on food spending as they feel the bite of the credit crunch', *Mail Online*, 30 October, www.mailonsunday.co.uk/money/article-1081933/US-consumers-cut-food-spending-feel-bite-credit-crunch.html, accessed January 2009

Friel, S. (2007) 'Unhealthy systems, unhealthy weight', in P. Horwitz (ed.) *Ecology and Health: People and Places in a Changing World*, www.vichealth.vic.gov.au/~/media/ProgramsandProjects/OtherActivity/EmergingIssues/Ecology%20and%20HealthPeople%20%20Places%20in%20a%20Changing%20World.ashx, accessed January 2009

Friel, S. and Broom, D. (2007) 'Unequal society, unhealthy weight – the social distribution of obesity', in J. Dixon and D. Broom (eds) *The Seven Deadly Sins of Obesity – How the Modern World is Making us Fat*, UNSW Press, Sydney

Friel, S., Walsh, O. and McCarthy, D. (2006) 'The irony of a rich country: Issues of access and availability of healthy food in the Republic of Ireland', *Journal of Epidemiology and Community Health*, vol 60, pp1013–1019

Friel, S., Chopra, M. and Satcher, D. (2007) 'Unequal weight: Equity oriented policy responses to the global obesity epidemic' *British Medical Journal*, vol 335, pp1241–1243

Friel, S., Marmot, M., McMichael, A., Kjellstrom, T. and Vågerö, D. (2008) 'Global health equity and climate stabilisation: A common agenda', *The Lancet*, vol 372, no 9650, pp1677–1683

Friel, S. Chatterjee, P. and Hawkes, C. (in preparation) *Social Determinants of Food and Nutrition Transitions: The Case of India*

Garrett, J. and Ruel, M. (2005) 'Stunted child-overweight mother pairs: Prevalence and association with economic development and urbanization', *Food and Nutrition Bulletin*, vol 26, no 2, pp209–221

Ghosh, J. (2002) *Social Policy in Indian Development*, United Nations Research Institute for Social Development, Geneva

Griffiths, P. and Bentley, M. (2001) 'The nutrition transition is underway in India', *Journal of Nutrition*, www.jn.nutrition.org/cgi/content/full/131/10/2692, accessed 10 February 2009

Grigg, D. (1995) 'The nutritional transition in Western Europe', *Journal of Historical Geography*, vol 22, no 1, pp247–261

Gupte, M. and Ramachandran, V. (2001) 'Epidemiological profile of India: Historical and contemporary perspectives', *Journal of Bioscience*, vol 26, no 4, pp437–64

Hawkes, C. (2002) 'Marketing activities of global soft drink and fast food companies in emerging markets: A review', in World Health Organization (ed.) *Globalization, Diets and Noncommunicable Diseases*, World Health Organization, Geneva

Hawkes, C. (2006) 'Uneven dietary development: Linking the policies and processes of globalization with the nutrition transition, obesity and diet-related chronic diseases', *Globalization and Health*, www.globalizationandhealth.com/content/2/1/4, accessed 22 December 2008

Hawkes, C., Eckhardt, C., Ruel, M. and Minot, N. (2004) 'Diet quality, poverty and food policy: A new research agenda for obesity prevention in developing countries', *International Food Policy Research Institute*, www.bvsde.paho.org/bvsacd/cd66/ CorinnaHawkes.pdf, accessed 10 February 2009

Hawkes, C., Chopra, M., Friel, S. and Thow, A. (2007) *Globalization, Food and Nutrition Transitions*, Background paper of the Globalization Knowledge Network, Commission on Social Determinants of Health, World Health Organization, Geneva

Hawkes, C., Chopra, M. and Friel, S. (2009) 'Globalization, trade and the nutrition transition', in R. Labonté, T. Schrecker, V. Runnels and C. Packer (eds) *Globalization and Health Pathways: Evidence and Policy*, Routledge, New York

Hinde, S. (2007) 'The car-reliant environment', in J. Dixon and D. Broom (eds) *The Seven Deadly Sins of Obesity: How the Modern World is Making us Fat*, UNSW Press, Sydney

Hong, T., Dibley, M., Sibbritt, D., Binh, P., Trang, N. and Hanh, T. (2007) 'Overweight and obesity are rapidly emerging among adolescents in Ho Chi Minh City, Vietnam, 2002–2004', *International Journal of Pediatric Obesity*, vol 2, no 4, pp194–201

ICIS (Interactive Chemical Information Software) Chemical Business (1994) 'Developing nations query Gatt's IPR agreement', 12 December 1994, www.icis.com/Articles/1 994/12/12/36262/developing-nations-query-gatts-ipr-agreement.html, accessed 22 December 2008

IMF (International Monetary Fund) (2001) 'Global trade liberalization and the developing countries', *Issues Briefs 08/01*, www.imf.org/external/np/exr/ ib/2001/110801.htm#i, accessed January 2009

Kantor, L. (1998) 'A dietary assessment of the US food supply: Comparing per capita food consumption with food guide pyramid servings recommendations', *Agricultural Economic Report No. 772*, US Department of Agriculture, Economic Research Service, Washington, DC, www.ers.usda.gov/Publications/AER772/, accessed 22 December 2008

Khamsi, R. (2007) 'Hunt for obesity gene yields a new suspect', *New Scientist*, 12 April, http://www.newscientist.com/article/dn11592-hunt-for-obesity-gene-yields-a-new-suspect.html, accessed 22 December 2008

Kuchler, F., Golan, E., Veryam, J. and Crutchfield, S. (2005) 'Obesity policy and the law of unintended consequences', www.ers.usda.gov/AmberWaves/June05/Features/ ObesityPolicy.htm, accessed 22 December 2008

Martinez, S. and Kaufman, P. (2008) 'Twenty years of competition reshape the US food marketing system', www.ers.usda.gov/AmberWaves/April08/Features/ FoodMarketing.html/, accessed 22 December 2008

Mendez, M. and Popkin, B. (2004) 'Globalization, urbanization and nutritional change in the developing world', *FAO Food and Nutrition Paper*, no 83, pp55–80

Mendez, M., Monteiro, C. and Popkin, B. (2005) 'Overweight exceeds underweight among women in most developing countries', *American Journal of Clinical Nutrition*, vol 81, pp714–721

Monteiro, C., Moura, E., Conde, W. and Popkin, B. (2004) 'Socioeconomic status and obesity in adult populations of developing countries: A review', *Bulletin of the World Health Organization*, vol 82, pp940–946

Morland, K., Diez Roux, A. and Wing, S. (2006) 'Supermarkets, other food stores, and obesity: The atherosclerosis risk in communities study', *American Journal of Preventive Medicine*, vol 30, no 4, pp333–339

Nielsen, S. and Popkin, B. (2004) 'Changes in beverage intake between 1977 and 2001', *American Journal of Preventive Medicine*, vol 27, pp205–210

OECD (2005) *OECD Fact Book 2005*, http://oberon.sourceoecd.org/vl=5453707/ cl=12/nw=1/rpsv/fact2005/, accessed 22 December 2008

OECD and FAO (2007) *OECD-FAO Agricultural Outlook 2007–2016*, Organisation for Economic Co-Operation and Development, Paris, and Food and Agriculture Organization of the United Nations, Rome

Pace, N., Seal, A. and Costello, A. (2008) 'Food commodity derivatives: A new cause of malnutrition?' *The Lancet*, vol 371, pp1648–1650

Papola, T. (2005) 'Workers in a globalising world: Some perspectives from India', in R. Smyth, C. Nyland and M. Vicziany (eds) *Globalization and Labour Mobility in India and China*, Asian Business and Economics Research Unit, Monash University, Melbourne

Parvanta, S., Brown, J., Du, S., Zhao, X. and Fengying, Z. (2008) 'TV use and snacking behaviours among children and adolescents in China', Paper presented at the Annual Meeting of the International Communication Association, Montreal, Quebec, www. allacademic.com/meta/p234027_index.html, accessed 22 December 2008

Popkin, B. (2002) 'The shift in stages of the nutrition transition in the developing world differs from past experiences!' *Public Health Nutrition*, vol 5, pp205–214

Popkin, B. and Gordon-Larsen, P. (2004) 'The nutrition transition: Worldwide obesity dynamics and their determinants', *International Journal of Obesity Related Metabolic Disorders*, vol 28 supp 3, ppS2–S9

Prentice, A. (2006) 'The emerging epidemic of obesity in developing countries', *International Journal of Epidemiology*, vol 35, no 1, pp93–97

Prentice, A. and Jebb, S. (2003) 'Fast foods, energy density and obesity: A possible mechanistic link', *Obesity Reviews*, vol 4, no 4, pp187–194

Rabobank (2007) *Strengthening the India–Australia Corridor in Select Food and Agribusiness Sectors*, Final Report submitted to National Food Industry Strategy, Rabo India Finance Ltd, Australia

Ray, D., Ugarte, D. and Tiller, K. (2003) 'Rethinking US Agricultural Policy: Changing Course to Secure Farmer Livelihoods Worldwide', Agricultural Policy Analysis Centre, University of Tennessee, Knoxville, www.inmotionmagazine.com/ ra03/APAC.pdf, accessed 22 December 2008

Reardon, T., Timmer, C., Barrett, C. and Berdegue, J. (2003) 'The rise of supermarkets in Africa, Asia and Latin America', *American Journal of Agricultural Economics*, vol 85, no 5, www.ssrn.com/abstract=474032, accessed 22 December 2008

Rosen, S. and Shapouri, S. (2008) 'Obesity in the midst of unyielding food insecurity in developing countries', www.ers.usda.gov/AmberWaves/September08/PDF/ ObesityCountries.pdf, accessed 22 December 2008

Swinburn, B., Egger, G. and Raza, F. (1999) 'Dissecting obesogenic environments: The development and application of a framework for identifying and prioritizing environmental interventions for obesity', *Preventive Medicine*, vol 29, no 6, pp563–570

United Nations Standing Committee on Nutrition (2000) *Fourth Report on the World Nutrition Situation*, United Nations Standing Committee on Nutrition, Geneva, http://www.unsystem.org/SCN/, http://www.ifpri.org/, accessed 22 December 2008

USDA ERS (2003) 'Foodreview: Weighing in on obesity', www.ers.usda.gov/ publications/FoodReview/dec2002/, accessed 22 December 2008

USDA ERS, Normile, M., Effland, A. and Young, C. (2004) 'US and EU Farm Policy – How Similar?' www.ers.usda.gov/publications/WRS0404/WRS0404c.pdf, accessed 22 December 2008

Uusitalo, U., Pietinen, P. and Puska, P. (2002) 'Dietary transition in developing countries: Challenges for chronic disease prevention', in World Health Organization (ed.) *Globalization, Diets and Noncommunicable Diseases,* World Health Organization, Geneva

WHO (2006) 'Obesity and overweight' *WHO Fact Sheet*, World Health Organization, Geneva, www.who.int/mediacentre/factsheets/fs311/en/index.html, accessed 28 November 2006

8
Explaining Patterns of Convenience Food Consumption

Lisa Schubert, Megan Jennaway and Helen Johnson

Introduction

Central to criticisms of contemporary dietary patterns, and almost irrespective of the focus of analysis – whether nutritional, environmental, ethical or cultural – is the 'problem' of convenience and fast foods. If we are to believe much of what we read, convenience foods stand out as being nutritionally inferior, as having production methods that are environmentally damaging and ethically indefensible, and as constituting and promoting food practices that are culturally degrading.

More often than not, the message about convenience food from food activists and nutrition policy-makers to those responsible for food provisioning at the household level is an unsubtle and unsupportive one: 'Cook unprocessed foods.' 'Cook at home.' 'Convenience foods are risky.' These sorts of messages fall into the category of scientists-cum-policy-writers trying to translate their knowledge to the real world, without such knowledge being adequately grounded in the lived experiences of those people whose everyday activities include feeding their dependants. The research reported on in this chapter adds to an emerging body of literature that seeks to redress this knowledge gap.

Specifically, the focus here is on explaining the meaning of convenience food consumption and the ways in which individuals, as primary family food provisioners (PFFPs), construct explanations of their behaviour related to convenience food. A review of existing literature on convenience food consumption patterns was conducted with an eye to identifying the conceptual framework, or discourse, that has informed the analysis presented in published research articles on the topic. This review was complemented by an ethnographic study in order to gain a deeper understanding of the reasons and motivations given by PFFPs to explain their food provisioning strategies.

Drawing on interview data, the discussion presents a critical analysis of the dominant research discourses in explaining convenience food consumption. The extent to which individual perspectives resonated with, and diverged from, these wider research discourses provide important insights into the influence of media and cultural representations on the way PFFPs conceived of their roles and responsibilities. The significance of these ethnographic insights for convenience food research and policy is synthesized in the concluding section.

Methods of investigation

Interview data are drawn from an ethnographic study based in Brisbane, Australia. The study was conducted between January 2002 and August 2006, and included 15 family households with working parents. The parents were professional and/or tertiary educated, and those in secure full-time employment earned above-average incomes. This sample was selected as a means of 'studying up' – a tradition in anthropology with a 30-year history (Nader, 1972; Shore and Nugent, 2002) – where the powerful groups in a society are examined for their insights and understandings regarding a particular system or problem. In this instance, convenience food consumption was explored in households that, apart from the limited or constrained time for family food provisioning that arises when combining parenting and paid employment, were well resourced overall. In-depth interviews were conducted with PFFPs on a minimum of two occasions, and each interview lasted between one and two hours. All PFFPs participating in the study – 14 of whom were female and 1 male – combined paid employment (full-time, part-time or casual) with the role of parenting dependant children. The interviews were semi-structured and discussion was wide-ranging around four key topics: the performance of family food provisioning; the impact of constraints or limitations in time available for food provisioning; household food strategies (see Schubert, 2008 for a description of this new construct); and preferred and actual family menus. Additionally, the study involved the collection of data from participant observation, family food diaries, and budgetary and expenditure records. All names used in this chapter are pseudonyms in order to protect informants' confidentiality.

The analysis presented centres on the ways in which PFFPs draw on dominant discourses represented in prior research when asked to talk about their strategies in managing to feed their households in the face of constraints on their available time. These discursive affinities are in many cases distinct from their 'actual practices'. Empirical evidence is employed to substantiate the importance of methods that do more than simply ask informants to account for what they do.

Nutrition behaviour research and dominant epistemologies – four frames for explaining convenience food consumption

The appeal and growth of convenience food consumption practices during the latter part of the 20th century has been of enduring interest to scholars from disciplines that encompass economics, cultural studies, sociology, nutrition, psychology and history. It is a topic that most people can relate to on a personal level, and one that many have strongly held views about. Thus, at a superficial level, the relationship between the rapidly evolving convenience food marketplace and consumer behaviour may seem easy to understand. However, we would suggest that the academic exploration of this topic from divergent disciplines, frameworks and methodologies reveals its complexity as a social phenomenon.

While the following account of relevant research revisits some of the territory addressed in the recent review paper by Jabs and Devine (2006), and in the work of Scholderer and Grunert (2005) towards the development of a frame analysis, it seeks to go beyond these efforts to examine a broader range of the disciplinary conceptual frames used by researchers to approach the question of convenience food consumption. The four frames to be discussed are:

1 household production;
2 convenience orientation;
3 food system;
4 consumer culture.

Table 8.1 summarizes key information about these four frames, including internal logic, policy implications and exemplars of research that has addressed the question of convenience food consumption. It should be noted that the policy platforms presented in this table are not necessarily the views or suggestions of the researchers quoted, but are included to demonstrate how different views have been taken up and injected into contemporary public health nutrition strategies. Finally, the fundamental epistemological limitations of each approach are presented. These limitations derive from the disciplinary boundaries applied, which have prevented researchers from capturing the realities, context and contingencies of everyday life within which decisions about food provisioning are made. An extended description of each of the disciplinary frames is then presented.

Household production (household economics) approach

This approach emphasizes that households are only capable of producing (doing) so much; households reaching or exceeding their limit need to outsource some products and services in order to manage activities. The trend towards increasing participation of PFFPs in paid employment has gone hand-in-hand with the trend towards food prepared outside the home. This latter economic trend has spearheaded investigations into potential efficiency gains through the renegotiation of prevailing divisions of household labour between spouses, the changing sphere of production for food provisioning, and the measurement of household expenditure on food prepared outside the home. However, the approach overlooks the many nonrational factors operating in dietary practices (for example, the moral economy of family care, as well as the contemporary

Table 8.1 *Four frames for approaching the study of convenience food consumption*

Frame	Indicative quote / mantra	Exemplary reference(s) using this approach	Policy suggestions to improve likelihood of healthy diets	Main weakness(es)
Household production (household economics) approach	There isn't enough time in the day to cook the way our mothers did … we just have more takeaways, and when I do cook it's something I can put together in 20 minutes	Ahuja and Walker, 1994; Devine et al, 2003	Ensure available food prepared outside the home options is compatible with achieving a healthy diet; promote efficiency at all stages of food provisioning	Assumes falsely that all consumers are rational individuals; assumes that healthy food prepared outside the home options is uniformly available to, and holds appeal to, all sociocultural groups; assumes that all consumers are willing and able to adapt and innovate with respect to their practices; assumes that renegotiation of tasks at home is an option available to all
Convenience orientation (consumer psychology) approach	I've got better things to do than cooking … this is quality time for the kids. I'm not going to throw that away for the sake of a home cooked dinner; When I'm alone, it's not worth putting in the effort	Candel, 2001; Jaeger and Meiselman, 2004; Carrigan et al, 2006	Ensure health messages specifically target those with a convenience orientation	Assumes falsely that those individuals with a 'convenience orientation' would necessarily be receptive to diet-related health messages
Systems approach	The way a society functions determines its food habits; McDonald's made me fat	Renner, 1944; Swinburn et al, 1999; Winson, 2004	Change or reject the dominant industrial food system; restrict marketing practices to vulnerable populations	Tendency to overemphasize structural considerations in analysis to the detriment of the understanding that can be contributed by a micro-level qualitative socio-cultural analysis of individual agents, whether they be food provisioners, producers or consumers; problematic if not grounded in a political economy framework
Consumer culture approach	I shop therefore I am	Gofton, 1995; Finkelstein, 2003	Unobtrusive and technological approaches should be taken by the food industry in order to make convenience foods and fast foods more consistent with requirements for healthy diets. Consumers can address any dietary shortcomings by using an 'insurance policy' approach, e.g. taking nutritional supplements, and buying fortified and functional foods to ensure nutritional adequacy of overall intake	Promotes technological and industry-led solutions to a social problem; drives food systems further towards an energy intensive model Encourages the medicalization of food via a medicine-food-industrial complex (see Scrinis, 2008 for an analysis of this development; see also papers by Dixon et al, 2006)

Source: the authors

anti-fast-food subtext in food and health messages), which can help explain some of the current resistance to transferring food provisioning activities from the private sphere in the face of the diminishing domestic time of women in paid employment.

A household production perspective refers to a rather technical interpretation of PFFP – in terms of the efficiency or inefficiency of an intentionally organized system of activity for the achievement of predefined objectives. When female PFFPs discussed the standard of meals, they frequently perceived the standard and/or style of a meal to be directly related to the preparation time available – a pressure felt more acutely in households with young children. Convenience foods in particular were seen as a way to make dinner possible, either in the case of a fully fledged fast-food meal or, alternatively, in a myriad of convenience food shortcuts that facilitated an abbreviated preparation time. In several households, experienced PFFPs took great pride in being efficiency experts, where every aspect of food provisioning was approached with great attention to how the job could be achieved in the least time possible. Sherrie, who held two part-time jobs in addition to having three children at home, typified this view:

> I make sure that I have a well stocked pantry and freezer, then I do a fresh grocery shop every weekend. I would have a pretty good idea of what we would be eating over the week. I'm lucky that there are a lot of meals that I can cook without a recipe ... if I am uninterrupted in the kitchen I can usually meet a scheduled meal time.

The limitations of this approach stem from an exclusive emphasis or overemphasis on household *production*, which restricts the discussion primarily to efficiency solutions and gender equity (that is, spreading the workload). These issues are only part of the problem, however, as the following analysis will make clear.

Convenience orientation (consumer psychology) approach

In contrast to the focus on household production, the disciplinary frame of consumer psychology links convenience-related behaviour to a broader convenience *orientation*. Here, convenience products include not only foods, but also non-food goods and services. Convenience foods can replace meals, beverages and snacks otherwise prepared by hand from mostly unprocessed ingredients, or could represent foods that did not previously exist; dishwashers and microwaves represent labour-saving devices; and paid domestic labour services, where duties include kitchen cleaning and food preparation, appeal to those with a convenience orientation. The convenience orientation approach represents the dominant orientation of commercially motivated market researchers. A convenience orientation is most commonly perceived as an innate or learned personality trait – an individual weakness or orientation – rather than something that evolves from multiple structural factors shaping behaviours (for an elaboration of this broader view, see Beardsworth and Keil, 1992).

The healthy convenience food market, which purports to deliver medicalized lifestyle-compatible dietary options, has emerged as the technological fix for the delivery of the two top consumer demands: convenience and health. But while directly matching market solutions to consumer orientation(s), there is a blurring of what it means to eat healthily.

It has been a popular theme in the literature that a preference for convenience foods sits in opposition to health as a motivation when making food choice decisions (that is, by choosing one, you are by definition rejecting the other). However, a significant proportion of this research has been carried out by engaging university students or other youthful populations as participants, and predates the expansion of the food industry into a healthy convenience food marketplace. In the present study, in contrast, many of the parents went to significant lengths to ensure that time-saving dietary practices were simultaneously aligned to their concept of a good diet for the family. While a convenience orientation was implied by participants with frequent references to 'laziness', this explanation has to be discarded in the light of a broader sociological analysis. The availability of healthy convenience food options also takes the explanation of actual practices beyond a laziness motivation.

Normal weekly menu patterns meant that for working women with young children, and with children who participate in a range of out-of-school activities, planning for other activities – such as community-based activities, and adult fitness and leisure pursuits – needed to have an in-built flexibility. For these PFFPs, planning purposively allowed for meal types that varied in their complexity, preparation time and shopping requirements to allow for situations where time limitations or otherwise constrained circumstances prevented what might fully qualify as a 'proper' meal (Murcott, 1982; Bugge and Almås, 2006). That PFFPs varied the amount of visible effort and measurable time that was made available for food provisioning was more a demonstration of their ability to manage everyday temporal and scheduling conflicts, and in no way implied that the women disregarded the nutritional value of the meal being offered.

Nonetheless, the stereotype of convenience foods as being the choice of lazy people remains strong in the psyche of many, as the following extract reveals. Grace, who combined working full-time in a senior teaching post involving regular after-hours work, caring for an active young family of three children, helping her husband with administrative support in his business, and entertaining from home on a regular basis, persisted in explaining her choice of certain convenience-orientated foods as being the result of her 'laziness'. As Grace explained, 'if I'm feeling particularly lazy, I know they are quite expensive, but [I buy] those bags [of] pre-cut vegetables'.

Grace presented what she sometimes did on a Friday night as not being an optimal way to feed her family. Her inability to muster the energy and effort was posed as a moral deficiency:

> Oh, fish and chips maybe on a Friday night, or a hamburger from the hamburger shop on a Friday night ... I don't know ... [it] just depends how lazy I'm being, sort of thing.

By contrast, Erin was frank in her admission that, as an employed sole parent of two teenagers, cooking at home had minimal appeal, and forcing her teenagers to eat family meals had even less. From her perspective, 'takeaways saved my sanity'. But if she was to be classified as a 'convenience consumer', she came to that orientation and behaviour because of past experiences and a current set of circumstances that left her with limited social support:

> When the kids were young I found that being – I call it 'sergeant major' – everything had to run as clockwork, I was very organized and had to have a diary to see who was doing what every day … I just did everything that needed to be fitted in and to be done. Now that they're teenagers they are much more independent and I find that their activities change so much … if I try to be organized it gets thrown out and then I get frustrated because I'd planned myself around what I'd organized and they throw a spanner in the works – I can't cope with that so I find it much easier now to take each day as it comes and just ride with it.

Erin felt that taking time to talk with both her daughter and her son was something she was conscious of – it just did not centre on the evening meal:

> Sometimes I'll pick the children up from school and I can't be bothered cooking dinner – you know cooking at home is my absolute – you know I hate having to cook at home, the whole idea of having to cook a meal every night, I dread it, so I'll pick the kids up from school and we may sort of say, 'Lets go to Sizzler on the way home?' So it's not a planned activity in that they're both always with me, it might be just one child or occasionally the two.

An emphasis on a convenience orientation approach, as exemplified in Erin's comments, tends to focus on individual personalities, skills or deficiencies:

> All of our friends, they're always cooking and having people over and entertaining. Maybe it might just be me [laughter]. I think it's more my dislike of the added pressures of being a single parent and being the only one who is there to do the running around for them and all that sort of thing – that's just my opinion.

Food system approach

Rather than setting the problem and the solution of convenience consumption within the boundaries of the individual, a food system approach sets out to demonstrate the interrelatedness of food production and processing approaches, and food consumption patterns and nutritional outcomes. According to this approach, a convenience orientation (in a given population) evolves as the result of changes in the ubiquitous industrial food system (because it is difficult for the population to do otherwise). Beyond a certain threshold of conformity, it makes little sense for an individual to 'swim against the tide'. Currently, our social, economic and physical environment promotes the consumption of recreational and non-basic foods that are profitable, energy-dense and nutrient-depleted (Winson, 2004; Drewnowski and Darmon, 2005; Lieberman, 2006; Linn and Novosat, 2008). Evidence from political economy, commodity chain analysis and a range of food system models leads to the conclusion that population dietary habits are increasingly shaped by dominant players in the food retail/ prepared food sectors and in global food processing industries. Convenience in food provisioning is shaped by marketing practices and their effect on making products appear desirable, even necessary (Shove and Southerton, 2000; Hamilton, 2003; Groves, 2004; Brewis and Jack, 2005). In Australia, the last two decades of food and nutrition policy have seen a marked shift in strategic emphasis whereby a systems approach, and changes simultaneously aimed at addressing marketing, economic and regulatory aspects of fast and convenience foods, have moved to centre stage.

The political climate has not always been receptive to this reorientation. The gross denial of this body of literature is illuminated in the mocking Australian media reports and commentaries that accompanied stories of individual litigation and class action suits in the US against the McDonald's corporation for contributing to obesity, with headlines such as 'Judge not swallowing McLawsuit' and 'Fat or fatuous, it's just another feeding frenzy for the killjoys' (Dalton, 2003; McGuinness, 2003). Indeed, media resistance continues to this day. Following a news report from one of a series of Australian Obesity Summits, an editorial in *The Australian* newspaper (25 February 2008) ran with the headline 'Exploding fat myths: We must stop expecting governments to do everything'. The editorial called for less government intervention and more self-control. Four months later, the same newspaper used the release of more conservative estimated trends in Australian childhood obesity rates to reiterate its ideological position in an editorial headed: 'The obesity epidemic that never was: Personal responsibility, not moral panic, is the key' (2 June 2008). Such media reports reflect a continued sympathy with pro-capitalist, laissez-faire, libertarian perspectives that project hostility at any suggestion, however evidence based, that we are not masters of our own diet.

In contrast, elements of popular culture have become highly critical of the food system in recent times, though such criticism is commonly paired with a celebration of the mavericks that rebel against the system and garner all their forces to act against the tide. In this study, PFFPs criticized, rebelled against and were distrustful of the food supply system. For some, like Jill, this was a dominant theme when she spoke about feeding her family. She and her husband Jamie commented on several occasions that they distrusted the fresh fruit and vegetable produce in supermarkets, were fearful of inaccurate labelling on imported foods, and were repeatedly disappointed with the quality of restaurant meals, even after careful and deliberate venue selection:

The food supply is now rubbish! I see how some of [my son's] friends eat. I've observed them at school and what they say when they come over for a play ... there is really some odd responses to how we eat [laughter]. I can't fathom it ... why would their parents let them eat like that? But it's everywhere isn't it? We choose to make the effort, but most people don't, do they? The food [fast food] is everywhere, it just overtakes them. I understand that, but it makes me sad. It's such a loss.

To compensate, Jill and Jamie injected significant energy into home provisioning, which included activities such as weekly market shopping, home bread baking, extensive 'scratch cooking' (where one starts from scratch with lots of relatively unprocessed ingredients), and homemade edible gifts for family, friends and work colleagues.

To view convenience food consumption purely as the consequence of an industrialized food system leaves food and nutrition policy-makers with two options: reorient the food system, or amplify messages about personal and parental responsibilities to choose good diets – strategies that people have unequal capacity to embrace. Neoliberal governments have so far mounted only weak responses to the former; hence the weight of political power has been directed at promoting the latter. Governmental responses have failed to take into account the full symbolic meaning or the socio-material aspects of convenience foods, and the changing attitudes to mundane aspects of food work that are now commonplace.

Consumer culture approach

The consumer culture approach proceeds from the assumption of a consumer society – generally considered to be a 20th century phenomenon (Schor, 1992) – in which the vast majority of people have a consumerist attitude or are living consumerist lifestyles. In a consumer culture, it makes sense for the market-place to be the source of solutions to limited or constrained time for food provisioning. In response, the convenience market-place has become increasingly proficient at providing alternatives for domestic food provisioning. In this approach, a convenience orientation represents a cultural shift in the way that people on the whole behave, rather than representing an identified personality trait. For all the discussion of 'Slow Food' (both the movement and the ethos) among the cultural élite, its prestige is inversely proportional to its accessibility and adoption. It is fast, convenient, food that has tangible status as modern food; it has become the motif for modern Australian society (Finkelstein, 2003), perhaps more so than in societies with an entrenched and historically rooted culinary culture. In a period where time scarcity has become a symbol of modernity (Godbey et al, 1998; Larsson and Sanne, 2005; Southerton and Tomlinson, 2005), the type of food that fits with this lifestyle must be suitably 'labour-lite', high-tech, minimalistic and streamlined. In consumerist societies there is a particular way of relating to consumer goods in which they take on central importance in the construction of culture, identity and social life.

In this study PFFPs, not unsurprisingly, looked to the market-place for solutions; however, they also looked for reassurance that matters of quality and health were not being undermined. Meal replacements for unplanned meals, or for one-off or extended periods when time for domestic food provisioning was significantly curtailed, were still considered in terms of their health implications – an occasional family fast-food meal was sanctioned because it was believed that the overall balance of the diet was retained, whereas more extensive replacement of homemade meals was only undertaken where PFFPs were convinced that nutritionally the meal was comparable.

It was a matter of pride for many of the PFFPs to be able to 'solve the problem of how to feed the family', and utilizing what the market-place had to offer was integral to their resolution of the problem. According to Sarah 'frozen organic kiddies' meals help us out ... I feel fine serving these because I am confident about what goes into them'.

Another way that the market provided solutions entailed a more medicalized view of the diet where vitamin and mineral supplements could be purchased and provided as an 'insurance policy' in case anything was lacking in the diet. Mia's concerns over her two daughters – which included a failure to display average growth patterns and episodes of constipation – were addressed in this way after consultation with her family doctor. As Mia stated, 'with the girls, they have good appetites now, but at various times I've had concerns ... and I now feel a lot more confident with them both taking a multivitamin every day'.

Overall, this study has shown that the diversified market-place was recognized by PFFPs as providing 'solutions' that could save time and support nutritional and social requirements, while also providing an insurance policy to address residual health concerns. Discourse analysis has revealed that each frame offers a different way of understanding dietary practices in general, and convenience foods and services, in particular. However, each is limited in its focus on only one dimension of food consumption. Moreover, ethnographic inquiry suggests that none of these approaches adequately takes account of how the everyday, repetitive and mundane dietary practices of PFFPs are constructed. Rather, prevailing social science explanations of everyday dietary practices reinforce the hegemony of these paradigms.

Using ethnographic data to better understand family food provisioning

The ability of ethnographic approaches to integrate micro-level, intermediate and macro-level data means they have significant potential to improve our understanding of the processes involved in contemporary dietary practices. Despite this potential, the use of these methods is infrequently reported in nutrition behaviour studies published in mainstream nutrition journals. To date, this approach has also had a limited role in informing current food and nutrition policy approaches addressing rising rates of diet-related chronic diseases.

In this study, household food strategies – largely portrayed as solutions to the problem of how to feed household members – were shaped by a complex of influences, including household resources, social institutions and moral responsibilities. Convenience foods are most often represented as something that enables consumers to save time and effort in food activities related to shopping, meal preparation and cooking, and consumption and post-meal activities (Buckley et al, 2007). Convenience foods also have symbolic (sometimes iconic) value, and the selection and/or incorporation of specific convenience food categories or types into dietary practices is mediated via a moral economy of care (McDowell et al, 2005), as well as household resources such as disposable economic capital, cultural knowledge and kitchen skills.

The defensiveness of, and self-deprecating comments made by, female PFFPs when discussing the quality of family meals and their efforts to ensure that household members were well fed was clearly evident in the interviews. Even when the task was clearly seen as a burden or a nuisance, no participant imagined any alternative to the private sphere and immediate household members in maintaining responsibility for managing family food provisioning. Gender roles were discussed, with men's relatively low contribution to food provisioning tasks being a point of contention. That said, efforts to challenge traditional gender ideologies pertaining to food provisioning work were only evident in a small number of dual income households.

Women who accepted their role of PFFP referred to juggling work commitments, family care and housework in ways that required a high level of organization (often at a personal cost), multi-tasking and long working days. As well, room for flexibility and contingency plans was deemed essential when less than optimal conditions arose. The reality of food provisioning thus involves a complex negotiation of strategies and priorities in households constrained in the amount of time available for food provisioning. While 'good nutrition' was identified as a desirable outcome for family members, and especially children, the household production of health was also managed through decisions that minimized stress, and balanced household production and food preparation outsourcing.

While the versatility and adaptability of PFFPs was clear in their own accounts of daily food provisioning practices, responses to questions regarding attitudes to convenience and fast foods and motivations for their use nonetheless tended to revert to one of the four disciplinary conceptual frames already identified and discussed. In the research reported here, women most often spoke about their roles in ways that reflected the categories identified in the literature; that is, in ways that were familiar, in that they reflected common media and cultural representations, were part of everyday language, and resonated with shared patterns and dominant voices.

When healthy eating messages repeatedly link ideas of good food and eating well to home-based food provisioning – 'Cook unprocessed foods.' 'Cook at home.' 'Convenience foods are risky' – the language and images widely used to transmit these messages perpetuate and reinforce assumptions around the right way to feed families, and the traditional gender ideology attached to this role. They rely on nostalgic models of what it is to eat well and feel well, without recourse to the 'ample evidence that food processing, family organization, gender roles and the nature of social bonds have all undergone profound change' (Poulain, 2002, p54).

In so much as it serves the interest of centrally constructed public health and nutrition messages to deconstruct/reconstruct notions of healthy eating, a rethinking of the fundamental attitudes to, responsibilities for and organization of domestic food provisioning is now needed. An analysis of these activities, akin to a social impact assessment that incorporates a consideration of dependency food work, would assist in the formulation of policies that aim to achieve improved population diets and to promote greater nutritional equity (without penalty to those carrying the bulk of its responsibility) by grounding such policies in the everyday reality of food provisioning.

A new ethos for culinary modernism

Rachel Laudan (2001), a food historian who writes expertly on population dietary change in both the distant and recent past, has criticized the trend to lambast culinary modernism by treating it ahistorically, by mistaking its excesses for its essence, and by refusing to acknowledge its essential utility. The essence of this message has been that the foods of culinary modernism are 'egalitarian, available more or less equally to all, without demanding the disproportionate amount of the resources of time or money that traditional foodstuffs did – [and thus allowing] us unparalleled choices not just of diet but of what to do with our lives' (Laudan, 2001, p42). The modern gastronome is more frequently adept at contrasting iconic 'junk food' with local artisan produce than with the numerous examples of affordable and still nutritious foods made possible by industrial processes. Of course the former contrast creates an evocative dichotomy, but the latter is perhaps even more important today and is brought into sharp focus when issues of nutritional equity are made central to the analysis. Laudan contends that the virtues of modern food need to be seriously considered and built into a new culinary ethos, one that:

> comes to terms with contemporary, industrial food, not one that dismisses it, an ethos that opens choices for everyone, not one that closes them so that a few can enjoy their labour, and an ethos that does not prejudge, but decides case by case when natural is preferable to processed, fresh to preserved, old to new, slow to fast, artisan to industrial (Laudan, 2001, p43).

One can follow this line of thought and still focus a critical gaze on the overabundance of highly processed foods, the largely unregulated food marketing environment that tips the scales towards a highly processed diet, and the political economy of the food retail sector. It is a nuanced argument in which a mature community of food and public health professionals and researchers should be engaged.

Taken seriously by food and nutrition policy-makers, such a stance could contribute to broader debates about how, as a society, we want to organize the feeding of cohabiting family members and, increasingly, of diverse household types. This discussion could encompass whose role it is to do the work, where meals are to be consumed and with whom, what food skills are worth retaining (and what new skills are worth developing), and how the food industry that is increasingly responsible for providing prepared meals should be regulated. Currently, debates about these topics are suffocated by moral posturing and the pervasive rhetoric associated with both gender norms and good diets. Liberating these debates would in itself be a good start.

Sociologically grounded accounts along these lines bring a sense of optimism to contemporary food habits and future directions (Beardsworth and Keil, 1997; Poulain, 2002). Based on a study of French food habits, Poulain (2002) offers a positive interpretation of the changes in contemporary food patterns that rids new habits of notions of infringement and guilt. He notes the poor fit between the mix of 21st century conditions shaping modern food habits to older, but still commonly promoted, habits (for example, three structured meals per day with snack avoidance). In a similar vein, Beardsworth and Keil (1992) refer to 'foodways in flux' to suggest that food habits are a potential barometer of social change.

In much the same way that critical analyses of the food system are opening up new possibilities on the production side, so critical micro-level studies can enliven debate and broaden options on the practical matter of ensuring that household members are well fed. In the main, the debate has not moved beyond an unhelpful position that espouses private responsibility by rational individuals, one that is silent on the gendered nature of this work. Further insights from feminist ethics and social policy literatures could draw on critical multi-disciplinary perspectives yet to be explored in the contemporary context.

Conclusion

This chapter has sought to highlight the limitations of prevailing attempts to clarify and explain why consumers in mainstream society have embraced convenience and fast foods. It also posits reasons why the fast-food alternative has surfaced in the late 20th and early 21st centuries as an increasingly accepted alternative to a more home-centred food production model.

Both professional and lay discourses offering explanations for contemporary convenience food consumption largely fall into one of the four frameworks presented here: household production, convenience orientation, food system, and consumer culture. By combining an analysis of these discourses in the social science research literature with interview data from an ethnographic study, the limitations of these approaches become clear. Importantly, despite quite divergent disciplinary frameworks, some common problems in the findings – including flaws in logic, a limiting ideology of personal responsibility and decontextualized data – mar their functional utility when transferring their lessons to food and nutrition policy.

Approaches that better integrate structure and agency in their understanding of dietary practices, that acknowledge both consumption and production in the household economy, and that attempt to provide a historically situated understanding of the convenience food and food provision service market-place, offer an opportunity to reinvigorate debate about population nutrition as enacted at the household level.

References

Ahuja, R. and Walker, M. (1994) 'Female-headed single parent families: Comparisons with dual parent households on restaurant and convenience food usage', *Journal of Consumer Marketing*, vol 11, pp41–54

Beardsworth, A. and Keil, T. (1992) 'Foodways in flux: From gastro-anomy to menu pluralism?' *British Food Journal*, vol 94, pp20–25

Beardsworth, A. and Keil, T. (1997) *Sociology on the Menu: An Invitation to the Study of Food and Society*, Routledge, London

Brewis, J. and Jack, G. (2005) 'Pushing speed? The marketing of fast and convenient food', *Consumption, Markets and Culture*, vol 8, pp49–67

Buckley, M., Cowan, C. and McCarthy, M. (2007) 'The convenience food market in Great Britain: Convenience food lifestyle (CFL) segments', *Appetite*, vol 49, pp600–617

Bugge, A. and Almås, R. (2006) 'Domestic dinner: Representations and practices of a proper meal among young suburban mothers', *Journal of Consumer Culture*, vol 6, pp203–228

Candel, M. (2001) 'Consumers' convenience orientation towards meal preparation: Conceptualization and measurement', *Appetite*, vol 36, pp15–28

Carrigan, M., Szmigin, I. and Leek, S. (2006) 'Managing routine food choices in UK families: The role of convenience consumption', *Appetite*, vol 47, pp372–383

Dalton, R. (2003) 'Judge not swallowing McLawsuit', *The Australian*, 24 January, p8

Devine, C. M., Connors, M. M., Sobal, J. and Bisogni, C. A. (2003) 'Sandwiching it in: Spillover of work onto food choices and family roles in low- and moderate income urban households', *Social Science and Medicine*, vol 56, pp617–630

Dixon, J., Hinde, S. and Banwell, C. (2006) 'Obesity, convenience and "phood"', *British Food Journal*, vol 108, pp634–644

Drewnowski, A. and Darmon, N. (2005) 'Food choices and diet costs: An economic analysis', *Journal of Nutrition*, vol 135, pp900–904

Finkelstein, J. (2003) 'The taste of boredom: McDonaldization and Australian food culture', *American Behavioural Scientist*, vol 47, pp187–200

Godbey, G., Lifset, R. and Robinson, J. (1998) 'No time to waste: An exploration of time use, attitudes towards time, and the generation of municipal solid waste', *Social Research*, vol 65, pp101–140

Gofton, L. (1995) 'Convenience and the moral status of consumer practices', in D. Marshall (ed) *Food Choice and the Consumer*, Blackie Academic and Professional, London

Groves, D. (2004) 'Gob smacked! TV dining in Australia between 1956 and 1966', *The Journal of Popular Culture*, vol 37, pp409–417

Hamilton, S. (2003) 'The economies and conveniences of modern-day living: Frozen foods and mass marketing, 1945–1965', *Business History Review*, vol 77, pp33–60

Jabs, J. and Devine, C. (2006) 'Time scarcity and food choices: An overview', *Appetite*, vol 47, pp196–204

Jaeger, S. and Meiselman, H. (2004) 'Perceptions of meal convenience: The case of at-home evening meals', *Appetite*, vol 42, pp317–325

Larsson, J. and Sanne, C. (2005) 'Self-help books on avoiding time shortage', *Time and Society*, vol 14, pp213–230

Laudan, R. (2001) 'A plea for culinary modernism: Why we should love new, fast, processed food', *Gastronomica: The Journal of Food and Culture*, vol 1, pp36–44

Lieberman, L. (2006) 'Evolutionary and anthropological perspectives on optimal foraging in obesogenic environments', *Appetite*, vol 47, pp3–9

Linn, S. and Novosat, C. (2008) 'Calories for sale: Food marketing to children in the twenty first century', *The ANNALS of the American Academy of Political and Social Science*, vol 615, pp133–155

McDowell, L., Ray, K., Perrons, D., Fagan, C. and Ward, K. (2005) 'Women's paid work and moral economies of care', *Social and Cultural Geography*, vol 6, pp219–235

McGuinness, P. (2003) 'Fat or fatuous, it's just another feeding frenzy for the killjoys', *The Sydney Morning Herald*, 11 February, p11

Murcott, A. (1982) 'It's a pleasure to cook for him: Food, meal times and gender in South Wales households', in E. Gamarnikow, D. Morgan, J. Purvis and D. Taylorson (eds) *The Public and the Private*, Heinemann, London

Nader, L. (1972) 'Up the anthropologist – Perspectives gained from studying up', in D. Hymes (ed.), *Reinventing Anthropology*, Pantheon Books, New York

Poulain, J. (2002) 'The contemporary diet in France: "De-structuration" or from commensalism to "vagabond feeding"', *Appetite*, vol 39, pp43–55

Renner, H. (1944) *The Origin of Food Habits*, Faber and Faber, London

Scholderer, J. and Grunert, K. G. (2005) 'Consumers, food and convenience: The long way from resource constraints to actual consumption patterns', *Journal of Economic Psychology*, vol 26, pp105–128

Schor, J. (1992) *The Overworked American: The Unexpected Decline of Leisure*, Basic Books, New York

Schubert, L. (2008) 'Household food strategies and the reframing of ways of understanding dietary practices', *Ecology of Food and Nutrition*, vol 47, pp254–279

Scrinis, G. (2008) 'Functional foods or functionally marketed foods? A critique of, and alternatives to, the category of "functional foods"', *Public Health Nutrition*, vol 11, pp541–545

Shore, C. and Nugent, S. (eds) (2002) *Elite Cultures: Anthropological Perspectives*, Routledge, London

Shove, E. and Southerton, D. (2000) 'Defrosting the freezer: From novelty to convenience', *Journal of Material Culture*, vol 5, pp301–319

Southerton, D. and Tomlinson, M. (2005) '"Pressed for time" – the differential impacts of a "time squeeze"', *The Sociological Review*, vol 53, pp215–239

Swinburn, B., Egger, G. and Raza, F. (1999) 'Dissecting obesogenic environments: The development and application of a framework for identifying and prioritizing environmental interventions for obesity', *Preventative Medicine*, vol 29, pp563–70

Winson, A. (2004) 'Bringing political economy into the debate on the obesity epidemic', *Agriculture and Human Values*, vol 21, pp299–312

9
Public Health and Moral Panic: Sociological Perspectives on the 'Epidemic of Obesity'

Stewart Lockie and Susan Williams

Introduction

In 2007, the number of people worldwide who were chronically underfed reached 923 million, some 75 million more than in 2003–2005 (FAO, 2008). By contrast, in 1999, over 1 billion adults and approximately 18 million children were overweight or obese (WHO, 2000). Neither rising food prices, nor rising food insecurity among the world's poor – especially landless and female-headed households (FAO, 2008) – appear to be slowing the spread of weight gain and obesity, a trend that has been associated, in particular, with populations undergoing socio-economic transformations associated with urbanization, modernization and globalization (WHO, 2000).

While the term 'epidemic' has been used to describe changes in the prevalence of obesity in developed countries such as the US and UK since at least the early 1990s, the World Health Organization's Consultation on Obesity in 1997 drew attention to the increasingly global nature of weight gain and obesity, observing that:

> *As standards of living continue to rise, weight gain and obesity are posing a growing threat to health in countries all over the world ... both developed and developing ... and affecting children as well as adults. Indeed, it is now so common that it is replacing the more traditional public health concerns, including undernutrition and infectious disease, as one of the most significant contributors to ill health* (WHO, 2000, pp1–2).

Further, the paradoxical coexistence of undernutrition and weight gain should not be viewed exclusively at the global level. Households containing both overweight and underweight individuals (generally obese adults and malnourished children) are common in middle-income countries (Prentice, 2006; see also Doak et al, 2005). At the same time, the diet of obese individuals is often nutritionally inadequate due to the predominance of energy-dense foods that are high in fat and/or sugar, but low in fibre, vitamins and minerals (Markovic and Natoli, 2009).

What does it mean, though, to be overweight or obese? These conditions are generally defined in terms of fat accumulation that is sufficient to increase the risk of psychosocial and/or medical morbidity. There are several ways in which this may be calculated. The body mass index (BMI) has been most widely used in epidemiological research since the 1970s as a convenient, acceptably accurate and low-cost measure of adiposity (or fatness) (Eknoyan, 2008). BMI is calculated as weight (kg)/height (m)^2. In adults, four BMI categories are used: underweight (<18.5), normal weight (18.5–24.9), overweight (25–29.9) and obese (>30) (WHO, 2006). By contrast, international measures for children and adolescents are age- and gender-specific to allow for the significant variability in age-related growth patterns. In adults, the interpretation of risk associated with BMI may also differ for different populations – especially for Asian and Pacific populations (WHO, 2006). The use of BMI in public health has been challenged, however, on the basis that its generalizability to non-Anglo Saxon populations and its sensitivity as a measure of adiposity are questionable. Although BMI correlates with total body fat, it is poorly correlated with fat distribution – particularly excess visceral abdominal fat, which is strongly associated with many obesity-related conditions such as cardiovascular disease, Type 2 diabetes and colon cancer (Field et al, 2001; Larsson and Wolk, 2007).

Despite these limitations, weight gain and obesity as defined by BMI are associated with increased risk of developing a number of health problems (see Table 9.1) including cardiovascular disease, Type 2 diabetes, osteoarthritis and some cancers. The risk of disease increases with increasing BMI (WHO, 2006). In Australia, the most significant obesity-related conditions (in terms of burden of disease) are cardiovascular disease (including coronary heart disease, stroke, hypertension, heart failure and peripheral vascular disease) and Type 2 diabetes. Cardiovascular disease is the leading cause of death and the second leading cause of disease burden in Australia (AIHW, 2008), with obesity attributed as the primary cause in 21.3 per cent of cases (Diabetes Australia, 2008). Type 2 diabetes is projected to be the leading specific cause of disease burden for males – and the second leading cause for females – by 2023 (AIHW, 2008). Similarly, obesity is recognized as the primary cause of 23.8 per cent of Type 2 diabetes cases (Diabetes Australia, 2008).

With such a substantial burden of disease attributed to weight gain and obesity, it is far from surprising that these conditions are so frequently framed in both the scientific literature and the mass media as an epidemic. Indeed, we would argue that the framing of obesity as an epidemic was so pervasive by

Table 9.1 *Relative risk of health problems associated with obesity*

Relative risk	Associated with metabolic consequences	Associated with weight
Greatly increased	Type 2 diabetes Gall bladder disease Hypertension Dyslipidaemia (raised blood lipids such as cholesterol) Insulin resistance Atherosclerosis	Sleep apnoea Breathlessness Asthma Social isolation/depression Daytime sleepiness/fatigue
Moderately increased	Coronary heart disease Stroke Gout/hyperuricaemia	Osteoarthritis Respiratory disease Hernia Psychological problems
Slightly increased	Cancer (breast, endometrial, colon) Reproductive abnormalities Impaired fertility Polycystic ovaries Skin complications Cataract	Varicose veins Musculo-skeletal problems Bad back Stress incontinence Oedema/cellulitis

Source: Australian Government (2009)

the late 1990s that it became the dominant narrative, or discourse, on weight gain and obesity. Researchers and medical professionals used the term with little or no qualification: the 'epidemic of obesity' screamed out of newspaper headlines. Yet, in more recent years, it seems that for every headline alerting readers to the spread and dangers of obesity there is another that questions the veracity of the epidemic narrative. For example, in January 2009, most of Australia's major newspapers carried stories claiming that the obesity epidemic was an illusion and, more specifically, that the childhood obesity epidemic was a myth. In the following month, the very same newspapers claimed, in contrast, that the childhood obesity epidemic was now affecting babies. While the latter claims are no less pervasive, the obesity epidemic narrative is increasingly used as a point of departure from which to debate the accuracy and consequences of claims regarding increasing body weight. The pervasiveness of this narrative, and the contestable knowledge claims associated with it, are worthy of sociological attention.

Our objectives in this chapter are twofold. The first is to review the existing evidence regarding changing patterns of weight gain and obesity with a view to establishing whether or not this is an issue that has claimed the attention of sociologists and other social scientists. The second is to review sociological contributions to the understanding of weight gain and obesity, and to comment on where a sociological research agenda might productively focus. While Australian data will be the focus of our empirical attention, empirical and theoretical contributions will also be drawn from a variety of countries for comparative purposes. This analysis indicates that there is very little about the obesity epidemic that is unique to Australia, or to anywhere else.

Are we witnessing an epidemic? Changing patterns of weight gain and obesity

The 1999–2000 Australian Diabetes, Obesity and Lifestyle Study found that rates of weight gain and obesity among urban Australian adults (calculated according to BMI using measured data) were 39 per cent and 21 per cent, respectively (Cameron et al, 2002). The prevalence of weight gain was considerably higher among men (48 per cent) than among women (30 per cent), while the prevalence of obesity was slightly lower among men (19 per cent) than among women (22 per cent). These rates were comparable with those reported for other developed countries, including the UK (17 per cent for men and 21 per cent for women) and Germany (19 per cent and 21 per cent), but slightly lower than those reported for the US (28 per cent and 33 per cent). Consistent across all of these countries was a steady increase in obesity, calculated according to BMI, with age, with levels peaking in the 55–64 year age group (Cameron et al, 2002). The 1995 data for Australian children (2–18 years) indicate that 15 per cent of boys and 16 per cent of girls were overweight at that time, and a further 5 per cent of both groups were obese (Magarey et al, 2001).

There are at least five aspects of obesity and overweight prevalence data that contribute to the construction of obesity as an epidemic or crisis. First, the data indicate a considerable increase in the prevalence of obesity, which more than doubled in both the US and Australia between 1980 and 2000 (Cameron et al, 2002). Even more dramatically, the prevalence of obesity among Australian boys (7–15 years old) more than tripled between 1985 and 1995, while the prevalence among girls in the same age group increased fourfold (Magarey et al, 2001). Since 2000, the data indicate that the prevalence of obesity in Australia may have stabilized, or at least that the rate of increase has slowed (see ABS, 1997, 2006; Barr et al, 2006; Gill et al, 2009). However, this brings us to the second aspect of obesity prevalence data of relevance here: namely, that irrespective of whether rates are stable or growing, approximately one in five adults in Australia and other developed nations are now classified as obese, and a further one in two as overweight. Crudely put, a lot of people are affected by weight gain and obesity, and are therefore likely to be affected by one or more associated health problems. The third indication of a crisis is that obesity and weight gain affect some groups more than others. In Australia, such groups among the adult population include those who have not completed a tertiary education, who come from a low income household, and/or who live in an area of relative disadvantage (ABS, 2007). Indigenous women, moreover, are 1.4 times more likely to be obese than the general population of Australian women (Phillips, 2008). Residents of outer regional, remote and very remote areas are classified as obese at higher rates (23 per cent) than are residents of inner regional areas (19 per cent) and major cities (17 per cent). A recent study of two rural areas in the Australian states of Victoria and South Australia reported 30 per cent of participants as obese, and 39 per cent as overweight (Janus et al, 2007). This correlation between obesity and various forms of social disadvantage leads some to argue that obesity needs to be seen as much as a social justice issue as a public health issue (Monaghan, 2005).

A fourth area of concern is the escalation of overweight and obesity among children, along with the recognition that overweight and obese children are more likely than their peers both to experience obesity as adults and to suffer disproportionate rates of chronic disease at younger ages (Speiser et al, 2005; Gill et al, 2009). These issues amplify the moral dimension of obesity narratives and either introduce, or reinforce, issues around parenting, maternal nutrition, advertising, schooling and so on. The fifth and final issue of relevance here is that high rates of weight gain and obesity are not solely a characteristic of the developed North, but also increasingly affect the populations of Asia, Latin America, the Middle East, Africa and the Pacific (Prentice, 2006). The so-called nutrition transition – the replacement of traditional diets, which are high in cereals and vegetables, with energy-dense Western diets – appears to accompany processes of urbanization and industrialization just as surely as do motorized transport, sedentary employment and passive entertainment (Popkin, 2001). Much like a pathogen-induced epidemic, therefore, the spread of historically high rates of weight gain and obesity has a spatial dimension, beginning in the US and thence spreading to Europe, to settler states such as Australia, and on to emerging economies and beyond (Prentice, 2006).

At a time when the proportion of residents of a given area that are now classified as obese has reached somewhere between a third and a half, the sheer visibility of seemingly excessive and potentially dangerous body fat is surely of concern. Yet, there are several aspects of the obesity epidemic narrative that have attracted criticism. One set of criticisms, which are related to the consequences of constructing the issue of changes in bodyweight as an 'epidemic', will be dealt with later in this chapter. Here, we are concerned with a second set of criticisms focused on the understanding of overweight and obesity from an epidemiological point of view.

To begin, it is alleged that the rate and level of increase in bodyweight has been overstated. According to Campos et al (2006) what we have seen has not been the exponential growth pattern typical of epidemics, but rather a small 'skewing' to the right of the population distribution of BMI – one that amounts to nothing more than an average weight gain among American adults of 3–5 kilograms over the course of a generation. In turn, these authors claim that such a small gain can be explained by the consumption of as little as 10 extra calories by an individual, the equivalent of a few minutes' less walking every day. While this weight gain has tipped many people over the threshold BMI values that are used to classify them as overweight or obese, the argument goes that this is likely to have few meaningful consequences for health. In particular, Campos et al (2006) claim there is limited evidence that anything other than extreme obesity is associated with increased mortality and that there are more documented risks from being underweight and from what is known as 'weight cycling' (or yoyo dieting) than there are from being overweight (see also Monaghan, 2005; Blair and LaMonte, 2006). They also claim that there are only a small number of conditions for which causal relationships have been established between fat tissue and disease, suggesting that statistical associations between weight gain/obesity and chronic disease may be better explained by treating obesity as a symptom of disease rather than as a risk factor. The poor record of public health interventions in encouraging long-term weight loss is also raised as an issue based on the documented risks of several weight loss methods, including diet drugs, surgery, eating disorders and fad diets, as well as the evidence that improving aerobic activity and fitness improves health independently of effects on bodyweight (see also Lee et al, 1999; Farrell et al, 2002; Monaghan, 2005; Blair and LaMonte, 2006). From this evidence, it is argued that the obesity epidemic narrative distracts attention from the far more important and achievable task of promoting higher levels of physical activity.

How robust is this argument? Certainly, it does not seem to square with the US Department of Agriculture's estimates that the 'average American' consumes almost 25 per cent more energy compared to that consumed 30 years ago (Rigby, 2006). However, focusing on what the average person living in any country does and does not do is potentially misleading. Campos et al's (2006) argument that shifting the BMI distribution curve at a particular population level translates into small average changes in bodyweight among individuals within that population misses the point of studying distributions in the first place. Changes in average weight – or even average BMI – are not particularly useful indicators of public health due to the potential for those individuals and sub-populations whose weight has not changed to pull down the average, and thus to mask weight gains among other sub-populations that are rather higher than average (Kim and Popkin, 2006). What is of interest, then, is how many people fall within problem categories, where those people come from, what has predisposed them to excessive weight gain and so on. It is well established, as discussed above, that some ethnic, socio-economic and other sub-populations experience significantly higher rates of weight gain and obesity than do others. In the US, increases in bodyweight have also been greater among adults already in the overweight and obese categories than among those in the normal weight category, resulting in a large increase in the proportion of people classified as morbidly obese (Kim and Popkin, 2006).

Further to these issues of classification is the misleading suggestion that increasing bodyweight has few negative health consequences, and that the re-classification of BMI with weight gain is purely arbitrary. Kim and Popkin (2006) accept Campos et al's (2006) argument that the relationships between BMI, adiposity (fatness), nutrition, physical activity and chronic health are complex and not always well understood. They also agree that nutrition and physical activity may each impact on chronic disease independently of any interaction with weight gain or obesity (see also Blair and LaMonte, 2006). It does not follow from this, however, that overweight and obesity do not function either as intermediate conditions, or as direct causes of chronic disease. Rigby (2006), for example, reports that only small changes in weight are required to increase risks of chronic disease starting from a normal weight BMI of around 21. He also points out that, in addition to mortality, there are a number of issues around quality of life and disability that warrant consideration in any assessment of the consequences of weight gain and obesity. Similarly, Hillier et al (2006; see also Blair and LaMonte, 2006) show that metabolic syndrome can be alleviated with modest weight loss. That consistent and long-term weight loss has proven difficult to achieve across so many public health interventions only suggests, according to Lawlor and Chaturvedi (2006), that extra importance should be attributed to prevention and to understanding key points of intervention during the life cycle.

Critics of obesity epidemiology highlight a number of important issues; namely, the complexity and uncertainty surrounding aspects of the relationship between BMI and health, the importance of targeting all risk factors for chronic disease and not simply the most visible, and the danger of assuming that an individual's bodyweight is the primary cause of chronic health conditions. Yet, this does not amount to a compelling case to dismiss weight gain and obesity as public health issues. Uncertainties and knowledge gaps may, in fact, contribute to an underestimation of the burden of disease arising from obesity (Canoy and Buchan, 2007). They may also be expected to contribute to what Dixon and Winter (2007) refer to as an environment of 'competing authorities', which exposes consumers to multiple conflicting messages – an environment that may have its own unmeasured impact on obesity epidemiology.

Causes of overweight and obesity

The prevailing view among health authorities is that weight gain and obesity result from a chronic imbalance between energy intake and energy expenditure (with intake exceeding expenditure) over an extended period of time (WHO, 2000). If we eat too much and/or exercise too little, we will get fat. However, the increasing prevalence of weight gain and obesity is not seen to result solely from overconsumption and inactivity, but from a range of environmental, social and behavioural factors that interact to determine energy intake and expenditure (WHO, 2000). Swinburn et al (2004) summarize those behavioural and environmental factors often put forward to explain weight gain and obesity, along with the strength of evidence currently available for each factor (see Table 9.2). They find 'convincing' evidence that factors such as sedentary lifestyles and a high intake of energy-dense foods increase the risk of weight gain/obesity. Heavy marketing of both energy-dense foods and fast-food outlets, as well as adverse social and economic conditions and the consumption of high-sugar drinks are identified to be 'probable' risk factors. Large portion sizes, frequent eating out, and yoyo dieting (rigid restraint followed by binge eating) are classified as 'possible' risk factors, while insufficient data are deemed available to determine the influence of alcohol on weight gain and obesity.

Physical activity and nutrition emerge from this analysis as the least controversial contributors to weight gain and obesity. Despite concerns that Australians are less active than in the past, physical activity patterns have remained relatively constant over the last 10 years. Moreover, approximately half of all adults are considered sufficiently active (AIHW, 2008) as to significantly reduce their risk

Table 9.2 *Evidence table for factors that might promote or protect against weight gain and obesity*

Evidence*	Decreases risk	No relationship	Increases risk
Convincing	Regular physical activity High dietary NSP (non-starch polysaccharides/fibre intake)		Sedentary lifestyles High intake of energy-dense foods#
Probable	Home and school environments that support healthy food choices for children Breastfeeding		Heavy marketing of energy-dense foods and fast-food outlets Adverse social and economic conditions (developed countries, especially for women) High-sugar drinks
Possible	Low Glycemic Index foods	Protein content of the diet	Large portion sizes High proportion of food prepared outside the home (western countries) 'Rigid restraint/periodic disinhibition' eating
Insufficient	Increased Eating frequency		Alcohol

Source: Swinburn et al (2004)

*Strength of evidence: the totality of the evidence was taken into account. The World Cancer Research Fund schema was taken as a starting point and was modified in the following manner: randomised controlled trials were given prominence as the highest ranking study design (RCTs not a major source of cancer evidence); associated evidence was also taken into account in relation to environmental determinants (direct trials were usually not available or possible).

#Energy-dense foods are high in fat and/or sugar; energy-dilute foods are high in non-starch polysaccharides (dietary fibre) and water, such as fruit, legumes, vegetables and whole grain cereals.

of cardiovascular disease, stroke, hypertension, Type 2 diabetes, osteoporosis, obesity, colon cancer, breast cancer, anxiety and depression (CDCP, 1996). There is a significant overlap, therefore, between those groups classified as overweight/obese and those classified as sufficiently active (independent of their BMI) to reduce the risk of chronic disease. Limited data are available on the total energy intake of Australians. However, the 2004–2005 National Health Survey found that the majority of Australians did not meet current nutrition guidelines – with 86 per cent consuming less than five servings of vegetables each day, 46 per cent consuming less than two servings of fruit each day, and with saturated fat accounting for 13 per cent of total energy intake (compared to the recommended level of <10 per cent) (NHMRC, 2003). Consuming more fruit and vegetables, and limiting the intake of high-fat foods reduces the total energy density of diets, thereby moderating weight gain and promoting weight maintenance (Savage et al, 2008). Australian studies have found that men, and people of lower socio-economic status, are more likely to have sub-optimal intakes of fruit and vegetables (AIHW, 2008).

As noted above, the importance of environmental and social factors in the prevalence of weight gain and obesity suggests that the task is not simply one of convincing people to eat a more nutritious diet – albeit, a more positive message than convincing them to eat less – and to take more exercise. Rather, the task is one of addressing the various ways in which contemporary societies have come to constitute what is referred to as an obesogenic, or obesity promoting, environment. Dixon and Broom (2007) summarize the features of the obesogenic environment in terms of the commodification of food preparation and leisure; time pressures; changing parenting practices such as the increasing treatment of children as 'consumers'; technology and sedentarization; car reliance; aggressive marketing; and competing/confusing messages about food and health. The interrelationships between these features are reflected in data concerning food consumption outside the home. In Australia, food purchased and consumed away from home now accounts for approximately one-quarter of total energy intake (Magarey et al, 2006). Consumption of foods purchased from fast-food outlets is becoming a regular behaviour for many people, with approximately one-quarter of Australians consuming fast food for dinner at least once per week (Scully et al, 2008) and the average Australian family spending 15 per cent of their food budget on fast food and takeaway foods (DAA, 2008). The consumption of foods prepared outside the home, in general, has a detrimental effect on energy and nutrient intakes (Burns et al, 2007) while the consumption of fast food is positively linked with weight gain and obesity (Rosenheck, 2008). Fast-food consumption is predicted by several factors: age (consumption decreases with increasing age), being a car driver, having children above the age of five years, not owning a home and, importantly, having higher household incomes (Mohr et al, 2007).

Biological theories posit that humans have an evolutionary preponderance towards weight gain (manifested in a preference for energy-dense foods, weak satiety and strong hunger traits), which makes them susceptible to obesogenic environments (Canoy and Buchan, 2007). We do not wish to debate this here. However, it is important not to substitute a simple behaviourist explanation for weight gain and obesity (for example, the lack of self-control) with an equally simple biological one. Dixon and Broom (2007) advance a social–ecological approach to the understanding of weight gain and obesity, one based on the acknowledgment that cumulative exposures to obesogenic environments promote changes in individual dietary and physical activity behaviours, with ensuing impacts on BMI and health. At the same time, such a model also recognizes that behavioural and biological processes can only be understood in the context of political, social and economic processes. Reduced physical activity, for example, can be at least partly explained by the fact that non-motorized transport and leisure are systematically discouraged by urban layouts, transport systems, retail and other geographies that make walking and cycling inconvenient, if not dangerous (Dodson et al, 2006). Limited access to practical and safe alternatives to car use disproportionately affects people living in outer suburbs characterized by low socio-economic status (Bostock, 2001). Conversely, these same communities are exposed to a higher-than-average concentration of fast-food outlets (Reidpath et al, 2002).

Sociological critiques: Public health crisis or moral panic?

The majority of sociological writing on weight gain and obesity falls into two camps. The first accepts the dominant epidemiological construction of weight gain and obesity as public health crises and seeks to contribute to the understanding of these crises through exploration of the environmental, social, political and economic dimensions of the obesogenic environment identified by Dixon and Broom (2007). The second camp, by contrast, challenges the framing of weight gain and obesity as a crisis or epidemic and instead reconceptualizes these conditions in terms of moral panic, as propagated by groups with an interest in the obesity epidemic narrative. In sociology, a moral panic is understood to be an exaggerated – and often irrational – outpouring of concern over perceived threats to social order. A moral panic most commonly develops during periods of rapid social and economic change. It is frequently directed at stigmatized minority groups and provides ideological support for attempts at social control. Use of this term is, therefore, deliberately provocative and emotive.

Reconceptualizing weight gain and obesity as a moral panic rests on two principal lines of argument. The first is that increases in the prevalence of weight gain and obesity do not fit traditional criteria for classification as an epidemic. They are not diseases that can be contracted or transmitted, and they are not growing at exponential rates. Within epidemiology, however, epidemics are not defined as the transmission of particularly virulent diseases but as the incidence or prevalence of illness or other health-related events outside the 'normal' range of expectations (Flegal, 2006). From this perspective, the classification of obesity as an epidemic is entirely appropriate (Flegal, 2006). A slightly more sophisticated take on this argument is offered by Boero (2007), who shifts the focus from adherence to technical definitions to the consequences of applying terminology to the particular issue of weight gain and obesity as it is constructed within public discourse. Boero (2007) points out that the rapid and seemingly indiscriminate spread of pathogenic epidemics like cholera and influenza played a major role in the rapid spread of fear and calls to vigilance in relation to these conditions. She argues, based on an analysis of US media reporting on obesity, that casting non-pathogenic phenomena in the same language helps to propagate fear, to privilege medical discourses and expertise, to open previously private domains of consumption and parenting to surveillance and intervention, and to legitimate the stigmatization of obese individuals. Further, these processes are gendered and racialized with women – particularly women from ethnic minorities – and their mothering practices singled out most frequently as targets of blame and reform (Boero, 2007). The sense of urgency engendered by the construction of obesity as an epidemic, for Boero (2007), feeds moral panic as well as the individualization and medicalization of what would better be understood as a social problem.

The second line of argument concerning the reconceptualization of weight gain and obesity as a moral panic draws on the challenges to obesity epidemiology posed by Campos et al (2006) and others. If weight gain and obesity are not the objective public health threats that the obesity epidemic narrative would have us believe, then the obvious questions for sociologists focus on who is propagating this narrative, what do they stand to gain from it and why are we so vulnerable to it? These issues are addressed by Monaghan, for example, by asking:

> *if, after controlling for smoking and other variables, physically fit people have similar mortality risk independent of body composition … why should clinicians tell a physically active person with a relatively high body fat per centage that this is unacceptable? Is it because body fat has become a highly visible, often enduring, deeply personalized corporeal marker for inferior social status in a way that smoking and hypertension are not?* (Monaghan, 2005, p310).

Elaborating on relevant dimensions of social status, Monaghan also contends that:

> *the highly publicised war against fat is about moral judgements and panic (manufactured fear and loathing). It is about social inequality (class, gender, generational and racial bias), political expediency and organisational and economic interests. For many everyday people, including men and boys (but more often women), it is also about striving to be considered good or just plain acceptable in a body-oriented culture … it is about occupational identity and relationships… All of this is independent of (potential) health problems commonly attributed to adiposity rather than highly consequential socio-economic factors* (Monaghan, 2005, p309).

Large food companies, medical researchers, public health agencies, politicians and the media are all easy targets of a moral panic critique which takes the rejection of obesity epidemiology as its starting assumption. The economic and political interests of these groups – combined with ideological commitments and negative attitudes to minorities – are claimed to legitimate the demonization of obesity despite the alleged lack of scientific evidence (Monaghan, 2005; Campos et al, 2006). This explanation is neat. It has even inspired a significant political movement for obesity acceptance (Sobal, 1995). But it is far from convincing. In fact, the conclusion that proponents of the view that weight gain and obesity should be considered public health issues are universally driven by self-interest, ideological blindness and/or social prejudice beggars belief (Kim and Popkin, 2006).

Drawing on the same critique of obesity epidemiology, Guthman and DuPuis (2006) attempt to develop a more historically informed understanding of obesity as moral panic by theorizing the obese body as a site in which the material and discursive contradictions of contemporary capitalism, and neoliberal attempts to regulate it, are played out. One of the more pervasive strategies of neoliberal governance, they note, is the devolution to individuals and communities of responsibility to solve the social and environmental problems generated by global capitalism (that is, by the individualization of social problems observed by Boero, 2007). In the case of obesity, however, citizens are not simply left to their own devices to deal with their weight while the food industry continues to promote and sell energy-dense and nutrient-poor foods. Personal responsibility, Guthman and DuPuis (2006) go on to argue, is construed simultaneously as the capacity to consume and as the potentially conflicting capacity to impose self-discipline. Overeating is both encouraged and vilified. This is probably true. However, even if capitalism and neoliberal attempts to govern it create contradictions and problems, to what and for whom are obese bodies and/or obesity epidemic narratives a solution, or even a partial solution? And how effective a solution could they be if the epidemic nature of overweight and obesity is not accepted in the first place? Guthman and DuPuis' critique is far more sophisticated than analyses that simply impute interests to anyone and everyone implicated in obesity and public health. Nonetheless, their critique generates two contradictions of its own: first, a contradiction between treating neoliberalism as a political rationality disconnected from the needs and goals of identifiable agents and institutions, and yet materialized in the practices and bodies of 'consumers'; and second, a contradiction between that same embodiment of obesity through overeating and a rejection of weight gain and obesity epidemiology.

We would suggest that all this still begs a question: what happens to conceptualizations of the obesity-epidemic-narrative-as-moral-panic if obesity epidemiology is not rejected? We would suggest that much of the underlying critique remains intact and is, in fact, strengthened. Stripped of the emotive language of moral panic, this critique has much to contribute in terms of understanding how several of the analyses presented – the construction of obesity as an epidemic within public discourses, the stigmatization of obese individuals and sub-populations, competing claims about the causes, consequences and potential solutions to increasing bodyweight, and so on – contribute to the competing/confusing messages about food and health that Dixon and Broom (2007) identify as components of the obesogenic environment. This point brings us full circle to those authors who accept that weight gain and obesity are serious public health issues, and suggest that the peculiar contribution of the sociological imagination to the resolution of these issues lies in understanding the obesogenic environment and how sub-populations and individuals interact with it (Dixon and Broom, 2007).

Although we will not offer a detailed review of the political economy literature in this chapter, we would suggest that research on the political economy of obesogenic environments is particularly advanced (even where this research has been undertaken without an explicit focus on obesity) and has a major contribution to make to population health and the identification of effective points of intervention. Fresh fruit and vegetables, for example, are what is known in the industry as a 'loss leader' – a product that retailers sell at minimal mark-up in order to encourage consumers into their stores.

Further, retailers are increasingly promoting themselves with signifiers of freshness, health and quality (Burch and Lawrence, 2005; and see Chapter 12 of this volume). However, processed foods are far more profitable than fresh foods. Winson (2004) consequently shows how major food retailers in Canada have increased the total shelf space, the number of sales locations and the promotional effort they devote to highly processed fatty, salty and/or sugary foods. Even fresh food sections are increasingly filled with a variety of pre-prepared food (from ready meals to pre-cut salad and vegetable mixes) that increase the value-added to retailers and reduce the affordability of fresh foods to consumers (Burch and Lawrence, 2005). Although retailers may not be able to control exactly what we buy – nor prevent us from purchasing from a rival retailer – the influence they exert through store layouts, allocation of shelf space and use of promotional materials, signage and so on, only needs to shift consumer decision-making at the margins to make a significant difference to health outcomes at a population level. As such, there is a very strong case for holding retailers accountable for their own claims to corporate responsibility. Similar arguments can be developed in relation to the planning of the built environment.

Although it is widely acknowledged that environmental changes more conducive to physical activity and healthy eating patterns are available to address weight gain and obesity at a population level (Hinde and Dixon, 2005), research into the ways individuals, families and other small groups interact with obesogenic environments is arguably less developed (although for a major contribution see Dixon and Broom, 2007). Such research, we would argue, is critical for understanding the non-genetic factors behind the vulnerability some people experience in relation to obesogenic environments, and the likely effectiveness of environmental interventions to address it. Small changes at a population level are extremely important. But so, too, are big changes at a local level, where multiple factors may combine to generate unexpected, unintended and undesirable outcomes. Bostock (2001), for example, has found that the reliance on walking as a mode of transport among single mothers without car access has compounded the social exclusion experienced by these women while also restricting their access to health services and food stores – thus obviating the potential health benefits of regular walking. Clearly, single mothers are particularly vulnerable to aspects of the built environment that render walking with small children dangerous and/or unpleasant. However, although renewing the built environment of lower-income neighbourhoods is clearly important in addressing the contradictory impacts of walking on single mothers, so too is the availability of transport options (such as public transport) that enable a wider range of mobility (Bostock, 2001).

Conclusion

Accepting the material reality of obesity and its consequences – even if it is accepted that our knowledge of weight gain and obesity is socially constructed and incomplete – raises the stakes. Stigmatization and discrimination are not straightforward tools of social control enabled by 'obesity talk'. They are both causes and consequences of rising bodyweights – components of a negative feedback cycle with potentially deadly consequences for those caught in it. Understanding and breaking the cycle of discrimination and obesity does not require that sociologists defer to the expertise of epidemiologists and population health specialists. Rather, it requires multiple disciplinary perspectives and genuine debate within and between those perspectives.

The importance of what Dixon and Broom (2007) refer to as a social ecology of weight gain and obesity is also widely recognized by population health specialists. Among other recommendations, Swinburn et al (2004) call for more research into: the processes through which low socio-economic status promotes overweight and obesity; the effectiveness of environmental modifications or interventions; the impact of labelling on consumer choice, food formulation and dietary patterns; and the development of indicators suitable for monitoring environmental influences on obesity and weight gain. These recommendations should not define a sociological research agenda, although they do suggest useful points of engagement for sociology with other disciplines and with public health agencies. The peculiar contribution of sociology, we have argued, lies in challenging the individualization of weight gain and obesity as social problems by unpacking the interests and processes involved in producing and reproducing obesogenic environments; by exploring how individuals interpret and experience potentially obesogenic environments; and, following Guthman and DuPuis (2006), by analysing how the body is constituted as a site of social regulation. In a political environment that favours a consumer model of citizenship, together with market-based solutions to the majority of social problems, difficult questions must be raised regarding opportunities for meaningful environmental intervention of the sort favoured by population health specialists.

References

ABS (1997) *National Health Survey 1995*, Australian Bureau of Statistics, Canberra

ABS (2006) *National Health Survey 2004*, Australian Bureau of Statistics, Canberra

ABS (2007) *Australian Social Trends 2007*, Australian Bureau of Statistics, Canberra

AIHW (2008) *Australia's Health 2008*, Australian Institute of Health and Welfare, Canberra

Australian Government (2009) *Promoting Healthy Weight*, Department of Health and Ageing report, www.health.gov.au/internet/main/Publishing.nsf/Content/health-pubhlth-strateg-hlthwt-obesity.htm, accessed 11 February 2009

Barr, E., Magliano, D., Zimmet, P., Polkinghorne, K., Atkins, R., Dunstan, D., Murray, S. and Shaw, J. (2006) *AusDiab 2005 The Australian Diabetes, Obesity and Lifestyle Study*, International Diabetes Institute, Melbourne

Blair, S. and LaMonte, M. J. (2006) 'Commentary: Current perspectives on obesity and health: Black and white, or shades of grey?' *International Journal of Epidemiology*, vol 35, no 1, pp69–72

Boero, N. (2007) 'All the news that's fat to print: The American "obesity epidemic" and the media', *Qualitative Sociology*, vol 30, pp41–60

Bostock, L. (2001) 'Pathways of disadvantage? Walking as a mode of transport among low-income mothers', *Health and Social Care in the Community*, vol 9, no 1, pp11–18

Boyce, T. (2007) 'The media and obesity', *Obesity Reviews*, vol 8, supp 1, pp201–205

Burch, D. and Lawrence, G. (2005) 'Supermarket own brands, supply chains and the transformation of the agri-food system', *International Journal of Sociology of Agriculture and Food*, vol 13, no 1, pp1–18

Burns, C., Jackson, M., Gibbons, C. and Stoney, R. (2007) 'Foods prepared outside the home: Association with selected nutrients and body mass index in adult Australians', *Public Health Nutrition*, vol 5, no 3, pp441–448

Cameron, A., Welborn, T., Zimmet, P., Dunstan, D., Owen, N., Salmon, J., Dalton, M., Jolley, D. and Shaw, J. (2002) 'Overweight and obesity in Australia: The 1999–2000 Australian Diabetes, Obesity and Lifestyle Study (AusDiab)', *Medical Journal of Australia*, vol 178, pp427–432

Campos, P., Saguy, A., Ernsberger, P., Oliver, E. and Gaesser, G. (2006) 'The epidemiology of overweight and obesity: Public health crisis or moral panic?' *International Journal of Epidemiology*, vol 35, pp55–60

Canoy, D. and Buchan, I. (2007) 'Challenges in obesity epidemiology', *Obesity Reviews*, vol 8, pp1–11

CDCP (Center for Disease Control and Prevention) (1996) *Physical Activity and Health: A Report of the Surgeon General*, US Department of Health and Human Services, National Center for Chronic Disease Prevention and Health Promotion, Atlanta

DAA (2008) *Fast Food and Take Away*, Dietitians Association of Australia, www.daa.asn.au/index.asp?PageID=2145834438, accessed December 2008

Diabetes Australia (2008) *The Growing Cost of Obesity in 2008: Three Years On*, Access Economics, Australia

Dixon, J. and Broom, D. (eds) (2007) *The Seven Deadly Sins of Obesity: How the Modern World is Making Us Fat*, UNSW Press, Sydney

Dixon, J. and Winter, C. (2007) 'The environment of competing authorities: Saturated with choice', in J. Dixon and D. Broom (eds) *The Seven Deadly Sins of Obesity: How the Modern World is Making Us Fat*, UNSW Press, Sydney

Doak, C., Adair, L., Bentley, M., Monteiro, C. and Popkin, B. (2005) 'The dual burden household and the nutrition transition paradox', *International Journal of Obesity and Related Metabolic Disorders*, vol 29, no 1, pp129–136

Dodson, J., Buchanan, N., Gleeson, B. and Sipe, N. (2006) 'Investigating the social dimensions of transport disadvantage – 1: Towards new concepts and methods', *Urban Policy and Research*, vol 24, no 4, pp433–453

Eknoyan, G. (2008) 'Adolphe Quetelet (1796–1874) the average man and indices of obesity', *Nephrology Dialysis Transplantation*, vol 23, no 1, pp47–51

FAO (2008) *The State of Food Insecurity in the World 2008*, Food and Agriculture Organization of the United Nations, Rome

Farrell, S., Braun, L., Barlow, C., Cheng, Y. and Blair, S. (2002) 'The relation of Body Mass Index, cardiorespiratory fitness, and all-cause mortality in women', *Obesity Research*, vol 10, no 6, pp417–423

Field, A., Coakley, E., Must, A., Spadano, J., Laird, N., Dietz, W., Rimm, E. and Colditz, G. (2001) 'Impact of overweight on the risk of developing common chronic diseases during a 10-year period', *Archives of Internal Medicine*, vol 161, no 13, pp1581–1586

Flegal, K. (2006) 'Commentary: The epidemic of obesity – what's in a name?' *International Journal of Epidemiology*, vol 35, no 1, pp72–74

Gill, T., Baur, L., Bauman, A., Steinbeck, K., Storlien, L., Fiatarone Singh, A., Brand-Miller, J., Colagiuri, S. and Caterson, I. (2009) 'Childhood obesity in Australia still remains a widespread health concern that warrants population-wide preventional programs', *Medical Journal of Australia*, vol 190, no 3, pp146–148

Guthman, J. and DuPuis, M. (2006) 'Embodying neoliberalism: Economy, culture, and the politics of fat', *Environment and Planning D: Society and Space*, vol 24, pp427–448

Hillier, T. A., Fagot-Campagna, A., Eschwege, E., Vol, S., Cailleau, M., Balkau, B., and the DESIR Study group (2006) 'Weight change and changes in the metabolic syndrome as the French population moves toward overweight: The DESIR cohort', *International Journal of Epidemiology*, vol 35, pp190–196

Hinde, S. and Dixon, J. (2005) 'Changing the "obesogenic environment": Insights from a cultural economy of car-reliance', *Transportation Research Part D – Transport and Environment*, vol 10, pp31–53

Janus, E., Laatikainen, T., Dunbar, J. A., Kilkkinen, A., Bunker, S., Philpot, B., Tideman, P., Titimacco, R. and Heistaro, S. (2007) 'Overweight, obesity and metabolic syndrome in rural southeastern Australia', *Medical Journal of Australia*, vol 187, no 3, pp147–152

Kim, S. and Popkin, B. (2006) 'Commentary: Understanding the epidemiology of overweight and obesity – a real global public health concern', *International Journal of Epidemiology*, vol 35, no 1, pp60–67

Larsson, S. and Wolk, A. (2007) 'Obesity and colon and rectal cancer risk: A meta-analysis of prospective studies', *American Journal of Clinical Nutrition*, vol 86, no 3, pp556–565

Lawlor, D. and Chaturvedi, N. (2006) 'Treatment and prevention of obesity – are there critical periods for intervention?' *International Journal of Epidemiology*, vol 35, no 1, pp3–9

Lee, C., Blair, S. and Jackson, A. (1999) 'Cardiorespiratory fitness, body composition, and all-cause and cardiovascular disease in men', *American Journal of Clinical Nutrition*, vol 69, pp373–380

Magarey, A., Daniels, L. and Boulton, T. (2001) 'Prevalence of overweight and obesity in Australian children and adolescents: Reassessment of 1985 and 1995 data against new standard international definitions', *Medical Journal of Australia*, vol 174, pp561–565

Magarey, A., McKean, S. and Daniels, L. (2006) 'Evaluation of fruit and vegetable intakes of Australian adults: The National Nutrition Survey 1995', *Australian and New Zealand Journal of Public Health*, vol 30, no 1, pp32–37

Markovic, T. and Natoli, S. (2009) 'Paradoxical nutritional deficiency in overweight and obesity: The importance of nutrient density', *Medical Journal of Australia*, vol 190, no 3, pp149–151

Mohr, P., Wilson, C., Dunn, K., Brindal, E. and Wittert, G. (2007) 'Personal and lifestyle characteristics predictive of the consumption of fast foods in Australia', *Public Health Nutrition*, vol 10, no 12, pp1456–1463

Monaghan, L. (2005) 'A critical take on the obesity debate', *Social Theory and Health*, vol 3, pp302–314

NHMRC (2003) *Dietary Guidelines for Australian Adults*, National Health and Medical Research Council, Commonwealth of Australia, Canberra

Phillips, A. (2008) *Rural, Regional and Remote Health: Indicators of Health Status and Determinants of Health*, Australian Institute of Health and Welfare, Canberra

Popkin, B. (2001) 'The nutrition transition and obesity in the developing world', *The Journal of Nutrition*, vol 131, pp871–873

Prentice, A. (2006) 'The merging epidemic of obesity in developing countries', *International Journal of Epidemiology*, vol 35, pp93–99

Reidpath, D., Burns, C., Garrard, J., Mahoney, M. and Townsend, M. (2002) 'An ecological study of the relationship between social and environmental determinants of obesity', *Health and Place*, vol 8, no 2, pp141–145

Rigby, N. (2006) 'Commentary: Counterpoint to Campos et al', *International Journal of Epidemiology*, vol 35, no 1, pp79–80

Rosenheck, R. (2008) 'Fast food consumption and increased caloric intake: A systematic review of a trajectory towards weight gain and obesity risk', *Obesity Reviews*, vol 9, no 7, pp535–547

Savage, J., Marini, M. and Birch, L. (2008) 'Dietary energy density predicts women's weight change over 6 years', *American Journal of Clinical Nutrition*, vol 88, no 3, pp677–684

Scully, M., Dixon, H. and Wakefield, M. (2008) 'Association between commercial television exposure and fast-food consumption among adults', *Public Health Nutrition*, vol 12, no 1, pp105–110

Sobal, J. (1995) 'The medicalization and de-medicalization of obesity', in D. Maurer and J. Sobal (eds), *Eating Agendas: Food and Nutrition as Social Problems*, Aldine de Gruyter, Hawthorne

Speiser, P., Rudolf, M., Anhalt, H., Camacho-Hubner, C., Chiarelli, F., Eliakim, A., Freemark, M., Gruters, A., Hershkovitz, E., Iughetti, L., Krude, H., Latzer, Y., Lustig, R., Pescovitz, O., Pinhas-Hamiel, O., Rogol, A., Shalitin, S., Sultan, C., Stein, D., Vardi, P., Werther, G., Zadik, Z., Zuckerman-Levin, N. and Hochberg, Z. (2005) 'Consensus statement: Childhood obesity', *The Journal of Clinical Endocrinology and Metabolism*, vol 90, no 3, pp1871–1887

Swinburn, B., Caterson, I., Seidell, J. and James, W. (2004) 'Diet, nutrition and the prevention of excess weight gain and obesity', *Public Health Nutrition*, vol 7, no 1a, p123

Winson, A. (2004) 'Bringing political economy into the debate on the obesity epidemic', *Agriculture and Human Values*, vol 21, pp299–312

WHO (2000) *Obesity: Preventing and Managing the Global Epidemic*, WHO Technical Report Series 894, World Health Organization, Geneva

WHO (2006) *BMI Classification*, World Health Organization, www.who.int/bmi/index.jsp?introPage=intro_3.html, accessed 9 February 2009

10
The Food Regulatory System – Is It Protecting Public Health and Safety?

Mark Lawrence

Introduction

Food regulatory systems are an integral component of modern food systems. Through their policy and food standard-setting activities, these systems of policy and law relating to food play a significant role in influencing food composition and food labelling and, in turn, public health. The primary objective when setting policy and food standards is 'the protection of public health and safety' (WHO and FAO, 2006; Office of Legislative Drafting and Publishing, 2008; FRSC, 2009). Yet, nowhere has this objective been clearly defined, nor has its implications for food regulation practice been critically examined.

The existence of food regulation has been traced to ancient times with historical writings revealing attempts by early civilizations to codify foods (WHO and FAO, 2006). From these beginnings to the present day, food regulations have tended to focus on addressing concerns related to food safety, fraud, misleading claims and adulteration. Yet, the modern food system has evolved dramatically from its early beginnings (and even from how it operated just one generation ago). A new order of public health challenges has emerged which also should command the attention of food regulators. One such challenge relates to dietary imbalances, which contribute significantly to the major preventable chronic diseases that afflict people in developed nations. A social justice imperative is at the centre of this issue, given that the burden of diet-related diseases such as cardiovascular disease, cancer, diabetes and obesity is disproportionately high among socially and economically disadvantaged communities (WHO and FAO, 2003; WHO Commission on the Social Determinants of Health, 2008). At the same time, rising food prices and diminishing food availability raise the likelihood of substantial food security concerns at local, regional and global levels. The founder of the Worldwatch Institute (in 1974) and the Earth Policy Institute (in 2001), goes so far as to argue that, '[T]he biggest threat to global stability is the potential for food crises in poor countries to cause government collapse' (Brown, 2009). A third contemporary challenge is environmental, given that the agricultural sector accounts for a substantial proportion of greenhouse gas emissions and is a major user of water and energy (Garnett, 2008).

A study of the setting of nutrition-related food standards in Australia and New Zealand would offer insights into the relationship between policy and law, and public health and safety in the food regulatory system. This chapter presents an analysis of the decision-making processes and outcomes associated with the setting of two food standards – one relating to standard-setting in the regulation of food composition, and the other to food labelling – within the Australian and New Zealand food regulatory system. The purpose of this research is to assess the nature and extent to which the objective 'to protect public health and safety' is enacted by the food regulatory system. A series of policy recommendations for the food regulatory system is presented in response to the findings of these analyses.

Background to the food regulatory system in Australia and New Zealand

In Australia and New Zealand the food regulatory system is the system of policy and laws relating to food (Australia and New Zealand Food Regulation Ministerial Council, 2009). The system operates to a food regulation model that comprises the following four structures:

- The Australia and New Zealand Food Regulation Ministerial Council (Ministerial Council), whose role is to develop domestic food regulation policy in the form of policy guidelines.
- A Food Regulation Standing Committee (FRSC) is responsible for coordinating policy advice to the Ministerial Council and ensuring a nationally consistent approach to the implementation and enforcement of food standards.
- An Implementation Sub-Committee (ISC) oversees a consistent approach to implementation and enforcement of food regulations and standards.
- Food Standards Australia New Zealand (FSANZ), formerly Australia New Zealand Food Authority (ANZFA), is a statutory authority responsible for developing all domestic food standards based on scientific and technical criteria, consistent with Ministerial Council policy (see Food Regulation Secretariat, 2009).

Standard-setting is one of the most commonly used strategies for the regulation of food in Australia and New Zealand and is undertaken by FSANZ. The legislation under which FSANZ operates states that among other objectives, when setting food standards, FSANZ must have regard to, 'the need for standards to be based on risk analysis using the best available scientific evidence' (Office of Legislative Drafting and Publishing, 2008). The concept of evidence-based practice implies a rational and objective basis to decision-making processes within the food regulatory system. However, the food regulatory system does not operate in a vacuum removed from external non-evidence-based inputs. For example, there are many stakeholders with vested interests regarding food regulations and they advocate to influence decision-making processes within the food regulatory system. It is relevant to be aware that whereas FSANZ maintains a public register of submissions it receives in relation to food standards decision-making, other committees and structures within the regulatory system are less transparent in their operation and decision-making processes. The extent to which the actions of these various stakeholders might shape decision-making processes depends often on how their interests align with the broader political setting within which the food regulatory system operates. Therefore, in order to gain insights into the less visible influences on decision-makers in the food regulatory system, it is valuable to consider the background to the establishment of the system and the orientation of the series of policy reviews that have continued to revise the structure and operation of the system over the past two decades.

The impetus for the establishment of the modern food regulatory system in Australia and New Zealand was the publication of the joint Industry Assistance Commission and Business Regulation Review Unit's (1988) *Report of an Inquiry into Food Regulation in Australia*. The report stressed the benefits to food manufacturers and the economic gains to the government that would be made from harmonizing and reducing food regulation across Australia. Many of the recommendations in the report were accepted by the Commonwealth, State and Territory governments and led to the then National Food Authority (NFA) being established in 1991 as a statutory authority operating under the National Food Authority Act 1991 (FSANZ, 2009a). The State and Territory governments agreed to adopt by reference into their food laws the food standards decisions prepared by the NFA and approved by a Ministerial Council. In 1996, the NFA became the Australia New Zealand Food Authority (ANZFA) – a bi-national government agency, when the Australian and New Zealand governments signed an agreement to establish one joint food standard-setting system under the Trans Tasman Closer Economic Relations (FSANZ, 2009a). Then in the early 2000s, ANZFA became FSANZ – the Australia and New Zealand food regulatory authority that exists to this day (FSANZ, 2009a).

The evolution of the roles, responsibilities and structures of the NFA, ANZFA and FSANZ has occurred against a series of regulatory reforms and governmental agreements (see selected examples in Table 10.1). The titles of several of these reform documents and agreements allude to their relationship to the larger neoliberal agenda of promoting innovation and increased choice by streamlining and reducing regulation (or so-called 'red tape'). In turn, the focus of these reform documents suggests their intended role in the implementation of this larger agenda. In practical terms, this neoliberal reform agenda strives

Table 10.1 *Twenty years of food-related regulatory reforms –*
selected examples

Report of an Inquiry into Food Regulation in Australia (Industry Assistance Commission and Business Regulation Review Unit, 1988)
Principles and Guidelines for National Standard Setting and Regulatory Action (Council of Australian Governments, 1995; 1997)
Food: A Growth Industry (The Blair Review), Final Report of the Food Regulation Review (Food Regulation Review Committee, 1998)
Council of Australian Governments, Inter-Governmental Agreement (2000)
Rethinking Regulation (The Banks Review), Report of the Taskforce on Reducing Regulatory Burdens on Business (Food Regulation Review Committee, 2006)
Simplifying the Menu: Food Regulation in Victoria (Victorian Competition and Efficiency Commission, 2008).

Source: the author

to secure minimal regulation, while claiming that a 'safe' food supply will be maintained – whatever safe means.

Understanding food regulatory policy decisions: A case study approach

In this section, two food-standard case studies are analysed in order to understand the way that the protection of public health and safety is interpreted and applied in the development of food regulation. The first case centres on the review of Food Standard A9 – Vitamins and Minerals, which was conducted in the 1990s and which enables a focus on food composition policy. The second case, the current proposal P293 – Nutrition, Health and Related Claims, is a study of food labelling policy under the present jurisdictional arrangements. The purpose of these analyses is to gain insights into the extent to which the focus of regulatory reform in relation to these particular topics has focused on public health and safety issues. The choice of these two particular case studies was based on their particularly powerful relationship with nutrition science in terms of their risk assessment as well as the nature of their health impact in their application. In addition, although they are distinct policy issues they overlap in their application. For instance, the ability to make nutrition, health and related claims is frequently contingent on the prior addition of vitamins and minerals to food products.

Food Standard A9 – Vitamins and Minerals

Responsibility for the review of Food Standard A9 – Vitamins and Minerals in the early to mid-1990s rested with the then Australian National Food Authority, the forerunner to FSANZ. The purpose of Standard A9 was to set out the provisions under which vitamins and minerals could be added to food products. At the time, an increasing number of fortified food products – such as fortified breakfast cereals and fortified fruit and vegetable juices – were being introduced into the marketplace for no apparent health reason, and with different combinations and levels of added nutrients. The Food Authority initiated a review of the Standard (NFA, 1992) with the intention of developing a public health and safety policy as a basis to clarify which products could be fortified, with which nutrients, and at what levels of fortification. In particular, the food standard review proposed a requirement for scientific evidence to demonstrate a public health need prior to permitting the fortification of food products.

This action by the NFA led to a particularly vexed and heated debate about what was meant by the protection of public health and safety, and what would constitute the role of the NFA in developing and implementing policy in this area. On the one hand, the majority of public health agencies and practitioners supported the NFA review, arguing that there was no evidence of any need for the majority of the fortified products that had entered the market-place up to that time (NFA, 1993). Instead, it was argued that fortification was being abused to promote the manufacture and marketing of so-called 'junk' foods. In contrast, a number of food manufacturers (particularly breakfast cereal manufacturers) took exception to the NFA's review of Standard A9, arguing that the requirement for an evidence-based justification of health needs prior to fortification would restrict trade opportunities as well as stifle food product innovation. Over a four-year period (1992–1995) there was heated debate between those stakeholders supporting, and those opposing, the review. Notably, certain food manufacturers were alleged to be particularly aggressive in lobbying senior government officials to oppose the NFA's review and challenge the work of NFA staff. For instance, shortly after the Chairperson of the NFA (who had led its policy position on food fortification) announced her resignation (NFA, 1994), the *Canberra Times* published an article in which the circumstances associated with the resignation were analysed. The newspaper article reported an allegation that, 'Ms Pincus felt obliged to go after being pressured by the Parliamentary Secretary in charge of food matters ... who had in turn been pressured by the [food] manufacturers' (Brough, 1994).

In 1994, the Ministerial Council voted 'behind closed doors' to reject its own NFA's policy recommendations related to the addition of nutrients into food products. Instead, it voted in support of a policy approach that aligned with the arguments of those food manufacturers actively opposed to the recommended changes to Standard A9 – the voting patterns and explanations of the individual Council members were not revealed. The Ministerial Council finally resolved that, unless there was evidence of harm, trade opportunities and innovation should not be restricted. This decision then placed the burden of proof on public health interests to demonstrate harm, rather than on food manufacturers to demonstrate a public health need.

Proposal P293 – Nutrition, Health and Related Claims

The more recent review of Proposal P293 – Nutrition, Health and Related Claims falls under the jurisdiction of FSANZ. The Proposal has been developed by FSANZ to bring the diversity of food labelling issues encompassed by

Nutrition, Health and Related Claims under one food standard. Among the many types of claims are: nutrition content claims, such as 'source of calcium'; general level health claims, such as 'food X is a good source of calcium and calcium helps build strong bones and teeth'; and high-level health claims, such as 'food X is a good source of calcium and will help prevent osteoporosis'. As such, the Proposal has had to contend with a range of questions. These included: should health claims be permitted on food products? If so, what level of scientific evidence is required to substantiate such a claim? And, are there certain food products that should not be permitted to make nutrition content claims and/or health claims?

Proposal P293 captures nutrition, health and related claims information for which there are strongly held differences of opinion among stakeholders. Most public health agencies and practitioners have argued the need for so-called 'disqualifying criteria' to determine those food products eligible to access nutrition content claims. They argue, for example, that a high-fat-containing product should not be able to be advertised as a good source of any particular nutrient – and, by implication, as a healthy food – as such a claim is inconsistent with the dietary guideline message to 'moderate fat intake' (NHMRC, 2003). In addition, these public health advocates have generally opposed policy that permits the use of high-level health claims, arguing that such claims are little more than a marketing tool to promote 'junk' foods. For instance, in his book *In Defense of Food*, Michael Pollan (2008) singles out health claims for particular attention. He recommends that people who want to eat healthy foods should avoid those that display a health claim – implying that such a claim is a marker of unhealthy food. Conversely, many food manufacturers argue that there should be no restrictions on the use of nutrition content claims on food products, irrespective of the consistency of that food product with the dietary guidelines (for example, see Wells, 2003). They state that such claims are simply technical statements relaying factual food composition information to citizens. In addition, they contend that all health claims are a legitimate nutrition education tool, and represent a practical way for food manufacturers to inform citizens about healthy eating.

In its preliminary assessment report for Proposal P293 – Nutrition, Health and Related Claims, FSANZ stated that it will adopt the Ministerial Council's advice, thereby permitting health claims under certain conditions (FSANZ, 2009b). There has been a lack of explanation from the Ministerial Council as to how its advice was formulated. In addition, FSANZ has resolved that there will be no disqualifying criteria for nutrition content claims. As a consequence of these policy decisions, many food products are permitted to be fortified and to display nutrition content claims, irrespective of their consistency with dietary guideline criteria. Reflecting this incongruence between nutrition content claims and actual food product attributes, Kellogg's Coco Pops was awarded the inaugural Parents' Jury 'Smoke and Mirrors' award in 2005 for inappropriate advertising to children (Parents' Jury, 2005). Among other concerns, the Parents' Jury pointed out that over one-third of the contents of a packet of Kellogg's Coco Pops (36 per cent by weight) is sugar.

The limits of Australia and New Zealand's food regulatory system

The preceding cases of decision-making in relation to food standards indicate limitations in the capacity of current policy processes to account for public health and safety within the food regulatory system. In particular, the findings from the case study analyses reveal that the purpose, governance and decision-making processes of the Australian and New Zealand food regulatory system are largely disengaged from contemporary public health considerations. The case studies highlight the often vexed and complex debates among stakeholders. They also illustrate that, more often than not, public health interests come off second best to food manufacturers and trade interests in such debates. We might ask how this occurs, given that protecting public health and safety is the primary objective in setting food regulation policy and food standards.

To begin to answer this question, it is necessary to recognize that the policy deliberations related to public health in the food regulatory system largely occur with no overarching food and nutrition policy to inform individual regulatory decisions. Thus, they are limited in being able to situate individual food standards decisions within a broader context. In the absence of a food and nutrition policy, the food regulatory system environment is dominated by a policy focus on regulatory reform (see Table 10.1). These reforms have dictated the context within which internal food regulatory system decision-making has and continues to be undertaken. The reviews consistently have been driven from the perspective of a neoliberal agenda. The neoliberal agenda is characterized by the pursuit of deregulation and the promotion of opportunities for food manufacturers to innovate and seek value-added opportunities for their products, especially in export markets. Invariably this agenda has created uncertainty towards what is meant by protecting public health and safety in the work of the food regulatory system, and resulted in challenges in balancing economic and public health interests in the setting of food standards.

A question mark therefore arises over the extent to which the Australian and New Zealand food regulatory system is effectively governed. A lack of transparency with decision-making processes – evident in the two case studies detailed above – is a particular concern at the Ministerial Council level, where the actual voting patterns and explanations for such voting are rarely fully revealed to the community. For instance, non-health ministers can be – and have been – elected by jurisdictions to serve as lead ministers on the Ministerial Council. From a public health perspective, it would be relevant to know the views and voting patterns of such non-health ministers on health-related food policy issues. Lack of transparency in decision-making also exists at the ministerial advisory level, particularly with regard to the workings of the FRSC, where there is no obligation to reveal the evidence or reasoning that underpin its decisions to the wider community. Additional governance concerns include the poor participation of citizens in the processes of the Australian and New Zealand food regulatory system, and uncertainties over how 'experts' are selected on to regulatory system committees and panels.

These governance concerns are not peculiar to the Australian and New Zealand food regulatory system. For example, in his commentary on the UK Food Standards Agency, Lobstein states that, 'The Food Standards Agency is far too cosy with big business: even the government seems to think it is no longer serving consumers' interests' (Lobstein, 2008).

The reversal of the burden of proof, which lies with consumers and public health advocates rather than with business, is a clear concern arising from the two case studies presented in this chapter. The protection of public health and safety was interpreted in terms of permitting fortification and nutrient content claims as long as there was 'no harm'. In the case of Standard A9, this resolution by the Ministerial Council signalled to the market-place that unless there was scientific evidence of an acute safety concern, liberal fortification of a range of food products was permitted. This has caused the non-transparency of food regulatory system decision-making processes to be exacerbated in at least two ways. First, because what was meant by 'no harm' was not defined. Second, and crucially, adequate mechanisms to monitor whether any harm was indeed occurring were not put in place.

In isolation, individual policy and food standards decisions may appear to have a relatively benign impact on public health. What harm could there be in adding a few nutrients to a food product, for example? And what harm could there be in permitting a food product to advertise the nutrients it contains? A closer look at the regulatory decision-making processes, as embarked upon in this research, illustrates that it is not until we start evaluating the cumulative outcome of individual decisions that we see patterns emerging. Moreover, it is only by examining the effects of multiple policy decisions that inconsistencies with public health guidelines are revealed, beyond what might be detected at the individual level.

For the cases investigated in this study, a two-step process played out that illustrates the cumulative effect of individual decisions. To begin, an outcome of decision-making associated with the Standard A9 case resulted in a highly processed, high sugar-containing product being fortified with a cocktail of nutrients. Then, the outcomes of the P293 review opened the way for the aggressive advertising of the product as one that is healthy for children. These experiences highlight that in protecting public health and safety the assessment procedures of the food regulatory system need to take account of the collective impact of individual policy and food standards decisions on health.

Further research that analyses the plethora of food products flooding the market-place under the watch of the Australian and New Zealand food regulatory system would provide additional insights into how public health may be better protected in this policy setting. For example, it would be useful to analyse the decision-making processes that have resulted in the flood of novel foods, functional foods and fortified foods onto the market-place, all of which have been accompanied by dubious claims about their capacity to optimize health, to provide energy and vitality, and to prevent various illnesses. If the evidence obtained from the research presented here were to be replicated for other case studies, it would further strengthen the argument that this particular food regulatory system is not keeping pace with changes in modern food systems.

Tim Lang has observed that the 'role of law in the governance of the relationship between food and public health is being altered by the changed structures and dynamics of modern food systems' (Lang, 2006, p30). This point is illustrated by the way food security and environmental sustainability are treated as 'externalities' in policy and food standard agendas by the current Australian and New Zealand food regulatory system. For example, in the Productivity Commission's most recent annual review of regulation in Australia, which encompassed a review of food regulation, the only reference to 'sustainability' was in the context of sustaining the economic objectives of food manufacturers (Productivity Commission, 2008) – a reference made without apparent irony.

Conclusions and recommendations

The evidence obtained from the case study analyses presented in this chapter indicates that the Australian and New Zealand food regulatory system is not adequately protecting public health. Whereas food and nutrition policies frequently promote the notion of 'making healthier choices the easier choices', the case studies suggest that the food regulatory system is instead fostering the proliferation of heavily marketed and highly processed, expensive foods with high fat, sugar and salt content. A major explanation for the processes and outcomes associated with the two case studies is the orientation of the broader regulatory reviews and governmental agreements within which the structure and operation of the food regulatory system has become framed. These reviews and agreements highlight that the food regulatory system needs to be viewed as operating principally as one 'cog' in the 'wheel' of the industrial economy – oriented preferentially towards constructing regulatory frameworks that help promote the development of new food ingredients, products and processes. Relatively less attention in these reviews and agreements was directed towards strengthening mechanisms for assessing and protecting the integrity of food and health relationships.

Food regulatory systems will continue to respond to a variety of (often competing) public health, economic, social, technological and political interests when setting policy and food standards. If the food regulatory system is to adequately protect the biological, social and environmental dimensions of public health, it must be comprehensively revised to ensure that it is more relevant and responsive to these multiple and interrelated challenges. The lack of an overarching food and nutrition policy is a central reason for the obvious disconnection between dietary guidelines and the system of policy and law that is designed to regulate food composition and labelling. Issues of governance and purpose have also emerged from this study. The analysis of two cases of regulatory review presented in this chapter thus gives rise to three policy recommendations for the revision of the Australian and New Zealand food regulatory system so that it is better equipped to protect public health nutrition, which centre on policy coherence, governance and the objectives of food policy and law. These three areas are described below.

Policy coherence

In terms of policy coherence, public health nutrition in Australia and New Zealand suffers from the absence of a coherent national food and nutrition policy. Hence, there is no overarching policy framework that informs the setting of policy or food standards in the regulatory system for these countries. Instead, much of the work of agencies such as FSANZ is framed within the context of high-level government policy which, originating with Treasury, is effectively dominated by the neoliberal agenda of deregulation that has prevailed since the early 1990s. With the public demand for a 'joined-up' food and nutrition policy response that simultaneously addresses health, economic, social and environmental issues, never has there been a more urgent time for Australia and New Zealand to initiate a Cabinet-level food and nutrition policy. The UK Cabinet Office's *Food Matters* policy document released in 2008 provides a positive example of what can be achieved (UK Cabinet Office, 2008). This policy document outlines joined-up interventions such as those that will integrate nutrition standards developed in the health sector into food service provision overseen by other government sectors. Also, it proposes that environmental sustainability criteria be integrated into such nutrition standards. One of the first objectives of such a policy document for Australia and New Zealand might be the 'reform of the reform agendas' to the extent that public health, social and environmental considerations all receive timely and sufficient attention.

Governance

Governance is a second important issue, with the Australian and New Zealand food regulatory system requiring greater transparency in relation to its decision-making processes. While much of the decision-making work of FSANZ is accessible in terms of the existence of a public register, the machinations of the FRSC and Ministerial Council are largely a 'closed shop'. The community is not informed who voted for what, or how and why decisions are made, beyond a vague commentary in an official communiqué. The reports prepared by the FRSC, along with ministerial voting patterns and a full and frank explanation of the issues discussed and how they were resolved, should all be provided to the public at the conclusion of each Ministerial Council meeting to enhance transparency. In addition, improved democratic processes related to decision-making are required. This relates to the process whereby experts are selected to serve on committees and panels within the regulatory system. It is noteworthy that, despite being affected by its decisions at every meal, the vast majority of the Australian and New Zealand population is not engaged with the food regulatory system. Mechanisms for the engagement of citizens, and the promotion of greater citizen participation in decision-making, are necessary steps to address this democratic deficit.

Protection of public health and safety

Third and finally, in relation to the protection of public health and safety, it is the position of FSANZ, FRSC and the Ministerial Council that the food regulatory system adequately accounts for the protection of public health and safety. This position is justified if the only measure of public health and safety related to relatively immediate safety concerns is informed by evidence from microbiological and toxicological studies. However, substantive public health issues related to chronic disease prevention, social equity and environmental sustainability are clearly relevant to a food regulatory system that seeks to protect public health and safety. These issues are largely overlooked by the food regulatory system in Australia and New Zealand at present. As such, a review of the system's primary objective is overdue. In particular, there is a need for an unambiguous definition of 'protecting public health and safety' – one that articulates the 'mainstreaming' of nutrition into the decision-making processes of the food regulatory system. Such a review would represent a worthy application of the exciting initiative of the Prince Mahidol Award Conference 2009 with its theme of 'mainstreaming health into public policies' (PMA, 2009).

References

Australia and New Zealand Food Regulation Ministerial Council (2009) 'Overarching Strategic Statement for the Food Regulatory System', www.health.gov.au/internet/main/publishing.nsf/Content/FB280282EE51D887CA256F190003B038/$File/Overarching%20Strategic%20Statement.pdf, accessed 13 May 2009

Brough, J. (1994) 'No tears for Pincus', *The Canberra Times*, 17 December, p4

Brown, L. (2009) 'Could Food Shortages Bring Down Civilization?' *Scientific American Magazine*, April 22, www.scientificamerican.com/article.cfm?id=civilization-food-shortages, accessed 11 May 2009

Codex Alimentarius Commission (2008) *Codex Alimentarius Commission Procedural Manual*, 18th edition, Joint FAO and WHO Food Standards Programme, World Health Organization and Food and Agriculture Organization of the United Nations, Rome

Council of Australian Governments (1995, 1997) *Principles and Guidelines for National Standard Setting and Regulatory Action*, Canberra

Council of Australian Governments (2000) Council of Australian Governments Inter-Governmental Agreement, www.foodstandards.gov.au/_srcfiles/31_Fina_signed-FRA2002.pdf, accessed 11 May 2009

Food Regulation Review Committee (1998) *Food: A Growth Industry (The Blair Review), Final Report of the Food Regulation Review*, AGPS, Canberra

Food Regulation Review Committee (2006) *Rethinking Regulation (The Banks Review), Report of the Taskforce on Reducing Regulatory Burdens on Business*, AGPS, Canberra

Food Regulation Secretariat (2009) *The Food Regulation Model*, www.sport.gov.au/internet/main/publishing.nsf/Content/foodsecretariat-system.htm, accessed 13 May 2009

FRCS (Food Regulation Standing Committee) (2009) *Overarching Strategic Statement for the Food Regulatory System*, www.health.gov.au/internet/main/publishing.nsf/

Content/FB280282EE51D887CA256F190003B038/$File/Overarching%20Strategi c%20Statement.pdf, accessed 11 May 2009

FSANZ (Food Standards Australia New Zealand) (2009a) 'Background', www. foodstandards.gov.au/aboutfsanz/background.cfm, accessed 11 May 2009

FSANZ (Food Standards Australia New Zealand) (2009b) *Final Assessment Report, Proposal P293 – Nutrition, Health and Related Claims*, www.foodstandards.gov. au/_srcfiles/P293%20Health%20Claims%20FAR%20and%20Att%201%20&%2 02%20FINAL.pdf, accessed 12 May 2009

Garnett, T. (2008) *Cooking up a Storm: Food, Greenhouse Gas Emissions and our Changing Climate*, Food Climate Research Network, Centre for Environmental Strategy, University of Surrey, UK

Industry Assistance Commission and Business Regulation Review Unit (1988) *Report of an Inquiry into Food Regulation in Australia, Part 1 – National Issues*, AGPS, Canberra

Lang, T. (2006) 'Food, the law and public health: Three models of the relationship', *Public Health*, vol 120, pp30–41

Lobstein, T. (2008) 'Board stiffs', *Guardian* newspaper on-line, www.guardian.co.uk/ commentisfree/2008/jan/07/boardstiffs/, accessed 3 December 2008

NFA (National Food Authority) (1992) *Full Assessment Report, Proposal 24 – Vitamins and Minerals*, National Food Authority, Canberra

NFA (National Food Authority) (1993) *Preliminary Inquiry Report, Proposal 24 – Vitamins and Minerals*, National Food Authority, Canberra

NFA (National Food Authority) (1994) 'Media release: NFA Chairperson announces resignation', 14 December, National Food Authority, Canberra

NHMRC (National Health and Medical Research Council) (2003) *Dietary Guidelines for Australian Adults*, AGPS, Canberra

Office of Legislative Drafting and Publishing (2008) *Food Standards Australia New Zealand Act 1991*, Federal Attorney-General's Department, Canberra, www. comlaw.gov.au/ComLaw/Legislation/ActCompilation1.nsf/0/2A3DE63AFBF7 C2EDCA257539000EA171?OpenDocument, accessed 12 May 2009

Parents' Jury (2005) 'Junk food ads slammed by Parents' Jury', www.parentsjury. org.au/downloads/2005_Awards_announcement_media_release.pdf, accessed 27 November 2007

PMA (The Prince Mahidol Award Conference) (2009) 'Mainstreaming health into public policies', www.pmaconference.org.com/, accessed 24 January 2009

Pollan, M. (2008) *In Defense of Food*, Penguin Press, New York

Productivity Commission (2008) *Annual Review of Regulatory Burdens, Chapter 3 – Food Regulation*, www.pc.gov.au/__data/assets/pdf_file/0017/83033/05-chapter3. pdf, accessed 3 December 2008

UK Cabinet Office (2008) 'Food matters: Towards a strategy for the 21st Century', www.cabinetoffice.gov.uk/strategy/work_areas/food_policy.aspx, accessed 24 January 2009

Victorian Competition and Efficiency Commission (2007) *Simplifying the Menu: Food Regulation in Victoria*, Melbourne

Wells, D. (2003) 'Talk to IBC Conference', www.afgc.org.au/cmsdocuments/ IBC%20Conference.pdf, accessed 24 January 2009

WHO and FAO (World Health Organization and Food and Agriculture Organization of the United Nations) (2003) *Diet, Nutrition and the Prevention of Chronic Diseases, Report of a Joint WHO/FAO Expert Consultation, WHO Technical Report Series 916*, WHO, Geneva

WHO and FAO (2006) *Understanding the Codex Alimentarius, 3rd Edition*, Secretariat of the Joint FAO/WHO Food Standards Programme, FAO, Rome, ftp://ftp.fao.org/codex/Publications/understanding/Understanding_EN.pdf, accessed 11 May 2009

WHO Commission on the Social Determinants of Health (2008) *Closing the Gap in a Generation: Health Equity Through Action on the Social Determinants of Health*, WHO, Geneva

11
The 'Wellness' Phenomenon: Implications for Global Agri-food Systems

David Burch and Geoffrey Lawrence

Introduction

In recent years there have emerged a number of discernible social trends involving the pursuit of a healthier lifestyle among consumers in the developed countries. These trends include:

- A desire by a growing number of people to take control of their health futures.
- The growth of new (often alternative) types of medical treatments that 'confront' medically based solutions to ill health.
- The marketing of thousands of new products designed to promote health (such as vitamins, diagnostic devices and nutritional supplements).
- Changing consumption patterns as a response to rising levels of obesity, cholesterol levels, and other diet-related illnesses.
- The movement of fast-food restaurants and supermarkets into the provision of a range of healthier choices in addition to their normal offerings.
- A repositioning by a number of major food companies into the provision of products with significant health claims (see Pilzer, 2007, ppvii-xviii).

As Western consumers have sought a healthier lifestyle through changing dietary patterns, so agri-food companies have transformed and expanded their product ranges. Novel food forms and new food categories, such as nutraceuticals and functional foods, have emerged to give substance to this so-called 'wellness revolution'. The purpose of this chapter is to trace the emerging alliances and strategic partnerships between the food and pharmaceutical industries, and to evaluate some of the implications of these relationships for long-established agri-food companies.

What are nutraceuticals? What are functional foods?

According to Hasler (1998) the term 'functional foods' appeared in Japan in the 1980s, while 'nutraceutical' was first used in 1989 by combining the words 'nutrients' and 'pharmaceuticals' (Kalra, 2003). The coining of this term indicates the growing recognition by the medical community, as well as the public, of the health-promoting effects of foods.

A recent industry study (Just-Food, 2006, p1) defined functional foods as 'foods that provide health benefits beyond basic nutrition'. Such benefits are achieved by adding new components to the original product, such as fibre, fish oil (which contains omega-3 fatty acids), vitamins and minerals, herbal extracts, proteins, phytochemicals (plant chemicals with disease-preventive qualities) and probiotics (beneficial bacteria) (see Just-Food, 2006, p1). Nutraceuticals are those substances which occur naturally in foods, but have been extracted to be sold in dosage form (Just-Food, 2006, p1). DataMonitor (2004) has extended this definition to include foods that confer health or medical benefits beyond what would normally be found in those foods: the purposeful addition of active, biological components converts a food substance into a nutraceutical. For example, folate (folic acid) can be added to staple foods for the purpose of preventing neural tube defects in babies, psyllium has been added to breakfast cereals in an attempt to reduce coronary heart disease and plant substances called phytosterols have been introduced to spreads like margarine as a means of reducing cholesterol levels (Bunge, 2004; Lawrence and Germov, 2008).

Since we are primarily interested in the wellness phenomenon and its impact on the corporate strategies embraced by agri-food companies, we will not dwell on the differences in constituents and production processes associated with nutraceuticals and functional foods. For our purposes, both terms refer to any new food products that have been manipulated in order to deliver perceived health benefits to consumers.

Nutraceuticals, functional foods and the life sciences paradigm

Writing about the growing importance of health concerns for the food and farming industries, Lang and Rayner (2001) and Lang and Heasman (2004) have argued that the industry has yet to live up to its public health promises. While farming in general, and food manufacturing and processing in particular, are expected to produce benefits to the public, to the environment and to the economy, the evidence suggests that the current system of food supply, based on a productionist paradigm, benefits the agri-food sector at the expense of both citizens and the environment.

In the face of this unsustainable paradigm (one based upon petrochemically derived pesticides and herbicides, plant monocultures, extensive water use and the factory farming of animals – see Gray and Lawrence, 2001), the food and agricultural industries of developed nations are faced with a choice between two new integrated approaches. The first is an ecological paradigm, which is effectively the antithesis of the productionist model: it puts a premium on organic and other sustainable modes of production, it emphasizes the importance of local foods that are pesticide free, and it is conscious of the importance of reducing food miles. The second approach is the so-called life sciences paradigm, which involves the use of new biotechnologies (genetically modified organisms) and nanotechnologies (manipulation of genetic and other materials at the level of 1 billionth of a metre) to 'fuse' farming and food manufacturing with bioscience.

The growth of the ecological paradigm – as evidenced by the increased production and consumption of organically certified produce – indicates that its influence will continue to be significant. Nonetheless, the life sciences paradigm appears to be growing even faster. In 2006, the global market for organic produce was some US$40 billion and was expected to grow at close to 20 per cent per annum (Organic Monitor, 2006). According to a DataMonitor (2004) report, the market for nutraceuticals alone was US$60.9 billion in 2003, and was growing at a rate of some 9 per cent per annum. Based on these developments, 'wellness' has been identified as a megatrend – one that would see sales in excess of US$200 billion towards the end of this decade as companies try to reinvent themselves for health-conscious consumers (see Wright, 2007).

There seems to be little doubt about where the food and agricultural industries see their future – that is, as an integral part of the life sciences paradigm. Those agri-food companies embracing wellness are increasingly coming to rely on various branches of bioscience (including biology, biotechnology, cellular biochemistry and, more recently, nanotechnology)[1] to provide the breakthroughs necessary for innovation in this rapidly developing industry. As a consequence, established food companies are entering into strategic alliances with pharmaceutical companies – with traditional distinctions between the two sectors fast disappearing.

The growth of the wellness industry

The first truly functional food – a yoghurt-like drink called Yakult – was developed by a Japanese microbiologist called Minoru Shirota and was first marketed in 1935. Shirota was inspired by the work of Elie Metchnikoff, who was a co-recipient of the Nobel Prize for Physiology in 1908 for his work on cell-mediated immunity and phagocytosis. Metchnikoff was interested in ways of enhancing human longevity and, inspired by the consumption of fermented milk by long-living Balkan populations, advocated the consumption of lactic-acid-producing bacteria in yoghurt and soured milk (Health Watch, 2007, p3). In his subsequent research, Shirota eventually isolated a strain of *Lactobacillus casei*, which 'could not only survive the acid conditions of the stomach and thrive in the intestine tract, but could out-compete potentially harmful organisms' (Health Watch, 2007, p3). Worldwide, some 24 million bottles of Yakult are consumed every day (Yakult, 2005).

From these small beginnings there has emerged a new global industry, in which all of the major companies involved in the agri-food supply chain participate – from input suppliers and commodity suppliers to processing companies, and including such names as Unilever, Kraft, Heinz, Archer Daniel Midland (ADM), Bunge, McDonald's, ConAgra, General Mills and Kelloggs (Harrison, 2000). Perhaps the most interesting example of a large well-established company strategically 're-configuring' itself to embrace the life sciences paradigm is that of Nestlé. Nestlé commenced operations some 140 years ago and is the world's largest food manufacturer. In its representation of itself today, it is no longer simply a food processor but 'the world's foremost Nutrition, Health and Wellness company' (Nestlé, 2008). Nestlé has undertaken a significant programme of research and development (R&D) in order to underwrite these claims. In March 2007, it began funding biotechnological research in New Zealand and Switzerland to develop probiotics for use in infant nutrition products, an innovation that aims to prevent upper respiratory tract infections in children (Nestlé Nutrition, 2007). In addition, Nestlé has expanded its operations in baby food through a series of acquisitions. In April 2007, the company paid some US$5.5 billion to acquire the US baby food brand Gerber from Novartis, and in July 2007 it purchased the Novartis medical nutrition group (Nestlé, 2007), thereby confirming its status as the second largest company in the healthcare nutrition industry.

There have been other significant corporate acquisitions that have further consolidated the company's shift into the wellness sector. In 2006, Nestlé paid US$600 million for Jenny Craig, the manufacturer of weight loss products and programmes. In the same year it paid US$670 million for Uncle Toby's, an Australian producer of cereals and snacks that has claimed its foods possess important nutritional benefits. The company also produces nutrition snacks such as Powerbar, drinks to aid weight loss and the 'Lean Cuisine' brand of diet-related ready meals. It now has a 'Nestlé Nutrition' division covering infant formula, baby food, medical nutrition, weight management and performance (sport) nutrition, as well as a Strategic Wellness Unit to 'drive' the idea of wellness throughout all of the company's main divisions (Nestlé, 2007).

There are numerous other examples which illustrate the trend by which established food companies are coming to embrace the wellness phenomenon. Campbell's Australia has a Centre for Nutrition and Wellness which is described as 'an information resource to help people of all life-stages understand the role that balanced nutrition plays in a healthy, active lifestyle' (Campbell's Australia, 2008). The company's website gives tips on diet, exercise and the nutritional value of foods. In an interesting move, the Coca-Cola company has funded a permanent research centre at the Academy of Chinese Medical Sciences in Beijing to 'promote Chinese wisdom in preventive holistic health through new and innovative beverages', using locally sourced herbs. This is partly in response to falling demand for full-sugar carbonated drinks, and is consistent with the company's decision to form its own 'Beverage Institute for Health and Wellness' (Coca-Cola, 2009).

The convergence of food and pharmaceutical companies

As indicated above, the 'wellness phenomenon' involves a blurring of the distinction between food and medicine, and between the nutritional and the clinical content of the products that consumers ingest. What is occurring is a convergence between the food and pharmaceutical sectors. This convergence has resulted from a wave of mergers and acquisitions alongside 'in-house' development of R&D facilities, which have together underpinned the capacity for new R&D initiatives based on strategic alliances with companies whose origins lie in the pharmaceutical, chemical, biotechnological and nanotechnological sectors.

There are numerous examples of the convergence between the food and pharmaceutical sectors that illustrate the trend we are analysing. An interesting example again involves Nestlé, and in particular its 'in-house' R&D arm known as Nestec. An early patent application granted to Nestec by the US Patent Office in 1994 (US Patent 5330755) involved a process for the production of an anti-diarrheic product based on carob. Later, in 1999, US Patent 5989350 was awarded granting Nestec rights over a heat-modified maize starch which improved the flowing properties of food preparations such as sauces, giving them a 'smooth and unctuous texture'. Similarly, US Patent 6174555, granted in 2001, awarded Nestec intellectual property rights over a coating for ice-based confectionery. The total number of patents awarded to Nestec by the US Patent Office between 1976 and the present day is 1319, most of which are associated with food and beverage ingredients, and food packaging (US Patent Office, 2009).

Another model of R&D development involves the establishment of a strategic alliance between two companies with closely related activities. For example, Proctor and Gamble, a leading producer of foods and food ingredients, has formed an alliance with Bunge, a major producer of bottled vegetable oils, to produce phytosterol ingredients for use in foods and pharmaceuticals. Proctor and Gamble is also seeking to reduce trans-fats and saturated fats in their food products as a means of addressing the heart disease and weight problems that many consumers face. The company has a line of functional ingredients that allow it to provide justification for such claims about the health and wellness benefits of its products (see Proctor and Gamble, 2005). Another company to adopt this approach is Cargill, the global commodity trader which has historically specialized in the procurement and export of grain, oilseed products, beef cattle and other commodities. In 2001, Cargill established its Health and Food Technologies Unit, with the aim of adding value to its traditional lines through the development of a range of functional ingredients, a strategy it progressed in collaboration with companies such as General Mills, Unilever, Coca-Cola, Pepsi-Cola and others seeking to endow their products with health attributes. Products being produced by Cargill include soy isoflavones designed to reduce a baby's susceptibility to rotavirus infections (and thus reduce the incidence of diarrhoea), glucosamine and chondroitin supplements for the improvement of joint functions, and a range of non-sugar sweeteners to reduce calorie intake (Buss, 2003).

The regulation of wellness foods

Convergence between the food and pharmaceutical sectors raises important issues relating to the regulation of wellness products, particularly when claims may be made about the medical benefits of a particular food line. When does a wellness product qualify to be defined as a commodity with clinical properties rather than just dietary benefits? What claims are allowed to be made for particular food wellness products in the absence of the kind of testing to which drugs are subjected? What needs to be done to ensure that wellness products are safe and do not have unknown side effects? Is it necessary to introduce regulations in order to ensure that the long-term effects of genetic modification are not harmful to humans or animals? And should nanotechnologies – which are not, presently, governed by international rules and protocols – be immediately subject to critical scientific scrutiny and state regulation (see Chapter 16)? These are among the major questions emerging in the present era, with all pointing to the desirability of the emergence of a more rigorous regulatory framework to govern the production, marketing and consumption of the novel wellness foods.

For example, one issue surrounding the production and marketing of wellness foods is the distinction between drugs (which are subject to testing and regulatory approval) and food products with alleged clinical benefits (which may not be subject to regulatory approval). The case of a red rice yeast supplement marketed by the US company Pharmanax is instructive in this regard:

> ... a novel HMG-CoA inhibitor extract from Monascus purpureus grown on rice, also known as red yeast rice, has demonstrated lipid improvement... Although red yeast rice has been used in China for over a thousand years, an FDA and pharmaceutical industry dispute has erupted regarding its classification as a supplement. This issue goes back to 1998 when Pharmanex, [which] was marketing a red yeast rice supplement at the time, was prohibited from selling its product due to its high levels of lovastatin – the chief ingredient in the cholesterol-lowering drug Mevacor. According to the Natural Products Association, Washington, D.C., FDA took the position that because the Pharmanex product, Cholestin, contained elevated levels of the active ingredient lovastatin found in prescription drugs, it was an unapproved new drug. Further, Pharmanex advertised the products emphasizing their lovastatin content. The NPA says Pharmanex eventually sued the agency, contending that the red yeast rice product was a dietary

supplement and should not be subject to drug regulation. Despite an initial ruling in 1998 favoring Pharmanex, on March 30, 2001, a decision by the Court of Appeals affirmed FDA's position and held that red yeast rice products containing significant amounts of the ingredient lovastatin are drugs subject to regulation by FDA. Pharmanex decided not to pursue the appeal (Adams, 2008).

Currently, such issues in the US are treated on a case-by-case basis under existing powers exercised by the Food and Drug Administration. But the difficulty of establishing a general system of regulation has been acknowledged by recent EU legislation. The main focus of EU food legislation and regulation has usually been on food safety, which covers functional foods as a matter of course. Legislation on the use of novel ingredients was introduced in 1997, which required a safety assessment on all foods and ingredients that were not in common use prior to that date. This requirement nonetheless proved to be of limited significance. It effectively covered only a few products and was criticized for stifling innovation since manufacturers of functional foods and food supplements could only make use of established ingredients and not newly developed products (Ottaway, 2007).

By 2000, over 80 proposals for improved safety legislation could be listed in a White Paper on Food Safety published by the European Commission (EC). One such proposal was for the creation of a General Food Regulation to lay down the principles of food law and to establish an independent Food Authority able to provide scientific advice and to undertake risk assessments. While this regulation (EC No 178/2002) was implemented in 2002, it did not create a specific framework for the regulation of functional foods (Coppens et al, 2006). In 2006, regulations were adopted to govern the addition of vitamins, minerals and certain other substances to food products, through the establishment of three lists, which covered prohibited substances, substances whose use is controlled by specified conditions, and substances placed under scrutiny and subject to a full safety evaluation (Ottaway, 2007). This was followed in 2007 by the introduction of a regulation on labelling, and a regulation on the making of health and nutrition claims for particular products. This regulation requires that only those claims included on an officially approved list of health and nutritional claims will be allowed to appear on labels and in advertising material (Ottaway, 2007).

The unprecedented expansion of production and consumption in nutraceutical and functional food products, and the associated scope for significant increases in the trade of such products, suggests the need for uniform standards to protect consumers. As with earlier cases of standard-setting in the food sector – namely, the emergence of standards for organic produce, and of standards for quality and safety set by global retailers – it seems likely that a regulatory system based on the equivalence of national standards, or a system of third-party certification administered by a body able to enforce this at the global level, will emerge at some point in the near future.

Explaining the wellness phenomenon

While we acknowledge that the health concerns of consumers play a large part in stimulating demand for wellness products, we believe that other factors are also important – factors that reflect the changing relationships along the agri-food supply chain. The argument is that, while in past decades food manufacturers such as Nestlé, Kellogg's, Heinz and Unilever have dominated market share in the sales of well-known branded food items, their share of the market is currently being eroded by those supermarkets that are competing with 'own brand' or 'private label' lines (Burch and Lawrence, 2007). The supermarkets – which once stocked only major food manufacturers' products – today carry and promote their own lines of breakfast foods, carbonated drinks, canned foods, frozen and chilled foods, and a host of other items across a growing range of product lines. The supermarkets have invested heavily in their own branding of quality food (and other) products, which now compete directly with the branded products on both quality and price. Importantly, as 'own brands', these products provide a higher return to the supermarket than do sales of the competing food manufacturers' brands (Burch and Lawrence, 2007). These conditions, in turn, provide a major incentive for the supermarkets to stack shelves with as much of their own products as possible, leading, over time, to the marginalization of other brands.

This drive towards the promotion of 'own brands' has been reinforced by the highly innovative practices of global supermarkets in the development of new products such as fresh 'ready meals', 'meal solutions' and other convenience foods, as well as by the global sourcing of fresh foods. These strategies, in turn, have come to challenge the dominance of established food processors. The response on the part of these established manufacturers has been an attempt to regain market share by moving into the production of a market segment which has not yet been occupied by supermarket 'own brand' products – namely, wellness products in the form of nutraceuticals, functional foods and a wide range of related products.

A second factor in the growth of the wellness industries is their use of the patent system and the related capacity to generate intellectual property rights in foodstuffs – a critically important form of protection at a time when proprietary brands are under attack from supermarket private labels. As indicated earlier, it is the fusion of the food manufacturing sector with the bioscience research sector that is creating opportunities for the kinds of innovation that had previously been absent among branded-product manufacturers. One of the other major benefits of such collaboration, though, is that the new wellness companies will be undertaking R&D for the production of food commodities and food ingredients. This means that now and for some years into the future, the intellectual property rights held by food companies will be protected by the patent system rather than by the ownership of brand products, where protection was afforded by copyright and brand names. The biosciences are now able to employ molecular-level changes that provide opportunities to alter what were once 'fixed' properties of foods, particularly with the novel addition of health-giving qualities.

Where applicable, patent ownership will provide a stronger form of protection for intellectual property than the ownership of brands, where the scope for producing similar products is substantial. As indicated by the examples of Nestec, Cargill and Kraft given above, the established food manufacturers have adopted a policy of innovation based on the latest advances in biochemistry, biotechnology and nanotechnology to create a wide range of health-based products. Here, wellness companies can promote themselves as conveying major health benefits, assisting them to compete with the supermarkets whose extensive advertising and corporate power has helped to position them as 'food authorities' (Dixon, 2007).

Finally, the growth of the wellness industry also reflects the 'greening' of many societies with consumers becoming more conscious about the nature of the ingredients in foods, the packaging of foods, and the distances over which food travels. Many consumers are coming to recognize the need to reduce energy use, to address pollution, to eliminate the 'food miles' that agricultural products travel where possible, to avoid eating foods that might compromise biodiversity and so forth. Green consumers are particularly interested in purchasing products from sustainable production systems – that is, systems that are less polluting than conventional agriculture (Lyons et al, 2001) and which produce foods that are less processed and are considered to be 'fresh', 'safe' and 'natural' (Warde, 1997). An important question for those promoting the life-science approach to novel foods is whether consumers will identify the new products as health giving (that is, 'natural') rather than as the manipulated creations of laboratory scientists (that is, 'unnatural').

The future of wellness companies

What will become of the wellness companies? Will they be the future of the food industry as people become more health conscious, or will consumers reject the very basis of the production of health/wellness products when they contain GMOs or are created via nanotechnologies? And what of the efficacy of the wellness model? Does it work in terms of providing solutions to the diet-related health issues faced by people throughout the world?

As Lang and Heasman (2004) have noted, the bioscience paradigm is based upon a reductionist model in which scientists interested in the health of the human body work with the basic components of life (genes, DNA, molecules) and seek to identify such things as gene expression and metabolic function as contributing to either disease, or to good health. The aim is to identify those molecular and/or genetic features of the human genome that might be altered, or might be acted upon, to improve the health of the individual. Scientists interested in nutrition also travel down the reductionist path, literally 'taking apart' genes and incorporating these into foods that people eat. The message here is that society must trust in science for the delivery of good health (Lang and Heasman, 2004, p38).

Related to this issue of reductionism is the tendency to focus upon individual solutions to the health problems faced by society as a whole. As part of the wellness revolution, nutrigenomics is a new science aiming to identify how food ingredients react with, and influence, bodily cellular performance. Hence, science might be able to determine how changes in an individual's diet may improve health and/or reduce disease, based on the particular genetic makeup of that individual. Once scientists know how dietary substances affect cells and genes, they can design particular foods and supplements to act on the body's molecular structure to produce certain health-based outcomes. It is easy to see the individualist trajectory at work here. Wellness will come to be associated with the health performance of the individual, not with the health of the wider society. Those with the financial resources to undertake the genetic screening, seek the biomedical advice and purchase the beneficial nutrients, might be expected to have enhanced health outcomes. But this approach will do little to address wider health problems faced by society. That is, in a world where the public health costs from poor diets, smoking and lack of physical exercise are at very high levels (Pierce, 2005, pxxiii), the focus of applied research investment might be more beneficial (that is, have wider positive benefits) if it targets health in its broadest sense. And, for the food industry, this might mean examining food production and distribution practices along the entire food chain, with the dual aims of eliminating waste and improving overall public health (Lang and Heasman, 2004, pp109–10).

Finally, in terms of the continuing problem for those food manufacturing companies developing wellness products in response to challenges from the supermarket sector, there is no reason to think that the supermarkets will not eventually move down a similar path and so erode the competitive edge which the food companies are seeking. Supermarkets in Australia are already attempting to define themselves as 'health authorities' to complement their status as 'food authorities' (Dixon, 2007). Woolworths ('the fresh food people') is Australia's market leader in grocery sales. It has over 700 supermarket outlets and serves up to 13 million customers each week. It claims to serve its customers by supplying 'fresh, healthy ... foods', and by 'offering expert nutritional advice [and] useful food handling and safety advice' (Woolworths, 2008). Woolworths also markets an own brand version of a 'Yakult-like' probiotic drink, which is produced in South Korea, while Tesco and other supermarkets are doing the same in the UK (*Irish Examiner*, 2006). Another company that has explicitly used the term 'wellness' is the UK supermarket Tesco, one of the leading private brand retailers in the world, with own brands accounting for over 50 per cent of its total food sales (O'Keefe, 2005, p31). Tesco has differentiated its products to appeal to different markets, with 'Tesco' as the conventional brand, 'Tesco Finest' for the higher-priced market, and 'Tesco Value' as the discount brand. It is at this higher price level that Tesco is entering the health area with premium brands such as 'Tesco Healthy Living', 'Tesco Fair Trade' and 'Tesco Organic' (Tesco, 2008).

Conclusion

The argument in this chapter is that as food manufacturers seek to maintain their market share and their profits in the face of pressure from supermarket own brands, they are invoking the health and wellness benefits of the products they sell. Furthermore, a number of the leading food manufacturers are now promoting themselves as wellness companies, making claims that their entire operations are based on the provision of healthy, nutritious and safe foods. This has, in part, been a response to the concerns of a growing number of consumers that the foods they are eating are overprocessed and chemically manipulated, and that their ingestion/digestion is partly responsible for poor health. Industrialized foods have, for example, been implicated in the increase in obesity, stroke, heart disease and cancer (Lawrence, 2004). By reinventing themselves as wellness firms, the food manufacturers are seeking to benefit from the 'revolutionary' wellness-related consumption patterns and personal health strategies of consumers in the developed world, as well as from the promotion of themselves as food authorities. However, at the same time as the food manufacturers are moving into the wellness sector, the supermarkets are pre-empting this shift with their own wellness strategies.

The most important concerns relate not so much to whether the supermarkets or the brand manufacturers are 'winning' in the market for wellness products, though, but relate instead to the efficacy and the impacts of the so-called 'wellness revolution'. Bioscience is at the core of many of the new products about which wellness claims are being made, and yet – as suggested earlier – bio-manipulated foods are not 'natural' foods. Are these the foods that consumers will embrace? What appears to be required in overcoming the health-related outcomes of poor eating habits is not the nutrigenomic promises of designer foods and wellness diets but, rather, a broader public health approach that would reduce the intake of junk foods and increase exercise levels in the population at large. In this vein, Lang and Rayner (2001) call for an integrated approach to food provisioning, which they term 'ecological public health'. This approach, they argue, should be a major priority of governments given its capacity to integrate the sustainability of food production, food safety and food nutrition, which together form the so-called 'three pillars' of future food policy. To date, governments in western countries have struggled with ways to ensure that environmental sustainability, food safety and nutrition are given equal importance in food provision.

Notes

1   A survey of European consumers in 2007 revealed that the majority of respondents rejected the use of nanotechnologies in food, despite that fact that they are already being employed in food production (Food Navigator, 2007).

References

Adams, C. (2008) 'Hearty nutraceuticals', *Nutraceuticals World*, 1 April, www. nutraceuticalsworld.com/articles/2008/04/hearty-nutraceuticals, accessed 24 March 2009

Bunge (2004) 'Bunge form alliance with Proctor and Gamble and Peter Cremer to sell phytosterol ingredients for foods and pharmaceuticals', www.pgchemicals.com/ resources/pr/ Bunge_TriParty_11-10-04.pdf, accessed 2 May 2006

Burch, D. and Lawrence, G. (2007) 'Supermarket own brands, new foods and the reconfiguration of agri-food supply chains', in D. Burch and G. Lawrence (eds) *Supermarkets and Agri-food Supply Chains: Transformations in the Production and Consumption of Foods*, Edward Elgar, Cheltenham, UK

Buss, D. (2003) 'The giant awakes', *New Nutrition Business*, vol 8, no 6, pp19–21

Campbell's Australia (2008) 'Centre for nutrition and wellness', www.campbellsoup. com.au/club/wellness.aspx, accessed 21 May 2008

Coca-Cola (2009) The Beverage Institute for Health and Wellness, at www. beverageinstitute.org, accessed 3 August

Coppens, P., Fernandes, M. and Pettman, S. (2006) 'European regulations on nutraceuticals, dietary supplements and functional foods: A framework based on safety,' *Toxicology*, vol 221, no 1, pp59–74

DataMonitor (2004) *Global Nutraceuticals: An Industry Profile*, DataMonitor, New York and London

Dixon, J. (2007) 'Supermarkets as new food authorities', in D. Burch and G. Lawrence (eds) *Supermarkets and Agri-food Supply Chains: Transformations in the Production and Consumption of Foods*, Edward Elgar, Cheltenham, UK

Food Navigator (2007) 'Consumers against nanotech in food, says BfR', www. foodnavigator.com/news/printNewsBis.asp?id=82217, accessed 12 December 2007

Gray, I. and Lawrence, G. (2001) *A Future for Regional Australia: Escaping Global Misfortune*, Cambridge University Press, Cambridge, UK

Harrison, J. (2000) 'In the spotlight: Unilever joins other food giants scrambling to get healthy', *Mergers and Acquisitions*, 1 June

Hasler, C. (1998) 'Functional foods: Their role in disease prevention and health promotion', *Food Technology*, vol 52, no 11, pp63–70

Health Canada (2002) 'Policy paper – nutraceuticals/functional foods and health claims on foods', Government of Canada, Ottawa, www.hc-sc.gc.ca/fn-an/label-etiquet/claims-reclam/nutra-funct_foods-nutra-fonct_aliment-eng.php, accessed 15 February 2009

Health Watch (2007) *Position Paper: Functional Foods*, www.healthwatch-uk.org/ Functional%20foods.pdf, accessed 9 February 2009

Irish Examiner (2006) 'Health drinks market set to grow by a third', 12 March

Just-Food (2006) 'An overview of the world's largest functional food companies', Aroq Limited, Bromsgrove

Kalra, E. (2003) 'Nutraceutical – definition and introduction', *AAPS PharmSci.*, vol 5, no 2, pp1–2

Lang, T. and Heasman, M. (2004) *Food Wars: The Global Battle for Mouths, Minds and Markets*, Earthscan, London

Lang, T. and Rayner, G. (2001) *Why Health is the Key to the Future of Food and Farming, A Report on the Future of Farming and Food*, www.agobservatory.org/ library.cfm?refID=30300, accessed 24 March 2008

Lawrence, F. (2004) *Not on the Label: What Really Goes into the Food on Your Plate*, Penguin, London

Lawrence, M. and Germov, J. (2008) 'Functional foods and public health nutrition policy', in J. Germov and L. Williams (eds) *A Sociology of Health and Nutrition: The Social Appetite*, Third Edition, Oxford University Press, Melbourne

Lyons, K., Lockie, S. and Lawrence, G. (2001) 'Consuming "green": The symbolic construction of organic foods', *Rural Society*, vol 11, no 3, pp197–210

Nestlé (2007) 'Wellness – nutrition and health', www.nestlé.co.uk/OurResponsibility/NutritionHealthAndWellness, accessed 17 October 2007

Nestlé (2008) 'Nestlé is.....', www.Nestlé.com/, accessed 21 May 2008

Nestlé Nutrition (2007) 'What's new?' www.Nestlénutrition.com/en/Tools/News.htm, accessed 17 November 2007

O'Keefe, M. (2005) 'Fresh food retailing: A growth story', *Farm Policy Journal*, vol 2, no 1, pp28–36

Organic Monitor (2006) 'The global market for organic food and drink: Business opportunities and future outlook', www.organicmonitor.com/700240.htm, accessed 9 February 2009

Ottaway, P. (2007) 'Supplements in Europe – a decade of intensive regulation', *Nutraceuticals International*, August, www.global.factiva.com.libraryproxy.griffith.edu.au/ha/default.aspx, accessed 24 March 2009

Pierce, M. (2005) 'Convergence of the health industry', *Leadership in Health Services*, vol 18, no 1, ppxxii-xxxi

Pilzer, P. (2007) *The New Wellness Revolution: How to Make Your Fortune in the Next Trillion Dollar Industry*, John Wiley and Sons, New Jersey

Proctor and Gamble (2005) 'P&G food ingredients: Bringing more to the table', www.pgchemicals.com/default.asp?page=ov, accessed 2 May 2006

Tesco (2008) 'Tesco healthy living', www.tescotracker.com/, accessed 21 May 2008

US Patent Office (2009) USPTO patent full text and image database, http://patft.uspto.gov/netacgi/nph-Parser?Sect1=PTO2&Sect2=HITOFF&p=1&u=%2Fnetahtml%2FPTO%2Fsearchbool.html&r=0&f=S&l=50&TERM1=Nestec&FIELD1=&co1=AND&TERM2=&FIELD2=&d=PTXT, accessed 15 February 2009

Warde, A. (1997) *Consumption, Food and Taste*, Sage, London

Woolworths (2008) 'Our story', www.woolworths.com.au/AboutUs/OurStory/, accessed 21 May 2008

Wright, R. (2007) 'The wild world of wellness', *Nutraceuticals World*, vol 10, no 8, p10

Yakult (2005) *The Shape of Health: Annual Report 2005*, www.yakult.co.jp/english/pdf/ar2005.pdf, accessed 5 March 2009

12
Supermarkets, Food Systems and Public Health: Facing the Challenges

Libby Hattersley and Jane Dixon

Introduction

Over recent decades, food systems around the world have become increasingly – and, some would say, excessively – concentrated, so that just a few large transnational corporations now control the vast majority of the world's food supply (Lawrence and Burch, 2007). In a period that has arguably heralded the emergence of a food regime based upon 'greening' tendencies among consumers (Burch and Lawrence, 2005; Friedmann, 2005), supermarkets have attained the balance of power and are said to be increasingly dictating what, where and how food is produced and consumed around the globe (see the contributions in Lawrence and Burch, 2007). These transformations have been well researched and documented (see Reardon and Beardegue, 2002; Lang and Heasman, 2004; Burch and Lawrence, 2007; McMichael, 2009). However, evidence regarding the health implications of this concentration of market power (in terms of both extent and market conduct) has been slower to emerge. Research in this area remains limited by lack of agreement over where responsibility for public health (beyond a narrow focus on food safety) lies in relation to the food system, as well as by the absence of an accepted framework for examining the multiple dimensions of food system-related health.

That supermarkets play a critical role in public health is undeniable, and credit has been given for their role in improving food safety and quality standards, fresh food availability and dietary diversity for many customers. As Lawrence and Burch (2007, p21) have said, the retail sector 'has an enormous capacity to deliver cheap, high quality, and wholesome foodstuffs to consumers'. At the same time, supermarkets have been criticized for externalizing the social, economic and environmental costs of their operations and ultimately adversely affecting the health and wellbeing of many communities worldwide, particularly those most vulnerable. These concerns have prompted supermarkets to place increasing importance on their role as leaders in corporate responsibility and as trusted authorities on diet and lifestyle. Whether this latter role, in particular, is deserved or even appropriate has not been adequately examined. We argue that the public health impacts arising from this sector require more government attention than they have received to date, given the unprecedented scale at which supermarkets are operating.

Drawing on evidence from a range of disciplines, including sociology, human geography, cultural anthropology, public health, and development and environment studies, this chapter deconstructs the multiple pathways through which supermarkets are influencing population health. It identifies the dominant industry and government responses to the issues faced and emphasizes the need for an integrated and systematic research agenda feeding into more effective public leadership, in order to address the challenges arising from supermarket-led food systems.

Deconstructing the relationship between supermarkets and health

There is increasing emphasis on the need for food policy and research that integrates the biological, social and environmental dimensions of health and sustainability (Lang, 2007; McMichael, 2007; Lang et al, 2009). The New Nutrition Science Project was launched in 2005 as a joint initiative of the International Union of Nutritional Sciences and the World Policy Forum. The aim was to reorient the nutrition discipline, declaring that 'the purpose of nutrition science is to contribute to a world in which present and future generations fulfill their human potential, live in the best of health, and develop, sustain and enjoy an increasingly diverse human, living and physical environment' (Beauman et al, 2007, p697).

The three major food system-related issues currently impacting on population health can broadly be defined as:

1 Inappropriate dietary patterns and high rates of diet-related disease (the biological dimension).
2 Adverse impacts on worker and community wellbeing, as well as widening social inequalities, as a result of inappropriate use of market power within the food supply system (the social justice dimension).
3 Food system-related environmental change, with subsequent feedback implications for food system sustainability and population health (the environmental dimension).

Supermarkets play a critical role in all three of these dimensions, as discussed below.

Supermarkets and diet-related health

The evidence for a relationship between dietary patterns and health is now well established. There is also a growing body of evidence available to indicate that dietary patterns are shaped by the local food environment: a composite of the mix of food retailing formats, ease of consumer access to particular outlets, the goods on offer in the local area, the relative cost of healthy and unhealthy food items, the cultural acceptability of particular foods, and area and sub-population characteristics (Morland et al, 2002; Cummins and Macintyre, 2006; White, 2007). While these impacts appear to be highly context-specific, all available evidence points to the powerful role that supermarkets play within local food environments. Evidence from the US, for example, has fairly consistently implicated supermarkets in the emergence of 'food deserts' due to preferential store siting in wealthier neighbourhoods and competitive displacement of small fresh food retailers (see Morland et al, 2002; Zenk et al, 2005). The result is that cheap, nutritious food becomes almost unobtainable in low-income neighborhoods, while supermarket presence in other areas has been found to have a beneficial impact on diet and related health outcomes (Morland et al, 2006).

Evidence from the UK, Australia and New Zealand does not consistently support the 'food deserts' concept, although it does suggest the existence of socio-economic and geographical differences in healthy food accessibility and affordability (see, for example, Wrigley et al, 2003; Burns et al, 2004; White et al, 2004; Burns and Inglis, 2006; Friel et al, 2006; O'Dwyer and Coveney, 2006; Winkler et al, 2006). Australia is a case in point, where a number of studies have determined that lower socio-economic and remote areas have to pay more for a healthy basket of food and have fewer fruit and vegetable varieties available (Burns et al, 2004; Burns and Inglis, 2006; Cancer Council NSW, 2007).

In developing countries and emerging economies, supermarkets and the foods they promote and sell have been implicated in the 'nutrition transition' towards the 'Western diet' – one that is high in fat, salt and sugar, and comes replete with associated health impacts (Hawkes, 2006). Wave theory has been used in economic geography to describe the different stages of supermarket penetration that are occurring across the globe. In the early and middle stages of penetration into a developing market, supermarkets sell fresh (and healthy) foods at higher prices than are generally charged by traditional fresh markets, while moving aggressively to establish price-competitiveness in processed foods (Minten and Reardon, 2008). This balance shifts slowly over time as supermarkets assume greater control over fresh food supply chains and gradually drop their prices of fresh fruit and vegetables. Meanwhile, significant numbers of small retailers are displaced due to urban planning regulations and declining customer numbers (Goldman et al, 1999; Schaffner et al, 2005; Minten and Reardon, 2008).

As yet, there is no consensus as to whether price trumps other factors with regard to food consumption patterns in developing markets. However, there is no doubt that the effects of food prices are experienced most strongly by those in society who possess the least purchasing power. In a systematic review of evidence from the UK and North America, White (2007) concluded that food preferences can act independently to predict food consumption and, for some groups (such as older adults and young people), food preferences are more important than accessibility or price.

Hawkes (2008) situates these issues within a broader assessment of the ways in which supermarkets can influence diet. Based on a review of the evidence provided by 22 studies, Hawkes identifies five such influences: supermarket locations, the foods they sell, the prices they charge, the strategies that they use to promote food categories and brands, and their nutrition education activities. Hawkes (2008) argues that supermarkets generally make a positive contribution to diets by increasing the size of the population that has access to affordable dietary diversity. At the same time, however, they can also contribute negatively by encouraging the consumption of processed and energy-dense foods through such means as promotions and pricing. Like White (2007) and others, Hawkes determines that food retailers can exert a significant influence on local food environments. Moreover, by displacing alternative food outlets, supermarkets may undermine the accessibility of healthy diets to 'marginalized' populations.

Hawkes (2008) arrived at two major conclusions in her assessment of supermarket influence over diets. First, supermarket influence is highly context-specific both geographically and socio-culturally. It is also very much dependent on the stage of a country's development. Second, supermarket food promotions may affect what foods consumers buy, as well as how much of the promoted product they buy. Their commercial interest in encouraging customers to buy and 'eat more' contradicts the advice of nutritionists and others to eat in moderation, both for health and environmental reasons (McMichael, 2007). In fact, Hawkes contended that the 'eat more' messages led by supermarkets contribute more to the 'obesogenic environment' that increasingly prevails in developed nations than does a more direct focus on individual energy-dense foods.

Supermarkets, community wellbeing and social justice

In addition to direct diet-related health impacts, supermarkets are thought to be playing a broader role in food culture. In their strategies of selling the concept of a time-poor 'convenience culture' – and of heavily promoting value-added and often highly processed 'meal solutions' – supermarkets have been criticized for contributing to the erosion of many of the norms and practices around home cuisine: namely, the intergenerational sharing of food knowledge, of preferred ingredients and of cooking skills (Ulijaszek, 2002). In promoting 'functional' processed food products by highlighting the presence or absence of specific nutrients, supermarkets have been implicated in the 'food reductionism' paradigm, which has itself been criticized for blurring and undermining distinctions between food and medicine, and between processed and unprocessed foods (Scrinis, 2008). Moreover, in stocking vast product ranges and constantly introducing 'novel' products, supermarkets have been criticized for contributing to choice overload (Nestle, 2002; Roff, 2007) and to nutritional confusion, with the result being a growing public perception of the need to look to some form of 'food authority' for guidance on diet (Dixon, 2007). At the same time, they are thought to be contributing to the homogenization and standardization of tastes and diets (Duchin, 2005). While these concerns are becoming increasingly widespread, supermarkets' impacts on social relations around food preparation and consumption have nonetheless received little empirical research attention thus far, and are thereby worthy of further exploration.

Other under-researched topics relating to the social dimension of health – although currently receiving growing attention – include the impact of supermarket power and contractual obligations on the occupational health and safety, socio-economic wellbeing (and livelihoods) of their suppliers, as well as the impact of these conditions on the social fabric of rural communities (Coe and Wrigley, 2007; Reardon et al, 2007). The growth in alternative food systems based on farmers' markets and community supported agriculture has been attributed to these concerns (Kirwan, 2004). A related issue is the potential for social impacts to arise within neighbour communities[1] as a result of job creation/displacement, changes in shopping behaviours and impacts on the financial viability of competing and complementary businesses.

Although power relations in the food system as a result of supermarket hegemony have been identified as a growing concern (Hughes, 2005; Harvey, 2007), the health impacts arising from supermarket conduct along the full length of the food supply system still require much greater attention. As Hawkes (2008) has noted in relation to dietary impacts, these influences are likely to be highly context-specific and affected by myriad geographic, demographic, cultural and socio-economic factors.

Supermarkets and an unsustainable food supply

While few would question the remarkable efficiencies introduced into modern food systems by supermarkets as a result of increased scales of operation and technological sophistication, few would also dispute that supermarket operations have a significant impact on the environment. The issue of global environmental change, food systems and human health is, in itself, a highly complex area. Nevertheless, the balance of available evidence now indicates that the global food production system is environmentally unsustainable, and that there is an urgent need to minimize further environmental damage if the future food needs of the world's growing population are to be met (McMichael et al, 2007; Cohen et al, 2008; McMichael, 2008).

At the most immediate level, environmental considerations arise from the location, size and nature of supermarket store development. Major supermarket chains have been criticized for favouring super-sized stores in 'town fringe' locations, which draw customers away from the traditional town centre and encourage car-based shopping (see, for example, Friends of the Earth, 2005). Research in France has found that shopping in a hypermarket emits four times more carbon dioxide than shopping at a local supermarket – due largely to the association of hypermarket shopping with car-dependency and increased travel distances (Beauvais, 2008). These problems cannot be seen as universal criticisms, however, as most major food retailers operate a diverse portfolio of retail formats, including small 'metro' stores in busy down-town areas, petrol station convenience stores, home delivery and on-line shopping (Pritchard, 2000). The environmental implications of these 'alternative' supermarket retail formats have received little research attention to date.

Beyond the retail store, supermarkets have received widespread negative publicity in relation to the environmental burdens that arise from their influence over food production, packaging and transport. According to a number of recent life cycle analysis studies, the most energy-intensive products to produce are energy-dense, animal-based foods – including fats and oils, and sweet snacks and drinks (Carlsson-Kanyama et al, 2003; Oresund Food Network and Oresund Environment Academy, 2008). These foods are heavily promoted through supermarkets and, in some of their retail formats (for example, in convenience stores at petrol outlets), these are almost overwhelmingly the only products available. Further, as discussed earlier, the 'eat more' approach to retailing widely adopted by supermarkets has been criticized for promoting excessive food purchasing, consumption and waste (Lundqvist et al, 2008). As such, it is an approach that contradicts recommendations to eat frugally, and to eat only what is necessary to promote and sustain health. Further criticism related to environmental impacts has been aimed at supermarkets for their global-sourcing strategies, long transport distances and refrigeration-dependent supply chains (Friends of the Earth, 2005; MacMillan et al, 2008).

Concerns over environmental change, growing food insecurity and a world population that is increasingly adopting the 'Western diet' (a diet that is high in animal products and processed foods), have encouraged a rash of media commentary and government-commissioned reports. A recent report commissioned by the Victorian State government in Australia – the country's second most populous state, and home to its horticultural food bowl – provided an increasingly familiar series of snapshots regarding the modern food system's contribution to environmental change (Larsen et al, 2008). Not surprisingly in the hot, dry country of Australia, concerns relating to climate change and water scarcity are at the fore. The report stressed that the biggest impact most individuals have on the environment is through the food they eat, with approximately half of the average Australian urban household's water use directly related to food (Larsen et al, 2008, p8). In turn, the grave implications of Australia's resource-hungry food supply for rural livelihoods and future food security were a central focus of the report:

> *Competition for water means that it will be increasingly used for 'high value' products (e.g. wine, almonds and dairy) often for export. As Australian and Victorian producers struggle with water*

> *scarcity and increasing costs, cheaper imports from international markets are filling market niches for basic food products such as fruit and vegetables. Under current conditions and excessive debt many producers are ceasing production, but reduced domestic production capability could undermine future food security* (Larsen et al, 2008, p16).

Despite growing civil society concerns for food system-related ecological damage and future food security, there nevertheless remains a paucity of data relating to all food system sectors, particularly between the farm gate and the household – the sphere dominated by supermarkets.

Responding to the challenges: The battle between citizens, governments and supermarkets

The majority of national governments across the world have demonstrated a strong and ongoing preference for self-regulation in the food retail sector, rather than for imposing what are seen as restrictive, costly and time-intensive governmental regulatory arrangements. However, from time to time, high levels of civil-society concern relating to retailer dominance and its wider social implications have led national governments to respond with various forms of public inquiry into the sector, all of which have focused on trading practices within the sector, on barriers to competition and on fair prices for consumers. By and large, these investigations have found some degree of abuse of supermarket power. However, the outcomes of such inquiries have not reached beyond the establishment of voluntary codes of conduct and watchdog monitoring schemes. This can only be seen as a form of political ambivalence – or, as Vorley (2007, p259) has put it, of 'political paralysis' – in the face of such a large and powerful sector.

While most governments have taken a hands-off approach, supermarkets have moved quickly and decisively to position themselves as authority figures in the food system. Facing growing media and civil society attention, they are increasingly juggling this heightened responsibility with the need to control brand image and reputation. For example, in order to manage consumer concerns and demands relating to food quality, supermarkets are leading the way in an 'audit culture' of quality assurance schemes and supply chain traceability (Campbell and Le Heron, 2007; Lawrence and Burch, 2007). This strategy enables supermarkets to offer a guarantee to their customers that the products they sell meet strict quality standards, and ultimately serves to re-embed trust in the industrial food system and the institution of the supermarket (Dixon, 2007).

One of the most important trends in supermarket-led control of the food supply is the growth of private label products, produced and sold under a supermarkets' own label, which compete directly with branded food products for shelf-space and are frequently priced more competitively (Burch and Lawrence, 2007). Own-brand lines enable retailers to exert significantly greater control over their supply chains, with substantial input into product specifications and quality assurance, along with the opportunity for greater returns. In moving into this area, retailers become de facto manufacturers, and are in a stronger position than traditional brand manufacturers to track consumer purchasing patterns and to innovate rapidly in response (Burch and Lawrence, 2005). With substantially greater control over their supply chains and with each product displaying the supermarket label, own-brands have become a key strategy for retailers to instill and nurture consumer trust and loyalty (Konefal et al, 2004). On the flip-side, however, supermarkets face significant risks in terms of brand reputation, and as a result they enforce strict food safety and quality assurance standards on their own-brand suppliers. It has been reported that the costs and risks associated with this greater emphasis on standards, traceability and the associated 'audit culture' are being passed up the supply chain, with growers and suppliers being required to bear these costs in order to access the market. Further, there is some evidence from the UK of increasingly direct and highly uneven relationships between supermarket chains and their international own-label suppliers, with poor labour conditions identified at production sites being a central issue of concern (Hughes, 2005).

In addition to the potential for costs and risks associated with quality assurance being passed to actors higher up in the supply chain (Hughes, 2005), with implications for supplier wellbeing, a number of concerns have been raised about limitations to the effectiveness of audits in evaluating labour standards. In identifying three waves through which retailer-led ethical audit management in the UK has developed – starting with retail-led social auditing of own-label suppliers, moving to third-party monitoring, and most recently to a focus on supplier self-evaluation – Hughes (2005) contends that ethical audit systems have become progressively more aligned with corporate pressures than with a moral drive to improve labour conditions at production sites.

Outside of their supply chains, the major supermarkets are increasingly using corporate social responsibility strategies to promote their contributions to community and environmental wellbeing, and to enhance their reputations as 'good corporate citizens' (Lawrence and Burch, 2007). These efforts generally promote three main domains: people, place and profit. At present, however, efforts are largely focused on the environmental aspects of place – and to a lesser extent on local community involvement – with health and wellness policies being a relatively new introduction (Dibb et al, 2008). It is rare to find assessments of the health of supply chain participants, possibly due to difficulties in getting suppliers to discuss their relations with supermarkets for fear of retribution.

As part of their position as trusted social institutions in Australia, super-markets are promoting and selling 'health' to their customers' and increasingly taking over the role of dietary and nutritional 'advisors' for the population (Burch and Lawrence, 2007 and see Chapter 11 in this volume). According to Hawkes (2008), core health and wellness strategies being led by supermarkets include the reformulation of own-brand products and the development of 'healthy' own-brand lines marked by the introduction of nutrition labels, along with the promotion of fruit and vegetables, and the implementation of nutrition education initiatives. Other strategies include the promotion and sale of organic products, and of novel and functional foods, with associated claims about their health-giving properties, together with partnerships between supermarkets, nutrition professionals and academics.

The risk supermarkets face with this strategy is an increasingly health- and marketing-savvy media and public. Australia's second largest supermarket chain, Coles Myer, has recently been forced to announce an intended re-design of its own-brand 'SmartBuy' logo following negative media reports over the logo's similarity to the official National Heart Foundation 'Tick', which is awarded to specific food products deemed to be 'healthier choices'. Media reports have argued that the national retailer has been intentionally deceiving its customers by conveying the impression that 'SmartBuy' products are healthier than they actually are, thus compromising the health of its customers, particularly those in lower-income brackets (Burke, 2009).

In the UK, the major supermarket chains have been particularly active in promoting commitments to environmental and ethical responsibilities, including the establishment of the Euro Retailer Produce Working Group's Good Agricultural Practice (EurepGAP) – now GlobalGAP – protocol for minimum standard-setting, and collaboration with other industries in high-profile voluntary codes of conduct such as the Ethical Trading Initiative and the WRAP (Waste and Resources Action Programme) campaign.

The critical concern arising from the array of issues canvassed above is whether a few big players in possession of an unprecedented level of market power can act as harbingers of ecological sustainability, food security and socially responsible food supply in the absence of any real government involvement. This question is of particular importance when the evidence repeatedly indicates that public concerns over the health impacts of supermarkets do not extend to behaviour change at the checkout (Lang and Barling, 2007).

The need for a new approach

Each of the issues raised in the preceding discussion pose questions about how the political, ecological, public health, and hence ethical, dimensions of supermarket operations can be assessed and regulated in a systematic and integrated way. The business-as-usual approach taken by industry and government – an approach that is largely confined to food safety, watchdog price monitoring, consumer complaints adjudication and corporate responsibility charters – is not sufficient in light of the scale of challenges facing the food system. These instruments are not designed to foster food security or socially just food systems; indeed, the extent to which they can promote environmentally sustainable and health-promoting food systems remains unclear.

There is an increasing emphasis internationally on the need for food system research that integrates these three dimensions. Tim Lang's (2007) ecologically integrated paradigm for food systems is an advance, with its three principles of a food supply geared to deliver health: societal responsibility based on a citizenship model; action on inequalities; and the development of robust ecological systems. We agree with Lang that ignoring this set of principles in a context of mounting food insecurity will consign food system actors to irrelevance.

In a recent examination of prevailing approaches to studying the community effects of industrially organized farming, Lobao and Stofferahn (2008) have identified a research approach that is highly pertinent to the study of an industrialized food supply more broadly, and especially to the activities of supermarkets. In keeping with agri-food scholarship, these authors described industrial farming in terms of vertical integration, contractual arrangements, dependence on hired labour and the legal status of corporations. Supermarkets share these features, especially as they extend to the production of own-branded foods and dominate supply chains for numerous commodities.

Lobao and Stofferahn (2008) argue that the impact on community wellbeing is the end result of three outcome categories: socio-economic wellbeing, community social fabric and environmental outcomes. These categories then framed an 'integrative research review' of 51 studies, from which the authors compiled a list of indicators applicable to each outcome category. The indicators applying to socio-economic conditions included: class structure, existence of services, employment growth, income and poverty levels, and income inequality. Community social fabric indicators ranged from demographic trends to 'features of community that reflect its stability and quality of social life', including community conflict, educational attainments, changes in social class structure, health status and civic participation (Lobao and Stofferahn, 2008, p222). Other indicators that reflect long-standing traditions in rural sociology and community studies more generally included changes in decision-making and fiscal pressures on local government. The environmental outcomes indicators related to the use of resources like water and soil, and to environmental conditions.

The authors observed that few studies took a multi-dimensional perspective focusing, instead, on the economic performance of actors in the supply chain. In describing directions for future research, Lobao and Stofferahn (2008, p229) noted that 'studies giving greater attention to conceptualizing and empirically assessing the direct and indirect paths' of industrialized farming are needed. Although industrialized food retailing has been under the microscope for less time than industrial agriculture, the same conclusions apply. In short, it is time to pay greater attention to conceptualizing and empirically assessing the direct and indirect paths of supermarket influence over the health of populations and environments.

Based on the evidence outlined above, we have developed the following diagram (see Figure 12.1) to depict the pathways between supermarket engagement in food systems, intermediary economic, social and environmental indicators, and population health.

In the middle-left of the figure, a basic food supply chain depicts the flow of a particular food product or commodity from production through consumption. As discussed earlier, modern food systems are being driven by the engagement

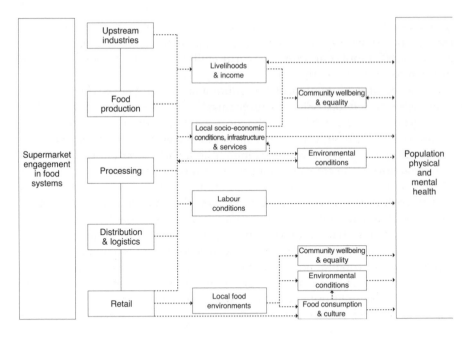

Source: the authors

Figure 12.1 *Pathways between supermarket operations, intermediary indicators and population health*

of supermarkets along the entire length of the supply chain, therefore this is depicted in the far left of the figure. Population health outcomes, the end-points of interest, are depicted to the far right. Finally, the major intermediary social, economic and environmental indicators currently known to be of interest in relation to food system-related health are depicted in the middle of the figure, with broken-dotted lines indicating where there is evidence of a relationship, or pathway, between components.

While this diagram is a work-in-progress and a simplified representation of what is a highly complex area, in the absence of an agreed upon framework for examining food system-related health we have found it a useful conceptual tool. As previously pointed out by Buttel (2001) and Marsden (2004), while recent years have seen rich engagement in empirical research relating to agri-food systems, there is a need, at the fundamental level, for a greater emphasis on theoretical and conceptual innovation. Concerted interdisciplinary effort in this regard would greatly enhance opportunities for systematic and coordinated empirical study, and ultimately the development of a more robust evidence base from which food system, and supermarket, performance can be measured.

Conclusion

This chapter has brought together evidence from a range of disciplines including sociology, human geography, cultural anthropology, public health, and development and environment studies to highlight the major pathways by which supermarket operations are impacting on population health. This is a complex area requiring more concerted research attention, given that the understanding of these issues is currently incomplete. In particular, there is an urgent need for greater effort in theoretical and conceptual development. There are also major gaps in evidence relating to supermarkets' role in shaping food culture, and particularly social relations around food preparation and consumption; the impact of supermarket-driven supply chain transformations on the social fabric of agricultural and related communities; and the interactions between food system-related environmental change and population health.

The critical role of supermarkets in public health is now rarely disputed, even from within the sector itself. However, without substantive policy initiatives to address food industry activities and their whole-of-society significance, supermarkets will remain in a position to 'pick and choose' the nature and extent of the health-promoting activities that serve their bottom line agenda. Innovation and collaboration in food system scholarship must be fostered in order to promote a more holistic understanding of food system-related health across government, the food industry and civil society, and to inform truly effective policy development and implementation.

Notes

1   The term 'neighbour community' is used to refer to the community within which a supermarket retail outlet is located.

References

Beauman, C., Cannon, G., Elmadfa, I., Glasauer, P., Hoffmann, I., Keller, M., Krawinkel, M., Lang, T., Leitzmann, C., Lötsch, B., Margetts, B. M., McMichael, A. J., Meyer-Abich, K., Oltersdorf, U., Pettoello-Mantovani, M., Sabat, J., Shetty, P., Sória, M., Spiekermann, U., Tudge, C., Vorster, H. H., Wahlqvist, M. and Zerilli-Marim, M. (2007) 'The principles, definition and dimensions of the new nutrition science', *Public Health Nutrition*, vol 8, no 6a, pp695–698

Beauvais, J. (2008) *Setting Up Superstores and Climate Change*, Beauvais Consultants, Tours, France

Burch, D. and Lawrence, G. (2005) 'Supermarket own brands, supply chains and the transformation of the agri-food system', *International Journal of Sociology of Agriculture and Food*, vol 13, no 1, pp1–18

Burch, D. and Lawrence, G. (2007) *Supermarkets and Agri-food Supply Chains: Transformations in the Production and Consumption of Foods*, Edward Elgar, Cheltenham, UK

Burke, K. (2009) 'Exposed: Home brand deception', *Sydney Morning Herald*, 17 January, p1

Burns, C. and Inglis, A. (2006) 'The relationship between the availability of healthy and fast food and neighbourhood level socio-economic deprivation: A case study from Melbourne, Australia', *Abstracts of the 10th International Congress on Obesity, Obesity Reviews*, vol 7, no s2, pp64–65

Burns, C., Gibbon, P., Boak, R., Baudinette, S. and Dunbar, J. (2004) 'Food cost and availability in a rural setting in Australia', *Rural and Remote Health*, vol 4, no 4, pp311–319

Buttel, F. (2001) 'Some reflections on late twentieth century agrarian political economy', *Sociologia Ruralis*, vol 41, no 2, pp 165–181

Campbell, H. and Le Heron, R. (2007) 'Supermarkets, producers and audit technologies: The constitutive micro-politics of food, legitimacy and governance', in D. Burch and G. Lawrence (eds) *Supermarkets and Agri-Food Supply Chains: Transformations in the Production and Consumption of Foods*, Edward Elgar, Cheltenham, UK

Cancer Council NSW (2007) *NSW Healthy Food Basket: Cost, Availability and Quality Survey 2007*, Sydney

Carlsson-Kanyama, A., Ekstrom, M. and Shanahan, H. (2003) 'Food and life cycle energy inputs: Consequences of diet and ways to increase efficiency', *Ecological Economics*, vol 44, pp293–307

Coe, N. and Wrigley, N. (2007) 'Host economy impacts of transnational retail: The research agenda', *Journal of Economic Geography*, vol 7, pp341–371

Cohen, M., Tirado, C., Aberman, N. and Thompson, B. (2008) *Impact of Climate Change and Bioenergy on Nutrition*, The International Food Policy Research Institute and Food and Agriculture Organization of the United Nations, Washington DC

Cummins, S. and Macintyre, S. (2006) 'Food environments and obesity: Neighbourhood or nation?' *International Journal of Epidemiology*, vol 35, no 1, pp100–104

Dibb, S., Eppel, S., Lang, T. and Rimmer, H. (2008) *Green, Healthy and Fair: A Review of the Government's Role in Supporting Sustainable Supermarket Food*, Sustainable Development Commission, London

Dixon, J. (2007) 'Advisor for healthy life: Supermarkets as new food authorities', in D. Burch and G. Lawrence (eds) *Supermarkets and Agri-Food Supply Chains: Transformations in the Production and Consumption of Foods*, Edward Elgar, Cheltenham, UK

Duchin, F. (2005) 'Sustainable consumption of food: A framework for analyzing scenarios about changes in diet', *Journal of Industrial Ecology*, vol 9, nos 1–2, pp99–114

Friedmann, H. (2005) 'From colonialism to green capitalism: Social movements and emergence of food regimes', in F. Buttel and P. McMichael, *New Directions in the Sociology of Development*, Elsevier, Oxford

Friel, S., Walsh, O. and McCarthy, D. (2006) 'The irony of a rich country: Issues of access and availability of healthy food in the Republic of Ireland', *Journal of Epidemiology and Community Health*, vol 60, pp1013–1019

Friends of the Earth (2005) *Checking Out the Environment? Environmental Impacts of Supermarkets*, Friends of the Earth, London

Goldman, A., Ramaswami, S. and Krider, R. (1999) 'Supermarket shopping adoption and the modernization of food retailing: Theory, method and application', *Department of Marketing Working Paper Series MKTG 99.134*, University of Science and Technology, Hong Kong

Harvey, M. (2007) 'The rise of supermarkets and asymmetries of economic power', in D. Burch and G. Lawrence (eds) *Supermarkets and Agri-Food Supply Chains: Transformations in the Production and Consumption of Foods*, Edward Elgar, Cheltenham, UK

Hawkes, C. (2006) 'Uneven dietary development: Linking the policies and processes of globalization with the nutrition transition, obesity and diet-related chronic diseases', *Global Health*, vol 2, pp1–18

Hawkes, C. (2008) 'Dietary implications of supermarket development: A global perspective', *Development Policy Review*, vol 26, no 6, pp657–692

Hughes, A. (2005) 'Responsible retailers? Ethical trade and the strategic re-regulation of cross-continental food supply chains', in N. Fold and B. Pritchard (eds) *Cross-Continental Food Chains*, Routledge, UK

Kirwan, J. (2004) 'Alternative strategies in the UK agro-food system: Interrogating the alterity of farmers' markets', *Sociologia Ruralis*, vol 44, no 4, pp395–415

Konefal, J., Mascarenhas, M. and Hatanaka, M. (2004) 'Governance in the global agro-food system: Backlighting the role of transnational supermarket chains', *Agriculture and Human Values*, vol 22, no 3, pp291–302

Lang, T. (2007) 'Food control or food democracy? Re-engaging nutrition with society and the environment', *Public Health Nutrition*, vol 8, no 6a, pp730–737

Lang, T. and Barling, D. (2007) 'The environmental impacts of supermarkets: Mapping the terrain and the policy problems in the UK', in D. Burch and G. Lawrence (eds) *Supermarkets and Agri-Food Supply Chains: Transformations in the Production and Consumption of Foods*, Edward Elgar, Cheltenham, UK

Lang, T. and Heasman, M. (2004) *Food Wars: The Global Battle for Mouths, Minds and Markets*, Earthscan, London

Lang, T., Barling, D. and Caraher, M. (2009) *Food Policy: Integrating Health, Environment and Society*, Oxford University Press, Oxford

Larsen, K., Ryan, C. and Abraham, A. (2008) *Sustainable and Secure Food Systems for Victoria: What Do We Know? What Do We Need to Know?* VEIL (Victorian Eco-Innovation Lab) Research Report No 1, Australian Centre for Science, Innovation and Society, University of Melbourne, Melbourne

Lawrence, G. and Burch, D. (2007) 'Understanding supermarkets and agri-food supply chains', in D. Burch and G. Lawrence (eds) *Supermarkets and Agri-Food Supply Chains: Transformations in the Production and Consumption of Foods*, Edward Elgar, Cheltenham, UK

Lobao, L. and Stofferahn, C. (2008) 'The community effects of industrialised farming: Social science research and challenges to corporate farming laws', *Agriculture and Human Values*, vol 25, pp219–240

Lundqvist, J., de Fraiture, C. and Molden, D. (2008) *Saving Water: From Field to Fork. Curbing Losses and Wastage in the Food Chain*, Paper 13, Stockholm International Water Institute, International Water Management Institute, Chalmers University of Technology and Stockholm Environment Institute, Stockholm

McMichael, A. (2007) 'Integrating nutrition with ecology: Balancing the health of humans and biosphere', *Public Health Nutrition*, vol 8, no 6a, pp706–715

McMichael, A. (2008) 'Environmental change, climate and population health: A challenge for inter-disciplinary research', *Environmental Health and Preventive Medicine*, vol 13, no 4, pp183–186

McMichael, A., Powles, J., Butler, C. and Uauy, R. (2007) 'Food, livestock production, energy, climate change, and health', *The Lancet*, vol 370, no 9594, pp1253–1263

McMichael, P. (2009) 'A food regime genealogy', *Journal of Peasant Studies*, vol 36, no 1, pp139-169

MacMillan, T., Alston, L., Segal, R. and Steedman, P. (2008) *Flying Food: Responsible Retail in the Face of Uncertainty*, UK Food Ethics Council, Brighton

Marsden, T. (2004) 'The quest for ecological modernization: Re-spacing rural development and agri-food studies' *Sociologia Ruralis*, vol 44, no 2, pp129–146

Minten, B. and Reardon, T. (2008) 'Food prices, quality, and quality's pricing in supermarkets versus traditional markets in developing countries', *Review of Agricultural Economics*, vol 30, no 3, pp480–490

Morland, K., Wing, S., Diez Roux, A. and Poole, C. (2002) 'Neighbourhood characteristics associated with the location of food stores and food service places', *American Journal of Preventive Medicine*, vol 22, no 1, pp23–29

Morland, K., Diez Roux, A. and Wing, S. (2006) 'Supermarkets, other food stores, and obesity: The Atherosclerosis risk in communities study', *American Journal of Preventive Medicine*, vol 30, no 4, pp333–339

Nestle, M. (2002) *Food Politics*, University of California Press, Berkeley

O'Dwyer, L. and Coveney, J. (2006) 'Scoping supermarket availability and accessibility by socioeconomic status in Adelaide', *Health Promotion Journal of Australia*, vol 17, no 3, pp240–246

Oresund Food Network and Oresund Environment Academy (2008) *Climate Change and the Food Industry: Climate Labelling for Food Products; Potential Limitations*, Oresund Food Network and Oresund Environment Academy, Copenhagen, Denmark

Pritchard, W. (2000) 'Beyond the modern supermarket: Geographical approaches to the analysis of contemporary Australian retail restructuring', *Australian Geographical Studies*, vol 38, no 2, pp204–218

Reardon, T. and Beardegue, J. (2002) 'The rapid rise of supermarkets in Latin America: Challenges and opportunities for development', *Development Policy Review*, vol 20, no 4, pp371–388

Reardon, T., Henson, S. and Berdegue, J. (2007) '"Proactive fast-tracking" diffusion of supermarkets in developing countries: Implications for market institutions and trade', *Journal of Economic Geography*, vol 7, pp399–431

Roff, R. (2007) 'Shopping for change? Neoliberalizing activism and the limits to eating non-GMO', *Agriculture and Human Values*, vol 24, no 4, pp511–522

Schaffner, D., Bokal, B., Fink, S., Rawls, K. and Schweiger, J. (2005) 'Food retail-price comparison in Thailand', *Journal of Food Distribution Research*, vol 36, no 1, pp167–171

Scrinis, G. (2008) 'Functional foods, functionally marketed foods? A critique of, and alternatives to, the category of "functional foods"', *Public Health Nutrition*, vol 11, no 5, pp541–545

Ulijaszek, S. (2002) 'Human eating behaviour in an evolutionary ecological context', *Proceedings of the Nutrition Society*, vol 61, pp517–526

Vorley, B. (2007) 'Supermarkets and agri-food supply chains in Europe: Partnership and protest', in D. Burch and G. Lawrence (eds) *Supermarkets and Agri-Food Supply Chains: Transformations in the Production and Consumption of Foods*, Edward Elgar, Cheltenham, UK

White, M. (2007) 'Food access and obesity', *Obesity Reviews*, vol 8, supp 1, pp 99–107

White, M., Bunting, J., Raybould, S., Adamson, A., Williams, L. and Mathers, J. (2004) *Do Food Deserts Exist? A Multi-Level, Geographical Analysis of the Relationship Between Retail Food Access, Socio-Economic Position and Dietary Intake: The Final Report*, The Food Standards Agency UK, London

Winkler, E., Turrell, G. and Patterson, C. (2006) 'Does living in a disadvantaged area entail limited opportunities to purchase fresh fruit and vegetables in terms of price, availability, and variety? Findings from the Brisbane Food Study', *Health and Place*, vol 12, no 4, pp741–748

Wrigley, N., Warm, D. and Margetts, B. (2003) 'Deprivation, diet and food retail access: Findings from the Leeds "food desert" study', *Environment and Planning A*, vol 35, pp151–188

Zenk, S., Schulz, A., Israel, B., James, S., Bao, S. and Wilson, M. (2005) 'Neighborhood racial composition, neighborhood poverty, and the spatial accessibility of supermarkets in metropolitan Detroit', *American Journal of Public Health*, vol 95, no 4, pp660–667

Part III
Towards a Sustainable Agri-food Future

13
Bodies, Bugs and Dirt: Sustainability Re-imagined in Community Gardens

Kelly Donati, Susan Cleary and Lucinda Pike

Introduction

For more than two centuries, community gardens have been increasingly recognized as a means of addressing the diverse and often divergent concerns of a range of city-based participants including local residents, governing authorities, private developers and community groups. They have played a role in 'fixing' a range of social, economic and ecological ills associated with living in the city. These gardens have:

- provided food for economically disadvantaged populations through allotments in 18th and 19th century Europe (Moselle, 1995; Crouch, 2003; Desilvey, 2003; Crouch and Ward, 2007);
- assumed moral and nationalist agendas through 'victory gardens' during the First and Second World Wars (Hynes, 1996);
- established their place within a constellation of public responses during the 1970s by food activists who advocated alternative strategies to mainstream food production and consumption (Belasco, 1989);
- been utilized by a number of grassroots community-development organizations involved in urban renewal projects in run-down neighbourhoods in American cities (Schmelzkopf, 1996; Smith and Kurtz, 2003).

Very recently, the community gardening movement was abuzz with excitement when US First Lady Michelle Obama made the public gesture (through a carefully orchestrated photographic opportunity) of planting a vegetable garden in the backyard of the White House, the first since Eleanor Roosevelt planted her 'victory' garden in 1943. In the face of the current global financial crisis, growing food in the city has taken on renewed economic significance in the form of 'recession gardens' (Sutter, 2009). This suggests, along with the persistence of urban agriculture in the cities of developing countries, that community gardening – and urban agriculture practices more broadly – will continue to gain momentum and intensify their future significance in Western cities (Castillo, 2003). Our aim in this chapter is to consider community gardening as an embodied and dynamic practice that brings 'other ideas into dialogue' with everyday lived experiences (Slocum, 2004, p778). We are interested in exploring how community gardens might contribute to an understanding of the 'living city', characterized by an earth-life nexus that, as Sarah Whatmore (2006, p601) suggests, has the potential to produce new ethical and political associations between human and non-human urban inhabitants.

Recent research on community gardens has variously focused on how these projects facilitate greater economic and social security by providing fresh food and by offering opportunities for meaningful community interaction (Moselle, 1995; Hynes, 1996; Lawson, 2005; Alaimo et al, 2008), as well as how they represent hybrid human-natural spaces that require constant care and the performance of mundane tasks to sustain them (Sander-Regier, 2008). In a related manner, inquiries have also been organized around the perceived moral vacuum of the modern urban living experience (Lawson, 2005). In this context, the practice of community gardening is framed by a moralizing discourse whose objectives overlap those of many sustainability policies and practices. For example, a study of community gardens as leisure spaces highlights the ways in which volunteers come together socially to garden, resulting in benefits such 'social capital', 'collective assets' and 'resource mobilization' for the greater good of the community. This can occur even if this was not necessarily the primary objective (Martin and Marsden, 1999; Glover et al, 2005, p450). Community gardens have also been problematized as instruments of neoliberal governmentality – that is, tools that play a role in shifting the social and economic responsibilities of the state to the community, thereby reproducing capitalist models and values of productivity, consumption and citizenship (Guthman, 2008; Pudup, 2008).

However, a focus on a politics of the problematic and an analytical (over)emphasis on the mechanisms of neoliberalism may hinder, as Edmund Harris suggests, the recognition of 'openings in practice … that support a politics of the possible' (2009, p62). We note, as Slocum (2004) has before us, that while the discourses and structures of neoliberalism have the potential to normalize and shape our approaches to sustainability, neoliberalism is not a complete strategy, nor does it tell the full story. Our interest in this chapter is not to critique or defend the well-founded and valuable analyses of community gardens. Having built collaborative relationships with many community gardening and urban agriculture organizations during and after our research, we are acutely sensitive as to why garden organizers and researchers emphasize the tangible, instrumental and goal-driven benefits of community gardens.[1] Rather than being critical of such approaches, which are often essential to securing land tenure or funding, we seek to highlight the forms of knowledge that might be excluded from such an approach and, through the lens of 'liveliness', to illuminate how the practice of urban food gardening exceeds both current policy objectives and understandings of sustainable cities more broadly. Along these lines, we suggest that the tangible and intangible pleasures of community gardens – aspects largely overlooked in a policy context – are not easily reducible to moral attributions, the structures of capitalism or even to the popular interpretations of sustainability.

The social, environmental and economic 'ills' of urban life and their remedies have been increasingly gathered under the broad umbrella of sustainability, generally understood as the capacity to maintain a social or ecological system over time (Whitehead, 2007). It is not difficult, we suggest, to draw parallels between today's 'sustainable consumer' and the moral citizen that social reformers sought to produce at the turn of the 19th century through the designation of allotment gardens in the UK and US. In a sense, the urban environment of today remains a moral bugbear that produces 'bad' consumption practices among urban citizens, just as the 19th century city was home to unproductive inhabitants who required moral 'rehabilitation' in the form of a greater connection to nature through gardening. And, as Pudup suggests, community gardens cultivate 'good' citizens with increased and measurable capacity for participating in neoliberal 'self-help technologies' (2008, p1228).

Nonetheless, we wish to move beyond these representational boundaries. We are interested in community gardens not in terms of how well 'green issues' can be 'bolted on to them' (Shorthose, 2000, p193), but instead as powerful sites of transformation which nurture what Lorimer describes as 'passionate, intimate and material relationships with the soil, and the grass, plants and trees that take root there' (2005, p85). As such, we point to notions of pleasure and liveliness as important – and yet underestimated – components of community gardens that contribute to an understanding of the ethical and political possibilities and practices of change. Within an urban context, we would like to dig a little deeper among the dirt and bugs, and open our inquiry to the small pleasures of the garden to see what forms of embodied knowledge, more-than-human relationships and new ways of thinking might emerge.

We approach our community garden case studies through the idea of embodied knowledge by drawing on Carolan, whose recent work on the understandings of the countryside moves beyond 'mere discursive constructs':

> *Mind is body. Consciousness is corporeal; thinking is sensuous. In short our understanding of space is more-than-representational. It is a lived process. To ignore how understandings of the countryside are embodied is to cut from our analysis a major (and indeed main) source of understanding* (Carolan, 2008, p409).

Of particular interest is Carolan's exploration of how farming and non-farming bodies relate differently to the sights, sounds, smells, tastes and tactile sensations of production agriculture in order to raise questions about how this might 'shape people's attitudes towards things like nature, the countryside and agriculture' (2008, p419). Just as Carolan suggests that lived and sensuous understandings of the countryside are knowledge-producing, we are interested in exploring how urban bodies can get a feel for living sustainably in the city beyond the more common 'institutionalized' and coherent understandings of social capital, community development and environmental conservation that tend to frame community gardens both in research and in practice. We suggest that sustainable urban life requires attentiveness to the embodied and transformative aspects of the more-than-human.

The following section offers a necessarily truncated description of research conducted on community gardens in Melbourne in early 2007. We approached our selected case study not for its quantifiable benefits, but in terms of the 'shared experiences, everyday routines and fleeting encounters' which enabled our participants to make shifts in their thinking and, from that, changes in their practices (Lorimer, 2005, p84). We then return to the intersection of 'liveliness' (the lively interdependence of the garden space), food, and discourses on urban sustainability, exploring how this intersection might be considered as something that animates and enlivens the city in ways that open up spaces of ethical and political possibility.

Liveliness in gardening practice

Our interest in the political and ethical possibilities of community gardens came about during research funded by the Hornery Institute, an Australian philanthropic body, and conducted in collaboration with Garden of Eden, one of the case studies in our research. The purpose of the primary research project was to document the various governance structures for community gardens in Melbourne, identify the benefits community gardens generate for the community, and highlight obstacles and challenges they face in order to inform the potential inclusion of a community garden project in a new master-planned community on the northern fringe of Melbourne. The project involved in-depth, semi-structured interviews with two to three gardeners and garden managers at four gardens around Melbourne. Participants were also provided with digital cameras and asked to take photos of things or spaces within the garden that had particular meaning to them. Though there were clear parallels in the responses of gardeners from three other community gardens that we studied, we have focused here on Garden of Eden because it allows us to explore the concept of liveliness in greater depth within the scope and constraints of this chapter. We also felt it was a particularly interesting garden because Garden of Eden was involved in a Work for the Dole (WFTD) programme[2] and was therefore the most institutionalized of all the spaces we considered.

While garden organizers felt strongly that community gardens have the potential to contribute to community health and wellbeing, many informed us that they struggled to quantify these benefits for government agencies in funding submissions. We also discovered that quantifying the benefits of community gardens was far more complex and multifaceted than we had imagined, and found ourselves ultimately questioning the temptation to align our findings with existing policy parameters (for example, 'community capacity building' or 'placemaking') in order to bring credibility to garden activities. Our sense was that framing community gardens in terms of desirable policy outcomes for creating sustainable communities largely failed to capture the essence of how community gardening might contribute to this process.

As the research progressed, we became increasingly interested in gardeners' reflections on how the space both produced, and allowed them to express, new forms of knowledge and understanding about how they lived in the city. What emerged from the research – and what we sensed intuitively from our own personal gardening experiences – was that gardening for pleasure was both powerful and transformative with broader political and ethical implications for thinking about urban sustainability.

Garden of Eden

Prior to its closure in mid-2007, Garden of Eden (GoE) was a community garden run by a not-for-profit association of the same name, located alongside the Albert Park Railway Track in inner Melbourne. Established in 2000, the garden comprised 18 raised vegetable beds, a herb garden, greenhouse, wood-fired oven, composting area, native garden, frog pond and a corner dedicated to wild vegetation and edible plants (such as figs, wild rocket and purslane). It was tended by participants in a WFTD programme which was managed by the Garden of Eden committee of management and small crew of staff.[3] The garden was designed and maintained according to the principles of permaculture, a way of living and producing food conceived by Bill Mollison in the 1970s. To the untrained eye, permaculture gardens sometimes appear to have an untidy, disorganized or laissez-faire approach to 'managing' ecological processes. This is, in part, because permaculture brings farming as well as smaller-scale modes of food production such as backyard gardening into contact with everyday life, such that humans, animals and crops coexist rather being separated into the regimented and rationalized compartments of production favoured by industrial agriculture.

Depending on employment circumstances and age, a typical WFTD gardener was placed at GoE for 15 hours a week over a 6-month period. The WFTD programme is underpinned by the principle of 'mutual obligation' that has come to characterize many federal 'self-help' welfare programmes in Australia (Van Gramberg and Bassett, 2005). As members of the WFTD scheme, the GoE mandate was the provision of a platform for learning and training to reduce social exclusion and to increase ecological literacy within the community. Though the intent of many WFTD programmes is to provide employment and training opportunities for the long-term unemployed, the reality as presented in the popular media and some research is that much of the work is often dreary and uninspiring for participants, with questionable training and learning gains. However, interviews with Rod, Suzie and Jon (pseudonyms) in this study presented us with a very different perspective on the

WFTD experience. For these gardeners, the work of gardening proved to be a richly textured process of learning, thinking and doing things in ways that were both embodied and lively. It enabled, we would argue, a sense of participation within a different kind of community – a pleasurable conglomeration of more-than-human entities that facilitated a different sensitivity and attentiveness to the broader issues of living in an urban environment.

For example, Rod – who was critically involved in overseeing the GoE project – began one of our conversations by reflecting on how the physical act of gardening and participation in the natural cycles of food production were potentially transformative experiences for many participants:

> *It's a ritualistic and sustained input over a lengthy period of time as the seasons change. While at Garden of Eden, you will see 'plant it, harvest it, eat it and save its seeds and replant it the next year' ... That immediate physical feedback that you get from being part of the programme is very powerful and inspires a lot of people. Even if they don't particularly have a leaning towards horticulture, it still provides a nurturing environment in which to spend a couple of days for a period of time when your life is not particularly pleasant when you are unemployed.*

Comments from other GoE participants also suggested that the mundane and dirty tasks of watering the garden, pulling weeds, turning compost and planting seedlings were not experienced as solitary government-imposed work. Instead, the garden provided a space for encounters between plants, compost, bugs and people that were personally, socially and ecologically productive, regardless of the institutional agenda that determined their participation in the project.

One WFTD participant, Suzie, spoke about how she loved the garden because it allowed her to grow food in the city with other people, and how she was keen to continue working there as a volunteer after she found employment: 'The funny thing is that I want that other job, but I want to keep coming here for two days or even one day a week.... I'd love to be part of something like this on an on-going basis as a volunteer'. Similarly, she reflected that: 'I'm learning new things every day, like how to propagate native mint. Jon showed me how... You're just always learning things when you are working with nature.' Clearly also appreciating the exchanges of knowledge in the garden, Jon later remarked that: 'Somebody might come up to me and ask me what a plant is. It's all about sharing. I've never really done that before, and it's a wonderful thing to do.'

The garden not only afforded new knowledge for participants and new opportunities for sharing this knowledge but, more importantly, it allowed for the development of embodied 'know-how' as opposed to formalized knowledge. Knowing how to propagate seedlings or distinguish weeds and pests from beneficial plants and bugs were part of the pleasure that inspired the gardeners to continue their participation in the garden and which, at the same time, contributed to the life of the garden itself. Along these lines, Suzie reflects on her experience in the garden as a metaphor for personal development and growth:

> *When you are working in nature, it's like you are working on yourself, like pruning back what you don't need, planting new seeds. The cycle of nature happens in all of us. So, when we are working in the garden, you know when you are out of balance, and you know when you are in tune with the whole thing.*

For Suzie, the garden was a space of interaction and exchange, an interdependant and mutually beneficial relationship in which the human and non-human flourish in each other's company: 'I notice when I'm here on my own, it's good. But it's just not the same or as enriching as when people are here. People are just as important as the plants. The plants thrive when people are here.' While the plants thrive in human company, Suzie finds that opportunity to observe the cycle of life equally enchanting and nurturing. When asked what part of the garden she loved the most, Suzie pointed us to the greenhouse: 'This is where all the little plants are nurtured until they are strong enough to go in the ground. It represents new life. The garden is such a beautiful place. It's such an amazing thing to watch things grow. I just love it.' In this sense, the gardeners and the plants, soil and seeds are intimately and vitally linked through the sharing of the garden space.

This interdependence was not a tidy or comfortable exchange for every gardener, however. The activities of the garden, and particularly the permaculture approach to gardening, produced organic but also disorderly systems for the creation and destruction of life. When asked what bothered him about the garden, Jon turned his attention to the composting area (see Figure 13.1):

> *Something that bothers me about organic stuff is that you have to have mess. You have to have an area set aside for mess, and that irritates me. But I know there's nothing you can do about it because that's the process of recycling, letting nature take its course to break down the organics.*

For Jon, the messiness disrupted the beauty of the garden, producing an unpleasant aesthetic that sat uncomfortably alongside the more attractive sections of the garden. While he was annoyed by unruly piles of decomposing matter and other materialities of the garden that were seen to be out of place, this mess had a function – 'letting nature take its course' – that he understood, despite his preference for a more tidy environment.

Suzie expressed an emergent flexibility with regard to the natural processes of the garden. Although the GoE garden managers encouraged planting according to the lunar cycle, her personal work schedule in the garden did not always allow this. When asked what made her proud of the garden, Suzie pointed to some plants she had recently planted out (Figure 13.2):

Source: Kelly Donati

Figure 13.1 *The mess of the composting area*

> *I planted a few crops in here ... black zucchini, tomatoes, corn and parsley. It's just beautiful. I see it as a boat with food in it. I didn't plant all of it, but some of it. I'm proud of my zucchini because we planted them outside of the lunar cycle, but they've gone really good! I realised I don't have to be quite so rigid... That's one of the things I'm learning here.*

Regardless of not having observed the lunar planting cycle, the seedlings in the 'food boat' had nonetheless come to life. Delighted that her crops had flourished, the flexibility of Mother Nature was for Suzie a lesson in being less rigid in her own ways of thinking and acting.

The garden creates openings for new ways for the gardeners to think about and express themselves in the world. Jon reflected on how his time and experiences in the garden had produced new creative and practical horizons for him – not only in terms of how it might improve his job prospects in

Source: Kelly Donati

Figure 13.2 *The 'food boat' garden bed*

horticultural landscaping, but in how it had inspired him to think differently about living in his environment. As a self-described country boy living in the city, horticulture was a way to connect to his previously rural life while gaining new knowledge that could be applied in novel and creative ways in the city:

> *This is what I really wanted to get into ... designing a sustainable lifestyle, a way of life. And now I'm here, working in a permaculture garden, which is wonderful because it's a whole different aspect to landscape design which I wasn't really clued up on. I wanted to come and experience permaculture as a community garden, and this [place] has inspired me. I submitted a design for the Don Fleming Student Award. I got some ideas from here and reworked them in different ways... I was selected for the top thirty in Australia, so I was really thrilled.*

Source: Kelly Donati

Figure 13.3 *Former wasteland transformed into a cultivated garden vista*

The garden environment, and the living things which comprised it, were often discussed in terms of the interaction between the wild and the cultivated. Asked what he loved about the garden, Jon walked to the 'wild' corner of the garden dominated by a 150-year old Moreton Bay fig tree and photographed the cultivated garden vista (Figure 13.3):

> *I've taken a photo from under these trees of that aspect looking over to the vines. It was wasteland, this whole garden; it was contaminated. [Now] I love the biodiversity of it. We have native trees here, and it's created a microclimate for the vegetables to grow there. I love that coming together of nature verging with something that is kept, and you can have them working in unison.*

For Jon, the garden represents an active vista in which nature and culture come together not as two dichotomous concepts, but as a new 'urban nature'

(Braun, 2005). The garden produces beauty from waste, creating diverse and liminal spaces between the cultivated and natural. This urban nature possesses its own lively potentiality. For Jon, it is the presence of the native trees, and not necessarily human intervention, that has created the conditions in which the vegetables can thrive.

It was from these conversations that we began to think of community gardens as spaces for bringing life into cities. Rod, Suzie and Jon sensed and sought out an engagement with the lively interdependence of the garden space, a pleasurable 'liveliness' that was arguably far richer and more complex than the benefits of physical exercise, fresh produce or skill development that may have interested government agencies and funding bodies. As the gardeners observed the plants following their natural life cycle, vegetables were no longer understood to be 'simply passive' forms of vegetation, but living things with their own likes and dislikes, becoming heterogeneously 'associated with activity and enlivened animation' that, in turn, brings life to both the garden and the human inhabitants of the garden (Hitchings and Jones, 2004, p15). The gardening community – comprised of much more than the gardeners who tend it – was shaped by lively 'forces of enchantment' that cultivated new attachments and associations between more-than-human inhabitants of the garden (Davies and Dwyer, 2007, p260). Gardeners, through the act of producing food in an urban environment, actively became part of a newly imagined food cycle.

Lively exchanges

Most gardeners are aware that, despite its pleasures, gardening is sometimes difficult and frustrating work that tests the best efforts and skill of even the most adept green thumb. Extreme heat (not uncommon during Melbourne's summers) scorches fruit and vegetables, and undoes an entire season's work in a very short space of time, while clouds can pass overhead without releasing a drop of rain. Pests and weeds will proliferate even as seedlings and plants stubbornly refuse to grow or yield fruit. The mess, frustrations and conundrums of gardening produce, in the evocative phrase of Renate Sander-Regier, 'tension in paradise' (2008, p8). Quoting garden writer Lorraine Johnson, she considers:

> 'garden failures' are 'full of wisdom and teaching ... a gentle tweak from the cosmos on the subject of control'. These lessons – in failure, negotiation, and compromise – help unfurl the gardener's physical and conceptual horizons (Sander-Regier, 2008, p10).

Yet gardeners persevere, unable to always control what transpires in the garden but nonetheless rising to the complex challenges of disease, pests and random acts of nature because of the pleasurable connections that even these very annoyances enable.

What is interesting for us is that these frustrations also require moments of reflection and decision about what response is needed. These moments of reflection may draw on formalized knowledge (for example, looking up a pest or problem in a gardening book) but also on gardeners' embodied knowledge and sensitivity to the needs of other life forms in the garden. Community gardens also appeared to represent for gardeners a nurturing and nurtured space that enabled the cross-pollination of ideas. We found that gardeners were often actively engaged in political questions about how to live sustainably and how to sustain themselves by eating and living more ethically. Not only at Garden of Eden, but also across all of our case studies, many community gardening organizers and practitioners were seeking to develop local responses to global issues such as climate change, increasing urbanization and inequities in the industrial food system. It became clear that at least some community gardens were hotbeds of environmental, cultural and social activism and learning – sites of civic engagement not because they were 'organized' as such, but because the act of growing food brought about a greater sense of interconnectedness with the earth's 'natural' and sometimes 'unnatural' rhythms in an urban environment where these patterns are often stifled by the everyday trappings and conveniences of city life.

Despite cities around the world and municipalities in Australia developing sustainable food policies, little is yet known about how pleasure and 'liveliness' might inspire more creative responses to sustainable urban living and the role that growing food in cities may play in this process. We need to consider the more-than-human aspects of city life, rather than simply considering food 'systems' in coherent, deterministic and human-centred terms. We consider it of concern that many 'rational strategies for initiating change' effectively reduce food to a commodity in which the economic and structural dimensions of agriculture are privileged over its aesthetic and sensual qualities as part of a 'living system' (Delind, 2006, pp124–125). In her critique of systems-based understandings of sustainable agriculture, Campbell similarly suggests that current approaches to food systems are too often approached as 'useful tools' that end up producing 'inhospitable', mechanistic and goal-driven understandings of sustainability that simply 'spits out food commodities' without creating genuine alternatives to industrial agriculture (1998, p57). As Delind warns, if '"we are what we eat," then we too are in the process of becoming commodities' (2006, p125).

As researchers and gardeners, we see the practice of community gardening – and urban food production more generally – as having considerable potential for imagining a radically different food system. The resulting more-than-human exchanges and interactions might contribute to what environmental ethicist Paul Thompson (1995, p19) calls a 'spirit of raising food and eating as an act of communion with some larger whole' – producing 'an ethic of farming, a philosophy of agriculture [that is] needed as much by those who eat as by those who farm'. Accordingly, ethics do more than provide us with a set of values that must be respected or goals to be achieved; rather, ethics become explicitly part of the choices we make when we design the 'tools' and strategies for working towards more sustainable cities. It is not necessarily through a commitment to goal-driven outcomes that the act of gardening expresses its political and ethical potentiality for, as Gibson-Graham reminds us:

> [i]f politics is a process of transformation instituted by taking decisions in an undecidable terrain, ethics is the continual exercising, in the face of the need to decide, of a choice to be/act/ think a certain way. Ethics involves the embodied practices that bring principles into action (Gibson-Graham, 2006, pxxvii).

While community gardens are often designed and managed with social and ecological change in mind, we suggest that this change does not necessarily happen because it is supported by government policy or even because it fits comfortably in a broader political framework for planning better cities. Instead, we suggest that the seemingly frivolous and private pleasures of gardening – that is, experiences that seem to sit outside the documentable benefits expected by more institutionalized and rational understandings of healthy bodies and communities – play an important role in setting the conditions for new political and ethical thinking. Our experience in speaking with GoE participants suggested that, even in a WFTD programme – arguably the most institutionalized of the garden projects we examined – the practice of gardening contributed to the process of imagining new possibilities for participating in urban life and interacting with the more-than-human world of food. We suggest that sustainability as a more-than-human condition exceeds the creation of goal-driven interactions between nature and culture. Engagement with the notion of sustainability must be lively – an embodied, enchanting and transformative interaction with the human and more-than-human world – not merely cognitive; not only ecological; but also pleasurable.

Conclusion

As we studied the four gardens in our research, we were surprised by the forms of more-than-human engagement that were not only pleasurable but that might also help us to imagine a more sustainable future. We use the word 'imagine' deliberately, because imagination and innovation are critical to the process of change and to thinking about the future by drawing creatively from past and present experiences. Although the act of growing food in the city might seem like a small gesture towards sustainability, it is often through these seemingly minor acts of pleasure and shifts in thinking that change happens.

Delind (2006) calls for academics and activists alike to make a case for food in our lives that goes beyond the rationalities of the market-place. Healthier and more engaged communities that may foster alternative ways of living and thinking are not always built on better policies but emerge from a greater attentiveness to the pleasures, liveliness and sensuality of the world in which we live. The practice of growing food has a fundamental and transformative role to play in this process:

If we are to do the work of building healthy bodies, landscapes, soils and cuisines, then we need spaces within which to regularly and freely come together, to talk, to complain, to sweat, to laugh, to oppose and debate, to reflect and to be awed. To this end, we will need to reintegrate agriculture, its rhythms, sensibilities and trappings back into our daily lives. Not only do we need to make such activity visible and accessible, we also need to make it convivial and sensual (Delind, 2006, p142).

With Delind's comment in mind, we read community gardens as urban geographies in which the mundane and everyday practices of gardening may produce new and more meaningful connections and networks with the more-than-human communities of the city. Our cities need more research attention and convivial conversations devoted to understanding the processes that allow the world to be seen in a new light, and which are the prerequisites for knowing and living differently, and more sustainably, in the world.

Notes

1   Such research is extremely useful for garden organizers who need to 'play by the rules' by demonstrating how community gardens are contributing in pragmatic and tangible ways to the goals of policies framed by a neoliberal governmentality perspective, including current sustainability policy.
2   The Work for the Dole programme aims to provide 'work experience placements for job seekers in approved activities which provide facilities and services to local communities' (see the Australian government's website, www.workplace.gov.au/workplace/Programmes/WFD/, accessed on 1 March 2009). The concept of mutual obligation assumes that the provision of welfare assistance should involve some return responsibilities for the recipient.
3   Beyond tending the on-site garden, Garden of Eden (GoE) also provided consulting and construction services for the Department of Human Services and worked in collaboration with other community organizations in designing and building new community gardens at public housing estates around inner-city suburbs of Melbourne.

References

Alaimo, K., Packnett, E., Miles, R. and Kruger, D. (2008) 'Fruit and vegetable intake among urban community gardeners', *Journal of Nutrition Education and Behavior*, vol 40, no 2, pp94–101

Belasco, W. (1989) *Appetite for Change: How the Counterculture Took on the Food Industry*, Cornell University Press, Ithaca, NY

Braun, B. (2005) 'Environmental issues: Writing a more-than-human geography', *Progress in Human Geography*, vol 29, no 5, pp635–650

Campbell, M. (1998) 'Dirt in our mouths and hunger in our bellies: Metaphor, theory-making and systems approaches to sustainable agriculture', *Agriculture and Human Values*, vol 15, pp57–64

Carolan, M. (2008) 'More-than-representational knowledge/s of the countryside: How we think as bodies', *Sociologia Ruralis*, vol 48, no 4, pp408–422

Castillo, G. (2003) 'Livelihoods and the city: An overview of the emergence of agriculture in urban spaces', *Progress in Development Studies*, vol 3, no 4, pp339–344

Crouch, D. (2003) 'Spacing, performing, and becoming: Tangles in the mundane', *Environment and Planning A*, vol 35, pp1945–1960

Crouch, D. and Ward, C. (2007) *The Allotment: Its Landscape and Culture*, Five Leaves Publications, Nottingham, UK

Davies, G. and Dwyer, C. (2007) 'Qualitative methods: Are you enchanted or are you alienated?' *Progress in Human Geography*, vol 31, no 2, pp257–266

Delind, L. (2006) 'Of bodies, place, and culture: Re-situating local food', *Journal of Agricultural and Environmental Ethics*, vol 19, pp121–146

Desilvey, C. (2003) 'Cultivated histories in a Scottish allotment garden', *Cultural Geographies*, vol 10, pp442–468

Gibson-Graham, J. (2006) *A Postcapitalist Politics*, University of Minnesota Press, Minneapolis

Glover, T., Parry, D. and Shinew, K. (2005) 'Building relationships, accessing resources: Mobilizing social capital in community garden contexts', *Journal of Leisure Research*, vol 37, no 4, pp450–474

Guthman, J. (2008) 'Neoliberalism and the making of food politics in California', *Geoforum*, vol 39, no 3, pp1171–1183

Harris, E. (2009) 'Neoliberal subjectivities or a politics of the possible? Reading for difference in alternative food networks', *Area*, vol 41, no 1, pp55–63

Hitchings, R. and Jones, V. (2004) 'Living with plants and the exploration of botanical encounter within human geographic research practice', *Ethics, Place and Environment*, vol 7, no 1–2, pp3–18

Hynes, H. (1996) *A Patch of Eden: America's Inner-city Gardeners*, Chelsea Green Publishing Company, White River Junction, VT

Lawson, L. (2005) *City Bountiful: A Century of Community Gardening in America*, University of California Press, Berkeley

Lorimer, H. (2005) 'Cultural geography: The busyness of being more-than-representational', *Progress in Human Geography*, vol 29, no 1, pp83–94

Martin, R. and Marsden, T. (1999) 'Food for urban spaces: The development of urban food production in England and Wales', *International Planning Studies*, vol 4, no 3, pp389–412

Moselle, B. (1995) 'Allotments, enclosure, and proletarianization in early nineteenth-century southern England', *The Economic History Review*, vol 48, no 3, pp482–500

Pudup, M. (2008) 'It takes a garden: Cultivating citizen-subjects in organized garden projects', *Geoforum*, vol 39, no 3, pp1228–1240

Sander-Regier, R. (2008) 'Earthways: Opportunity, community and meaning in the personal garden', *The Brock Review*, vol 10, pp1–20

Schmelzkopf, K. (1996) 'Urban gardens as contested space', *The Geographical Review*, vol 85, pp364–381

Shorthose, J. (2000) 'Micro-experiments in Alternatives', *Capital and Class*, no 72, Autumn, pp191–207

Slocum, R. (2004) 'Consumer citizens and the cities for climate protection campaign', *Environment and Planning A*, vol 36, pp763–782

Smith, C. and Kurtz, H. (2003) 'Community gardens and politics of scale in New York City', *The Geographical Review*, vol 93, pp193–212

Sutter, J. D. (2009) 'Recession gardens' trim grocery bills, teach lessons', *CNN*, 2 April, www.cnn.com/2009/LIVING/04/01/recession.garden/, accessed 2 May 2009

Thompson, P. (1995) *Spirit of the Soil: Agriculture and Environmental Ethics*, Routledge, London

Van Gramberg, B. and Bassett, P. (2005) *Neoliberalism and the Third Sector in Australia* (Working Paper 5/2005), School of Management, Victoria University of Technology, Melbourne

Whatmore, S. (2006) 'Materialist returns: Practising cultural geography in and for a more-than-human world', *Cultural Geographies*, vol 13, no 4, pp600–609

Whitehead, M. (2007) *Spaces of Sustainability: Geographical Perspectives on the Sustainable Society*, Routledge, London

14
Biofuels: Finding a Sustainable Balance for Food and Energy

Sophia Murphy[1]

Introduction

As the damage wrought by reliance on fossil fuels becomes ever clearer – manifest in the form of climate change, air pollution, the release of carcinogens and more – the appeal of a biomass-powered energy system is obvious. In some respects, biomass-powered energy is not new: people have gleaned and cultivated energy from the biomass around them for millennia. They have burned wood and dung, kept draft animals to pull their ploughs, made candles from wax, and used compost to provide heating and cooling. Billions of people around the world currently rely on these forms of biomass to meet their energy needs. Yet, the recent love affair with biofuels in many of the world's industrialized, as well as developing, countries – demonstrated in the tripling of global biofuel production between 2000 and 2007 – has little in common with those traditional biofuel practices.

The modern biofuels[2] industry links two issues high on the global policy agenda: food and energy. Both agriculture and energy consumption in developed countries have changed beyond recognition with the advent of fossil-fuel derived energy, particularly oil. Energy consumption has increased astronomically, with agriculture now one of the biggest users. As the writer Michael Pollan (2006) describes, agriculture has been transformed from a solar-powered activity into a sector that runs on fossil fuels.

For some, biofuels present an opportunity to assist the estimated 2.4 billion people worldwide who currently lack access to sufficient energy to meet their simple daily needs (UN-Energy, 2007). For these advocates, biofuel technologies represent a decentralized solution to energy shortages by using locally available and cheap materials to meet a basic human need. In contrast, opponents argue that biofuels are an outcome of the unquenchable thirst for energy by a minority of the world's population – a minority that uses the majority of the world's resources. Growing demand for biofuels has also established a platform for ongoing conflict related to land, water and air quality that the poor cannot hope to win, particularly in the context of the current configuration of global trade and investment rules.

For some environmentalists, biofuels reflect the possibility of a locally available, decentralized and renewable source of energy that uses abundantly available crops and waste products from agriculture to generate power. For farmers in developed countries, a number of whom have formed cooperatives and invested heavily in the sector over the past five years, biofuels promise an opportunity to buoy depressed commodity prices with new demand and an opportunity to add value close to home. Developed country governments talk about the opportunities for biofuels to establish energy independence – reducing the need for oil imports. Meanwhile developing country governments hope they will be able to turn biofuels into a new stream of foreign exchange revenue. Biofuel technology might also provide local communities with the opportunity to generate some of their own energy needs, whether they use cooking fat from a local McDonald's store to make biodiesel, or the otherwise discarded stalks of sweet sorghum, grown as cattle feed, to make ethanol. Business, too, sees promise in biofuels, including the promise of significant returns on investment. Reflecting this optimism, a number of global agribusiness firms, oil companies, Wall Street investors and entrepreneurs have invested heavily in the sector in recent years. Big name investors include tycoons Richard Branson, George Soros, Bill Gates and Vinod Khosla. The global oil company Royal Dutch Shell also recently announced that it would put all of its research and development money for renewable energy exclusively into biofuels.

Critics, in contrast, see a very different picture. They link biofuels to both recent food price surges, and to a spate of colonial-style land grabs in which foreign investors and foreign governments acquire the right to land and water in much poorer countries, at the expense of the livelihoods and food security of local people. They argue that biofuels allow rich consumers to believe climate change might be mitigated without any changes in their energy consumption. For some environmentalists, biofuels paint a misplaced green glow on what remains fundamentally a fossil-fuel based energy supply. They see much of the investment in the sector supporting an unsustainable and oil-dependent agricultural production model, built on monocultures and petroleum-based inputs, as well as what are all too often appalling working conditions for the labourers involved. For these critics, the dramatic increases in world commodity prices in 2007 and 2008 proved that biofuels were taking food from the mouths of the hungry. Among the critics of biofuels, business is also well represented. The largest opposition, particularly in the US, comes from industrial meat producers that include Tyson and Smithfield, and the industry groups representing food processors, such as the Grocery Manufacturers Association. Opposition to biofuels from these companies stems, at least in part, from their significant new and competing demand for agricultural commodities that would otherwise be used as animal feed or as additives in processed food.[3]

Amid these competing claims, where does the truth lie? As the scientific evidence starts to accumulate – examining issues as diverse as energy efficiency, water use, relative greenhouse gas emissions, land use, trade and food security – it seems many of the boldest promises made for biofuels are, indeed, misleading. Some claims have been proven factually wrong, while others depend on a series of other, supporting, measures that have not been taken. Importantly, the evidence is mounting that decentralized, locally controlled sources of energy will have to be protected by regulation; the market will otherwise simply reinforce existing unequal market power relationships.

Few of the criticisms levelled at biofuels reside exclusively within the technology itself. Rather, biofuels throw into stark relief the limits of industrial food and feed production. Industrial agriculture is strongly associated with social inequity, environmental pollution, and the hugely disproportionate economic and political power of transnational agribusinesses and energy companies. Biofuels cannot be better than the agricultural and energy systems that they link to. Biofuels create an opening for better energy, and even agricultural, practice but there are significant risks given biofuels are directly tied to an unsustainable system of production.

This chapter examines, in some detail, the arguments surrounding the biofuels debate. The analysis begins by explaining why biofuels have excited so much interest in the last five years and why, increasingly, they attract so much criticism. The chapter also evaluates the extent to which biofuel technology might contribute towards a broad set of goals, including poverty eradication, sustainable agricultural production systems, and the quest to find a sustainable balance between food, agriculture and energy needs.

Biofuels: Background to the issues[4]

The focus of this chapter is on biofuels now in commercial distribution – often referred to as first-generation biofuels. While beyond the scope of this chapter, it is important to also identify those second- and third-generation biofuels currently under development, or with limited commercial application. Second-generation biofuels are generally defined as those made from the cellulose in plants. Cellulose-to-liquid-fuel technology continues to be difficult and commercial viability remains elusive. Meanwhile, third-generation biofuels will use algae – an idea that is still only in an exploratory phase of development. In contrast, today's commercial biofuels sector consists of bio-ethanol and biodiesel: bio-ethanol is derived from sugar cane, maize and, to a lesser extent, wheat; and biodiesel is derived from palm oil, canola (also called rapeseed), soybeans and, most recently, jatropha (a group of succulent plants that can grow in dry conditions and poor soils, while producing up to 40 per cent oil). Apart from jatropha, these crops are all grown for food, feed and industrial processes, and are widely traded in international markets as commodities. On the whole, these crops are overwhelmingly grown in monocultures and are bought, processed and shipped by only a small number of multinational firms. The biggest biofuel users are the European Union (EU), the US and Brazil, while China and India are also emerging as big users (IEA and OECD, 2007, p15). In terms of biofuel production, Brazil and the US have dominated the market for a number of decades. Together, they account for over 75 per cent of world ethanol production (Brazil uses sugarcane and the US uses maize). Meanwhile, the EU produces almost 80 per cent of global biodiesel supplies, with almost half of global biodiesel production occurring in Germany, using canola (UNCTAD, 2006).

Biofuels are not a new idea. Ford's Model T engine was designed to run on ethanol, and Diesel (the inventor of the diesel engine) thought that plant matter would provide the energy for his machines (Pahl and McKibben, 2008). But biofuels had a limited presence over the 20th century. Indeed, at the same time as interest and support for biofuels faded during these years, politics, investments and technology all played their part in supporting the expansion – and eventual dominance as an energy source – of fossil fuels. The oil cartels (along with the automobile industry) proved to be powerful lobbyists in assisting fossil fuel expansion. Oil is also relatively cheap to extract and refine, and easy (and safe) to transport. Importantly, oil is also incredibly energy-rich. The science of measuring energy balance (what is the net energy gain from a given form of fuel) is controversial. Assumptions about where the oil comes from (out at sea? tar sands?) makes a big difference to the equation, because not all oil is equally accessible. Similarly, assumptions about how crops are grown and where, and what kind of energy is used for the processing into biofuel, also make a big difference to the final results. Ethanol production creates a by-product, distillers grain, that is a protein-rich animal feed and valuable in its own right. At this time, oil remains markedly more efficient than any kind of biofuel, with more than twice the net energy yield than the most energy efficient biofuel (ethanol derived from cane sugar). The energy efficiency of any biomass used to produce liquid fuel depends significantly on the choice of on-farm inputs and how the energy needed to make the biofuel (generally heat and electricity) is derived. A less industrialized agricultural system will produce a more energy efficient crop. All the same, none of the biofuels available comes close to the energy return available from fossil fuels today.

In the 1970s, agribusinesses such as Archer Daniels Midand (ADM) – which dominated sugar and maize processing and trade – started to look for new markets for the products they made, including ethanol. Agribusinesses persuaded a series of national policy-makers in the US to include subsidies and targets for fuels that included an ethanol blend (Keeney, 2009). At the same time, Brazil also began to develop its ethanol industry, which is now the most well-established in the world. Reflecting this, over 90 per cent of vehicles in Brazil currently run on so-called 'flex-fuel' – either ethanol or petrol – allowing drivers to choose the fuel they want to use, while 45 per cent of Brazil's fuel for its light fleet vehicles (mainly cars and motorcycles) is derived from sugar cane (Grunwald, 2008). Not only does Brazil have a surplus of ethanol to export (at the same time as it is investing heavily to further expand its exportable surplus), it also has the technologies and equipment to sell to other countries to enable them to produce their own ethanol. Brazil is seeking to export flex-fuel cars to those developing countries that have the means to generate biofuels cost effectively.

The evidence presented above points to the extent to which Brazil has established itself as a world leader in biofuels. In contrast, the biofuels industry has, until recently, remained small in the US. Then, in the 1990s, interest in ethanol was revived under the impetus of clean air legislation. Ethanol contains oxygenates that allow petrol to burn more cleanly. California's clean air legislation has played an important role in generating interest and investment in commercial biofuels production in the US. Other states, such as Minnesota, mandated state targets for ethanol use starting in the 1990s. The Minnesotan experiment was one of the earlier public policy interventions to support biofuels and it included several important provisions: privileging local (in-state) ownership; financing and marketing preferences for farmer-owned ethanol producers; and, built-in obligations on producers to respect public as well as private objectives for the industry (Morris, 2006a).

In the few short years since biofuels have emerged, they have come to dominate debates relating to both energy and agriculture. As recently as 2006, much of the debate centred on how to manage risks and develop strong standards to meet stringent environmental and social goals. In 2009, many are concerned that the environmental and economic costs entailed by the sector are too big to justify, making the public support provided to the biofuels sector by governments unacceptable. Oxfam International, in its briefing paper *Another Inconvenient Truth*, summarized this view of the problem: 'Biofuels are presented in rich countries as a solution to two crises: the climate crisis and the oil crisis. But they may not be a solution to either, and instead are contributing to a third: the current food crisis' (Oxfam International, 2008, p2).

A critical look at the arguments for biofuels

This section reviews some common arguments made in support of biofuels, as well as the criticisms of those arguments.

Energy dependence

In both the US and in Europe, the biofuels industry and policy-makers who support the sector have argued that biofuels will enable greater energy independence via a reduction in the demand for fossil fuels. However, this argument is largely specious in practice: the technology is intimately linked to fossil fuels – both in the production of feedstock and in its final use. The production of biofuel feedstock overwhelmingly occurs on farms and plantations that rely heavily on fossil fuel-derived inputs – from fertilizers to pesticides to the fuel to power the machinery used to plant and harvest the crops. In addition, most biofuels are currently blended with fossil fuels, either gasoline or diesel, to varying percentages. In short, biofuel is attractive precisely because it works with the existing infrastructure.

The boldest advocates claim that biofuels will contribute to 'energy independence' by reducing dependence on oil imports. Yet, the US Department of Energy estimates biofuels will provide just 2.9 per cent of total US energy needs by 2010. By way of comparison, oil imports are expected to supply over half US liquid fuel requirements over the same time period (Keeney, 2009). The land that would be required, should biofuels become a significant share of the liquid fuel market, is staggering. The target of 35 billion gallons (132.49 billion litres), approved by the US Congress in December 2007, is equivalent to roughly 12 per cent of current liquid fuel usage in the US. This target is not realistic. Globally, biofuels met just over 1 per cent of total demand for liquid fuels in 2006 (Howarth et al, 2009). Even with the rapid development of new technologies related to biofuels, the sector's potential to make a major contribution to current liquid fuel consumption is tightly constrained by the natural resource limits on arable land and freshwater supplies.

It is clear that the net energy contribution from biofuels will only ever be small. Given climate change and the ecological crisis facing intensive agricultural production systems (see Chapters 1 and 2 of this volume), the attention focused on the biofuels sector risks distracting money and attention from fundamental energy reforms that are urgently needed.

Others argue, however, that although biofuels cannot ever account for a large share of liquid fuel use at today's levels of consumption (levels that continue to grow), they might make a much greater relative contribution in a radically reshaped energy economy. As US energy expert David Morris (2006b) points out, it is one thing to provide 5 or even 20 per cent of the fuel in a petrol or diesel blend for a typical car engine, as biofuels now do. It is quite another to provide the fuel for a back-up motor in a primarily electric car, something biofuels could do without oil (Morris, 2006b). If energy policy were to tackle the need to (radically) reduce total consumption in countries such as the US, as well as find ways to support increased reliance on alternatives to fossil fuels, possibly including biofuels, energy independence might be a more plausible objective. For countries where energy use is very low and large parts of the population have little access to liquid fuels (because fossil fuels are prohibitively expensive), biofuels on a local scale are an attractive alternative to expanding demand for imported oil.

New markets for excess production – or a driver of unsustainable production?

Biofuels have promised to provide new opportunities for rural regions of the developed nations. For government officials in both the US and Europe, biofuels looked like a useful new outlet for otherwise unwanted commodities. In an era of plentiful commodities, biofuels were an easy sell. In the upper mid-western US, where corn (for ethanol) and soybeans (for biodiesel) are grown in abundance, farmers have welcomed the technology, and some have formed cooperatives to invest jointly in the production facilities to make their own fuel (Morris, 2006a). Biofuels offered the chance to build value-added industry in these rural areas, where jobs and new investments were badly needed. They also offered an alternative to global markets, creating a domestic market for what farmers produced, and in which farmers had a better chance of securing a share in value-adding through processing. Farmers also received higher prices for their crops as demand increased.

In practice, however, biofuels have not played a straightforwardly positive role in rural economies. In the absence of any system of supply management, higher prices quickly spurred an increase in production, leading to more production and new pressures on uncultivated arable land in a number of biodiverse and ecologically sensitive areas (Fargione et al, 2008). The EU had initially introduced payments to encourage producers to shift into biofuel feedstock production, but so many farmers took up the scheme that by 2007 the payments were discontinued. In both the EU and the US, large areas of land have come out of conservation reserve programmes since commodity prices started to rise around 2004, a trend that accelerated dramatically in 2007 and 2008. Ambitious (and many would say unrealistic) mandates for minimum use and other incentives to stimulate biofuels use have created relatively secure new markets for increased production of crops that can be used as feedstock. Yet, the result has been more land devoted to biofuel feedstock rather than sustained higher prices for the commodities involved.

The indirect land-use effects of biofuels are one of the greatest concerns raised by biofuels critics. Land-use change includes the carbon released into the atmosphere when new land is brought into cultivation, or when new methods of cultivation increase greenhouse gas emissions. The effects are most marked when ecosystems such as peat bogs and rainforests are either mined for lumber and/or developed for agriculture (Oxfam International, 2008). Even if biofuels are grown sustainably on land that is well suited to feedstock, the expansion of acreage for biofuels displaces the food (or feed) production that had previously taken place. Since the demand for these crops remains, food and feed production is increasingly pushed on to more marginal land, or into areas where the land has not been cultivated before. If this new land is forested (as it is in the Amazon) or is peat land (as in Indonesia and Malaysia), very significant levels of greenhouse gases are released. It may take decades, even centuries, to sequester enough carbon to make up for the initial carbon release when native vegetation is destroyed (see Searchinger et al, 2008; Howarth et al, 2009).

The concern that demand for biofuels has powerful effects on decisions related to land use – especially in developing countries – is not only related to carbon reserves and climate change. It is also linked to a loss of biological diversity. Much of the land being brought into cultivation since the time of biofuel expansion is especially rich in biological life (Keeney and Nanninga, 2008). The loss of this biodiversity through farming is irrevocable. Even on well-established farmland, biodiversity and soil health suffer when changing costs and commodity prices render the production of monoculture crops (such as maize) more lucrative. To maintain or enhance soil fertility, land does much better if maize is grown in rotation with other crops, particularly legumes (which fix nitrogen in the soil), and forage crops such as alfalfa (Mallarino and Pecinovsky, 2009). However, the drive for ethanol has led many farmers to drop these rotations. The adoption of continuous maize crops is only possible in the short term, and reduces the biological diversity of the soil.

The science of measuring the impacts of biofuels on indirect land use is new and controversial. While many of the problems identified by critics point to indirect land use issues, it is also difficult to lay all the blame on biofuels. Arable land is under pressure from all sides – to grow food, animal feed and fuel. There is, however, a critically important difference with biofuels: the demand is potentially infinite. While food and animal feed are arguably limited by human appetite, demand for fuel theoretically has no limit. While the pressure to open new land to cultivation exists with or without biofuels, adding biofuels complicates the economics, the politics and the regulations required to foster sustainability objectives.

Biofuels in commercial use increase the demand for those crops that are strongly associated with agriculture's contribution to greenhouse gas emissions. While any crop grown in an industrial system – a system reliant on oil-powered machinery and inputs such as fertilizer that are derived from petroleum products – is a problem for the climate, regardless of its end use, biofuels crops are among the largest greenhouse gas pollutants. For example, most maize production is heavily dependant on nitrogen fertilizers. If those fertilizers are overused, they encourage such intensive microbial activity that the soil's organic carbon is depleted (Khan et al, 2007). The effect on soil is akin to burning, and it leaves the soil less productive. Fertilizer overuse is widespread across the corn belt of the US, leading to nitrate and pesticide contaminated surface and ground waters, and hypoxia (low oxygen) where rivers that drain large agricultural areas, such as the Mississippi River drainage basin, run into the sea. The Gulf of Mexico estuary has a large 'dead zone' – or hypoxia problem – along the coast of Louisiana and Texas (USGS, n.d.). Nitrous oxide – produced as a by-product of nitrogenous fertilizers – is a significant greenhouse gas, one emitted from row-crop cultivation as well as from aquatic ecosystems that are down river from agricultural production. It is generated through the use of nitrogen fertilizers in quantities greater than the soil can absorb. It has 300 times the effect on the global energy balance ('climate forcing' power) than an equivalent weight of carbon dioxide, such that nitrous oxide's overall contribution to climate change is far more significant than was previously understood (Howarth et al, 2009). These are not new problems, but demand for biofuels is exacerbating them.

The impact of biofuels on water resources is another important concern for many critics. Biofuel production relies on intensive water use; it takes roughly four litres of water to produce a litre of ethanol at the plant (a 4:1 ratio), in addition to the water required for the feedstock (Keeney and Muller, 2006). This can vary enormously – a recent study from the University of Minnesota that compared ethanol production on a state-by-state basis, counting both the water used in crop production and at the processing plant, showed a range from 6:1 water to ethanol in Iowa (almost all of which comes from rain), to 96:1 in

South Dakota and 2100:1 in California (Chiu et al, 2009). The wide differences in these ranges relates to the percentage of corn that is irrigated in each state – Iowa had the lowest percentage of irrigated corn, while in California much of the corn crop is irrigated. As such, any national average of such widely differing numbers has to be viewed with extreme caution. Likewise, any further demand on water in some regions is a matter of public concern, but this is not the case in all regions, given that water availability varies considerably from place to place. From a public policy perspective, the expansion of the ethanol industry to areas where water is already scarce presents a significant problem. Water management might be improved via the introduction of regulations and/or tighter criteria for minimum-use mandates that address water use concerns. However, the likely effectiveness of any such regulations would have to be carefully weighed in different national and local contexts.

Oil refinery and ethanol production are not dissimilar in their demands on the water system, but if the biofuel feedstocks are produced on irrigated land, the water cost jumps significantly. In their environmental assessment of biofuels, Howarth et al (2009, p6) suggest that '[t]he water requirements of biofuel-derived energy are 70 to 400 times larger than other energy sources such as fossil fuels, wind or solar.' While this range is enormous, even at the lower end of increased water use, it is obviously an issue that needs attention when planning the development of the biofuel sector.

Food security

The dramatic increase in biofuel production in the past few years has created a clear – if not somewhat complex – link between the price of maize and the price of oil that has increased volatility in agricultural commodity markets. It has exacerbated world hunger by making it harder for net-food importing developing countries to predict the cost of their food imports.[5]

Biofuels are blamed for much of the increase in commodities prices for the year ending June 2008 (see Chapters 1 and 6, this volume). A widely cited World Bank report claimed as much as 75 per cent of the price increases of 2007–2008 were due to biofuels (Mitchell, 2008). Another, widely cited, report from the International Food Policy Research Institute (IFPRI) put the number at 30 per cent (Rosegrant, 2008). Actual use (as opposed to the speculation triggered by anticipated demand) was in fact relatively modest: industry analyst Licht (2008) reports that ethanol production used 4.49 per cent of the global grains supply in 2007, and biodiesel used 7.63 per cent of the combined global supply of soybean oil, rapeseed and palm oil. At the same time, it seems clear that investors projected significant growth in demand for grain, based in part on relatively high use targets set by both US and EU governments. That assumption, further pushed by poor harvests in key export producers such as Australia, and entirely unrelated factors in financial markets, sent billions of dollars into speculative investment in commodity indices, driving prices much higher than the 'fundamentals' (supply and demand) seemed to warrant (de la Torre Ugarte and Murphy, 2008). There were also direct effects on the cost of food: feed represents roughly 50 per cent of the cost of raising meat in industrial-scale facilities, and biofuels have created a direct competition for several of the most common feedstuffs, particularly maize (Westcott, 2007).

Demand for biofuels also began at a time when global stocks of many grains were already in decline. In one of the most important agricultural policy changes initiated by the US government, its programme of farmer-owned commodity reserves was eliminated in 1996. The political pressure for this move came primarily from multinational agribusinesses, which resented the lost opportunity for hedging and speculating on price movements that resulted from the stocks. The US is a major grower of a number of agricultural commodities for world markets; this change ended an important instrument for limiting volatility in world prices. Structural adjustment programmes (and their successors, poverty reduction strategies) designed by the World Bank and International Monetary Fund (IMF) encouraged developing countries to abandon their national and regional grain reserves as well. The global stock situation also shifted markedly early in the 2000s with the decision of the Chinese government to eliminate a considerable portion of their (very large) food reserves. The volatility of food prices the world over through 2007 and 2008 called into question the wisdom of ending such stocks.

Just as interest in biofuels was growing, matched by steadily larger targets for their use in a number of countries, so world stocks of many commodities were reaching all time lows. Belief that increasingly integrated global markets would provide stability should domestic harvests fail apparently outweighed the fundamental issue that there was not much grain in reserve should a major food grain exporter (say the US or Australia) fail to produce an adequate supply. The food price crisis of 2007 and 2008, however, showed how difficult getting supply and demand right using a 'just in time' system for agriculture is – with millions of people paying the price in hunger.

Biofuels cannot be blamed for the global policy of low food stocks. That has come about as a result of government choices to cut public stocks (for instance in the US and the EU), the demands of structural adjustment programmes, and the subsequent poverty reduction strategies devised by the World Bank and IMF. Yet, while biofuels are not behind the decision to leave the management of food stocks to the private sector, clearly biofuels represent an important new demand at a time of stress in the food system. In 2002–2003, year-ending stocks of grain fell below 25 per cent for the first time since the early 1980s. A 25 per cent year-end stock means there is enough grain for one quarter (three months) of the year's demand.

A number of factors contributed to the decline in global food reserves. The most important was the implementation of policies over the 1990s that reduced or eliminated public grain stocks in some of the largest producer and consumer countries. As mentioned earlier, the 1996 decision of the US government to end its policy of holding stocks, a policy that had been in place since the 1930s, had global implications. The decision was strongly endorsed by multinational agribusinesses, which are well-positioned to benefit from speculating on volatile prices because of their superior access to both market information and global supplies. For many of these firms, adding biofuels into the demand for the grains they supply (and process) is a logical, self-interested way to keep commodity markets buoyant. With regard to the EU, it has also changed its policies through the 1990s to eliminate its stocks (European Commission, n.d.). At the same time, the conditions attached to the World Bank and IMF structural adjustment programmes pushed developing countries to abandon local and regional reserves of grain. Given the access to cheap foreign grains, local reserves were viewed as expensive and unnecessary.

It seems clear that the mood of 2004 – 'what shall we do with all this maize and soy?' – has vanished. In a report published by the Farmland Trust, three economists from Purdue University describe this change as a move from a paradigm of surplus to one of shortages:

> *The transition from surplus stocks or 'too much' to 'too little' came quickly for most agricultural commodities from 2006 to 2008. Once that thin line was crossed, prices were 'unbolted' as everyone asked what the value of food should be in a world of 'too little'* (Tyner et al, 2008, p11).

The 2008 Farmland Trust report looks at the factors that drove higher food prices in 2007 and early 2008. The report concludes that demand for corn for ethanol production is a bigger factor than demand for oilseeds to produce biodiesel. Within the oilseed sector, demand for feed grew roughly twice as much as demand for oilseeds for industrial purposes (including biodiesel production), but growth in rapeseed use (as opposed to soy oil or palm oil) was overwhelmingly the result of EU policies that turn rapeseed into biodiesel (Tyner et al, 2008, p19).

More hopefully, it is possible to argue that the world is not entering a period of scarcity so much as a period of transition. This could lead to more productive and more ecologically sustainable agricultural production and distribution systems. Either way, there is no doubt that hunger has been increasing, together with price volatility, both of which are matters of serious concern for all governments concerned to respect their peoples' right to food and the future of their agriculture. Policies that worsen people's access to food have no place when hunger is already a desperate problem for more than a billion people worldwide.

Conclusion: A future for biofuels?

Many of the criticisms levelled at biofuels could arguably just as well be levelled at industrial food and feed production. If the maize, canola or soybeans were not used for biofuels, there might be less overall pressure on land. But the demand for animal feed is large and growing (much larger than the demand for biofuels), and chances are the demands on land, water and air would change little should biofuels be taken out of the equation. Indeed, the loudest protests over ethanol policy in the US have come from livestock companies such as Tyson, which has paid the price with higher commodity prices, in part driven by biofuels demand, and from the US grocery industry. If biofuels somehow magically 'disappeared' from the world economy, the problems associated with biofuels production described here would not similarly disappear: the problems lie in agricultural production systems and their lack of sustainability in industrialized (and most industrializing) societies. Yet, without tighter regulation, biofuels risk adding more fragility to an already fragile world.

Biofuels have very visibly connected three 'elements' that are more deeply linked than is commonly understood: energy, water and agriculture. Modern industrial agriculture is, in fact, deeply dependent on fossil fuels for its high-level productivity. For all the gains in output, the dependence of industrial agriculture on the petroleum industry makes it unsustainable (see Weis, 2007; and Chapters 2 and 6, this volume). Industrial agriculture is a large net contributor to greenhouse gas emissions; it is a big user (and too often waster) of water; it mines the soil, failing to replace the nutrients it needs to grow crops; and it creates dependencies that have undermined family owned agriculture the world over, turning independent businesses into easily exploitable links in a production chain (see Patel, 2007).

There is also a growing body of evidence demonstrating the limits of industrial agriculture: productivity gains have slowed to almost nothing, suggesting that as demand continues to increase, we need a new approach if the world's people are to be fed. The work of scientists and experts included in the International Assessment of Agricultural Knowledge, Science and Technology for Development (IAASTD, 2008) suggests that profound changes in agri-food systems are needed. Such changes will not just include new technologies, but will also include changes in trade and investment rules, as well as new consideration for the social and cultural knowledge wrapped up in agricultural practice, and new respect for the power – and the limits – of the planet's biosphere. A growing number of agro-ecological experiments point the way to a new approach for raising yields: measuring not the output per plant (and discounting the inputs required to get the best yields), but instead measuring the total productivity of a given parcel of land. Agro-ecology focuses on mixed cropping systems, and ensuring that different components of the farm contribute to the overall output (for example by using nitrogen-rich poultry manure instead of inorganic fertilizers; or, avoiding the use of pesticides in rice paddies, which kill fish that would otherwise live in the paddy waters).

The biofuels sector is young and growing fast. It is shaped by, and often dependent upon, a wide variety of public policies, many of which are still in flux. The sector is also dependent on agricultural output, commodity production costs and oil prices. Uncertainty about the future of biofuels also relates to the still unfinished business of establishing credible environmental and social standards for biofuels. Much of today's commercial production meets a narrow, but important, set of standards, including lower greenhouse gas emissions than regular gas, cleaner burning fuel and better engine performance through higher octane levels. Yet, most biofuels fail important sustainability tests and raise still unsolved issues for global agriculture more generally.

It is not biofuels as such that create the economic, environmental and social problems articulated throughout this chapter. Rather, these problems stem from the industrial agricultural system and the deregulated markets in which production and exchange takes place. Problems are also related to their positioning within a finite set of fragile, if renewable, resources and the apparently insatiable human appetite for energy. Governments need to move with far more care in charting out an appropriate course for biofuels so that they do not end up subsidizing poor practices and missing the opportunity to steer public investment into truly sustainable energy sources.

Notes

1   The author wishes to thank Dennis Keeney, Shiney Varghese, Ben Lilliston, Jim Kleinschmit, Mark Muller and André Lambelet for their comments, disagreements, ideas and edits. She also wishes to thank Kristen Lyons and Tabatha Wallington for their warm encouragement and patience, and the Agri-Food Research Network for the invitation to turn these thoughts into a chapter. The mistakes are all mine.
2   This chapter uses the term 'biofuels' throughout. It is the most common term for the sector. However, the alternative term 'agrofuels' is also commonly used, and appears throughout this book.
3   Some of the biggest firms, such as Cargill, are on both sides of the divide over biofuels: their grain operations profit from higher commodity prices, while their meat processing businesses lose out.
4   A wide range of materials is available to introduce the sector for those who are unfamiliar with it, including: UNCTAD (2006); UN-Energy (2007); IEA and OECD (2007); Doornbosch and Steenblick (2007); Oxfam International (2008); various papers from the International Institute for Environment and Development; Worldwatch Institute (2007).
5   A net food importing country is one that depends on food imports to meet the food needs of its population.

References

Chiu, Y.-W., Walseth, B. and Suh, S. (2009) 'Water embodied in bioethanol in the US', *Environmental Science and Technology*, vol 43, no 8, pp2688–2692

de la Torre Ugarte, D. and Murphy, S. (2008) *The Global Food Crisis: Creating an Opportunity For Fairer and More Sustainable Food and Agriculture Systems Worldwide*, EcoFair Trade Dialogue Discussion Papers, no 11, October, Heinrich Böll Stiftung and Misereor, Germany

Doornbosch, R. and Steenblik, R. (2007) *Biofuels: Is the Cure Worse Than the Disease?* OECD, SG/SD/RT(2007)3, 11–12 September, Paris

European Commission Directorate-General for Agriculture and Rural Development (n.d.) *The Common Agricultural Policy Explained*, ec.europa.eu/agriculture/publi/capexplained/cap_en.pdf, accessed 26 May 2009

Fargione, J., Hill, J., Tilman, D., Polasky, S. and Hawthorne, P. (2008) 'Land clearing and the biofuel carbon debt', *Science*, vol 319, no 5867, pp1235–1238

Grunwald, M. (2008) 'The clean energy scam', *Time*, 27 March, US

Howarth, R., Bringezu, S., Bekunda, M., de Fraiture, C., Maene, L., Martinelli, L. and Sala, O. (2009) 'Rapid assessment on biofuels and environment: Overview and key findings', in R. Howarth and S. Bringezu (eds) *Biofuels: Environmental Consequences and Interactions with Changing Land Use*, Proceedings of the Scientific Committee on Problems of the Environment (SCOPE), International Biofuels Project Rapid Assessment, 22–25 September 2008, Gummersbach, Germany, Cornell University, Ithaca, US

IAASTD (International Assessment of Agricultural Knowledge, Science and Technology for Development) (2008) 'Executive Summary of the Synthesis Report', April, www.agassessment.org/docs/IAASTD_GLOBAL_SDM_JAN_2008.pdf, accessed 31 March 2009

IEA and OECD (2007) *Renewables in Global Energy Supply. An IEA Fact Sheet*, International Energy Agency, France

Keeney, D. (2009) 'Ethanol USA. Viewpoint', *Environmental Science and Technology*, vol 43, no 1, pp8–11

Keeney, D. and Muller, M. (2006) *Water Use by Ethanol Plants: Potential Challenges*, Institute for Agriculture and Trade Policy, Minneapolis, www.agobservatory.org/library.cfm?refid=89449, accessed 25 May 2009

Keeney, D. and Nanninga, C. (2008) *Biofuel and Global Biodiversity*, Institute for Agriculture and Trade Policy, Minneapolis, www.agobservatory.org/library.cfm?refid=102584, accessed 25 May 2009

Khan, S., Ellsworth, T. and Boast, S. (2007) 'The myth of nitrogen fertilization for soil carbon sequestration', *Journal of Environmental Quality*, vol 36, pp1821–1832

Licht, F. (2008) *World Ethanol and Biofuels Report*, vol 6, no 15

Mallarino, A. P. and Pecinovsky, K. (2009) *Effects of Crop Rotation and Nitrogen Fertilization for Corn on Yields of Corn, Silage Corn, Soybean, and Oats*, Iowa State University Extension, 20 April, www.agronext.iastate.edu/soilfertility/, accessed 25 May 2009

Mitchell, D. (2008) 'A note on rising food prices', World Bank, Washington, DC, as cited in Eide, A. (2008) *The Right to Food and the Impact of Liquid Biofuels (Agrofuels)*, Food and Agriculture Organization of the United Nations, Rome, www.fao.org/righttofood/publi08/Right_to_Food_and_Biofuels.pdf, accessed 26 May 2009

Morris, D. (2006a) *Ownership Matters: Three Steps to Ensure a Biofuels Industry That Truly Benefits Rural America*, Institute for Local Self-Reliance, Minneapolis

Morris, D. (2006b) 'The once and future carbohydrate economy', *The American Prospect*, 19 March

Oxfam International (2008) *Another Inconvenient Truth: How Biofuels Policies are Deepening Poverty and Accelerating Climate Change*, Oxfam Briefing Paper No 114, June, Oxfam International

Pahl, G. and McKibben, B. (2008) *Biodiesel: Growing a New Energy Economy*, Second Edition (revised), Chelsea Green Publishing, Vermont, US

Patel, R. (2007) *Stuffed and Starved: Markets, Power and the Hidden Battle for the World Food System*, Black Ink, Melbourne

Pollan, M. (2006) *The Omnivore's Dilemma: The Search for a Perfect Meal in a Fast-food World*, Bloomsbury, London

Rosegrant, M. (2008) 'Biofuels and grain prices: Impacts and policy responses', Testimony before the US Senate Committee on Homeland Security and Governmental Affairs, 7 May, www.ifpri.org/pubs/testimony/rosegrant20080507.asp, accessed 26 May 2009

Searchinger, T., Heimlich, R., Houghton, R., Dong, F., Elobeid, A., Fabiosa, J., Tokgoz, S., Hayes, D. and Tun-Hsiang, Y. (2008) 'Use of US croplands for biofuels increases greenhouse gases through emissions from land-use change', *Science*, vol 319, no 5867, pp1238–1240

Tyner, W., Abbot, P. and Hurt, C. (2008) *What's Driving Food Prices?* Farm Foundation Issue Report, US, www.farmfoundation.org, accessed 26 May 2009

UNCTAD (2006) *The Emerging Biofuels Market: Regulatory, Trade and Development Implications*, United Nations Conference on Trade and Development, Geneva and New York

UN-Energy (2007) 'Sustainable bioenergy: A framework for decision makers', UN-Energy, New York, esa.un.org/un-energy/pdf/susdev.Biofuels.FAO.pdf, accessed 26 May 2009

USGS (US Geological Survey) (n.d.) *The Gulf of Mexico Hypoxic Zone*, toxics.usgs.gov/hypoxia/hypoxic_zone.html, accessed 26 May 2009

Weis, T. (2007) *The Global Food Economy: The Battle for the Future of Farming*, Zed Books, London

Westcott, P. (2007) 'U.S. ethanol expansion driving changes throughout the agricultural sector', *Amber Waves*, September, US Department of Agriculture, Washington, DC, www.ers.usda.gov/AmberWaves/September07/Features/Ethanol.htm, accessed 26 May 2009

Worldwatch Institute (2007) *Biofuels for Transport: Global Potential and Implications for Sustainable Agriculture and Energy in the 21st Century*, Worldwatch Institute, Washington, DC and Earthscan, London

15

Examining the Mythologies of Organics: Moving beyond the Organic/Conventional Binary?

Hugh Campbell, Chris Rosin, Solis Norton, Peter Carey, Jayson Benge and Henrik Moller[1]

Introduction: Debating organic mythologies

The turn of the 21st century marked a crossroads for organic agriculture. By 2002, when the research project detailed in this chapter was being designed, organic agriculture had emerged as a commercial force that incorporated many producers and retailers on a global scale. It was also a time when the new visibility of organic agriculture, coupled with a global debate over the role of genetically modified organisms (GMOs) in conventional agriculture, resulted in a high-profile public debate between promoters and detractors of organic agriculture. This chapter reflects on this public debate, using data produced by the Agriculture Research Group on Sustainability (ARGOS) project. The ARGOS project is a longitudinal social–ecological study of over 100 farms and orchards in New Zealand using organic, conventional or an environmentally oriented management system (usually an integrated management system that is designed to eliminate chemical residues from the final product and/or adheres to sets of 'best practice' guidelines around nutrients, water and energy). This chapter provides the first opportunity for a group of scholars working on the project to consider the broad pattern emerging out of the preliminary research results.

During the years leading to the establishment of the ARGOS project, publicly debated critiques of organic agriculture came from two completely different directions. First, the emergence of global controversy over GMOs in agriculture resulted in the significant elevation of organic agriculture as a claimed alternative system to mainstream agriculture. This prompted a backlash from scientists advocating the adoption of GMOs, which is best symbolized by the high-profile and widely cited attack on the 'Urban myths of organic farming' by Trewavas, published in the March edition of *Nature* in 2001 (Trewavas, 2001). From the other direction, Pollan (2001) and others questioned whether commercial organic agriculture was consistent with the purer sustainability claims of either the original organic philosophies, or the more recent ideas about sustainable food systems. In short, they charged organic agriculture with having sold out through commercialization. Both sides agreed, in largely pejorative terms, that organics was a fraud or an act of deception against the consumer – a charge that subsequently became the subject of vociferous counter-claiming by advocates of the new commercial organic sector.

This vigorous public debate certainly raised the public image of organic agriculture as an alternative system of food production. It is more questionable whether either its high-profile science critics, or its staunch defenders, did justice to the deeper and less reactionary currents of academic discussion, which focused more constructively on the role of organics in achieving agricultural sustainability. This chapter suggests that the heightened media claims and counter-claims around the virtues or fraudulence of organics were fuelled in the early 2000s by wider ideological commitments concerning the future direction of agriculture (and agricultural sustainability). As such, media debates about organics became organized around key mythologies – claims that have political meaning and significance, but that are only loosely connected, or are completely disconnected, from the markedly less sensationalist science discussions that were occurring during that time in a number of related fields of scholarship.

Such debates around organic mythologies were influential during the establishment of the ARGOS project, which took shape around 2002. The preliminary results of the project thus shed light on some of the key claims mobilized both for and against organic agriculture at that time. This chapter also forms a useful starting point for a judicious re-framing of several key questions about organic agriculture and its potential contribution to global agendas around agricultural sustainability.

The media mythologies of organics: From Trewavas to Pollan

Even a fairly shallow examination of the organics debate in the early 2000s, as it was portrayed in the popular media, reveals that the role of science quickly becomes problematic. There are a number of reasons for this contemporary phenomenon, which centre on the politicization of science in public controversies. A quick search on the internet will turn up numerous websites full of sceptical claims about organic agriculture. These sites all devote some part of their discussion to 'debunking the myths' of the alleged positive benefits of organic farming and food, or to demonstrating scientific proof of the fraudulence of the positive claims regarding the benefits of organic farming. Organic trade associations like the UK Soil Association have mobilized a similar set of counter-claims – again declaring that there is strong scientific evidence to support their position. Both sides are, at best, guilty of 'cherry-picking' scientific findings to support their claims. At the height of this debate, it was almost impossible to engage in any sustained discussion about the kinds of scientific methodologies that could reliably inform such debates at anything more than a superficial level.

Most of the anti-organic websites support their claims by citing the high-profile critique of organic agriculture published by Trewavas in *Nature* in 2001. This item forms the emblematic centrepiece of the public science–sceptic position on organics.[2] Notable scientists who were taking an active role in media debates, like anti-'junk science' campaigner Lord Taverne (*Guardian*, 2004) cited such work and argued that consumers are being 'conned' by organic marketing claims. At the farthest end of this spectrum, lobbyists like public relations expert Dennis Avery (see Avery, 1995) were hired by agribusiness-funded organizations in the US to coordinate a public campaign against organic agriculture.[3]

The strong claims against organics that are reproduced in this kind of media discussion tend to cluster around the following seven issues:

1   Organic agriculture produces food with no scientifically demonstrable nutritional benefits to consumers.
2   Organic farming experiences significantly declining yields compared to conventional approaches.
3   Organic farming represents a flawed agronomic approach that will reduce profitability or lose money outright for farmers who convert to organic approaches.
4   Organic soil management leads to unavoidable long-term declines in soil fertility.
5   Organic systems have unacceptable long-term risks with regard to pest control.
6   The 'natural' pesticides used in organic systems are just as dangerous as synthetic pesticides.
7   Organic systems provide no wider environmental benefits to agro-ecosystems.

Most of the abovementioned critical commentary has been advanced by media advocates of mainstream agriculture, by public supporters of GM technologies and by sceptics seeking reasons to rally around 'science' versus 'mumbo jumbo' explanations. In response, the newly commercializing organics industry – and its professional allies, such as the UK Soil Association – were also eager to select positive 'science' findings and to popularize them through the media as a means of countering the claim that organics was a fraud. What emerged from this latter response was something of a problem in itself: a framing of organic agriculture as the panacea for all agricultural ills.

As indicated at the outset of this chapter, however, the two sides of this media debate are not entirely clear cut – a simple demarcation of agricultural science-informed sceptics and organic industry-aligned advocates simply does not hold. Rather, the emergence of a commercial organic food industry has also provoked a third position: a sustained and challenging critique originating in the alternative agriculture movement itself, buttressed by the broad support of a number of popular commentators. Put simply, some argue that commercial organic agriculture has 'sold out', or failed to live up to the promise of genuine alternative and sustainable forms of farming. Symbolized by Pollan's widely cited attack in his *New York Times* article 'Behind the organic-industrial complex' (2001), this critique relies less on any recourse to scientific evidence and more on an amalgam of normative political desires and insights from wider philosophies of sustainability. In other words, it posits how alternative agriculture 'ought' to be and concludes that commercial organics does not fit this image.[4]

This particular critique of commercial organics is mobilized around the dynamic that, once commercializing pressures have developed in an alternative sector, these pressures inform the guiding logic of the sector to a greater extent than do environmental concerns. The profit motive drives further development of the sector and, guided by this economic logic, new recruits into organic agriculture will be motivated by the desire to secure financial premiums rather than environmental sustainability. Simplified into a set of guiding logics about the evils of commercial organics, four claims about the consequences of these commercial pressures seem to dominate the communications of these critics:

1 That commercial organic production has less beneficial outcomes than 'authentic' organics as practised by local, small-scale, philosophically committed members of the organic social movement.
2 That there is a cultural convergence of commercial organic production with the views and practices of conventional agriculture.
3 That new recruits to organic agriculture in commercial settings are motivated primarily by financial gain.
4 That, in the long run, organic producers in commercial contexts will reproduce the same problematic outcomes associated with conventional agricultural production.

What emerges from the arguments put at both ends of the anti-organics continuum – as represented by Trewavas and Pollan, respectively – is a tendency towards a false binary between organic and conventional agriculture, a *fallacy of composition* (or at least of hasty generalization) in which an idealized but problematic category (whether organic or conventional) is constructed in order to critique the category that is being defined in opposition. In Trewavas's case, and most certainly that of users who subsequently cited his article, a few items of specific evidence are generalized to establish a unitary category of good, scientifically proven, 'non-organic' agriculture while disqualifying the category of 'organics'. In Pollan's case, false categories of both organic and conventional agriculture emerge – with the differences between the two collapsing as 'organic' increasingly converges on conventional agriculture as the former is commercialized.

This is the binary opposition that confronted the ARGOS project when it was being designed in 2002. What made this problem even more interesting was that such binaries are not merely media-based, academic or heuristic constructs. The undeniable commercial expansion of certified organic agriculture at a global scale meant that, through the mechanism of new market audit schemes and certification-based systems of food governance, 'organic' has been mobilized as a uniform institutional category within the global systems of food trade. Put another way, organic certification performs the same magic that we are criticizing among its academic detractors. It creates a unitary operating category called 'organic' in the marketplace, which bundles together myriad subtle differences and styles of production under one label. As the following narrative will reveal, the preliminary results of ARGOS indicate that the project design was instrumental in enabling ARGOS research to clearly differentiate between production systems. As such, the research demonstrates that organic (as a market audit category) involves scientifically defensible differences relative to non-organic production. It also holds the potential to create a set of insights that supersede the whole organic/conventional binary as an academically useful construct.

Methods for a sustainability science of agriculture?

When the research group was designing the ARGOS project in 2002 (see Manhire et al, 2003), a series of methodological challenges were identified:

1 That real-world dynamics in farming systems create endless problems in terms of establishing defensible comparisons between systems.
2 That sustainability issues tend not to respect disciplinary boundaries, making some kind of engagement with multidisciplinary and transdisciplinary approaches necessary.
3 That existing comparisons of complex farming systems involving either very small numbers of farms or a single 'split-farm' – while allowing a dense technical focus – are next to useless for gaining more generalizable social scientific insight.
4 That existing social science studies of sustainable agriculture often struggle to integrate ecological dynamics.

In response to these challenges, the ARGOS research group deployed a longitudinal study design incorporating over 100 farms and orchards in the sheep/beef, dairy and kiwifruit export sectors, arranged in geographically contiguous panels of organic and non-organic management systems.[5] The panel design has some obvious benefits. The panels were organized in triplet clusters in different localities to try to control for ecological variation across landscapes, thus addressing the first point above. Ideally, the three farm/orchard types share contiguous boundaries and were comprised of similar family-run commercial farms of reasonably similar size. The ARGOS design was therefore able to compare different management systems across similar soil (and wider landscape, ecology and climate) profiles.

The second key design feature was to include a wide range of measures and observations across the range of social, economic and ecological dynamics present on farms/orchards, which contributed to an understanding of the sustainability of management systems (point 2 above). This allowed for a much more comprehensive integration of some of the financial and performance data (such as yield data) to be examined in conjunction with ecological outcomes, such as farm biodiversity or water and soil quality (thus responding to point 4 above).

Third, the sheer number of farms in the panel design meant that ARGOS could identify some of the depth of comparative material usually obtainable from single or paired farm studies, but broadened out with greater statistical power to a group of over 100 farms/orchards (point 3). This inevitably required a trade-off, however, between the analytical depth achievable from intense case studies and the wider zone of inference gained by studying a larger group.

In trying to solve some of the identified methodological challenges, ARGOS also made several key compromises. In particular, the decision was made to specifically concentrate analysis at the farm scale, rather than some other cross-cutting scale – such as the community, catchment, region or nation – so as to examine the intersection of economic, social and ecological characteristics. In addition, it was decided that ARGOS would specifically study family farms engaged in commercial-scale agriculture. The farms would be selected to represent the 'norm' of commercial-scale farms rather than other forms of farming enterprise, which might have identified different sustainability outcomes to the institutional forms of farming chosen. Finally, New Zealand's highly export-oriented, developed world, temperate agricultural economy – one based around family farming rather than corporate agriculture – together with the highly educated and unsubsidized nature of its agricultural sector, mean that the ARGOS findings will potentially be generalizable. New Zealand is a paradigmatic example of the kind of developed world food producers currently supplying global-scale procurement chains for large high-end retailers like UK supermarkets and European Union (EU) cooperatives. Indeed, New Zealand family farmers are the suppliers to Pollan's Organic–Industrial Complex.

In summary, ARGOS deployed a complex array of interdisciplinary measures designed to understand how farm-level interactions around organic, integrated and conventional management play out over time. It is deliberately focused on commercial-scale family farms undertaking production for global export industries. Although it does not resolve all the methodological challenges associated with comparing the relative merits of organic and non-organic management, it does try to address the need for a more integrative, multidisciplinary approach to understanding agricultural sustainability. This kind of methodological approach – often called 'sustainability science' – is designed to address sustainability questions that do not respect disciplinary boundaries and are unlikely to be understood through a reductionist focus on component parts of complex systems.[6]

Re-examining some of the key mythologies

Due to the challenge of summarizing the full spectrum of results emerging from 100-plus ARGOS farms and orchards, the following section provides a brief review of findings around some of the central scientific claims made in the mythologies debate. As such, it will probably give little comfort to either side in the organic mythologies debate. Moreover, ARGOS does not yet undertake nutritional analysis of food from ARGOS farms and orchards. The project, nonetheless, harnesses an array of complex measures around issues of yield, financial performance, soil fertility, pest management, biodiversity on farms and social differences between farmers using different management systems – the analysis of which does go some way toward understanding the dynamics of organic and non-organic management systems.

Yield

A central issue in the organic mythologies debate was the so-called 'yield gap'. This was one of the key claims in Trewavas (2001) – made without any recourse to scientific citation – and one of the most widely cited. Trewavas claimed that conventional agricultural systems could produce as much as organic systems on only 50–70 per cent of the land area. This was restated, in the popular press, as a claim that organic farming methods produced only half the yield of conventional farming. Contributors like Avery translated this 'yield gap' into the compelling argument that organics would exacerbate world hunger and/or destroy biodiversity by requiring the conversion of extensive tracts of habitat into farmland in order to meet world food demands. In response, the UK Soil Association and others cited studies which showed a negligible or non-existent yield gap in organic farms.

In contrast to these contestable and unjustified claims, the ARGOS project was able to generate comparative data between both organic and non-organic panels of farms and orchards over consecutive years. The ARGOS design meant that yields could be compared as an aggregate of the difference between paired organic and non-organic farms and orchards, rather than by the less useful measure of mean yield across single panel types (Benge et al, 2009). The results for the kiwifruit sector showed a significant difference in yield between organic and non-organic orchards growing the same variety of kiwifruit. Over a number of years, organic orchards generally produced about 20–30 per cent less than the same area of a non-organic orchard. It is noteworthy that the ARGOS data are also consistent over the best part of the last decade. While the 'gap' between organic and non-organic systems does vary from year to year, it has remained consistent over the longer term even while both systems have gradually increased their productivity. Interestingly, compared with industry data from the mid-1990s, *all* of the systems are outperforming the industry's conventional production as measured in 1997 (Campbell et al, 1997, p23).

In both the sheep/beef and kiwifruit sectors, the comparison of organic and non-organic systems was made more complex by the fact that some farms and most orchards use integrated management systems, which incorporate environmentally oriented modifications to conventional production methods. Taking this into account, organic sheep and beef producers were only slightly less productive than conventional producers (by 15 per cent), but significantly less productive than integrated management producers (by 30 per cent). The same dynamic was evident in the kiwifruit industry in the mid-1990s with integrated management being the most productive system.

The long-term nature of the ARGOS yield data thus offers greater insight than previous generalizations based on single-year data on relative yields, particularly as relative yields may relate to other important aspects of the farm systems. One immediate observation from preliminary ARGOS data is warranted. The 'yield gap' between organic and non-organic seems to hover between 20 and 30 per cent – a figure significantly less than the 30–50 per cent range cited by Trewavas (2001) and subsequent sceptics in making scientific claims about organics. It is, nevertheless, a wider gap than the 'nil gap' claim organic proponents from places like the Rodale Institute have made (see LaSalle et al, 2008).

Financial performance

As a logical corollary to 'yield gap' arguments, critics have suggested that organic premiums are fragile, and will eventually lead to financial ruin for farmers. A variant on that argument is that organic farmers in Europe are unfairly subsidized by the EU and would otherwise be financially unviable. These contentions have been countered by organic organizations with widely publicized claims that organic growers were accessing super-premiums compared to their failing conventional peers.

In contrast to these claims, the financial performance of ARGOS organic and non-organic producers turned out to be relatively comparable. Despite the complete absence of any form of subsidy for organic production, early results reported in Saunders et al (2007) suggest that there were no significant differences between the profitability of organic and non-organic systems. No important differences appeared across four years of data from three sectors. The similarity among sector results most probably derives from lower yields in organic systems combined with the presence of a market premium and lower input costs. This finding shows that neither the strong claim that organics will lead to financial ruin, nor the claim that organics is generating exceptional profits, can be sustained when looking at aggregate results from organic producers, although there was, admittedly, considerable variation in the performance of individual organic producers.

Soil fertility

Claims centred on the issue of soil fertility lie at the heart of many scientific debates around organics. If an orthodox position is taken, then organics is claimed to 'mine the soil' and will, in the long run, require external subsidies of inputs or suffer reduced productivity. Strong organic proponents argue the exact opposite – that organic management is the only way to maintain soil health through promoting biological activity in the soil as the key long-term source of nutrients.

Four years of soils research on the ARGOS farms and orchards has allowed a much more complex array of data to be built up than has been available to date. Carey et al (2009) document a range of significant differences between organic and non-organic systems among the ARGOS panels. However, an even more significant point is that the ARGOS clustered-panel design allowed these differences to be identified in a way that simple averages of each panel could not. Organic farms and orchards tended to have some better soil characteristics – such as lower soil density, higher water-holding capacity and higher earthworm numbers – than their non-organic neighbours.

The ARGOS results clearly show that soils are the most frequent area of demarcation between organic and non-organic systems (as might be expected given that soil fertility is at the centre of organic management practices). Furthermore, it is equally evident that a highly sophisticated study design is needed to identify which differences stem from organic management and which do not. Most of the science upon which sceptical claims about the inevitable collapse of soil fertility in organic regimes rests fails to achieve this level of methodological rigour, let alone provide a basis for wider understanding of the sustainability of farm systems. On this issue, the ARGOS data clearly support a more optimistic view of the potential contribution of organic management to agricultural sustainability.

Biodiversity and pest management

While most of the biological action in agriculture seems to happen in the soils, there are wider biodiversity issues emerging across the ARGOS panels. The first interesting point is that Maegli et al (2007) have found few differences in the biodiversity impacts of organic and non-organic management (once soils are excluded). Insectivorous birds are more abundant on organic farms, spider diversity and abundance is higher in the shelterbelts (hedgerows) typically found on organic dairy farms, and plant biodiversity in – and under – shelterbelts is higher in organic kiwifruit orchards. Invertebrate communities are restructured in streams flowing through organic and other sheep/beef farms – there were more species per sampling site, especially of sensitive groups like mayflies, stoneflies and caddisflies in organic streams and overall higher abundance of invertebrates within organic farms. These differences are probably associated with a mixture of habitat availability on farms, and the direct impact of organic management on biodiversity.

The lack of sprays makes it slightly more likely for birds to inhabit organic farmscapes. However, larger gains are more likely to emerge from the tendency of organic producers to allow more woody vegetation and grassy sward to grow on their properties, rather than to denude the landscape to create the 'tidy' appearance characteristic of more conventional farms and orchards.

A myth about weed management is also put to rest by the ARGOS data: organic producers are not suffocating under an intolerable weed burden. There were no significant differences in the presence of weed species between organic and non-organic ARGOS panels, nor was there evidence that organic producers are achieving this kind of parity by using excessive 'natural' pesticides (Blackwell et al, forthcoming). Organic sheep/beef farmers spend more time controlling weeds, but less money on chemicals, equipment and contractors than do their conventional and integrated management counterparts to achieve this equivalence in weed prevalence.

Social differences

The centrepiece of one set of critical claims about organics is that certified organic growers cannot be differentiated according to any particular social or cultural characteristics compared to non-organic growers. Put simply, the argument is that certified organic growers may well be conventional growers who are solely pursuing organic production for the financial reward. In contrast, the ARGOS social research data demonstrate that there are noteworthy – albeit at times subtle – differences in the ideas, practices, values and subjective understandings of organic and non-organic panel members. These differences are not always aligned in the ways expected by some commentators, however.

The notion of 'environmental orientation' captures the extent to which the positive aspects of farming are associated with the qualities of the farm environment (such as biodiversity, water quality and soil quality). Rosin et al (2007) show that organic and non-organic producers do exhibit noticeable differences in terms of their orientation towards particular qualities of the farm environment, environmental practices and the way they understand and value environmental aspects of farm production. This does not collapse into a simple binary between organic/environmentally positive and non-organic/ environmentally negative categories, however. Rather, organic growers value particular components of their farm environment quite highly, especially the biological aspects of soil fertility and general farm/orchard 'environmental health'. Non-organic growers also value specific environmental aspects of their farm system very highly, and many non-organic sheep and beef farmers draw a particularly strong link between farm environmental health and the health and welfare of their animals.

Elaborating on this point, Fairweather et al (2009) demonstrate that behind the social categorization of particular growers as 'conventional' or otherwise lies a heterogeneous array of orientations towards the environment. Here, the variation within the panels is highly instructive. While the organic panel generally does align with strongly positive orientations towards the environment, the other panels also contain growers who are environmentally positive (though these panels also exhibit a variety of other positions). Two conclusions are immediately obvious. First, the strong critique of commercial organic agriculture as representing a token attempt to use environmental criteria for commercial gain is not borne out by the ARGOS data on organic growers. Rather, the organic certification system does provide a form of demarcation that signifies a group of commercial growers with strongly environmentally oriented ideas and values. Equally relevant is that the opposite does not apply: conventional growers are not universally without any positive environmental orientation. The non-organic panels also contain, to varying degrees, environmentally positive and proactive practitioners – although a greater number of non-organic producers are strongly production-oriented rather than environmentally oriented. Put simply, organic certification does demarcate a socially desirable set of characteristics by organic growers – but this group is not exclusive.

Discussion and conclusions: Beyond the organic/conventional debate

In aggregate, these results begin to suggest that emerging market certification systems do, in fact, demarcate a style of orchard and farm management that is measurably different in its effects and impacts relative to its rival categories. These differences can be attributed to two possible processes: a) commercial certified organic (and certified integrated) management shifts farm practice – and a key set of environmental outcomes – modestly along the continuum away from some of the negative environmental outcomes of mainstream agriculture; or b) these alternative certification systems act as a mechanism to categorize producers who were already attempting some of these more progressive activities prior to entering a certification scheme.[7] In either case, sceptical claims regarding the fraudulent nature of organic management, along with the associated claims of public deception, are not justified. In the New Zealand context, a well-structured and interdisciplinary science programme did not replicate the worst-case effects previously found in studies of isolated aspects of organic farming and repeated by the likes of Trewavas in the public organics debate. Similarly, the arguments made by the likes of Pollan are overstated. Commercial organic agriculture is not on a course to becoming 'conventionalized' or indistinguishable from mainstream practices. Rather, early analysis of ARGOS data indicates that key areas of farming activity are slightly better, or at least no worse, on organic farms in comparison to their counterparts. Commercial organic production in New Zealand does make a positive difference in some of the key areas that challenge the future sustainability of global agriculture.

Beyond making the point that certified commercial organic systems do exhibit a number of differences with regard to the social and ecological dynamics of farms, the ARGOS data raise a whole set of related questions and challenges about sustainable agriculture:

- There is an urgent need to move beyond simple binaries between organic and conventional management. At best, 'organic' now represents only one rather broad-brush category – one created by a comprehensive market audit system – among a myriad of possible approaches to good environmental practice. In contrast, 'conventional' is so heterogeneous as to make the category meaningless in anything other than a pejorative sense.
- There is also a need to unravel a diverse range of integrated management practices from those of conventional farming in popular discourse, and to follow closely the degree to which integrated management secures a

particular pathway to market – with associated social and environmental impacts – through new institutional retailing practices.

- While ARGOS data show that organic and integrated management systems (as current commercially derived, audit-based pathways to market) do affect outcomes at the farm level, other ways of explaining farm outcomes also need to be examined. Alongside market-audit pathways exist other ways of organizing and recognizing farm practice that may have an equally significant impact on outcomes. Such approaches include: a) regional dynamics (as implied by geographical indicators for food); b) farm sub-cultures with desirable qualities (which are being targeted for special labelling status by the Slow Food movement); c) community-networks of action (such as the Landcare movement in Australia); and, d) new regulatory devices like integrated catchment management. The attention to farming categories must nonetheless continue to acknowledge that much of the activity on farms is due to the voluntary actions of individual farmers and their families.

- Conventional farm management seems to comprise a range of approaches – from what some call 'conservative conventional' (farming that is well within the capacity of systems) through to highly 'productivist conventional' (that is, maximum output from maximum input strategies). We need to recognize that there is an important group of conventional farmers who are already strongly committed to a range of environmental goals on their farms. Due to the predominance of 'conventional' producers in many farm sectors (for example, the New Zealand sheep/beef industry), this latter group might actually be responsible for the greatest positive impact on overall landscape management. Put simply, moderate change by the majority in the industry has the potential to exceed the impact of major change by a small minority.

Ultimately, the organic mythologies debate deserves credit for creating the context in which these subsequent and more nuanced questions about the sustainability of commercial agriculture systems have been recognized. This was achieved by the organics movement, in part, through the introduction of a serious 'alternative' to mainstream agriculture and by establishing a precedent that eroded many of the taken-for-granted certainties and categories on which traditional agricultural science was founded. In creating the possibility of alternative ways of both producing and retailing food, organics opened up a window not only for its own particular variant on agricultural production, but also for a proliferating range of alternative understandings and insights into how we organize and value agricultural systems. The result is that the world of sustainable agriculture is undergoing a period of creative elaboration across institutional, consumer, political and methodological levels. The ARGOS project is one participant in a new wave of 'sustainability science' methodologies in agriculture that now seeks to move well beyond the old debates around the fraudulence and validity of organics to understand how organics fits into wider patterns, dynamics and potentials across all agricultural systems.

Notes

1   The authors are all members of the Agriculture Research Group on Sustainability (ARGOS). We would like to thank other members of ARGOS for their contribution to the ideas behind this chapter – particularly Jon Manhire, John Fairweather, Lesley Hunt, Glen Greer, Caroline Saunders, Dave Lucock and Komathi Kolandai.
2   An added complexity in the use of Trewavas's work is that even though it has been widely cited to support mainstream agriculture, much of his critique is actually based on comparing organics with integrated management systems rather than 'conventional' systems – a distinction that is consistently missed in media discussion of his work.
3   While agricultural scientists like Trewavas made an early appearance in this public debate, the longer-term scientific discussion of key claims and processes around organics seemed to quite quickly disconnect from this media activity and continued along its own academic lines (much more out of the public view) with positive and negative attributes of organics being discussed as part of wider discussions of biological and ecological processes on farms.
4   Identifying these three political positions in the organics debates of the early 2000s provides ample context to understand the problems being faced by the ARGOS Project. Suffice to say that reality was even more complex, with significant internal debates about organics standards taking place within the organic social movement itself, as well as subsequent retailer-level discussion of new standards and requirements for organics like animal welfare and energy auditing.
5   The way that ARGOS constructed panels of non-organic management systems was important, as the ensuing argument in this chapter will demonstrate. The investigation of these systems revealed multiple styles, including experiments with more environmentally oriented production, in different industry sectors. For example, the New Zealand kiwifruit industry has not used conventional production methods since 1998, so panels of integrated management systems were constructed to compare with the organic panels. In the sheep/beef industry, integrated management and conventional panels were constructed.
6   For a review of this kind of methodological approach see the journal *Sustainability Science*.
7   The distinction between these two dynamics is sociologically fascinating. Are producers that are demarcated by audit schemes simply creating a consumer package and brand for activities they were already doing, or does entry into the scheme also change management practice in good ways? Only over much more time will the ARGOS data – particularly in the dairy sector – be able to address this distinction.

References

Avery, D. (1995) *Saving the Planet with Pesticides and Plastic: The Environmental Triumph of High-Yield Farming*, Hudson Institute, Washington, DC

Benge, J., Emanuelsson, M., Lucock, D. and Manhire, J. (2009) *Management and Production Features of ARGOS Farms and Differences between Production Systems*, ARGOS Research Report, www.argos.org.nz/research_results.shtml, accessed 5 March 2009

Blackwell, G., Lucock, D., Moller, H., Hill, R., Manhire, J. and Emanuelsson, M. (forthcoming) 'Prevalence and diversity of broad-leaved herbaceous plants on sheep/beef pastures in the South Island', *NZ Journal of Agricultural Research*

Campbell, H., Fairweather, J. and Steven, D. (1997) *Recent developments in Organic Food Production in New Zealand: Part 2, Kiwifruit in the Bay of Plenty*, Studies in Rural Sustainability no 2, Department of Anthropology, Otago University, New Zealand

Carey, P., Benge, J. and Haynes, R. (2009) 'Comparison of soil quality and nutrient budgets between organic and conventional kiwifruit orchards,' *Agriculture, Ecosystems and Environment*, vol 132, pp7–15

Fairweather J. R., Rosin, C., Hunt, L. and Campbell, H. (2009) 'Are conventional farmers conventional? Analysis of the environmental orientations of New Zealand farmers,' *Rural Sociology*, vol 74, no 2, pp430–454

Guardian (2004) 'The costly fraud that is organic food', 6 May

LaSalle, T., Hepperley, P. and Diop, A. (2008) *The Organic Green Revolution*, Rodale Institute, Kutztown, Pennsylvania

Maegli, T., Richards, S., Meadows, S., Carey, P., Johnson, M., Peters, M., Dixon, K., Benge, J., Moller, H., Blackwell, G., Weller, F., Lucock, D., Norton, D., Perley, C. and MacLeod, C. (2007) *Environmental Indicators from Alternative Farm Management Systems: Signposts for Different Pathways to Sustainable Primary Production in New Zealand?* ARGOS Research Report 07/12, www.argos.org.nz/research_results.shtml, accessed 5 March 2009

Manhire, J., Campbell, H. and Fairweather, J. (2003) *Pathways to Sustainability: Comparing Production Systems across Four Sectors of New Zealand Agriculture*, CSAFE Discussion Paper no 2, Centre for the Study of Agriculture, Food and Environment, University of Otago, New Zealand

Pollan, M. (2001) 'Behind the organic–industrial complex', *New York Times Magazine*, www.nytimes.com/2001/05/13/magazine/13ORGANIC.html

Rosin, C., Hunt, L., Fairweather, J. and Campbell, H. (2007) *Social Objective Synthesis Report: Differentiation among Participant Farmers/Orchardists in the ARGOS Research Programme*, ARGOS Research Report 07/13, www.argos.org.nz/research_results.shtml, accessed 1 March 2009

Saunders, C., Greer, G. and Zellman, E. (2007) *Economics Objective Synthesis Report*, ARGOS Research Report 07/11, www.argos.org.nz/research_results.shtml, accessed 1 March 2009

Trewavas, A. (2001) 'Urban myths of organic farming', *Nature*, 410, pp409–410

16
Nanotechnology and the Techno-Corporate Agri-food Paradigm

Gyorgy Scrinis and Kristen Lyons

Introduction

Technological innovations have played a significant role in shaping and transforming the products, production practices and socio-economic structures of agri-food systems over the past century. From the adoption of mechanical harvesters to new hybrid seed varieties, technological innovations have been associated with profound social, economic and environmental change. Over the past two decades, technoscientific innovations have also been at the heart of many controversies, crises and political struggles across the food system – including struggles over genetically modified (GM) foods, genetic erosion and contamination, the factory farming and cloning of animals, chemical pollution, the public health impacts of processed foods, the 'food miles' associated with the long-distance transportation of fresh and packaged foods, the corporate control of farmers and markets, and food scares such as 'mad cow' disease.

Nanotechnology represents the most recent and most powerful set of technologies being applied across the food system. A new range of nano-scale techniques, materials and products are currently being developed and are at the early stages of research and commercialization across all agri-food sectors, including agricultural production, food manufacturing, food packaging and retailing.

Nanotechnology generally refers to a range of techniques for directly manipulating materials, organisms and systems at a scale of 100 nanometres or less – one nanometre being a billionth of a metre. Nanotechnologies provide new and more powerful means to engage with, manipulate, and control nature and materials at the level of atoms, molecules, genes, cells and bits of information

– what we refer to as the 'nano-atomic level of engagement with nature'. Nanotechnology can be understood not so much as a separate and distinct techno-scientific field, but rather as a new techno-scientific platform, whereby a range of existing disciplines – such as molecular biotechnology, chemistry, materials science and information technologies – are able to shift their focus down to the molecular level (ETC Group, 2003). Within the food system, this is achieved via the development of nano-chemical technologies, nano-biotechnologies and nano-information technologies.

These technologies are promoted as offering a range of benefits across the agri-food system, including productivity and efficiency gains, environmental benefits such as reduced chemical usage and adaptation to changing ecological conditions, and more nutritious and safe foods. In so doing, nanotechnologies – like other recent technological revolutions and innovations, such as genetic engineering – are being positioned as a necessary 'techno-fix' to the crises facing global food production (such as the need to feed a growing population) while also meeting the challenges of climate change and other forms of ecological degradation (Hinsliff, 2009). Yet, presenting nanotechnologies as offering narrowly framed technical advances and benefits ignores the substantive role that technologies also play in shaping, maintaining, and transforming the existing structures, cultures and ecologies of food production and consumption.

Nano-scale technologies are currently being developed within — and are primarily being used to entrench and extend – the dominant paradigms of agri-food production, distribution and consumption, and their associated technological and economic structures. In the agricultural sector, nano-industrial forms of production will extend and deepen the chemical-industrial and genetic-industrial agricultural paradigms. In food manufacturing, nano-processing techniques will facilitate the further development of processed-reconstituted foods, as well as of a new range of nutritionally engineered or 'functional foods'. In doing so, they will expand the nutritionally reductive paradigm of 'nutritionism' upon which the scientific legitimacy and marketing claims of these food products are based (Scrinis, 2008a). Nano-packaging and identification innovations will also be used to facilitate the long-distance transportation, long shelf-life, supply-chain tracking and monitoring of the food supply – all of which could support an increasingly globalized, export-oriented and supermarket-dominated food system.

While these technologies are being developed and applied within particular agri-food paradigms, they may also directly change the form of the structural, cultural and ecological relations they mediate by such means as transforming production practices; changing our understanding of food and nutrition; transforming our relationship to nature; and extending the reach of commodification practices, intellectual property rights and corporate power.

This chapter outlines a range of nanotechnological applications across the agri-food sector and examines the ways these might extend or transform the existing practices, relations and structures of the food system. We also consider how the emerging regulatory regime – together with emerging civil society and consumer opposition, and competing corporate and sectoral interests –

might shape or impede the development and trajectory of nanotechnological innovations.

Nano-industrial agriculture

In the agricultural sector, nanotechnological innovations are being researched and applied in the areas of plant and animal breeding, chemical pesticides, veterinary medicines and satellite-mediated 'precision farming' systems. These nano-industrial applications will largely be geared towards both the fine-tuning, and creation, of new efficiencies and capabilities within large-scale, monocultural, chemical and capital-intensive styles of farming – as well as offering short-term sticking plaster solutions to emerging agro-ecological problems. At the same time, they may facilitate further corporate concentration of, and control over, agricultural inputs and producers. This emerging *nano-industrial* or *nano-corporate* paradigm of agricultural production has strong continuities with – and indeed is likely to frame and encapsulate – the genetic-industrial paradigm associated with the introduction of GM crops since the 1990s (Scrinis, 2007).

One of the first nano-industrial applications is the development of nano-chemical pesticides – or nano-pesticides – which are pesticides that contain nano-scale chemical toxins. Nano-scale formulations of new and existing pesticidal toxins offer a range of novel properties, such as increased toxicity, stability or dissolvability in water as compared to larger-scale molecules of the same chemical toxins. At the same time, the nano-encapsulation of pesticidal toxins offers new possibilities for the controlled or targeted release of pesticides, such as in the alkaline environment of certain insects' digestive systems, or under specific moisture and heat levels (ETC Group, 2004; Kuzma and VerHage, 2006; FoE, 2008). The increased toxicity of nano-pesticides and the ability to more precisely control the quantities and conditions under which pesticides are released could result in a reduction in the volume of chemical pesticides being applied in specific situations, thereby reducing input costs and environmental pollution (Kuzma and VerHage, 2006). However, nano-pesticides – like GM herbicide-tolerant and *Bt*-insecticidal crops – could also further entrench and extend the chemical approach to pest control by exploiting these new efficiencies and the expanded range of options for pesticidal delivery they offer. Nano-scale pesticides also introduce a new range of possible health and environmental hazards due to their increased toxicity and their ability to penetrate the surface of food crops. Their enhanced dissolvability may lead to the contamination of wider geographical areas. Encapsulated toxins may also be released in the gut of non-target living organisms. While such nano-pesticides may already be commercially available, there is presently an absence of labeling or public disclosure requirements for nano-scale chemicals (Bowman and Hodge, 2007).

Nano-scale wireless sensors are another industrial innovation, being developed to assist in the real-time monitoring of crops, animals and soils. Nano-sensors could detect the presence of plant pathogens and may be used to trigger the release of pesticides. These nano-sensors would form a part of so-called 'precision farming' systems, involving the use of information technologies and geographical positioning systems to more precisely micro-manage the application of pesticides, fertilizers and irrigation systems. It is large-scale, capital-intensive farms that are likely be able to adopt and benefit from the potential cost-savings, efficiencies and productivity gains of these integrated technological packages.

There is also a range of nanotechnological innovations being developed specifically for animal production systems. They include the use of micro- and nano-fluidic systems for the mass production of embryos for breeding; drug delivery systems able to penetrate inaccessible parts of an animal's body; more biologically active drug compounds; and sensors for monitoring livestock health and locations (ETC Group, 2004; Ajmone Marsan et al, 2007; Scott, 2007). Australian researchers are developing needle-free nanoparticle vaccine delivery systems enabling the more targeted and effective vaccination of cattle, the magnetic properties of which would simultaneously enable the surveillance of treated animals (Mittar, 2008). In fish-farming operations, developments include nano-scale water cleaning products, along with nanocapsulated vaccines that would be released into the water, absorbed into the cells of the fish and activated using ultrasound (ETC Group, 2004). In the context of large-scale, intensive, factory-farming or close-confinement livestock operations, such innovations offer efficiency and productivity gains, together with the further adaptation or re-engineering of animals to the requirements of this mode of animal production.

The convergence and integration of nanotechnologies and biotechnologies offer new avenues for plant and animal breeding, including new techniques for facilitating the development of genetically engineered crops. For example, researchers are attempting to use nanoparticles, nanofibres and nanocapsules to introduce foreign DNA and chemicals into cells (FoE, 2008). The emerging field of synthetic biology promises a more radical approach to genetic engineering and plant breeding (ETC Group, 2007; Ribeiro and Shand, 2008). Rather than just cutting and pasting genes from one existing genome into another, bioscientists are developing a number of strategies for synthesizing novel living organisms, including the engineering of synthetic DNA. These advances in plant breeding techniques could enable the introduction and control of a wider range of genes and character traits into crops – including drought-tolerant and 'climate-ready' genes (ETC Group, 2008). The seed-chemical corporations that currently control the global market for genetically modified crops have also shown great interest in developing traits such as the ability to control the reproductive capabilities of seeds and to link the expression of crop traits to external chemical triggers. Nano-genetically engineered seeds could, thereby, facilitate the further technological and corporate integration of seed, chemical and other agricultural inputs.

Nano-industrial food processing and nano-engineered functional foods

In the food manufacturing sector, the development of a new range of processing techniques and additives is under way which variously aim to modify food flavour and texture, speed of processing, heat tolerance, shelf-life, nutritional profile and nutrient bioavailability. These 'nano-engineering' applications are likely to support the continued development of a growing range of cheap, processed and convenience foods. But it is the engineering of supposedly healthier 'functional foods' that are the most common examples given to illustrate the benefits of nano-food innovation (Moraru et al, 2007). The development and marketing of these nano-functional food products are framed within – and are likely to extend and transform – the nutritionally reductive paradigm of 'nutritionism' that currently dominates scientific and popular understandings of the relationship between food and bodily health (Scrinis, 2008a).

As Sanguansri and Augustin (2006, p547) note:

> *The next wave of food innovation will ... require a shift from macroscopic properties to those on the meso- and nano-scales, as these subsequently control the hierarchical structures in food and food functionality.*

Nanotechnology will not only extend the ability of food technologists to fractionate foods down to their nano-scale component parts, but will also provide new techniques for the reconstitution and transformation of these individual food components, before being reassembled to form 'processed-reconstituted' foods.

One of the broad aims of these innovations will be to achieve productivity gains and cost savings in the production of relatively cheap, processed and convenience foods. For example, a German company, Aquanova, has developed nano-sized food additives that accelerate the processing of industrial sausage and cured meats (FoE, 2008). The development of nano-scale formulations of existing flavour or nutrient additives may also enable a reduction in the quantities – and therefore the costs – of these additives, while achieving the same processing functionalities.

Nanotechnology also enables the introduction of new qualities and character traits into foods and food ingredients. Nano-structured food ingredients and nanoparticles in emulsions, for example, are being developed in an attempt to control the material properties of foodstuffs. Their application such as in the manufacture of ice cream to increase texture uniformity is a case in point (Rowan, 2004). The development of food ingredients able to reproduce the creamy taste and texture of full-fat dairy products would enable the production of very low-fat ice cream, mayonnaise and spreads (see Chaudhry et al, 2008). In addition, Unilever has reported breakthroughs in the development of stable liquid foams that may improve the physical and sensory properties of food products, as well as the ability to aerate products that currently do not contain air (Daniells, 2008). This aeration is also seen as a means of reducing the caloric density of foods. The food company Blue Pacific Flavors has developed its Taste Nanology process for engineering ingredients with more concentrated flavours by targeting specific taste receptors, making it possible to remove the bitter taste of some additives and to reduce the quantities of additives required (Anon., 2006).

In another set of applications, nano-encapsulation techniques are being developed as part of a strategy to harness the controlled delivery of nutrients and other components in processed foods. The aim is to enhance a number of functionalities, such as to 'provide protective barriers, flavour and taste masking, controlled release and better dispersability for water-insoluble food ingredients and additives' (Chaudhry et al, 2008, p244). Nanocapsules have been produced through the development of self-assembled nanotubes using hydrolyzed milk proteins (Chaudhry et al, 2008). Food companies are already utilizing micro-capsules for delivering food components such as omega 3-rich fish oil, while masking the taste and odour of the fish oil. These nano-encapsulated fish oils are being developed as a means of enhancing the bioavailablity, stability and transparency of food components (Zimet and Livney, 2009). A recent study claimed that the encapsulation of curcumin – the phytochemical found in turmeric and claimed to have antitumour and anticarcinogenic properties – in nanoemulsions increased the bioavailability of this compound (Wang et al, 2007). A nanocochleate nutrient delivery system has also been developed and is claimed to 'protect micronutrients and antioxidants from degradation during manufacturing and storage' (Chaudhry et al, 2008, p244).

Nanotechnology also holds out the more distant promise of nutritionally interactive foods able to change their nutritional profile in response to an individual's allergies, dietary needs or food preferences (FoE, 2008). Chen and Shahidi (2006, p36) describe this promise of personalized nutrition, which is based on the development of targeted delivery systems:

> ... advances in nanotechnology may lead to multifunctional nanoscale nutraceutical delivery systems that can simultaneously detect and recognize the appropriate location, analyze the local and global needs, decide whether or how much of the payload should be released and monitor the response for feedback.

Such futuristic applications not only assume the ability to precisely understand and manipulate the nutrient properties of foods and their effects on particular bodily functions, but also to target and address the precise nutrient needs of individuals.

Nanotechnology, thereby, provides a range of approaches to the cost effective production of so-called 'functional foods', or foods with modified nutrient profiles and novel traits – foods that might be more accurately termed 'nutritionally engineered foods' or 'functionally marketed foods' (Scrinis, 2008b). Yet, there is reason to question the individual and public health benefits of these nutritional modifications. Like all 'functional foods', the claimed health benefits of nutritionally engineered nano-foods are based on a nutritionally reductive and decontextualized understanding of food and nutrients, and their relationship to bodily health. This dominant ideology or paradigm of 'nutritionism' typically involves the reduction of our understanding of food to its nutrient composition, such that it tends to replace and undermine other ways of understanding food and the body (Scrinis, 2008a). This often takes the form of a more simplified focus on single nutrients. Nutritionally reductive scientific knowledge has been translated into reductive dietary advice, as well as being translated directly into *nutritionally reductive technological practices*, whereby the nutrient profiles of foods are engineered to reflect the nutritional trends and fetishes of the day. The efficacy of these nutritional modifications assumes not only that these single nutrients can be manipulated individually, but also that they can deliver health benefits in isolation from the foods themselves and the nutrient matrix in which they are contained (Jacobs and Tapsell, 2007).

The marketing of these nutrient content and health benefit claims is also typically focused on the single nutrients added or subtracted, thereby distracting attention from the overall nutrient profile and quality of the foods. A focus on the link between nutrients, foods and internal bodily functions, such as cholesterol absorption or blood sugar levels, is now increasingly common in popular dietary advice and food marketing campaigns. Nano-functional food innovations will provide new avenues for the production of these 'functional' foods intended to target particular bodily functions. These nano-engineered foods will thereby reinforce the shift to this latest 'functional' stage or era of nutritionism, opening up new possibilities for the commodification of nutrients, nutritional knowledge and food products.

The introduction of nano-scale components in foods also raises novel health concerns, particularly in terms of their toxicity. For example, as Pustzai and Bardocz (2006) note in their review of the health risks of nano-scale food components, nanoparticle versions of the food additives titanium oxide and silicon dioxide are already being used in foods and have been approved as GRAS (generally recognized as safe) by the US Food and Drug Administration. Yet, they argue that there is already sufficient scientific evidence to indicate that these nanoparticles are cytotoxic (that is, toxic to cells), and that their incorporation into foods has occurred without appropriate safety testing.

Nano-food packaging and supply chain monitoring

The most advanced sector of nano-food innovations has been in the development and commercialization of food packaging applications, with up to five hundred nano-packaging products already on the market (FoE, 2008) Nano-engineered food packaging materials aim to better control the conditions in which fresh and prepared foods are contained so as to reduce the rate of food spoilage and to enhance its durability, transportability, shelf-life and 'freshness'. In these ways, nano-packaging innovations could facilitate an increase in the use of food packaging, enabling an expansion of the range of packaged foods, the distances these foods are transported, and the time and range of conditions under which they are able to be both transported and preserved (FoE, 2008).

Some nano-packaging materials are designed to reduce gas and moisture exchange, and UV light exposure, or to emit antimicrobials and antioxidants, with the goal of keeping food 'fresher' for longer – or at least slowing deterioration. Commercial examples include the use of nanocomposite barrier technology by Miller Brewing to create plastic beer bottles. The plastic contains nanoparticles that provide a strong barrier between carbon dioxide and oxygen, which enables beer to retain its effervescence (and shelf-life) for longer (ETC Group, 2004). DuPont has also produced a nano titanium dioxide plastic additive – DuPont Light Stabilizer 210. By reducing UV exposure, DuPont claims its barrier technology will minimize the damage to food contained in transparent packaging (El Amin, 2007). Nano-packaging materials are also being developed to interact with the foods they contain, such as the ability to 'release nanoscale antimicrobials, antioxidants, flavours, fragrances or nutraceuticals into the food or beverage to extend its shelf-life or to improve its taste or smell' (FoE, 2008, p16).

This interactive, chemical-release packaging is being developed to respond to specific trigger events. For example, packaging may contain nanosensors that are engineered to change colour if a food is beginning to spoil, or if it has been contaminated by pathogens. To do this, electronic 'noses' and 'tongues' will be designed to mimic human sensory capacities, enabling them to 'taste' or 'smell' scents and flavours (ETC, 2004). In Scotland, UV activated nano titanium dioxide is being utilized to develop tamper-proof packaging materials, while in the US carbon nanotubes are being incorporated into packaging materials to detect micro-organisms, toxic proteins and food spoilage (El Amin, 2007).

Nano-scale barcodes and monitoring devices are also being developed and commercialized. This includes nano-scale radio frequency identification tags (RFid) able to track containers or individual food items. These RFid tags could also transmit information after a product leaves the supermarket, unless the tags are disabled at the checkout register (ETC Group, 2004). The nanotech company pSiNutria is also developing nano-based tracking technologies, including an ingestible BioSilicon which could be placed in foods for monitoring purposes, but could also be eaten by consumers (FoE, 2008). Supermarkets would use nanosensors to monitor product sales and expiry dates, thus reducing the lead time for product re-ordering (Kuzma and VerHage, 2006). Nanosensors may thereby improve management efficiency for those large-scale retailers able to absorb the costs of nano-monitoring and identification techniques.

The use of nanomaterials in food packaging poses a number of potential new health and environmental hazards. Nanomaterials in food packaging and food contact materials may unintentionally migrate from the packaging and into foods, and thereby increase the likelihood of nanomaterial ingestion (Chaudhry et al, 2008; FoE, 2008). Active and chemical-release packaging, and food contact materials designed to deliberately release substances such as flavours, odours or nutritional additives raise similar concerns. Nanomaterials in food packaging may also be released into the environment, posing a range of ecological hazards (FoE, 2008).

Techno-ecological transformations: From an instrumental to a reconstitutive logic of control

While there is a diverse range of applications of nanotechnological applications within and across all sectors of the agri-food system, a number of common characteristics or rationalities can be identified. These technological characteristics may directly or indirectly shape, extend and transform the ecological and socio-economic relations, practices and structures that they mediate.

Nanotechnologies introduce a greatly enhanced ability to manipulate and reconstitute nature at the nano-atomic level. Nanotechnology enables the deconstitution of nature and systems down to their component atoms, molecules, genes, bits, cells and other parts; the transformation or rearrangement of these component parts; and the reconstruction or reconstitution of organisms, materials and devices from the ground up. These reconstitutive practices go beyond the instrumental control, use and exploitation of whole objects of nature, and also beyond the fragmentation of nature and food into their component parts, for they also enable the further transformation and re-engineering of these parts in order to achieve specific ends.

In being reconstituted in these ways, nature is not simply encountered as raw material to be used as an input to the production process, nor encountered as a constraint to be overcome, but can instead be more directly harnessed as a productive force in the quest for capital accumulation and corporate control (Goodman et al, 1987; Kloppenburg, 1988; Boyd et al, 2001). Just as the new biotechnologies have been used to harness the reproductive qualities of DNA, nanotechnologies are being used to harness the self-assembling properties and other novel features of materials at the nano-scale (Dupuy, 2007).

One of the primary aims of nanotechnological innovation is likely to be the fine-tuning of large-scale, standardized, mechanized and resource-intensive systems of production, with the aim of increasing productive output or achieving new efficiencies. Examples include the potential for nano-chemical pesticides to be used more sparingly and precisely; the use of nanosensors to enable the more precise management of inputs within large-scale farming operations; and new food processing techniques and additives for reducing costs and wastage. At the same time, these large-scale standardized systems can also be rendered increasingly *flexible* by adapting agricultural systems to the ecological challenges of climate change and reduced water availability, or by enabling food manufacturers and retailers to more quickly adapt to changing consumer demands for convenience and nutritionally enhanced foods.

Nanotechnology may facilitate a higher degree of *uniformity* across the agri-food system, while enabling a new level of product and system *differentiation*. Nature and materials are increasingly encountered as being constructed from a set of uniform, standardized and interchangeable nano-scale building blocks, as foods, seeds and other inputs are able to be broken down into their constituent parts. Uniformity is in a sense being extended to the nano-atomic level. This nano-atomic uniformity would overlay and potentially extend the genetic, cellular, chemical and organic levels of uniformity that already characterize food production systems. At the same time, nanotechnology can also be used to re-differentiate these highly uniform and standardized inputs, products and systems, such as through the selective introduction of novel traits into crops or processed foods, or the micro-management of small areas within large-scale farms.

These technical capabilities enable both the inputs and outputs of agricultural and food manufacturing systems to be rendered increasingly interchangeable. For example, a range of crops could be used as biomass inputs to be transformed into a range of food or fuel products, and food ingredients can be reconstituted to mimic the properties of fats. This logic of interchangeability and 'substitutionism' further intensifies competition between the suppliers of these inputs and products (Goodman et al, 1987; Lawrence and Grice, 2008). But it also tends to increase competition between the purchasers of food products, as in the use of crops for food versus biofuel – a situation that may have contributed to recent global food price increases (Gordon, 2008; Piesse and Thirtle, 2009).

While new agri-food technologies have facilitated the production of highly standardized and processed food products, alternative agri-food trajectories based on principles of quality and diversity have also emerged, such as the rise and expansion of organic produce, and the renewed demand for fresh and wholefood products. Many of these alternative trajectories have not involved technologies such as genetic engineering, and have in some cases been positioned in direct opposition to GM crops (Wilkinson, 2002). Due in part to their broader range of applications across the food system, nanotechnological innovations appear to have greater potential to support certain aspects of 'quality' food production and distribution, such as through the use of nano-packaging for transportation of high-value foods, reduced application of chemical inputs, the nutritional engineering and 'enhancement' of foods, the facilitation of more comprehensive supply chain monitoring, and so on. The organic industry has nonetheless resisted the introduction of nanotechnological inputs to date (Lyons, 2008).

In terms of environmental impacts, nanotechnological innovations may, in specific circumstances, either ameliorate or intensify existing levels of resource use, pollution emissions, soil and water degradation, and loss of biodiversity in particular instances. For example, nano-pesticides and precision farming may in some cases allow the more targeted and reduced use of chemical inputs on the farm. At the same time, nanotechnological innovations may facilitate the overall expansion of large-scale and resource-intensive systems of farming, food manufacturing and distribution, and the ecological problems associated with them.

Nano-scale technologies also introduce novel forms of ecological and health hazards, such as the potential toxicity of nanoparticles used on the farm or added to processed foods and food packaging. Despite the enhanced level of precision associated with the nanotechnological manipulation of nature at the atomic and molecular level, there is nevertheless still a considerable lack of precision in understanding and being able to control the consequences of these nano-atomic level manipulations (Dupuy and Grinbaum, 2006; RCEP, 2008).

Techno-corporate appropriation and integration

In *From Farming to Biotechnology*, Goodman and colleagues (1987) identified the appropriation by capitalist industries of traditional agricultural inputs and farming practices, as well as food processing and food preparation practices, as a central dynamic of the modern industrial food system. The concept of industrial appropriation conflates the two otherwise distinct processes of technological and economic appropriation. First, there is the initial technological appropriation of the discrete practices of food production and preparation via the development of technological instruments, inputs and food products, with the aim of extending control over nature and the technical process. Second, there is the subsequent economic appropriation of these discrete inputs and products through the processes of commodification, patenting, and corporate appropriation and control.

The nanotechnological platform provides new avenues for such technological and economic appropriation. New possibilities for the technological embodiment of farmers' pest management within controlled-release nano-pesticides, and for the appropriation of consumers' knowledge of health and safety through nutritionally engineered foods and 'smart' food packaging, illustrates this potential. The patenting of nano-scale materials, organisms and products itself entails an extension of techno-commodification practices to the nano-atomic level, new possibilities for the control of products, markets and producers and, therefore, new avenues for capital accumulation. Nanotechnology extends and shifts the logic of technological and economic appropriation to the nano-atomic level of nature, in contrast to earlier forms of control and commodification that operate via the genetic and (micro) chemical levels.

A further distinction can be drawn between the initial appropriation of distinct practices, on the one hand, and the subsequent integration of these appropriated practices, on the other. The initially discrete technological and economic appropriations of food production and preparation practices have increasingly been integrated by means of further technological innovation in the form of technological packages – such as integrated seed-chemical packages – that have in turn facilitated the corporate integration and concentration of ownership and control of the food system. The integration and alignment of GM crops and particular herbicides in the form of herbicide-tolerant crops is a notable example.

Nano-scale technologies will facilitate the further re-integration and convergence of technologies, inputs and products across the food system, whether in the form of technology packages sold to farmers, or health-convenience packages sold to consumers (Dixon et al, 2006). The development of smart, interactive, environment-sensitive or cybernetic materials and products is important in this respect. For example, nano-sensors would form a part of the precision-farming packages aimed at integrating and coordinating various mechanical, chemical and irrigation technologies, while food processing techniques may combine and integrate the nutritional and convenience traits of food products. Some nanotechnological innovations may have cross-sector applications – such as the potential for using nano-encapsulation techniques to encapsulate both pesticides and nutrients. The development of food monitoring and surveillance applications also facilitates the vertical integration and coordination of agri-food supply chains, from farm inputs to supermarket checkouts and beyond.

To the extent that it is primarily the larger agri-food corporations that are able to develop, patent and market the new techniques and products of nanotechnology, these innovations will enable corporations to extend their market dominance within particular agri-food sectors, and will facilitate the corporate concentration of ownership and control across the food and non-food industries. The ETC Group draws a direct connection between technological convergence and corporate convergence, arguing that technological convergence is 'driving new and unprecedented corporate alliances across all industry sectors', such as the convergence of the food and pharmaceutical industries facilitated by the new biotechnologies (ETC Group, 2008, p5).

Global agri-food corporations have extended and consolidated their ownership and control of the global food system enormously over the past few decades (Weis, 2007; Hendrickson et al, 2008). McMichael (2005) and Friedmann (2005) have described this shift as one from the earlier 'mercantile-industrial' food regime to a 'corporate' or 'corporate-environmental' global food regime. At the same time, technologies of production, distribution and coordination have become increasingly central to the restructuring, integration and corporate concentration of food systems over this period. We therefore refer to the 'techno-corporate' character of the contemporary food regime – or the techno-corporate food paradigm – in order to highlight the dominance and centrality of both corporate and technological structures across the global food system, as well as the close interconnection between technological and corporate relations and forms of control (Scrinis, 2007; Scrinis and Lyons, 2007). Nanotechnology and other recent techno-scientific forms, such as genetic engineering, can to a significant extent be characterized as *corporate technologies*, in the sense that corporations not only predominantly own and control the technologies and their associated patents and products, but are also using these technologies as one of their primary strategies for integrating and extending their control over suppliers, for reducing or eliminating competitive markets, and for meeting shifting consumer demands (Heffernan, 1999; Boyd, 2003; Scrinis and Lyons, 2007; Otero, 2008).

Friedmann (2005) argues that the contemporary 'corporate-environmental' food regime is, in part, being maintained through the ability of corporations to selectively address a range of civil society consumer demands for higher standards in terms of quality, health and environmental standards, but that they do so by creating two distinct global markets targeted at wealthy and poor consumers:

> *The corporate-environmental food regime encapsulates two distinct corporate strategies for privileged and cash-poor customers across the globe... [T]he distinction between fresh, relatively unprocessed and low-chemical input products on one side and highly engineered edible commodities composed of denatured and recombined ingredients on the other, describes two complementary systems within a single emerging food regime* (Friedmann, 2005, p258).

Just as agri-food corporations are able to span the divergent trends and markets across the global food system, nano-scale technologies may also have the potential to span and lend a degree of technological unity to these distinct corporate strategies and trajectories – such as by augmenting the mass production of cheap standardized foods and by potentially enabling the production and distribution of more environmentally benign or quality-enhanced food products and production techniques. These technologies will also enable corporations to more rapidly and flexibly respond to – and adapt their large-scale production and distribution systems to – these changing market and ecological conditions.

This new round of technological innovations has the potential to reinforce and accelerate the corporate-based technological treadmill upon which primary producers, food manufacturers and consumers have been captured. This is because the 'nanotechnological treadmill' will be added to, and will overlay, the existing chemical and genetic treadmills, as well as the contemporary 'nutrient treadmill'. Nanotechnological innovations also threaten to progress the types of agri-food system restructuring that have undermined and displaced small-scale producers, manual agricultural work and the demand for particular commodities. Agricultural applications such as nano-pesticides and nanosensor-enabled precision farming systems, for example, may expand the use of mechanical and chemical technologies, or automate other skilled tasks or decision-making practices, and thereby threaten to further reduce and displace farm labouring work.

Conclusion: Regulation of, and resistance to, nano-food innovations

While these nano-food innovations are at a relatively early stage of research and commercialization, their development is being driven by corporate agri-food interests – largely in the absence of nano-specific regulations or public scrutiny. It remains to be seen whether the emerging regulatory regime, together with resistance from a range of possible sources – civil society organizations, consumers, particular agri-food sectors such as organics and competing corporate interests – might retard or re-direct the developmental trajectories of nano-food applications.

Until recently, there have been no national or international regulations to specifically target nano-food products, nor are there internationally agreed protocols for assessing the toxicity or environmental impacts of nanoparticles (Institute for Food and Agriculture Standards, 2006; Bowman, 2008). However, by early 2009, two significant moves along these lines had been made: the Canadian government introduced the world's first nano-specific regulations, calling for mandatory reporting on the use of nano-materials (Anon., 2009); and the European Parliament proposed that food produced via nanotechnology processes undergo risk assessment prior to approval, and called for the clear labelling of nano-foods. The outcome of this proposal may set a precedent for other countries and regions (European Parliament, 2009).

As has been the case with GM crops, the dominant discourse and the emerging regulatory regime for nano-foods is so far contained within a 'benefits versus risks' framework, whereby the claimed benefits of nanotechnological innovation promoted by industry and governments are taken as given, and with only a narrow range of (primarily toxicological) health and environmental 'risks' acknowledged as requiring regulation and management. Nevertheless, these early developments in nano-food regulation can be expected to have a number of flow-on effects. The introduction of risk assessment procedures may increase understanding of the risks associated with the production and consumption of nanotechnologies which might, in turn, improve the capacity to monitor and mitigate these risks. This would be a significant achievement given growing concerns over the products of nanotechnology: for example, the UK Royal Commission on Environmental Pollution (RCEP, 2008) has acknowledged that some manufactured nanomaterials may present hazards to human health and the environment, while the British Royal Society has urged caution in developing nanotechnologies, citing the very limited eco-toxicological research related to nanomaterials (RS and RAE, 2004).

It is possible that other countries and regions may follow the lead of Canada and the European Union in developing nano-specific regulations and labelling requirements, especially those seeking to comply with international standards to maintain international market access for agriculture and food exports. At the same time, it is also possible that corporate actors will take advantage of current regulatory gaps, relocating nano-related testing and commercialization activities to unregulated countries and regions. In these circumstances, nano-foods could end up being sold in those countries unable or unwilling to regulate health, safety and other issues. This may result in a similar situation as has occurred with GM crops over the last decade where, in response to the introduction of tighter regulations and consumer resistance in the north, production and consumption of GM crops and foods shifted from Northern to Southern countries (McMichael, 2001). If the same trend occurs with nanotechnology, this may leave countries in the South as the testing ground for the new nano-foods.

In recent years, civil society groups have become increasingly active in their opposition to agri-food nanotechnologies. Friends of the Earth and the ETC Group have led international calls for moratoria on the release of any products of nanotechnology until adequate assessment, regulation, labelling requirements and public involvement in decision-making related to nanotechnologies are established (ETC Group, 2004; FoE, 2008; Lyons and Scrinis, forthcoming). These and other civil society groups have also highlighted the role of nanotechnology in the ongoing commodification and corporatization of agriculture and food systems.

Nano-food applications also raise many issues of concern to consumers, evoking responses reminiscent to those associated with GM foods (Kearnes et al, 2006). In one Swiss survey, a majority of consumers did not want to eat nano-foods, or foods wrapped in nanopackaging (Siegrist et al, 2007). Similarly, a US survey reported that only 7 per cent of survey respondents were prepared to purchase foods produced using nanotechnology, while 62 per cent wanted more information about the health risks and benefits prior to considering buying nano-foods (Peter D. Hart Research Associates, 2007).

Many questions remain regarding the extent to which the concerns raised by civil society groups and the public will shape future trajectories of the nano agri-food industries. In recent years a number of models for public engagement have been proposed in an attempt to give voice to the broad range of concerns associated with the development of nanotechnologies. Many of these models, however, have been criticized both for the limited extent to which diverse interest groups have been included in deliberative dialogue, and for the gaps between processes of deliberation and the actual formation of policy and regulations related to nanotechnologies (Lyons and Whelan, forthcoming, 2009). These limits to public participation may exacerbate mistrust in regulators, thereby fuelling opposition to nano-foods. This was certainly the outcome of deliberative governance approaches related to GM foods, whereby consumers' lack of trust in regulatory structures heightened their perceptions of the risks of eating GM foods – circumstances that have, in part, resulted in global opposition to GM crops and consumer boycotts of GM foods (Cocklin et al, 2008).

Acknowledging the growing uncertainty associated with future nano-food applications, the organic agri-food sector has taken steps to exclude nanotechnologies. In 2008, the UK Soil Association – the world's oldest organic certifier – prohibited the listing of products and processes derived from nanotechnology from its organic standard due to the unknown ecological and health risks associated with exposure to nano-particles. Organic certifiers around the world – including the Biological Farmers of Australia – are beginning to follow this lead, and it is likely other more general food standards may move to exclude nano products and processes (Lyons, 2008).

It is not yet clear how supermarkets and the retail sector will respond to nano-food applications. On the one hand, we might expect their support for nano applications, such as remote sensing and tracking devices that offer improvements in the efficiency of tracking and sales information, or nano-packaging materials that offer marketable characteristics – such as longer shelf-life – to consumers. On the other hand, due to their sensitivity to consumer opposition and the potential loss of market share, supermarkets might also exclude nano-foods and other nano-based products, as they did in the controversy over GM foods, when many retailers in the UK went GM-free in response to consumer backlash. German supermarket chain Metro has already responded to consumer opposition by recalling consumer loyalty cards that utilized nano-based identification tags (Busch, 2008).

While the corporate science sector continues to invest heavily in nano agri-food research and development, the commercial success and developmental trajectory of nano-food applications are yet to be determined. Many scientists and government agencies are joining civil society groups to call for effective risk assessment procedures related to nano-food products and processes. At the same time, on-going opposition from the organic sector, retailers and other players in the agri-food sector, as well as community acceptance or rejection of public participation processes, will play a vital role in shaping the trajectory of this agri-food technology.

References

Ajmone Marsan, P., Tramontana, S. and Mazza, R. (2007) 'Nanotechnologies applied to the analysis of the animal genome', *Veterinary Research Communications*, vol 31, no 1, pp153–159

Anon. (2006) 'Flavor firm uses nanotechnology for new ingredient solutions', *Food Navigator*, www.foodnavigator-usa.com/news/ng.asp?n-flavor-firm-uses, accessed 27 March 2009

Anon. (2009) 'World's first mandatory national nanotechnology requirement pending', media release, www.nanotechproject.org/news/archive/7061/, accessed 28 January 2009

Bowman, D. (2008) 'Governing nanotechnologies: Weaving new regulatory webs or patching up the old?' *Nanoethics*, vol 2, no 2, pp179–181

Bowman, D. and Hodge, G. (2007) 'A small matter of regulation: An international review of nanotechnology regulation', *Columbia Science and Technology Law Review*, vol 8, pp1–32

Boyd, W. (2003) 'Deep structure and the problem of monopoly in agricultural biotechnology', in R. Schurman and D. Kelso (eds) *Engineering Trouble: Biotechnology and its Discontents*, University of California Press, Berkeley

Boyd, W., Prudham, W. and Schurman, R. (2001) 'Industrial dynamics and the problem of nature', *Society and Natural Resources*, vol 14, pp555–570

Busch, L. (2008) 'Nanotechnologies, food and agriculture: Next big thing or flash in the pan?' *Agriculture and Human Values*, vol 25, pp215–218

Chaudhry, Q., Scotter, M., Blackburn, J., Ross, B., Boxall, A., Castle, L., Aitken, R. and Waekins, R. (2008) 'Applications and implications of nanotechnologies for the food sector', *Food Additives and Contaminants*, vol 25, no 3, pp241–258

Chen, H. and Shahidi, F. (2006) 'Nanotechnology in nutraceuticals and functional foods', *Food Technology*, March, pp30–36

Cocklin, C., Dibden, J. and Gibbs, D. (2008) 'Competitiveness versus "Clean and Green"? The regulation and governance of GMOs in Australia and the UK', *Geoforum*, vol 39, pp161–173

Daniells, S. (2008) 'Unilever breakthrough could take food foams to new level', *Food Navigator*, 12 March, www.foodnavigator.com, accessed 1 February 2009

Dixon, J., Hinde, S. and Banwell, C. (2006) 'Obesity, convenience and "phood"', *British Food Journal*, vol 108, no 8, pp634–645

Dupuy, J. P. (2007) 'Some pitfalls in the philosophical foundations of nanoethics', *Journal of Medicine and Philosophy*, vol 108, pp237–261.

Dupuy, J. P. and Grinbaum, A. (2006) 'Living with uncertainty: Toward the ongoing normative assessment of nanotechnology' in J. Schummer and D. Baird (eds) *Nanotechnology Challenges: Implications for Philosophy, Ethics and Society*, World Scientific Publishing, Singapore

El Amin, A. (2007) 'Carbon nanotubes could be new pathogen weapon', *FoodProductionDaily.com Europe*, www.foodproductiondaily.com/news/ng.asp?id=79393-nanotechnologypathogens-e-coli, accessed 13 November 2008

ETC Group (2003) *The Big Down. Atomtech: Technologies Converging at the Nano-Scale*, Action Group on Erosion, Technology and Concentration, Canada

ETC Group (2004) *Down on the Farm. The Impacts of Nano-Scale Technologies on Food and Agriculture*, Action Group on Erosion, Technology and Concentration, Canada

ETC Group (2007) *Extreme Genetic Engineering: An Introduction to Synthetic Biology*, Action Group on Erosion, Technology and Concentration, Canada

ETC Group (2008) 'Patenting the "climate genes" ... and capturing the climate agenda', *ETC Group Communique*, Issue 99

European Parliament (2009) 'Novel foods, MEPs set new rules', www.europarl.europa.eu/news/expert/infopress_page/067-52498-082-03-13-911-20090324IPR52497-23-03-2009-2009-false/default_en.htm, accessed 24 March, 2009

Friedmann, H. (2005) 'From colonialism to green capitalism: Social movements and the emergence of food regimes', in F. Buttel and P. McMichael (eds) *New Directions in the Sociology of Development*, Elsevier, London

Friends of the Earth (FoE) (2008) *Out of the Laboratory and on to our Plates: Nanotechnology in Food and Agriculture*, Friends of the Earth, Australia

Goodman, D., Sorj, B. and Wilkinson, J. (1987) *From Farming to Biotechnology: A Theory of Agro-Industrial Development*, Basil Blackwell, New York

Gordon, G. (2008) 'The global free market in biofuels', *Development*, vol 51, no 4, pp481–487

Heffernan, W. (1999). 'Biotechnology and mature capitalism', paper presented at the 11th Annual Meeting of the National Agricultural Biotechnology Council, Lincoln, Nebraska, June 6–8.

Hendrickson, M., Wilkinson, J., Heffernan, W. and Gronski, R. (2008) 'The global food system and nodes of power', Report to Oxfam America

Hinsliff, G. (2009) 'New science could defeat food crises', *The Observer*, 8 February

Institute for Food and Agriculture Standards (2006) 'An issues landscape for nanotechnology standards: Report of a workshop', Michigan State University, Michigan

Jacobs, D. and Tapsell, L. (2007) 'Food, not nutrients, is the fundamental unit in nutrition', *Nutrition Reviews*, vol 65, no 10, pp439–450

Kearnes, M., Grove-White, R., Macnaghten, P., Wilsdon, J. and Wynne, B. (2006) 'From bio to nano: Learning lessons from the UK agricultural biotechnology controversy', *Science as Culture*, vol 15, no 4, pp291–307

Kloppenburg, J. R. (1988) *First the Seed: The Political Economy of Plant Biotechnology*, Cambridge University Press, Cambridge, UK

Kuzma, J. and VerHage, P. (2006) *Nanotechnology in Agriculture and Food Production. Anticipated Applications*, Woodrow Wilson International Center For Scholars, Washington D.C.

Lawrence, G. and Grice, J. (2008) 'Agribusiness, genetic engineering and the corporatisation of food', in J. Germov and L. Williams (eds), *A Sociology of Nutrition: The Social Appetite*, Third Edition, Oxford University Press, Melbourne

Lyons, K. (2008) 'Nanotech food and farming and impacts for organics', *Australian Certified Organics*, Winter, pp30–31

Lyons, K. and Scrinis, G. (forthcoming 2009) 'Nano-engineered foods and the corporatisation of the agri-food system', in K. Gould and B. Torres (eds) *Nanotechnology, Social Change and the Environment*, Rowman and Littlefield

Lyons, K. and Whelan, J. (forthcoming 2009) 'Community engagement to facilitate, legitimize and accelerate the advancement of nanotechnologies in Australia', *NanoEthics*

McMichael, P. (2001) 'The power of food', *Agriculture and Human Values*, vol 17, no 1, pp21–33

McMichael, P. (2005) 'Global development and the corporate food regime', in F. Buttel and P. McMichael (eds) *New Directions in the Sociology of Development*, Elsevier, London

Mittar, N. (2008) 'Nanotechnology, vaccine delivery systems and animal husbandry', Paper presented at the Science in Parliament Briefing on Nanotechnology – Ultra-Small Particles, Mega Impacts: Queensland's Future With Nanotechnology, 28 August, Brisbane

Moraru, C., Panchapakesan, C., Huang, Q., Takhistov, P., Liu, S. and Kokini, J. (2007) 'Nanotechnology: A new frontier in food science', *Food Technology*, vol 57, no 12, pp24–29

Otero, G. (2008) 'Neoliberal globalism and the biotechnology revolution: Economic and historical context', in G. Otero (ed.) *Food for the Few: Neoliberal Globalism and Biotechnology in Latin America*, University of Texas Press, Austin

Peter D. Hart Research Associates (2007) 'Awareness of and Attitudes Toward Nanotechnology and Federal Regulatory Agencies: A Report of Findings Based on a National Survey Among Adults', Conducted on behalf of: Project On Emerging Nanotechnologies, the Woodrow Wilson International Centre For Scholars, Washington, DC, http:www.nanotechproject.org/file_download/217

Piesse, J. and Thirtle, C. (2009) 'Three bubbles and a panic: An explanatory review of recent food commodity price events', *Food Policy*, vol 34, pp119–129

Pustzai, A. and Bardocz, S. (2006) 'The future of nanotechnology in food science and nutrition: Can science predict its safety?' in G. Hunt and M. Mehta (eds) *Nanotechnology Risk, Ethics and Law*, Earthscan, London

RCEP (2008) *Novel Materials in the Environment: The Case of Nanotechnology*, Royal Commission on Environmental Pollution, London

Ribeiro, S. and Shand, H. (2008) 'Seeding new technologies to fuel old injustices', *Development*, vol 51, no 4, pp496–503

Rowan, D. (2004) 'How technology is changing our food', *The Observer*, 16 May

RS and RAE (2004) *Nanoscience and Nanotechnologies: Opportunities and Uncertainties*, Royal Society and Royal Academy of Engineering, London

Sanguansri, P. and Augustin, M. (2006) 'Nanoscale materials development – A food industry perspective', *Trends in Food Science and Technology*, vol 17, pp547–556

Scott, N. (2007) 'Nanoscience in veterinary medicine', *Veterinary Research Communications*, vol 31, no 1, pp139–144

Scrinis, G. (2007) 'From techno-corporate food to alternative agri-food movements', *Local–Global*, vol 4, pp112–140

Scrinis, G. (2008a) 'On the ideology of nutritionism', *Gastronomica*, vol 8, no 1, pp39–48

Scrinis, G. (2008b) 'Functional foods or functionally-marketed foods? A critique of and alternatives to, the category of functional foods', *Public Health Nutrition*, vol 11, no 5, pp541–545

Scrinis, G. and Lyons, K. (2007) 'The emerging nano-corporate paradigm: Nanotechnology and the transformation of nature, food and agri-food systems', *International Journal of the Sociology of Food and Agriculture*, vol 15, no 2, pp22–44

Siegrist, M., Cousin, M-E., Kastenholz, H. and Wick, A. (2007) 'Public acceptance of nanotechnology foods and food packaging: The influence of affect and trust', *Appetite*, vol 49, pp459–466

Wang, X. Jiang, Y., Wang, Y., Huang, M., Ho, C. and Huang, Q. (2007) 'Enhancing anti-inflammation activity of curcumin through O/W nanoemulsions', *Food Chemistry*, vol 108, no 2, pp419–424

Weis, T. (2007) *The Global Food Economy: The Battle for the Future of Faming*, Zed Books, London

Wilkinson, J. (2002) 'Genetically modified organisms, organics and the contested construction of demand in the agrofood system', *International Journal of Sociology of Agriculture and Food*, vol 10, no 2, pp3–11

Zimet, P. and Livney, Y. (2009) 'Beta-lactoglobulin and its nanocomplexes with pectin as vehicles for w-3 polyunsaturated fatty acids', *Food Hydrocolloids*, vol 23, pp1120–1126

17
Conclusion – Big Choices about the Food System

Tim Lang

Introduction

In the mid-20th century, the world's food system was set on a different course to its earlier trajectories. Policy and actions on food supply, which had previously been subject either to national (and often local) efforts or to the vagaries of war, famine and circumstance, were given different directions. This post-Second World War settlement represented the triumph and hard work of many food analysts from the natural, medical and social sciences of the day (Vernon, 2007; Lang et al, 2009). They seized the chance offered by the world's dire experience of two World Wars, agricultural trade slumps and famines to offer a new policy package to policy-makers. It is hard for those of us who inherit this post-1940s policy framework to appreciate the ambition, timing and brilliance of what was achieved with this new approach, or to appreciate the hard work that fleshed it out and delivered it. The word 'paradigm' is frequently used in policy analysis, sometimes too loosely. But if ever the word was appropriate in food policy, the 1940s was such an occasion.

These food analysts were daring enough to suggest that the gloomy Malthusian scenario – where population growth exceeds the growth possibilities of agricultural output – could be banished. In its place, science and human endeavour would triumph over the fixed laws of Nature. Modern agricultural and scientific research already showed that Nature could be tamed and even unleashed. A judicious mix of State support + Capital + Science could accelerate food output, banish waste and make people healthier. This package would need to be underpinned by welfare so as to rebuild the financial 'pull' (Keynesian demand factors) and to ensure some degree of distributional justice. Many social and natural scientists in the 1930s and 1940s had documented the dire health and livelihood effects of not earning enough to be able to buy food (International Labour Office, 1938; British Medical Association, 1939). And they had seen, in the UK for example, the social advantages of rationing in the Second World War (Hammond, 1951; Titmuss, 1958). Rationing may have been unpopular and cumbersome, but it ensured that the weak were not penalized and that health inequalities narrowed. People were fed reasonably well, whatever their social station.

Another key to the policy package concerned the state. The 1930s were, like today, a time of massive restructuring in capitalism and society. Then, as now, the ideological stakes were high; market logic dominated but was under critique from those with the view that progress should be tailored around benefiting the many not the few. The food policy progressives took a more considered position. Governments, they argued, needed to ease the booms and slumps of farming's climate and crop failures (Boyd Orr, 1943; Mackintosh, 1944). The state should invest in infrastructure through marketing support, storage, and advice or extension systems to increase farm output. Science could work for the public good on the land by helping to unlock farming potential as well as, further down the supply chain, via the application of scientific principles in storage, factories and the kitchen. Importantly, the overriding ethos was that a combination of changes was needed. Science, capital investment and the state were, alone, incapable of transforming food production to meet social needs, but together they might.

To some extent (arguably a large extent) – as we now know – the package succeeded. Production went up, and in a manner its architects would be proud of. At a similar time, the number of hungry people fell. The package unleashed productivity, fed billions more, made food cheaper, reduced senseless post-harvest waste, increased choice, lightened diets, and invented and used technologies to transform what and how we eat. That picture has been much documented over recent years (Maxwell and Slater, 2004). Again, it is hard for people living or brought up in affluent Western societies to appreciate the transition. Trips to low-income countries could remind us of the restricted choice that this new ethos confronted. No wonder it was defined as progress itself.

The package hit difficulties in the early 1970s, when the oil crisis exposed how much it depended on non-renewable resources (see also Chapter 6, this volume). Famines in Sudan and Bangladesh resuscitated the Malthusian nightmare. But, ironically, it was oil-money (namely, Rockefeller Foundation funds) that saved the day with a new generation of plant breeding, known as the Green Revolution. A new phase of progress was championed within the new paradigm. At the same time, however, some more fundamental critiques surfaced which have consolidated today. The production-oriented model was criticized, firstly for its contribution to environmental degradation (Carson, 1962; UNEP, 2009), secondly for its heavy reliance on fossil fuels – particularly petroleum oil (Leach, 1976; Jones and Woodward, 2002; Garnett 2008) – and, thirdly, for the distortion of diets, and the model's implication in the growth of diseases associated with over- and mal-consumption (Keys et al, 1950; Keys, 1970; WHO, 2002; WHO and FAO, 2003; WCRF and AICR, 2007). This last critique was particularly galling. The underlying rationale of the policy was to increase quantity, and now medical epidemiologists were producing evidence suggesting the ubiquity of fats and sugary processed foods caused harm.

While these policy doubts grew, accompanied by resistance from vested interests, the pace and scale of change ushered into food – the legacy of which we have to face today – should be acknowledged. Almost everything in supply chains changed with the Green Revolution: how food is grown, where, what happens to it, its routes to the consumer, who controls those processes and so on (see Chapters 11 and 12, this volume). Great tribute needs to be paid to those social and natural scientists who have documented this process, probing behind the rhetoric and asking: whom does this serve (Goodman and Watts, 1997; Burch et al, 1999)? At the consumer end, there has been a parallel revolution. How people eat, what they eat, as well as their assumptions about food, have been altered, subjected to extraordinary marketing and mass psychological transformation (Lawrence, 2004; Hawkes, 2007).

Policy now faces dilemmas

While the understanding and data about this transition have been built up over the last 30 years, policy-making has not been as sure-footed. The gap between evidence and policy has widened, atrophied, been ignored or, perhaps, belatedly acknowledged. The resurgence of concerns about food security covered in this book, and elsewhere, is testament to the frustration felt about that state of affairs. Siren voices talk again of doom and gloom – Malthus' last laugh? But there is hope, too. Some see a future in another round of hi-tech investment (but see for a critique Chapter 16, this volume); others propose small-scale and sustainable agriculture (see Chapter 13, this volume). These policy dilemmas are being articulated and debated in academia, industry, farming and think-tanks. The scale of the task today is daunting, even compared to the heroic actions of the mid-20th century thinkers, and policy movers and shakers.

Today, at the world level, we have inherited a fissured set of institutions in which to debate this. Food governance is split: globally, regionally, nationally and locally. Political power has fragmented, while economic power has concentrated into the hands of huge corporations. This is the challenge of what I have termed food democracy: making food systems accountable to, and for, the public good.

Nowhere is this democratic challenge more evident than in the state of institutions themselves. The United Nations (UN) has been the key champion of the mid-20th century paradigm. To some extent it was created in the image of this paradigm, borne out of the hope and the ashes of the Second World War (Boyd Orr, 1966; Shaw, 2007). Reading the accounts of the 1943 Hot Springs Conference, where President Roosevelt gathered the Allies to discuss post-war agricultural reconstruction, one senses the vision and optimism (Hot Springs Conference, 1943). Things could, and should, be run differently, they argued. And better institutions would be needed, grouped under the UN. Some were new versions of League of Nations' entities: the World Health Organization

(WHO) and International Labour Organization, for example. But the Food and Agriculture Organization (FAO) was new, created in 1945. The UN 'family' has since grown to include bodies such as the World Food Programme (founded 1960), the UN Environment Programme (1972), the UN Development Programme (1965), and the UN Conference on Trade and Development (1964), along with connected bodies such as the Intergovernmental Panel on Climate Change (IPCC, 1988). In food policy, as befits an area that had grown and succeeded by integrating policy across sectors, there was an attempt to bind the various efforts made by such organizations. In 1997, the UN's Administrative Committee on Coordination (ACC), the liaison for the heads of the UN Agencies, established a Sub-Committee on Nutrition which worked under what was surely the longest acronym in the UN: the Administrative Committee on Coordination/Sub-Committee on Nutrition (ACC/SCN), now known, more simply, as the SCN.

If this policy architecture was not complex enough, the more important fissure has been between the UN and the Bretton Woods bodies, also designed to restructure capitalism and economies after the Second World War. The 1944 Bretton Woods Conference was to economics what Hot Springs was to food and agriculture. But its institutional legacy has been more powerful, creating in its wake the World Bank (1945) and the International Monetary Fund (1946). Like the UN, it too inherited earlier institutions, notably the Bank for International Settlements, itself created by the Hague agreements in 1930. Although there were attempts to include food and agriculture in the workings of the General Agreement on Tariffs and Trade (GATT) created in 1948, these moves were blocked (ironically by the US). Only when a new GATT was signed at Marrakech in 1994 did food and farming receive global political commitment to be disciplined by neoliberal economic logic, subsidy reduction and tightly defined economic rationality. There was also pressure for the creation of the Organisation for Economic Co-operation and Development (OECD), founded in 1948. Alongside these macro-economic bodies has been the growth of significant political gatherings such as the G8, and now the G-20, where powerful countries meet, discuss and agree on future policy direction.

In some respects this plethora of institutions, sketched above, is a fine testament to democracy and human political ingenuity. But the net effect – felt as food challenges loom today – is that food policy and food security are split. Just when we need to integrate public health nutrition, environment, economy, social justice and food systems, the institutions that ought to do so are split both organizationally and intellectually. The net effect is policy 'cacophony' on the one hand – a wall of policy noise due to many competing voices (Lang and Rayner, 2007) – and inertia and inflexibility on the other, as a consequence of the sheer size and range of institutions (Lang et al, 2009). The complexity of the modern picture for food production, health and the environment – the new food security challenge – is in part impaled on that dilemma. Which body could make the requisite leap? Who has the political leadership capacity? Who has the vision? Reading the countless statements, communiqués and plans of action that come from these bodies, there is only one conclusion possible. There is a dire gap between evidence, policy and practice.

This account should not lead to pessimism. We should not forget that the fundamental challenges addressed by earlier generations of food scientists had their effect. Gone, the optimists today plead with us, are the Old Gods of Necessity, Need and Nature, as well as the Old Demons of Hunger, Ill-health and Cost (Dyson, 1996; Smil, 2000). Now, food is plentiful, good and more affordable for billions of people. The worlds of Nature, Labour and Production, say these optimists, have now been squeezed into different shapes.

Unfortunately, as we also know, food nirvana – decent, health-enhancing food for all, produced in ways that do not adversely affect future generations – has not been achieved. While the 1940s 'productionist' vision judged success largely by raising output – where quantity was the key goal – today we know that the food system's efficacy has to be judged against more complex and broader criteria: environmental (climate change, water, soil, sound land use), health (obesity alongside hunger, escalating healthcare costs, safety – in other words, public health and nutrition), social (widening inequalities within and between nations, see Chapter 7, this volume), cultural (marketing excess, perversion of needs), ethical (animal welfare, decent labour conditions), and economic (rapid concentration distorting markets, internalization of full costs) (Lang et al, 2009).

Even measured against its own baseline – the core goal of banishing hunger – the record of the productionist paradigm has slipped. Since 1996, availability of food per capita has fallen. Meanwhile, the absolute numbers of hungry people have risen (FAO, 2006a; FAO, 2008a). To make matters worse, barely a nation on earth is now not witness to some, if not all, of the problems associated with what Professor Barry Popkin has memorably termed the 'nutrition transition', as everyday food cultures (those complexes of meanings, routines and realities) have been recast (Popkin, 2002, 2003, 2009). More people suffer obesity and overweight globally in the 2000s than underweight and hunger (see Chapter 9, this volume). With trade liberalization came 'Western' marketing, soft drinks, and other culinary aspirations to parts of the world that had not experienced their delights.

In sum, the institutions that ideally ought to give a lead to the new vision for food security – and to food generally – are restricted by their own complexity. That challenge needs resolving. And the more coherent picture needs to be articulated more effectively. This requires the multitude of 'single issue' bodies to think beyond their particular policy concerns: coherence requires campaigners on hunger to take more note of obesity, those on development to see better the perils of unfettered trade liberalization, those concerned about biodiversity to acknowledge the importance of building food systems that enhance it rather than 'park' it. In short, the evidence requires food policy to be coherent, not divisive, and not ad hoc.

The global concerns: A blip or structural?

Some voices argue that such talk is premature and deviatory. Actually, they say, the core problem is really distribution. It is rightly pointed out that, globally, there is enough food to feed the world, as measured in calories per capita, if only it were better distributed. According to this analysis, food security is a matter of distributional justice, and the challenge is to make markets work more efficiently, to smooth out barriers to effective distribution and to raise output for the future. But even if the problem of gross mal-distribution could be resolved – a highly charged political issue – the distributional analysis underplays, or even fails to recognize, the critical issue of *how* should this food be produced? On this, the evidence is overwhelming. Sustainability has to be the basis on which the world produces food and ensures healthy consumption for all (UNEP, 2009). Along with other voices, as many of the contributors to this book argue, food security can only be achieved if food systems become sustainable.

The challenges ahead are serious. Without in any way resorting to neo-Malthusian prognoses, the new picture is one of unparalleled effort: more food has to be produced for a world population rising to 9 billion by 2050, from less land, with rapidly emerging water stress, with problems for fertility and soil structure, added pressures on land use, with uncertain but finite fossil fuel sources, at a time of financial instability, with energy 'crunches' after a century of building in reliance on fossil fuels, with inexorable urbanization affecting not just the rural infrastructure and labour force but often occurring on fertile land where many cities first sprouted due to their potential to feed people. What makes this picture so real is not just the evidence, which is real enough, but also the coincidence of these factors. Each would be hard enough to tackle on its own, but together they compound the complexity.

One thing is agreed – more food needs to be produced, in sustainable ways, with less waste, and in a manner that takes account of the new nutritional picture dominated by the coincidence of overconsumption, underconsumption and mal-consumption. The question remains: how is this to be achieved? Reviewing this global situation, Professor John Beddington, the UK Government's Chief Scientific Adviser, has spoken of a coming 'perfect storm' of rising demand, stagnant production and climate change (Beddington, 2009). The chair of the IPCC, a Nobel Peace Prize winner, has urged people in the West to eat less meat and dairy (Jowit, 2008; see also Chapter 2, this volume). Some see technologies such as genetic modification and a new era of hi-tech industrialized farming (such as intensive hydroponic greenhouses) as the way forward, dismissing more sustainable lower-input agriculture as irrelevant. But the systematic International Assessment of Agricultural Knowledge, Science and Technology for Development, co-initiated and led by the current Chief Scientist at the UK's Department for Environment, Food and Rural Affairs (Defra), suggests that more ecological solutions, based on engaging and supporting small farmers, could yield the most dramatic change (IAASTD, 2008). Reliance on single technology solutions is unlikely to resolve the complex array of problems ahead which are partly social, partly environmental, and partly about control over food systems (Tansey and Rajotte, 2008).

Although the last few years have seen political recognition of this picture grow right across the institutional divide sketched above – a recognition that has brought with it some coherence to the political rhetoric, if not to the funding – the signs were there for some time that the rate of increase in food productivity of previous decades was already slowing down (see Chapter 5, this volume). In 2005–2008, world food commodity prices rocketed, sending global food security rapidly up the international political agenda and rekindling neo-Malthusian debates (FAO, 2008b). A long-arranged intergovernmental meeting in Rome in June 2008, hosted by the UN's Food and Agriculture Organization, became a crisis meeting, leading to promises of increased aid, of more research and development, and of better trade arrangements (FAO, 2008c).

Figure 17.1 depicts the rise of global commodity prices from 2005, gradually at first but then rapidly, only to fall back. Figure 17.2 gives the picture for key food commodities in the year from April 2008 to April 2009. Prices were in fact already falling when the governments met at FAO in Rome in June 2008. Does this mean that the concerns about future food security were either misplaced or a blip? Most analysts currently think not (Evans, 2008; Ambler-Edwards et al, 2009; Evans, 2009). Few doubt that we are at a 1940s moment when big decisions need to be taken about the way forward. This book has summarized some of that thinking.

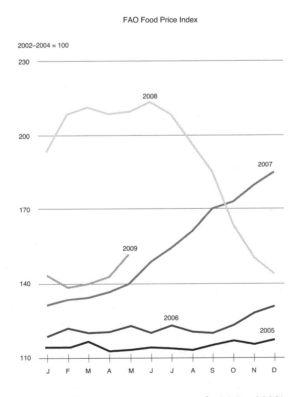

Source: www.fao.org/worldfoodsituation/en/ (accessed 12 May 2009)

Figure 17.1 *FAO Food Price Index 2005–2009*

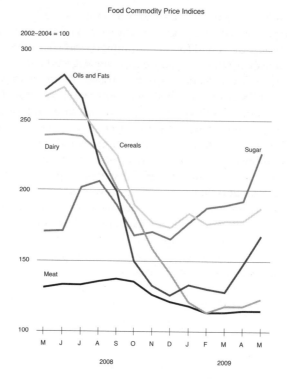

Source: www.fao.org/worldfoodsituation/en/ (accessed 12 May 2009)

Figure 17.2 *Commodity prices 2008–2009*

Redefining food security for the 21st century

So just what is food security? Indeed, is the term meaningful or useful in policy? The term food security can mean all things to all people. Simon Maxwell showed how it has been used in nearly 200 different ways across the world (Smith et al, 1993). Yet, despite this variability – or perhaps because of it – food security continues to feature in local, national and international food policy discourse.

The definition most commonly cited is that of the FAO. The FAO proposes that food security 'exists when all people, at all times, have access to sufficient, safe and nutritious food to meet their dietary needs and food preferences for an active and healthy life' (FAO, 2008a). The FAO's definition of food security is sometimes translated as being about three As: accessibility, affordability and availability. To some extent, this is apple pie and motherhood. Who could be against the everyday formulation of the UK's definition, thus: '[w]e believe that global food security means everyone having enough to eat' (Defra, 2008, p1). The UK's Sustainable Development Commission on which, to declare an interest, I am Land Use and Food Commissioner, proposed an additional clause: '... in a way that does not compromise future generations' ability to feed themselves sustainably and healthily' (Sustainable Development Commission, 2008, p1). The question is what does 'sustainably and healthily' mean exactly? How does it translate into actual growing or farming? What does this mean for diet? What are the cultural signposts for consumers? How does it link to land-use pressures? How does this fit within the Common Agricultural Policy? Does this apply to all produce? How is it to be delivered? The questions abound.

My own view is that, while research and practice is needed to flesh out quite what sustainable food systems are, all countries and food systems can safely assume that the conventional 3As approach to food security is no longer adequate. Nor is it good enough to bolt on the word sustainability. A mindset needs to change, too. Food security can only come from making food systems sustainable. That they are not is amply evidenced. My own proposed definition (Lang, 2009) is that we need policies to promote a sustainable food system, locally, nationally and globally:

- where the core goal is to feed everyone sustainably, equitably and healthily;
- which addresses needs for availability, affordability and accessibility;
- which is diverse, ecologically sound and resilient;
- which builds the capacities and skills necessary for future generations.

By 'sustainably' here, we mean meeting criteria to judge food production and consumption for their impact on several grounds:

- Environmental: climate change and greenhouse gas emissions, water use, land use, biodiversity and waste.
- Health: safety, nutrition, access and affordability.
- Quality: fresh or seasonal where appropriate, and local if meeting other criteria.
- Social values: animal welfare, ethics, working wages and labour conditions, and equality of distribution.

The challenge for supply chains is how to translate these complex but real demands into the business model. My colleagues and I have presented our model elsewhere (Lang et al, 2009), but the interesting and heartening fact is that some businesses are beginning to address some of these demands, which suggests that it is possible (Lang, forthcoming 2009). The challenge is to level the playing field to encourage all to begin the process of improving food systems measured against all these impacts.

Renewing capacities: Land and labour

The transition that lies ahead is awesome. There should be no doubt about that. How can the attention of policy-makers be captured? This requires organization and determination, of course, but also better concepts that 'speak' to policy. The new food security debate could, perhaps, talk more about capacities. For food systems to be sustainable, the capacity of soil, people and economies need to be refocused. The question of labour and skills is particularly pressing; however, it is a topic that does not receive its due level of policy attention or political priority. This was not a mistake made by the mid-20th century thinkers. They knew that farmers and growers needed help (Stapledon, 1935; Kuczynski, 1942). Today, development NGOs rather than governments primarily wear this mantle. Agriculture is still the world's largest employer, with about 40 per cent of the world's population employed in agriculture, largely at a subsistence level (Halweil, 2000). Of the approximately 1.1 billion men and women working in agricultural production in the mid-1990s, nearly half did so on a waged basis (FAO, 1996). Although the value of food production in 2000 was only about 3 per cent of gross world product, the agricultural labour force accounts for approximately 22 per cent of the world's population, and 24 per cent of GDP in countries with per capita incomes of less than US$765 – the low-income developing countries as defined by the World Bank (see Millennium Ecosystem Assessment Program, 2005).

Millions of these workers earned the lowest wages in the rural sector, lower even than the amount required to subsist. Farming is both hard work and hazardous (Hurst et al, 2005). Globally, agriculture accounts for at least 170,000 occupational deaths each year, half of all fatal accidents. Even in a rich country like the UK, the farm is the most dangerous place of work, if measured by the likelihood of the worker being killed while at work (Health and Safety Executive, 2008).

This must change. Working on the land or with fragile crops requires great persistence and dedication. In the past, rich countries created agricultural extension services, a model which was taken to the developing world. These are expensive, and suffered the financial cuts unleashed on agriculture by the financiers and accountants under the Washington Consensus, the neoliberal backlash to the socially progressive mid-20th century economic policy-formers (Williamson, 1989). Whereas the latter saw a benign role for the state, the former abhorred it. Developing countries should be weaned of handouts was the clear message.

We need to be bold again today, confident that the financial house of cards built in the name of decluttering the economy has fallen (Tett, 2009). Sustainability – on the land and in health – requires skills to be developed, new sharing to be forged across professions and disciplines. It makes no sense for consumers any more than farmers to be encouraged to lower carbon emissions while ignoring the issue of scarce water, or to think only about CO_2 reduction while ignoring ecosystems and biodiversity support (see Chapter 14, this volume). The mid-21st century needs improvement on all these fronts. Given food's impact, new skills and awareness will be essential. That requires education, research and support. Private consultancies or short-term aid are not the answer.

But capacity building is not just a matter of people. The soil is the thin crust on which food production centrally depends. In 2009, two centuries after the birth of Charles Darwin, it is good to remember that he – a liberal progressive – found soil to be the wonder of wonders. Again, it was an issue central to the mid-20th century policy-makers whose legacy we now need to reform (Stapledon, 1935; Balfour, 1943; Drummond, 1944). Aquaculture and hydroponics have a role, of course but, fundamentally, future food needs to harvest solar power (to make plants grow) as it interacts with soil-based growth. A key conflict is over land use – how to use or cover soil. Everywhere, there is fierce competition between uses for land: food, fuel, carbon and water sinks, biodiversity, amenity, transport and identity, competition that the growth of mega-cities will accentuate. Urbanization has often been by seashores or estuarial plains with rich soil (Crawford and Marsh, 1989), whereas now, prime land is often given to housing.

A new focus on land use is a priority, not least since a subtle 'imperialism' is in existence. For example, one calculation for London – a city that grew centuries ago – estimated in 2003 that the city's total footprint was 48,868,000 global hectares (gha), or 6.63gha per capita. London's actual land use far exceeds its spatial geography. If this was made more equitable to reflect London's portion of the world's 'bio-capacity', its footprint ought to shrink to 1,210,000gha, or 0.16gha per capita (Lyndhurst and Greater London Authority, 2003). London's food has been estimated to be 41 per cent of its total footprint. To turn this into its global fair share would require Londoners each to consume 70 per cent less meat, to ensure that local seasonal unprocessed food makes up more than 40 per cent of their diet, and to cut waste by a tonne a year. For the UK as a whole, a shift from the current diet to a healthy diet would reduce the footprint of the average UK consumer from 0.82gha to 0.64gha per person (Frey and Barrett, 2007). Meat consumption accounted for 46 per cent of the conventional diet's footprint, followed by dairy products (9 per cent) and alcoholic drinks (8 per cent).

Patterns of wealth and purchasing power give developed-world consumers a reach they perhaps underestimate: the use of land elsewhere without owning or being responsible for it. Rightly, much attention has been given recently to a new generation of country-to-country land deals (Grain, 2008; von Braun and Meinzen-Dick, 2009). These are important, but small, steps compared to the hidden footprint that has developed over recent decades with the globalization of food sourcing to feed the affluent. Food retailers are key agents in this process.

Refocusing policy around sustainable diets

What consumers eat has a direct impact on both their health and the health of the planet. Yet messages to consumers – let alone messages from consumers down the supply chain – are muddled. Should consumers prioritize health or climate change when choosing their diet? Water or waste reduction? Eat fish because it is good for them? Not eat fish because stocks are in stress? The obvious answer is all of these. But how? The evidence is strong to do all of it, and yet collectively it makes too little sense. In truth, there is no clarity for consumers about what a sustainable diet might look like, or what the principles and matrices might be for judging it. Policy-makers and scientists urgently need to clarify how to fuse guidelines on health and environment, not least because these guidelines ought to inform policy as well as advice to farmers and growers on what the market needs, and how to achieve it. For decades, policy has been taken in a different direction: 'let the market decide' has been the mantra. Of course, the message coming from responsible companies, farmers, consumers and scientists is that the big picture needs to be clarified. What should I do: eat fish or not? I cannot do both.

The case for fusing guidelines about the health and environmental impacts of diet, and for rethinking what unrestrained choice does to human health, is overwhelming. A study in Europe found that food, drink, tobacco and narcotics (taken for data reasons together) accounted for an estimated 20–30 per cent of the environmental impact of all consumption by European consumers. Meat and meat products (including meat, poultry, sausages or similar) were the largest contributor, accounting for 4–12 per cent of the impact on global warming of all consumer products (Tukker et al, 2006). The Stern Report estimated that agriculture and food are considerable sources of greenhouse gas emissions (Stern, 2006). Farm animals (globally) have been calculated to be responsible for 31 per cent of greenhouse gases, and fertilizers for 38 per cent of nitrous oxide (N_2O). While farm animals' methane effects have been rightly highlighted (FAO, 2006b), the effects of fertilizers have received less attention – despite being more potent. In rich consumer-societies, such as the UK, the cumulative effect is 19 per cent (Garnett, 2008). Of that, agriculture accounts for the greatest proportion (7.5 per cent), with the remainder made up by fertilizer manufacture (0.7 per cent), food manufacture (1.8 per cent), packaging (1 per cent), transport within the UK (1 per cent) home-related use (2.3 per cent), retail (1.7 per cent), catering (1.5 per cent), and waste disposal (0.4 per cent). Thus, agriculture accounts for about half of food's total greenhouse gas emissions, with the other half evenly spread across processes after the farm gate through to domestic use.

Diet's environmental impact is not restricted to greenhouse gas emissions; it also has impacts on water, waste and energy, for example. How one farms or grows food varies the amount of water used, but the case for thinking about water generally and the hidden trade in 'embedded' or 'virtual' water is pressing (Allan, 2003). Dutch and UK data suggest that 1kg of beef, for example, requires 10,000–20,000 litres of water, and that a cup of black coffee represents 140 litres of embedded water (Chapagain and Hoekstra, 2004; Chapagain and Hoekstra, 2006; Chapagain and Orr, 2008). More research is needed on how these figures vary by method of production and location.

Waste is an even clearer issue. Despite the assumption that modern food practices would reduce waste – not least due to insecticides and better storage such as refrigeration – it appears that rich consumer societies have merely changed *how* they waste. Savings in some sectors have been replaced by waste elsewhere. In the UK, for example, where food retailers now aim for zero waste – meaning that they do not discard food – an estimated one-third of purchased food is thrown away by consumers, the equivalent of 6.7 million tonnes of food every year, most of which is avoidable. About one-sixth of that is thrown away whole, untouched or unopened (WRAP, 2008). On energy reliance, it is widely accepted that many of the productivity gains in the food sector in the 20th century came about by using non-renewable fossil fuels to replace human and animal labour (Pimentel and Pimentel, 1996; Haber, 2007).

The (re)democratizing agenda

The picture painted here, and throughout this book, is sobering. The heartening thing is that realization is growing that the current situation is not acceptable. A new approach to food security is emerging. The case for imagination, for leadership, and for better planning, vision and energy is becoming clear. A process of change is looming. We must face this, rather than be frightened of it. It needs engagement rather than the bland 'box-ticking' of too many stakeholder processes, where consultation is too often token; it needs real, deep accountability alongside verve and daring. Business-as-usual is not an option; nor is it desirable to wait for circumstances to legitimate a return to dirigisme, or economic planning and control by the state, whether by benign ruler or shock. Too many people are already being crushed by the failings of the food system. To that extent the neoliberals were not only right, but they have won. Market logic *has* unleashed consumer rights. But food rights and planetary survival capacities have been trampled in the process. Institutions need reformulating. Hugely more thought needs to be given to how people might be encouraged to change. We all have a real vested interest in seeing diet as part of the move to sustainable societies. At the same time, we are all locked into a partial notion of progress. Barriers to change are systemic, so change must be systemic, too. The discourse about food security symbolizes the need to integrate nutrition, environmental sustainability and social justice. No other food-policy thinking passes the laugh test.

References

Allan, J. (2003) 'Virtual water – the water, food and trade nexus: Useful concept or misleading metaphor?' *Water International*, vol 28, pp4–11

Ambler-Edwards, S., Bailey, K., Kiff, A., Lang, T., Lee, R., Marsden, T., Simons, D. and Tibbs, H. (2009) *Food Futures: Rethinking UK Strategy*, Chatham House Report, Royal Institute of International Affairs (Chatham House), London

Balfour, E. (1943) *The Living Soil*, Faber and Faber, London

Beddington, J. (2009) *Chief Scientific Advisor's Speech to UK Sustainable Development 2009 conference*, news.bbc.co.uk/1/hi/uk/7951838.stm, accessed 18 March 2009

Boyd Orr, J. (1966) *As I Recall: The 1880s to the 1960s*, MacGibbon and Kee, London

Boyd Orr, S. (1943) *Food and the People. Target for Tomorrow No 3*, Pilot Press, London

British Medical Association (1939) *Nutrition and the Public Health: Proceedings of a National Conference on the Wider Aspects of Nutrition*, 27–29 April, British Medical Association, London

Burch, D., Goss, J. and Lawrence, G. (1999) *Restructuring Global and Regional Agricultures: Transformations in Australasian Agri-Food Economies and Spaces*, Ashgate, Aldershot, UK

Carson, R. (1962) *Silent Spring*, Houghton Mifflin and Riverside Press, Boston, Cambridge, Mass

Chapagain, A. and Hoekstra, A. (2006) *Water Footprints of Nations*, vols 1 and 2, UNESCO–IHE Value of Water Research Report Series No. 16, UNESCO, Paris

Chapagain, A. and Hoekstra, A. (2004) *Water Footprints of Nations*, vols 1 and 2, UNESCO–IHE Value of Water Research Report Series No. 16, UNESCO, Paris

Crawford, M. and Marsh, D. (1989) *The Driving Force: Food, Evolution and the Future*, Heinemann, London

Defra (2008) *Ensuring the UK's Food Security in a Changing World*, Department for Environment, Food and Rural Affairs, London

Drummond, J. (1944) *Charter for the Soil*, Faber and Faber, London

Dyson, J. (1996) *Population and Food: Global Trends and Future Prospects*, Routledge, London

Evans, A. (2008) *Rising Food Prices: Drivers and Implications for Development*, Written Evidence to House of Commons International Development Committee Inquiry into Food Security, Center on International Co-operation (New York University) and Royal Institute for International Affairs (Chatham House), New York and London

Evans, A. (2009) *The Feeding of the Nine Billion: Global Food Security for the 21st Century*, Chatham House Report, London

FAO (1996) *Farm Wage Labour: Poorest of the Rural Poor*, Food and Agriculture Organization of the United Nations, Rome, www.fao.org/docrep/x0262e/x0262e19. htm, accessed 23 Jan 2008

FAO (2006a) *The State of Food Insecurity in the World 2006: Eradicating World Hunger – Taking Stock Ten Years After the World Food Summit*, Food and Agriculture Organization of the United Nations, Rome

FAO (2006b) *Livestock's Long Shadow – Environmental Issues and Options*, Food and Agriculture Organization of the United Nations, Rome

FAO (2008a) *Declaration of the High-Level Conference on World Food Security: The Challenges of Climate Change and Bioenergy*, 3–5 June, Food and Agriculture Organization of the United Nations, Rome, www.fao.org/fileadmin/user_upload/ foodclimate/HLCdocs/declaration-E.pdf, accessed 30 May 2009

FAO (2008b) *State of Food Insecurity in the World 2008: High Food Prices and Food Security – Threats and Opportunities*, Food and Agriculture Organization of the United Nations, Rome

FAO (2008c) *Special Programme on Food Security*, Food and Agriculture Organization of the United Nations, Rome, www.fao.org/spfs/en, accessed 17 May 2009

Frey, S. and Barrett, J. (2007) *Our Health, Our Environment: The Ecological Footprint of What We Eat*, International Ecological Footprint Conference 'Stepping up the Pace: New Developments in Ecological Footprint Methodology, Applications', Cardiff, www.brass.cf.ac.uk/uploads/Frey_A33.pdf, accessed 30 May 2009

Garnett, T. (2008) *Cooking Up a Storm: Food, Greenhouse Gas Emissions and Our Changing Climate*, Food and Climate Research Network, University of Surrey, Guildford, UK

Goodman, D. and Watts, M. (eds) (1997) *Globalising Food: Agrarian Questions and Global Restructuring*, Routledge, London

Grain (2008) *Seized! The 2008 Land Grab for Food and Financial Security*, Grain, Barcelona

Haber, W. (2007) 'Energy, food, and land – the ecological traps of humankind', *Environmental Science and Pollution Research International*, vol 14, no 6, pp359–365

Halweil, B. (2000) 'Where have all the farmers gone? *World-Watch*, vol 13, no 5, pp12–28

Hammond, R. (1951) *Food: the Growth of Policy*, HMSO and Longmans, Green and Co, London

Hawkes, C. (2007) *Marketing Food to Children: Changes in the Global Regulatory Environment 2004–2006*, World Health Organization, Geneva

Health and Safety Executive (2008) *HSE Statistics 2007/08*, Health and Safety Executive, London, www.hse.gov.uk/statistics/index.htm, accessed 30 May 2009

Hot Springs Conference (1943) *Final Act of the Hot Springs Conference*, 18 May–3 June 1943, Hot Springs Virginia, US, www.worldfooddayusa.org/?id=16367, accessed 29 May 2009

Hurst, P., Termine, P. and Karl, M. (2005) *Agricultural Workers and their Contribution to Sustainable Agriculture and Rural Development*, Food and Agriculture Organization of the United Nations, International Union of Foodworkers, International Labour Organization, Rome and Geneva

IAASTD (2008) *Global Report and Synthesis Report*, International Assessment of Agricultural Knowledge, Science and Technology for Development, London

International Labour Office (1938) *The Worker's Standard of Living. Studies and Reports Series B (Economic Conditions)*, International Labour Office of the League of Nations, Geneva

Jones, A. and Woodward, L. (2002) *Eating Oil*, EFCR Pamphlet Series, Policy Research Development, Elm Farm Research Centre, London

Jowit, J. (2008) 'UN says eat less meat to curb global warming', *The Observer*, London, www.guardian.co.uk/environment/2008/sep/07/food.foodanddrink, accessed 28 May 2009

Keys, A. (1970) 'Coronary heart disease in seven countries', *Circulation*, vol 41, supp 1, pp1–211

Keys, A., Brozek, J., Henschel, O. and Mickelsen, H. (1950) *The Biology of Human Starvation*, University of Minnesota Press, Minneapolis

Kuczynski, J. (1942) *A Short History of Labour Conditions in Great Britain 1750 to the Present Day*, Frederick Muller, London

Lang, T. (2009) *Food Security and Sustainability: The Perfect Fit*, Sustainable Development Commission, London

Lang, T. (forthcoming 2009) 'From "value-for-money" to "values-for-money": The challenge of ethical food for food policy in Europe', *Environment and Planning A*, Special Issue on Ethical Food-Scapes

Lang, T. and Rayner, G. (2007) 'Overcoming policy cacophony on obesity: An ecological public health framework for policymakers', *Obesity Reviews*, vol 8, supp, pp165–181

Lang, T., Barling, D. and Caraher, M. (2009) *Food Policy: Integrating Health, Environment and Society*, Oxford University Press, Oxford

Lawrence, F. (2004) *Not on the Label*, Penguin, London

Leach, G. (1976) *Energy and Food Production*, IPC Science and Technology Press for the International Institute for Environment and Development, Guildford, UK

Lyndhurst, B. and Greater London Authority (2003) *London's Ecological Footprint: A Review*, Greater London Authority, London

Mackintosh, J. (1944) *The Nation's Health*, The Pilot Press, London

Maxwell, S. and Slater, R. (2004) *Food Policy Old and New,* Basil Blackwell, Oxford

Millennium Ecosystem Assessment Program (2005) *Ecosystems and Human Well-being: Synthesis,* Island Press, Washington, DC

Pimentel, D. and Pimentel, M. (1996) *Food, Energy and Society,* Colorado Press, Niwet, CO

Popkin, B. (2002) 'An overview on the nutrition transition and its health implications: the Bellagio meeting', *Public Health Nutrition,* vol 5, no 1A, pp93–103

Popkin, B. (2003) 'The nutrition transition in the developing world', *Development Policy Review,* vol 21, pp581–597

Popkin, B. (2009) *The World is Fat: The Fads, Trends, Policies and Products that are Fattening the Human Race,* Avery and Penguin, New York

Shaw, D. (2007) *World Food Security: A History Since 1945,* Palgrave Macmillan, London

Smil, V. (2000) *Feeding the World: a Challenge for the Twenty-First Century,* MIT Press Books, Boston and Massachusetts

Smith, M., Pointing, J., Maxwell, S. et al (1993) *Household Food Security, Concepts and Definitions: An Annotated Bibliography,* Institute of Development Studies, Brighton

Stapledon, S. (1935) *The Land: Now and Tomorrow,* Faber and Faber, London

Stern, N. (2006) *The Stern Review of the Economics of Climate Change. Final Report,* HM Treasury, London

Sustainable Development Commission (2008) *Sustainable Development Commission Response to the Defra Discussion Paper 'Ensuring the UK's Food Security in a Changing World',* Sustainable Development Commission, London, www.sd-commission.org.uk/publications/downloads/Response_EnsuringUKFoodSecurity.pdf, accessed 29 May 2009

Tansey, G. and Rajotte, T. (eds) (2008) *The Future Control of Food: A Guide to International Negotiations and Rules on Intellectual Property, Biodiversity and Food Security,* Earthscan and IDRC, London and Ottawa

Tett, G. (2009) *Fool's Gold: How Unrestrained Greed Corrupted a Dream, Shattered Global Markets and Unleashed a Catastrophe,* Little Brown, London

Titmuss, R. (1958) *War and Social Policy. Essays on the Welfare State,* Allen and Unwin, London

Tukker, A., Huppes, G., Guinee, J., Heijungs, R., De Koning, A., Van Oers, L., Suh, S., Geerken, T., Van Holderbeke, M., Jansen, B. and Nielsen, P. (2006) *Environmental Impact of Products (EIPRO): Analysis of the Life Cycle Environmental Impacts Related to the Final Consumption of the EU–25,* European Commission Joint Research Centre, Brussels

UNEP (2009) *The Environmental Food Crisis: The Environment's Role in Averting Future Food Crises. A UNEP Rapid Response Assessment,* United Nations Environment Programme, Geneva

Vernon, J. (2007) *Hunger: A Modern History,* Harvard University Press, Cambridge

von Braun, J. and Meinzen-Dick, R. (2009) *'Land Grabbing' by Foreign Investors in Developing Countries: Risks and Opportunities,* Policy Brief No. 13, Washington, DC, www.ifpri.org/pubs/bp/bp013.asp, accessed 17 May 2009

WCRF and AICR (2007) *Food, Nutrition, Physical Activity and the Prevention of Cancer: A Global Perspective,* World Cancer Research Fund and American Institute for Cancer Research, Washington, DC and London

WHO (2002) *World Health Report 2002: Reducing Risks, Promoting Healthy Life,* World Health Organization, Geneva

WHO and FAO (2003) *Diet, Nutrition and the Prevention of Chronic Diseases. Report of the Joint WHO/FAO Expert Consultation,* WHO Technical Report Series, No. 916 (TRS 916), World Health Organization and Food and Agriculture Organization of the United Nations, Geneva

Williamson, J. (1989) 'What Washington means by policy reform', in J. Williamson (ed) *Latin American Readjustment: How Much has Happened*, Institute for International Economics, Washington, DC

WRAP (2008) *The Food We Waste*, Waste and Resources Action Programme, Banbury, UK

Index